Global Entrepreneurship

T0293686

This second edition of a *Choice* Outstanding Academic Title improves coverage of the global environments in which entrepreneurs operate. In *Global Entrepreneurship: Environment and Strategy*, Nir Kshetri explores and illuminates the economic, political, cultural, geographical, and technological environments that affect entrepreneurs as they exploit opportunities and create value in economies around the world.

Grounded in theory, the book begins by laying out the concepts, indicators, and measurements that have unique impacts on entrepreneurs in different regions. This framework sets the scene for a close examination of global variations in entrepreneurial ecosystems and finance. Kshetri methodically examines entrepreneurship patterns in diverse economies through the lenses of economic system, political system, culture and religion, and geography (both by country and by continent)—and for the first time, includes an entire chapter on entrepreneurship in Latin America.

All new for this edition, *Global Entrepreneurship* offers case studies at the end of each chapter to illustrate relevant concepts, as well as two detailed cases in an appendix, to encourage broader reflection. The book is accompanied by online resources, bringing additional value for instructors and students in entrepreneurship and international business classes.

Nir Kshetri is Professor at Bryan School of Business and Economics, University of North Carolina-Greensboro, USA.

Global Entrepreneurship

Environment and Strategy

Second Edition

Nir Kshetri

Routledge
Taylor & Francis Group

NEW YORK AND LONDON

First published 2019
by Routledge
711 Third Avenue, New York, NY 10017

and by Routledge
2 Park Square, Milton Park, Abingdon, Oxon, OX14 4RN

*Routledge is an imprint of the Taylor & Francis Group, an
informa business*

Library of Congress Cataloging-in-Publication Data
Names: Kshetri, Nir, author.
Title: Global entrepreneurship environment and
strategy / Nir Kshetri.
Description: 2 Edition. | New York: Routledge, 2018. |
Revised edition of the author's Global entrepreneurship, 2014.
Identifiers: LCCN 2018021279|
ISBN 9781138311206 (hardback) |
ISBN 9781138311213 (pbk.) | ISBN 9780429458996 (ebk)
Subjects: LCSH: Entrepreneurship. |
Entrepreneurship—Developing countries.
Classification: LCC HB615 .K76 2018 | DDC 658.4/21—dc23
LC record available at https://lccn.loc.gov/2018021279

ISBN: 978-1-138-31120-6 (hbk)
ISBN: 978-1-138-31121-3 (pbk)
ISBN: 978-0-429-45899-6 (ebk)

Typeset in Bembo
by codeMantra

Contents

Chapter 1

Global Entrepreneurship
The Current Status, Definitions, Types, and Measures

This chapter's objectives include:

1   To demonstrate an understanding of the current Global Entrepreneurial Revolution.
2   To identify the major trends and forces shaping the Global Entrepreneurial Revolution.
3   To analyze various metrics in order to measure the determinants, performance, and impacts of entrepreneurship in an economy.
4   To apply the tools and concepts learnt in the chapter to asses an economy's entrepreneurial performance and success.
5   To demonstrate an understanding of the international heterogeneity in the development of entrepreneurship and entrepreneurial capability.

A Global Entrepreneurial Revolution

A number of trends and indicators point toward the fact that entrepreneurship has become a truly global phenomenon. One such indicator concerns the appetite for entrepreneurial ventures. Highly successful entrepreneurial firms are found across the world. In the 2017 Forbes' global list of the 2,000 biggest public companies, 58 countries were represented.[1] Moreover, companies from emerging markets such as Colombia, Saudi Arabia, South Africa, Turkey, and UAE were featured in the Forbes' 2017 list of 100 Top Regarded Companies (www.forbes.com/top-regarded-companies/list/#tab:rank). Various forces and events have shaped this global entrepreneurial revolution.

Favorable Attitude toward Capitalism and Social Acceptance of Entrepreneurship

One important trend facilitating a global entrepreneurial revolution and growing entrepreneurial spirit concerns a favorable attitude toward free market capitalism. Note that capitalism is the foundation of entrepreneurship.

According to a Gallup poll conducted in 2010, 61% of Americans had a positive view of capitalism and about the same proportion had a negative view of socialism. In 2016, 60% in the U.S. had a positive view of capitalism, which is unchanged from 2010.[2]

Among the most encouraging developments in the global entrepreneurial arena has been the acceptance of the ideas of free market capitalism in countries with a history of socialism. For instance, in a 2009 Global Attitudes Survey conducted by the Pew Research Center, the proportions of respondents agreeing to the statement "Most people are better off in a free market economy, even though some people are rich and some are poor" were 79% in China, 65% in Poland, and 51% in Russia. As a point of comparison, the corresponding proportion was 41% for Japan, which is historically a capitalist country. Likewise, according to a survey conducted by the Yury Levada Analytical Center, about 80% of young Russians said that they had successfully adapted to capitalism.[3] This does not mean that these young Russians have a favorable attitude toward the country's wealthy business tycoons, also known as the "oligarchs." Nonetheless, they have readily and enthusiastically accepted the idea that free market economy is good for the society.

The development of a successful entrepreneurial society rests upon social acceptance of entrepreneurship and entrepreneurial activities. Positive developments on this front are worth noting in emerging economies. For instance, a survey conducted by YouGov, which was released in 2010, found that about 50% respondents in China and India believed that their societies were more welcoming of entrepreneurial activities compared to a decade ago.[4]

Responses of Policy Makers

In response to the demands of various forces and as their own priority, policy makers in most countries are directing efforts to encourage entrepreneurship among local communities and promoting the creation of entrepreneurial societies. They have realized the potential contributions of entrepreneurship to economic growth and development. According to the World Bank's Doing Business 2018 report, between June 2016 and June 2017, 190 economies tracked by the World Bank undertook 264 business reforms. Among the most common reforms in 2016/2017 were those related to reducing the complexity and cost of regulatory processes to start a business and getting credit. These were followed by trading across borders.[5]

Young People's Engagement in Entrepreneurial Activities

One of the most encouraging trends in global entrepreneurship in recent years is young people's desire to be entrepreneurs and their engagement in entrepreneurial activities in emerging economies. For instance, according to the World Bank, 40% of Latin American youth have reported a desire to become an entrepreneur.[6] Likewise, according to a survey conducted by the telecom provider Ooredoo in 2014, 83% of Qatari youth said they would like to be entrepreneurs.[7] The proportions for other GCC countries were Saudi Arabia, 81%; UAE, 79%; Kuwait, 78%; Bahrain, 69%; and Oman, 69%. In other Arab countries, young people have demonstrated high levels of entrepreneurial inclination. For instance, according to a 2009 Gallup Poll conducted among Arab youth who did not own businesses, the proportions that were planning to start their own businesses "in the next 12 months" were 38% in Tunisia, Comoros, and Iraq; 39% in Djibouti; and 46% in Sudan.[8]

Likewise, at the time of starting their companies, the average ages of founders in Saudi Arabia's fastest growing 100 companies were in the 30–33 years range in 2009 and 2010.[9] These are big achievements for these countries, where entrepreneurship is a relatively new phenomenon.

While only 1.6% of Chinese college graduates started businesses in 2011, some young entrepreneurs have been highly successful. They have started many successful entrepreneurial ventures such as introduction of Disney movies to the country, efficient health care delivery, cutting-edge online games, and web applications.[10]

Various Types of Capitalism and Their Influences on Entrepreneurial Activities

Capitalism is the foundation of entrepreneurial opportunities. In capitalistic economies, the means of production are mostly privately owned and a market economy operates. That is, economic decisions are influenced by competition, supply, and demand. However, it would be erroneous to conclude that only one form of capitalism exists. There are a number of variations in the way capitalism functions across the world.

At least four prevalent forms of capitalism have been identified: (i) entrepreneurial, (ii) big firm, (iii) state directed, and (iv) oligarchic.[11] Entrepreneurial capitalism is characterized by the presence of high-impact entrepreneurs with radical ideas in which small, innovative firms play a major role. Note that high-impact entrepreneurs are people involved in launching and growing of companies with an above-average impact on the creation of jobs and wealth.[12] Some examples include the founders of companies such as Twitter, Uber, Apple, Facebook, Yahoo, Microsoft, and Google. These entrepreneurs possess capability to bring innovative products, services, and business models that meet marketplace needs. The U.S. is viewed as a fertile place for high-impact entrepreneurs due to its pro-private sector culture and a smaller state sector compared to Western European countries.

In a big firm capitalism, radical entrepreneurship tends to be absent and the economic growth is mainly driven by the government through the collaboration with big businesses. This form of capitalism is prevalent in Japan and some European countries. Japan has many innovative large firms, but the country has among the lowest per capita rate of entrepreneurial activities.

Some developing countries such as China have found state-guided capitalism as a way to achieve economic growth (Chapter 8). In such model, the government guides the market, typically by supporting few industries that are expected to perform well. For one thing, the deep entrenchment in the economy allows the Chinese government to intervene quickly and produce desired outputs. The cash-rich Chinese government has also been pressuring as well as providing a wide range of incentives for its firms to expand overseas.

In an oligarchic capitalism, a small group of individuals and families control the majority of the national wealth and power, in some cases with the support of corrupt politicians. This form of capitalism is thus associated with and facilitated by "politically embedded cronyism."[13] In this form of capitalism, entrepreneurs use political power, capital, and social networks to maximize economic rewards. That is, a small group of wealthy people tend to maintain a grip over the country's economy, polity, and society.[14] In some cases, oligarchic capitalism is characterized by a symbiosis of political and economic elites. That is, political elites such as rulers, elected officials, party leaders, and bureaucrats are also economic elites or successful entrepreneurs. In such a system, state incumbents may generate and maintain uneven distribution of property rights, which favor a few private actors. There tends to be a limited role of societal groups.

This system may serve as a tactic of survival for a ruling regime. In some economies such as Ukraine, powerful oligarchs tend to provide financial resources to the ruling elites, and in return, they exert a strong influence on government policies. For instance, three top oligarchs[15] in Ukraine reportedly played key roles in supporting the former President Kuchma's regime. Some developing economies in Asia (e.g., India), Africa, Latin America (e.g., Colombia), and the Middle East have also exhibited characteristics of this form of capitalism. Despite the existence of certain elements of a market economy and political democracy, this form of capitalism lacks a true market system.

Variation in Entrepreneurial Activities across the World

While the general trend discussed above suggests a growth in entrepreneurial ventures worldwide, significant cross-country variation exists in entrepreneurial success and a number of features of entrepreneurship. This section sheds light on some of the important international differences in various aspects of entrepreneurial opportunities, behaviors, and performance.

First, economies worldwide differ drastically in terms of their populations' willingness to engage and actual engagement in entrepreneurial ventures as well as the nature of entrepreneurial activities pursued. For instance, only 0.18% of the population in Indonesia is engaged in entrepreneurial activities[16] compared to about 7.5% in the U.S.[17] According to a Global Entrepreneurship Monitor (GEM) study, less than 1% of Indonesians wanted to start a business compared to 14.5% in the U.S. dominance of the economy by natural resource-based industries such as mining and agriculture, lack of access to capital for small businesses, and poor education for would-be entrepreneurs appear to be important factors contributing to Indonesia's weak entrepreneurial performance.[18]

Qualitative Differences

In addition to the quantitative variations, qualitative differences also exist in entrepreneurial activities worldwide. While an increasing number of people in developing countries have started businesses, high-impact entrepreneurship is severely lacking. Many developing countries do not provide environment to produce highly successful entrepreneurs such as Microsoft founder Bill Gates and Wal-Mart founder Sam Walton. These countries' entrepreneurship landscapes mainly consist of small-scale entrepreneurs such as peasant farmers, street hawkers, market vendors, owners of small restaurants, and florists. For instance, while India has some high-performing global firms such as Wipro, TCS, and Infosys, the country lacks behind developed and some developing countries in terms of high-expectation business launchers per capita.

Motivation and Intended Goals of Entrepreneurial Activities

People across the world also differ in terms of motivation and intended goals of entrepreneurial activities. While most people in industrialized countries engage in entrepreneurial activity to take advantage of business opportunities, necessity or the lack of other opportunities is an important driver in most developing economies. Moreover, entrepreneurial success may mean different things to entrepreneurs from different political, social, and cultural environment. For instance, according to the 2009 GEM report, proportionately more Chinese entrepreneurs than those in the U.S. are motivated by the desire to make money. The GEM study found that fewer than 40% of Chinese entrepreneurs started businesses to have more independence, and more than 60% of them did so to increase their income. On the contrary, in the U.S., only about 40% of entrepreneurs start businesses to increase income, while almost 60% do so to gain more independence.[19] This means that compared to U.S. entrepreneurs, Chinese entrepreneurs are more likely to measure their "success" in terms of the wealth they generate than in terms of personal autonomy.

Gender Bias and Other Types of Disparities in Entrepreneurship

A large gender bias in access to resources and the participation rate of entrepreneurial activities is probably the most serious concern. Worldwide only 30% of small- and medium-sized enterprises (SMEs) that are formally registered are owned and run by women.[20]

The lack of gender equality in labor laws prevents women to work and earn more relative to men. In 104 economies, women are not allowed to work at night or in certain jobs such as manufacturing, construction, energy, agriculture, water, and transportation. These laws affect more than 2.7 billion women.[21]

It would be helpful to compare countries with different levels of gender equity in entrepreneurial performance. On the 2018 Mastercard Index for Women Entrepreneurs (MIWE), New Zealand topped the list. Sweden, Canada, the U.S., and Singapore made it to the top five in the index.[22] Bangladesh was rated lowest (57th) on the list. While women's engagement as business owners in Bangladesh was high (25.9%), women entrepreneurs in the country encounter a great number of barriers and challenges. The lack of financial inclusion is a serious problem facing women entrepreneurs in the country. Other major challenges include the lack of women in business leadership and professional and technical positions, the lack of access to tertiary education, poor supporting conditions for SMEs, low quality of governance, and adverse cultural perception of women entrepreneurs.[23]

Studies have found that women's low rate of participation in entrepreneurship is due to the lack of supports such as access to advice, money, and training rather than the lack of basic traits. For instance, an analysis of data from cross-country Business Environment and Enterprise Performance Survey (BEEPS) suggested that female-managed firms were less likely to obtain a bank loan than male-managed ones. Moreover, for the approved loan applications, female entrepreneurs were charged higher interest rates than their male counterparts.[24] A study of the UAE's Dubai School of Governance showed that many aspiring female entrepreneurs in the Gulf Cooperation Council (GCC) region lack confidence in business skills, which discourages them from seeking access to money. Moreover, lenders' low confidence in women's business skills leads to women's inadequate access to money in GCC countries. Likewise, according to a Gallup Poll conducted in GCC countries, women in these countries are less likely than men to have access to a mentor who can give them advice on managing a business.[25]

Other types of disparities—affecting people disadvantaged because of their social and economic backgrounds—are important too. Institutions in some economies have built-in biases that systematically favor the participation of certain segments of the population in entrepreneurial activities. For instance, in Indonesia's lucrative business sectors such as mines, palm oil plantations, and oilfields, only influential people are granted a business license.[26] Likewise, observers have noted that potential entrepreneurs in India, who have graduated from a less well-known university or those who belong to a poor family, face difficulties in getting funding.[27]

Effects of Political, Cultural, and Other Broad Environmental Factors

The World Bank's annual "Doing Business" report is probably the most well-known and most often referenced source to compare entrepreneurial climate in economies worldwide. As indicated in Figure 1.1, various geographical regions and economic groups differ widely in the number of procedures, time, and cost required in starting a business. Organization for Economic Co-operation and Development (OECD) economies are among the best performers. For instance, according to the World Bank's annual "Doing Business 2018" report, out of 185 economies, the overall rank of New Zealand, an OECD country was No. 1. In New Zealand, starting a new business requires only one procedure, which can be completed in half a day and costs only 0.3% of the country's per capita GDP.

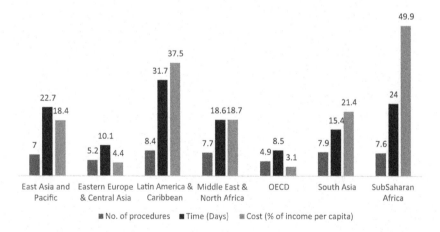

Figure 1.1 A Comparison of the Number of Procedures, Time, and Cost Required in Starting a Business across Different Regions in the World.

Source: The World Bank "Doing Business 2018" (www.doingbusiness.org/rankings).

Singapore, South Korea, and Hong Kong, which ranked #2, #4, and #5, respectively, in the World Bank's annual "Doing Business 2018," have driven the overall performance of East Asia and Pacific. In Singapore, starting a new business requires three procedures, which can be completed in 2.5 days and costs 0.5% of the country's per capita GDP.

The worst performers, especially in terms of the cost required in starting a business, are Sub-Saharan African (SSA) economies. In Somalia, which ranked 190, a potential entrepreneur needs to complete nine procedures to start a business, which takes an average of 70 days and cost 204% of the country's per capita GDP. Likewise, enforcing a contract in the country takes an average of 575 days.

As to the cultural context, desire for business ownership varies across countries.

According to the 1997/1998 ISSP Module on Work Orientations/General Social Survey, the proportion of people who say they would prefer to be self-employed varied from 26.9% in Norway to 79.9% in Poland.[28] The same survey found that proportion of self-employment varied from 6.1% in the then East Germany to 30.2% in Poland. According to the 2009 Eurobarometer Survey on Entrepreneurship, among the surveyed countries, the strongest preference for self-employment was in China and the weakest was in Japan: 71% Chinese and 39% Japanese preferred to be self-employed.[29]

People across the world also differ in the way they view entrepreneurs and entrepreneurship. In some societies, a negative societal perception of entrepreneurs leads to a lower propensity to engage in entrepreneurial activities. According to the 2009 Eurobarometer Survey, 49% of Europeans had a good opinion about entrepreneurs (Figure 1.2). The corresponding

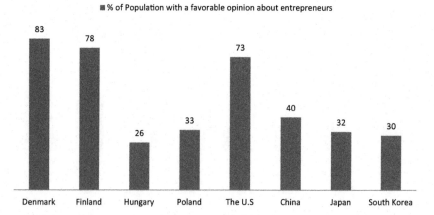

Figure 1.2 **Proportion of Populations with a Favorable Opinion about Entrepreneurs.**
Source: 2009 Eurobarometer Survey.

proportions for other professions were liberal professions (lawyers, doctors, architects, etc., 58%; civil servants, 35%; top-managers, 28%; bankers, 25%; and politicians, 12%). As shown in Figure 1.2, while the western capitalist societies have a good opinion about entrepreneurs, some collectivist and post-socialist societies express a less favorable opinion.

Definitions and Types of Entrepreneurial Activities and Their Variations Worldwide

We follow the OECD's definition of entrepreneurship, entrepreneurial activity, and entrepreneurs. Entrepreneurship is defined as—the phenomenon associated with entrepreneurial activity.[30] Entrepreneurial activity is the enterprising human action in pursuit of the generation of value, through the creation or expansion of economic activity, by identifying and exploiting new products, processes, or markets. Entrepreneurs are those persons (business owners) who seek to generate value, through the creation or expansion of economic activity, by identifying and exploiting new products, processes, or markets. Global entrepreneurship, on the other hand, can be defined as a discipline of study and practice focused on comparative analysis of entrepreneurship across economies with diverse environmental settings.

Productive, Unproductive, and Destructive Entrepreneurship

Entrepreneurs tend to maximize their own wealth, power, and prestige by means of entrepreneurial activities, which can have positive as well as negative effects to the society.

To consider the societal effects of entrepreneurial ventures, the concepts of productive, unproductive, and destructive entrepreneurship are employed.[31] Pivotal to this view is the idea that a society's rules of the game determine the distribution of these various forms of entrepreneurship.

Free-market entrepreneurs rely on competition, supply, and demand and engage in socially and economically useful activities, which help generate jobs and wealth and hence are productive. The most obvious examples are entrepreneurial activities that take place in high-growth industries, which create jobs and lead to technological innovations are productive ones.

Unproductive entrepreneurial activities are those that contribute little or nothing to economic growth. Activities involving wealth distribution through political and legal channels such as lobbying are considered to be unproductive entrepreneurial activities.[32] Some analysts consider entrepreneurial activities related to activities such as trades on crude oil as unproductive. One estimate suggested that the world's daily crude oil consumption amounted 85 million barrels in the mid-2010. However,

1.1 billion barrels of crude oil is traded daily.[33] Some observe that entrepreneurial activities of a large proportion of the world's billionaires are unproductive. A Canberra Times article commented on the Forbes' list of 1,011 billionaires published in March 2010 put it best:

> Too few of the world's billionaires can claim to be honest-to-God productive entrepreneurs who have enlarged the economic pie by dint of hard work, imagination, risk taking and innovation although thankfully a useful proportion do populate the list. But a depressingly large number constitute a ragbag of monopolists, oligarchs gifted assets and profits by the state, mega-financial engineers or just family plutocrats. And once on the list you tend to stay there; there is little churn. The arteries of capitalism are hardening.

In destructive entrepreneurship, entrepreneurs are engaged in detrimental activities such as those related to criminal and quasi-criminal behaviors, which lead to net social loss. The idea here is that if the perceived benefits of engaging in illegal entrepreneurial activity exceed their costs, some entrepreneurs are likely to engage in destructive entrepreneurship. Some examples include activities involving illegal drug production, organized crime extortion, and corruption. While lobbying is described above as an unproductive entrepreneurial activity, it can also be viewed as destructive entrepreneurship since a significant amount of resources are typically wasted by companies in lobbying efforts.[34] In many cases, the lobbying efforts are mostly directed toward acquiring a monopoly right. This type of entrepreneurship may be destructive since monopoly rights often lead to a welfare loss, which means that the losses to the society would outweigh the gains.[35]

Entrepreneurship Indicators

To explore the heterogeneity discussed above in more detail, in this section, we introduce several entrepreneurship indicators. There have been international efforts to develop and measure various entrepreneurship indicators. The OECD/EUROSTAT framework stands out as the most developed efforts to conceptualize, measure, and compare entrepreneurial activities in OECD countries. This framework for entrepreneurship indicators consists of three main building blocks: determinants, performance, and impacts. Ahmad and Hoffmann provide a useful analogy to understand interrelationships among them: Assume that passengers would like to go from point A to point B by time t (policy objective, Impact). There may be various means of transport available. Factors such as a car's engine size and fuel consumption rate are the Determinants. During their journey, passengers are informed about their current status about the direction and time by technologies such as speedometers and GPS readings (the Performance indicators). Note too that different passengers (policy makers) would like to go to different places and get there at different times (different impacts), using different modes of transport (determinant).[36]

Determinants of entrepreneurship are the factors that affect entrepreneurial performance. We discuss various determinants of entrepreneurship in terms of three categories: (a) regulatory framework; (b) values, culture, and skills; and (c) access to finance, market, R&D, and technology.

Entrepreneurial performance measures are the entrepreneurial actions that are instrumental in delivering the impacts of entrepreneurs and entrepreneurship. Put differently, target indicators used in measuring entrepreneurial performance tell the progress toward achieving the ultimate objectives. Indicators related to creation, survival, and mortality rates of various types of firms are used to measure entrepreneurial performance. Birth and concentration rates of high-growth enterprises and gazelle enterprises could provide even better measures of entrepreneurial performance. OECD defines high-growth enterprises are those with average annual growth rates (in employees or turnover) greater than 20% for over a three-year period, and with ten employees at the beginning of the observation period.[37] High-growth enterprises up to five years old are referred to as gazelles. Note that these performance indicators are only the means to achieve various entrepreneurial goals, rather than an end in themselves.

Entrepreneurial impacts reflect the value created by entrepreneurs and entrepreneurship and are the ultimate objectives that policy makers want to accomplish. Various objectives such as job creation, economic growth, poverty reduction, and the formalization of the informal sector have been identified.

In this section, we mainly focus on the determinants and impacts of entrepreneurship.

Entrepreneurial Impacts Indicators

Job Creation

Regional and national-level studies have found that entrepreneurship is positively related to job creation. A high proportion of net job creation in the U.S. is attributable to startup ventures that are less than five years old. Likewise, a comparison of different regions across Germany indicated that in the 1990s, regions with higher startup rates experienced higher employment growth.[38]

Job creation has been a critical policy challenge faced by many governments, especially in emerging economies. In fact, unavailability of job opportunities for young citizen is an important factor that contributed to the toppling of governments in many Arab countries. For instance, the proportions of the youths that neither work nor study range from 21% in

Jordan to 49% in Yemen.[39] For citizens in the Arab world, especially for those under thirty, addressing the lack of quality jobs is arguably no less important than human rights, the rule of law, and political freedoms. An estimated 100 million jobs need to be created in the region by 2020.[40]

Economic Growth

High economic growth rates of economies such as Ireland, Taiwan, and Singapore can be attributed to entrepreneurial activity.[41] Various measures of entrepreneurship are found to have positive effects on economic growth. The GEM has found that national entrepreneurial activity—as measured by the share of people actively involved in starting a new venture and/ or managing a business less than 42 months old—has significant positive correlation with subsequent economic growth rate. GEM data also suggest that there are no countries with high levels of entrepreneurship and low levels of economic growth.[42] A possible indicator of entrepreneurship is the number of competitors since the introduction of a new product or the startup of a new firm is an entrepreneurial act. In this regard, a study of manufacturing firms in the U.K. indicated that an increase in the number of competitors positively affected economic growth as measured by total factor productivity growth.[43]

Using the share of SMEs as a measure of entrepreneurship, researchers have found similar results. A study of manufacturing industries conducted in 13 European countries indicated that a higher share of small businesses led to higher output growth in subsequent years. The results indicate that industries with a high share of small enterprises relative to the same industries in other countries performed better in terms of output growth during the subsequent three to four years.[44]

Formalization of the Informal Sector

Significant entrepreneurial activities take place in the informal economy (also referred to as undeclared, shadow, black, or underground economy). Informal economic sectors encompass direct subsistence workers (self-employed, unpaid family workers, and domestic servants who are usually the lowest paid workers), informal salaried workers, and informal entrepreneurs. In some economies such as Georgia, informal economy also includes those with double employment. That is, most workers in the informal sector received formal wages and also engage in nonreported income-generating activities, in most cases at the formal employment workplaces.[45]

Various potential advantages to formal sector participation include police and judicial protection (and less vulnerability to corruption and the demand for bribes), access to formal credit institutions, the ability to use formal labor contracts.[46] Formal sector participation also leads to greater access to a wider marketplace including foreign markets that would allow these businesses to specialize and make them more productive and competitive. Most informal businesses pay lower wages and have lower growth rates than formal ones. They also have poorer safety records, are less likely to pay taxes, and are targets of corrupt government officials.[47]

According to the economist Hernando de Soto, there are two main barriers to poor people's access to the formal economy. The first barrier is associated with unreliable record-keeping systems in developing countries. Second, individuals in these countries face an environment of distrust and uncertainty that can lead to their unwillingness to give information about themselves and their transactions to their own governments, and other actors. For instance, the information can be used against them, which increases their vulnerability.[48] Various sources of uncertainty include burdensome regulations, defective policies, and procedures. Corruption, bureaucracy, red tape, and a lack of simple legal rules tend to discourage entrepreneurs from registering their businesses. Factors such as high tax rates and the absence of monitoring and compliance of both registration and tax regulations also decrease the attractiveness of formal registration.[49] A high proportion of entrepreneurial firms in developing countries thus remain informal, because formalization entails significant costs.

Although precise estimates regarding the size of informal economy are hard to come by, various attempts have been made to estimate the size of informal sectors as a proportion of the GDP and total employment. In general, the proportion of informal economy tends to be higher if a country is economically less developed.

The Peruvian economist Hernando de Soto, who is well known for his work on informal and unofficial economy, argues that the lack of formal title to unregistered houses, small business assets, and other properties costs the world economy US$9 trillion in "dead capital."[50] These assets have owners but no formal documentation. Accounting for the gains that have been foregone due to the failure to register their assets, which have instead accrued to the formal economy counterparties, a recent revised estimate of the loss to owners of assets without formal documentation has been put at US$20 trillion.[51]

A large informal sector would reduce a country's development potential and act as a constraining factor to fight against poverty. Formalization, on the other hand, can encourage and stimulate entrepreneurial activities. Studies have also shown that people who have a formal title to their property are likely to invest up to 47% more in businesses.[52]

Poverty Reduction

Entrepreneurial activities contribute to poverty reduction through a number of mechanisms. One of the most important ways in which entrepreneurship would help poor people get out of the poverty trap is through job creation.[53] In this regard, it is worth noting that in developing countries, the private sector accounts for about 90% of jobs, and poor people consider self-employment and availability of jobs as the two most important ways to improve their lives. There is more. Entrepreneurial activities lead to higher degree of availability and low prices of goods and services consumed by poor people. A further mechanism whereby entrepreneurship can contribute to poverty reduction is through increased taxes. Taxes to corporations and commercial transactions are the main sources of government revenues, which can be invested in health, education, and other public goods targeted to the poor.[54] In addition, increased taxes would also allow direct income transfers to poor household through government aids.

While some developing economies have experienced significant economic growth, the lack of mechanisms to trickle down the benefits to the poor represents a fundamental challenge facing them. The benefits of economic growth in most developing economies are highly concentrated and disproportionately distributed to the well-connected and wealthiest individuals. For instance, while Indonesia's GDP growth rate has been substantial (6%–7%), there has been relatively little job growth and only wealthy elites have benefitted from the economic growth. Likewise, about ten families control more than 80% of the stock in India's largest corporations.[55]

Determinants of Entrepreneurship

A study conducted in European countries found that very little of the difference in a worker's propensity to engage in self-employment is explained by observable characteristics of the worker.[56] This means that various aspects of the business environment such as government regulations, societal perception of entrepreneurship, and access to finance and other resources affect individuals' ability and willingness to engage in entrepreneurial activities. As noted earlier, key determinants of entrepreneurship include (a) regulatory framework; (b) values, culture, and skills; and (c) access to finance, market, R&D, and technology.

In Chapter 2, we discuss these factors as key elements of an entrepreneurial ecosystem with special emphasis on the roles of policy and regulation and illustrate them with a number of success stories. Since the lack of finance is arguably often the biggest roadblock for potential entrepreneurs to materialize the goal of starting their own businesses, in Chapter 3, we undertake an in-depth treatment of the various sources of entrepreneurial finances and their variation across the world.

In Chapters 4–10, we examine the above key determinants of entrepreneurship in the contexts of a range of economies such as OECD countries

(Chapter 4), economies in Former Soviet Union and Central and Eastern Europe (FSU&CEE) (Chapter 5), Gulf Cooperation Council (GCC) economies (Chapter 6), Africa (Chapter 7), China (Chapter 8), India (Chapter 9), and Latin America (Chapter 10). In Appendix 1, we make use of these factors to analyze two developing world-based entrepreneurial firms.

Regulatory Framework

Government policies and actions affect the costs, risks, and barriers to competition faced by entrepreneurial firms and hence the range of opportunities that are potentially profitable. While there have been a lot of complaints about high tax rates in some economies, studies have shown that there are other bigger obstacles. In some countries, poor infrastructure, burdensome regulation, contract enforcement difficulties, crime, and corruption can amount to over 25% of revenues or over three times of what firms pay as taxes.[57] While there are a variety of mechanisms by which laws, regulations, and policy would affect a country's entrepreneurial performance, this section focuses on three major aspects: corporate bankruptcy laws, labor regulations, and property rights.

CORPORATE BANKRUPTCY LAWS

Corporate bankruptcy laws are among the most discussed issues. This issue is important as the average time taken by bankruptcy proceedings is less than two years in industrialized countries compared to 4.5 years in South Asia. U.S. corporate bankruptcy law has been a role model for many countries. In an attempt to provide reorganization opportunities for corporations experiencing financial difficulties, dozens of countries are upgrading their regulative institutions. For instance, since 2002, the U.K. has passed a series of Enterprise Acts, which aim to make it easier for failed entrepreneurs to enjoy a fresh start. China's new bankruptcy law adopted in 2007 has made restructuring of insolvent firms easier. Some Islamic countries, which still have a negative view of bankruptcy, are also adopting more lenient bankruptcy laws. The U.S. Department of Commerce's Commercial Law Development Program (CLDP) reported that it advised GCC economies such as Oman, Bahrain, and the UAE on new draft Insolvency Laws.[58]

According to the World Bank, during 2004–2009, 59% of industrialized economies improved corporate bankruptcy laws. The proportions for developing countries were 33% in East Asia, 22% in Latin America, 16% in the Middle East, and 13% in South Asia.[59] Inefficiency in legal systems and retributive attitudes toward the debtor have made the adoption of American corporate bankruptcy law difficult in developing countries.

LABOR REGULATIONS

Some labor regulations limit businesses' capacity to grow and compete in the global economy. In India, for instance, companies with more than 100 employees require government permission to dismiss workers. In order to fire a worker in Burkina Faso, an employer is required to re-train a worker, find another job, and pay severance package equivalent to 18 months' wages.[60] Similarly, firing workers is almost impossible in Venezuela. Furthermore, many employees in the country want nation-alization of their companies so they can become government employees, which have better perks and a higher level of job security than most private firms.[61]

PROPERTY RIGHTS

Clear property rights would allow entrepreneurs to use the assets as collat-eral and thus increase their access to capital. Especially for entrepreneurial firms that rely heavily on intellectual property (IP), they face a unique challenge in economies with weak IP protection laws and enforcement mechanisms. In most industrialized countries, duties and obligations to one's former employer, confidentiality clauses, and noncompete agree-ments would prohibit a departing worker from taking valuable information with them. Observers have noted that such agreements are ineffective in some economies such as Russia. For instance, an employee in the Russian internet advertiser, System.ru reportedly took the firm's entire client data-base to a newly formed rival.[62] In this regard, strong property rights allow an existing company to prevent other entrepreneurs from starting their own ventures using the IP developed by the former. Conversely, young startups that own strong property rights can be in a position to compete against established companies.

Values, Culture, and Skills

Values, culture, and skills are composed of many different elements. One economy may outperform another on some elements but fall behind on others. For instance, according to Ernst & Young's (EY) G20 En-trepreneurship Barometer 2013 (www.ey.com/gl/en/services/strategic-growth-markets/ey-g20---entrepreneurship-culture), the U.S. was found to have the best entrepreneurship culture overall. However, it is argued that Europe outperforms the U.S. on some components of val-ues, culture, and skills. For instance, some have noted that advantages of Europe over the U.S. include more stable workforce, relatively less hostility to immigrants and a large number of high-quality engineering schools.[63]

VALUES AND CULTURE

The underlying values and culture of a society affect the entrepreneurial patterns. First, societies across the world vary in their propensity to take risks. In the Arab world, for instance, large corporate bureaucracies are found to be risk averse. The lack of a tradition of private entrepreneurship in many of the economies in Former Soviet Union and Central and Eastern European countries is arguably related to an underdeveloped risk-taking culture in the absence of local norms and social networks providing support for such a culture.[64] Managers with experience in state-owned enterprises in these economies tend to be risk averse. Likewise, some suggest that Chinese tend to have a low risk-taking propensity.

In some societies, family and social obligations act as barriers to productive entrepreneurship. Entrepreneurs are expected to provide jobs and even redistribute their wealth and income to the members of their extended family and to the society. For instance, accumulating a huge amount of wealth is still a delicate subject in China, and some people in the society expect entrepreneurs to provide socialist benefits. Some Chinese entrepreneurs are thus still sensitive to the society and the communist party that resist ideas related to the ownership of private property.

The concept of high- and low-context cultures would help us understand the international differences in entrepreneurial orientation.[65] In high-context cultures such as those of Asia and the Middle East, which are characterized by relational and collectivist values, people prefer to enter well-established institutions and organizations. For instance, in Japan, employment in large corporations is viewed as more prestigious and respected than in the U.S. Thus, in Japan, more educated and qualified people tend to gravitate toward careers in large corporations. Likewise, a survey conducted in 2010 indicated that 52% of Arab population in 15–29 age group preferred government employment over a private sector job. Moreover, 45% of aspiring entrepreneurs in the region preferred a public sector job.[66]

Cultural differences are also linked to difference in personal characteristics between entrepreneurs and people with other occupations. For instance, a comparative study of Japan and the U.S. showed that entrepreneurs in Japan had significantly different personal characteristics than managers of large corporations. Silicon Valley entrepreneurs, on the other hand, showed less personality differences with managers from large corporations.[67]

Religions and ethical systems are also linked to entrepreneurial performance. For instance, Confucianism, some forms of Christianity, and Judaism arguably play roles in shaping habits and values that promote economic success including the belief that people can influence their destinies. For instance, it is argued that the Jewish faith arguably is learning-based, not rite-based, which encourages a belief in progress and personal accountability.[68]

ENTREPRENEURIAL SKILLS

Economies worldwide exhibit a high degree of heterogeneity in terms of education systems' ability to prepare students for entrepreneurship. This is important as a study conducted with self-employed individuals enrolled in a Peruvian micro-finance program indicated that even a little entrepreneurship training can significantly enhance the business performance.[69]

For instance, researchers have found that one reason for Chinese graduates' lack of preparedness to entrepreneurship concerns the Chinese education system that is traditionally based on rote learning. A number of surveys have indicated that while critical thinking is encouraged in the West, this aspect is not emphasized in China. The lack of skills and experiences to manage various types of entrepreneurial ventures has hindered Chinese companies' international expansion activities. For instance, China is reported to have a large number of venture capitalists interested in funding U.S. startups, they lack skills and experience to manage venture investments.[70]

The lack of entrepreneurial education and training has also been a matter of concern in EU economies. According to a Flash Eurobarometer study conducted in 2009, 39% of EU respondents agreed with the statement "My school education gave me the skills and know-how that enabled me to run a business" compared to 67% in the U.S. Similarly, with respect to another statement "My school education helped me to develop my sense of initiatives—a sort of entrepreneurial attitude," 49% of EU respondents agreed compared to 73% in the U.S.[71]

A related point is that entrepreneurial firms face difficulty in finding skilled talent. Especially, SMEs are reported to face difficulties in finding and retaining skilled and highly qualified personnel. In Canada, a study indicated that 55% of all SMEs and 80% of mid-sized businesses reported this as a major barrier to growth.[72] In the U.K., about 20% of SMEs reported challenges in finding people with the right skills.[73] Among high-growth firms, 50% reported such problems.[74]

Access to Finance, Market, R&D, and Technology

ACCESS TO MARKETS

Access to and demands of an entrepreneurial firm's products in the domestic and foreign markets are a critical factor determining the attractiveness of entrepreneurial activities. In addition to private demand, procurement regulations and policies that give priority to new companies in government contracts for goods and services would create better opportunities for potential entrepreneurs.

On the other hand, the lack of antitrust laws in some economies leaves anticompetitive conducts entirely unregulated. In such economies, one or a few dominant firms misuse their market power, in some cases by forming anticompetitive collusion or anticompetitive mergers, which create entry barriers to new firms and deter entrepreneurship. For instance, in Mexico, markets that lack competition account for 30% of consumer spending, which has forced Mexicans to spend 40% more than they would in the presence of a better antitrust laws and enforcement.[75] A Canberra Times article commented on Mexican billionaire Carlos Slim, who overtook Bill Gates as the world's richest man in Forbes' list published in March 2010:

> ...Carlos Slim made his fortune from being the monopolist who controls 90 per cent of Mexico's telephone landlines and 80 per cent of its mobile phone subscribers. The OECD notes that he charges among the highest usage fees in the world.[76]

As of 2011, in half of Mexico's 400 local areas, only Slim's company had the infrastructure to make calls to landlines. It is estimated that the average costs of home and business landlines in Mexico are 45% and 63% more than the OECD averages, respectively.[77]

ACCESS TO FINANCE

Entrepreneurs need capital in all phases of business life. A critical practical challenge that most potential entrepreneurs face is the ability to acquire the capital, from access to early seed funds to access to the stock markets. In general, initial wealth is positively related to an individual's entry into entrepreneurship.[78] When there is limited credit availability and the entrepreneurs' initial capital requirements are substantial, low-wealth households face higher barriers to starting an entrepreneurial venture.

Unavailability of bank loans in many developing economies is partly due to improper management of assets rather than unavailability of funds. Banks in many developing countries have adopted too conservative lending policies as reflected in the liquidity ratio of liquid assets to total deposits. They tend to maintain high proportions of their assets in liquid forms such as cash, deposits with other banks, central bank debt, and short-term government securities. In a study of a sample of 35 developing countries, the mean of liquidity ratio was 45% and the ratio was 126% in Argentina compared to 2% in the U.K. and 6.5% in the U.S.[79]

Access to finance is thus a more serious obstacle in less developed economies than developed ones. For instance, according to the World Bank's Enterprise Surveys, access to finance was identified as a key obstacle for 45% of firms in SSA to their businesses compared to 13% in OECD countries. In many developing economies, access to financial services is a broader economic and social problem. For instance, in Bogotá and São Paulo, fewer than 40% of families have access to the financial system.[80]

Likewise, according to an Adviser of the Central Bank of Nigeria, 60% of Nigerians are underbanked.

Entrepreneurs rely on a variety of funding sources to support their entrepreneurial activities. There are important differences across economies in terms of the availability and sources of finances. SMEs account for less than 4% of the total loans of three of China's four largest banks. Consequently, most of the entrepreneurial funding in China is reported to come from unofficial, informal, and even illegal channels. According China's central bank, Wenzhou city's 89% of people and 57% of enterprises have borrowed money from such channels, who reportedly pay interest rates as high as 10% for 30 days, which translates to 214% for a year.[81] Quoting a Wenzhou businessman, an Economist article explained that there were 100,000 people in Wenzhou city who could raise as much as one billion yuan (US$150 million) each within forty-eight hours.[82]

R&D AND TECHNOLOGY

Access to technology greatly facilitates entrepreneurial activities. According to a report of the Internet Innovation and the Small Business and Entrepreneurship Council, a small business startup can save over US$16,000 by using high-speed broadband. For instance, high-speed broadband allows working from home rather than in the office, reducing costs associated with travel and office space. Similarly, due to lower startup costs for an online shop-front, Internet-based technologies can provide small firms the opportunity to overcome the limitations of size and compete more effectively and/or in larger markets with bigger-sized establishments. According to an EU-commissioned study on internationalization of SMEs, a firm's e-commerce adoption is positively correlated with its chance of being active in export or import markets.

Access to technology is limited in many developing and least developed countries due to unavailability and the lack of affordability of ICT hardware, software, and services. As Figure 1.3 shows, there is wide variation in fixed and mobile broadband prices across economies with various developmental stages. The real irony here is that the poorer the economy, the higher the price of broadband access.

Finally, R&D would provide opportunities for high-quality entrepreneurship and enhance an entrepreneurial business's competitiveness. R&D would help create new inventions and innovations, which can be used to develop new products, services, or processes. Firm- and country-level studies have linked R&D activities with high entrepreneurial performance. A comparison of East Asian economies indicated that successful entrepreneurial economies were with a higher R&D performance.[83] At the firm level, the probability of successfully launching a new product increases with an increase in R&D investment. R&D activities affect performances of new

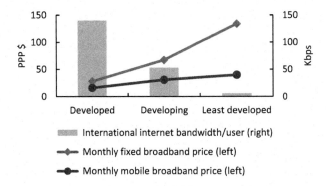

Figure 1.3 Monthly Fixed and Mobile Broadband Prices and Bandwidth Availability (2016).
Source: ITU (2016). ICT facts and figures 2016. Switzerland Geneva, June 2016.

and existing firms via different mechanisms, and perhaps in different contexts. Since most startups are less likely to have a direct access to large R&D facilities, they often rely on employees who have gained R&D-related knowledge and experience in previous employers. In this way, while existing firms engage in R&D activities to improve existing products, startups benefit from knowledge spillovers and the existing stock of knowledge by combining in new and innovative ways to launch new products.[84]

Becoming a Successful Entrepreneur in Different Countries

While entrepreneurial traits such as a high need for achievement, innovative thinking, creativity, breakthrough ideas, high risk-taking propensity, perseverance, and flexibility are more or less universal for becoming a successful entrepreneur, the ability to fit to the environment is no less important. The success of an entrepreneur interested in starting entrepreneurial venture in multiple countries may hinge on the ability to learn and adapt to the unique environmental contexts, overcome the challenges, and take advantage of the various international differences. For instance, an entrepreneur needs to have a good understanding of the market and market dynamics; knowledge about customers' needs and wants; the ability to acquire financial resources and recruit people with appropriate knowledge, skills, and experience; and manage them. An entrepreneur who successfully manages these factors in one institutional setting does not necessarily mean that he/she can do so in other settings.

In some cases, the fact that important ingredients are missing in the economy means that entrepreneurial firms need to take extra efforts and measures. For instance, due to the lack of entrepreneurial education in India, the country's successful companies invest heavily in employees through extensive training and development in firm-specific skills. One study found that firms in the country's IT industry provide 60 days of formal training to newly hired employees and they are paid during the period. Some firms go even further. For instance, Tata Consultancy Services is reported to have a seven-month training program for science graduates in order to convert them into business consultants, and every employee in the company gets 14 days of formal training annually.[85]

In some countries, entrepreneurial successes have to be achieved within a culture that is hostile to capitalism and entrepreneurship. While small-scale entrepreneurs may not be in a position to change such perception, large organizations, either singly or in cooperation with other organizations or the government agencies, can take measures to change negative social image associated with entrepreneurs and entrepreneurship. In many emerging economies, a market economy does not function well. In these economies, institutional rules related to entrepreneurship tend to be incomplete, ambiguous, and sometimes conflicting with one another. In countries with underdeveloped market economy, some entrepreneurs also take initiatives to create new market institutions. Such entrepreneurs are also known as institutional entrepreneurs.

Financing sources that are common in industrialized countries such as bank loans or personal and business credit cards are not readily available in most developing countries. In such cases, alternative sources such as informal financing may be more appropriate. Entrepreneurs can also take advantage of special sources such as subsidized government financing in some countries.

Relevant cultural, religious, and spiritual networks also help increase market access for some entrepreneurs. Some examples include entrepreneurs utilizing the Mouride Brotherhood in Senegal and the Gambia, and Indian Sikhs.[86] Many followers of the Mouride Brotherhood, with roots in Senegal's Touba, for instance, work as street vendors selling sunglasses, bags, and souvenirs and other small-scale entrepreneurial activities in Western countries such as Italy, France, Spain, and the U.S., Mouridism preaches the responsibility to look after others within the Brotherhood. The followers of the Brotherhood, abroad and at home, donate to the Brotherhood, which in turn provides business loans and other helps to other followers. Likewise, studies conducted among immigrants living in Europe, Americas, and Australia have indicated that diaspora-based networks from China, India, Pakistan, South Korea, Sri Lanka, Vietnam, and other parts of the world help immigrants from their countries of origin to access resources and develop business ideas as well as facilitate market access.[87]

Finally, the true success of an entrepreneurial activity, irrespective of wherever it has been carried out, can only be assessed by the impact it has upon the society, the economy, and the environment. Entrepreneurial activities need to be performed in such a way that they minimize negative impacts and maximize positive impacts on the society, the economy, and the environment.

Creating an Entrepreneurial Economy and Society

Policy makers keen to improve entrepreneurial outcomes can take various measures. Policy interventions can be oriented to create rewards for productive entrepreneurial activity and levy penalties for unproductive or destructive ones. An improvement in the legal system in areas such as contract and property rights and favorable tax policy is a promising way to stimulate productive entrepreneurial activity. There is also a need to infuse and nurture a value system and culture in which creating jobs is encouraged more than getting a job.

Various entrepreneurial outcome indicators discussed above can be improved by encouraging foreign multinationals to engage in local procurement, sourcing, and collaborate with local suppliers, distributors, and retailers to create value and increase efficiency in the supply chain. For instance, Nestle sources milk locally from nearly 150,000 Pakistani farmers. A study on Unilever in Indonesia shows that by supporting such linkages the company created approximately 90 additional jobs for each direct job created in the company.[88] Evidence from economies such as China and Taiwan indicates that linkages to MNCs could provide an efficient channel to gain access to technical know-how.[89]

The most promising entrepreneurial activities are those that encourage the participation of the most underrepresented population segment and produce positive impacts on the economy, the society, and the environment. To take an example, female entrepreneurs in Mali use solar energy to dry mango products and market them.[90] Government support to such activities could significantly contribute to creating a successful entrepreneurial society. In particular, reducing gender disparity in access to resources can lead to better entrepreneurial outcomes. One study found that agricultural productivity can be increased by as high as 20% in SSA, if women's access to land, seed and fertilizer, and other resources is increased to the same level as men's.[91]

Research has also indicated that individuals who have gained access to training and education are likely to have an improved entrepreneurial orientation. For instance, it was found that over 70% of students that participated in Young Enterprise entrepreneurship program developed positive attitudes toward starting their own businesses. Likewise, half of the trainees that graduate from the International Labor Organization's (ILO) training program start a new business.[92]

In light of the various benefits that can arise from the formal sector, policy makers should formulate strategies to formalize the informal sector.

Formalization of the informal sector is likely to contribute in a significant way to poverty alleviation. The Peruvian economist De Soto, for instance, describes poor people as small entrepreneurs, who have been stuck in a poverty trap because their wealth is informal. While formalization of the informal wealth may likely to face opposition from businesses and national elites, a strong government, public funding, an efficient bureaucracy, and substantial legal changes may help accomplish this goal.[93]

Not all firms are created equal. In order to achieve higher rates of economic growth and jobs creation, policy incentives need to be established to encourage high-quality or high-expectation companies instead of just the firm birth rates. One way to achieve this would be to reduce incentives and support for the establishment of low-quality companies. Some suggested that the government should act like a venture capitalist and encourage only innovative companies.[94]

Concluding Comments

Entrepreneurs contribute to the national economy in several ways. Some of the important mechanisms associated with entrepreneurs' role in generating wealth and income include creating jobs, providing competition to the existing businesses, helping to improve productivity by bringing innovations in product and process, introducing new goods and services, reducing prices of exiting products, advancing technological development, and enhancing the competitive position of an economy.

While societal, governmental, and economic environments for entrepreneurship have dramatically improved and entrepreneurial activities have exhibited an explosive growth rate worldwide in recent years, significant international differences exist with respect to the availability and structure of entrepreneurial opportunities as well as the impacts, performance measures and various determinants of entrepreneurship.

Considerable variation across population segments can be observed in the willingness and abilities pursue and respond to entrepreneurial opportunities. In some economies, a large gender gap in the participation in entrepreneurial activities exists, which can be attributed to differential access to resources, differential societal expectations, and differential opportunities for men and women. It is thus essential to design appropriate policy intervention in light of the fact that increased female participation in entrepreneurial activities has a strong positive impact on the society and the economy of any country.

Unaffordability and unavailability of Internet and broadband have hampered entrepreneurial activities in some developing and least developed countries. However, improving connectivity and decreasing Internet and broadband prices provide hope for underprivileged potential entrepreneurs from these countries.

End of Chapter Questions

1   Why is it important to formalize the informal sector?
2   What are the various forms of capitalism? Give an example of a country, which has a prevalence of each form of capitalism.
3   What is oligarchic capitalism? How does it affect a country's economic development?
4   What is destructive entrepreneurship?
5   How are the indicators related to determinants, entrepreneurial performance and entrepreneurial impacts related?
6   How can unproductive and destructive entrepreneurship be discouraged?
7   Please select an economy that is among the most friendly to small businesses and another economy that is among the least friendly to small businesses. Do some research on determinants of entrepreneurship in these countries and compare them. What conclusions can you draw?

End of the Chapter Case: Blockchain-Based Land Registry and Formalization of the Informal Sector in Developing Economies

A large proportion of poor people in developing economies lack property rights. For instance, in most African countries, over 90% of rural areas are not registered.[95] Ghana's 78% of land is unregistered.[96] There is a long backlog of land-dispute cases in Ghanaian courts.[97]

One estimate suggested that over 20 million rural families in India do not own land and millions more lacked legal ownership to the lands where they built houses, lived on, and worked.[98] Land titles in the country fail to guarantee the owner's complete rights. The records of property transactions are on paper and are not updated. An upshot is that widespread disputes occur over ownership of land.[99]

In some economies, land owners have been the victims of predatory behaviors of government officials. In Honduras, for instance, there have been instances in which government officials have altered titles to registered properties. Some government officials allocated properties with altered titles to themselves. The country's bureaucrats got beachfront properties by altering the titles.[100] They also allegedly accept bribes in exchange for property titles.

Blockchain can be used to provide a tamper proof evidence of land ownership, which can help to overcome the aforementioned challenges. In addition, blockchain-based land registry can also provide incentives and pressures for small informal businesses to formalize. This is important because informal businesses often tend to avoid attention and like to keep their activities secret. Digitization of their economic activities, however, forces them to be more transparent.

What Is Blockchain?

Blockchain is the technology underlying bitcoin and other cryptocurrencies. We follow the definition of blockchain provided in a 2018 Internal Report of the National Institute of Standards and Technology.[101] According to the report, blockchain can be viewed as a decentralized ledger that maintains records of a transaction simultaneously on multiple computers. After a block of records is entered into the ledger, the information in the block is mathematically connected to other blocks. In this way, a chain of records is formed. Due to this mathematical relationship, the information in a block cannot be changed without changing all blocks in the chain. Any alteration of information in a block would create a discrepancy that is likely to be noticed immediately by others in the network. Blockchain-based ledgers thus do not require record-keepers to trust each other. In this way, the dangers associated with data being stored in a central location by a single owner do not apply to blockchain.

Blockchain-Based Property Registration Projects in Some Developing Economies

More and more developing economies are looking toward blockchain for securing property rights. Some blockchain-based property registry projects that are being considered or undertaken in developing economies are summarized in Table 1.1.

In a blockchain-based land registry system, property-related transactions can be recorded securely with GPS coordinates, written description, and satellite photos.[102] Digitally certified documents (e.g., land title) are put on the land owner's account by a certifier such as a property lawyer or a government agency. The certifier often needs the subject's permission to do so. After putting on the blockchain, certifiers do not have access to the data. The introduction of more sophisticated features into a blockchain-based registry system allows a high degree of security and privacy as well as other features for property owners. Thus, blockchain-based land registry systems are likely to be complete, efficient, and effective.

The Republic of Georgia represents probably the most advanced use case of blockchain deployment in land registry. Bitcoin company BitFury and the Georgian government signed a deal to develop a system for registering land titles using the blockchain.[103] BitFury built the software and tested land title registrations. The Peruvian economist Hernando de Soto is involved in the project. The government has also committed to use blockchain to validate property-related government transactions.[104] In February 2017, BitFury and the Georgian National Agency of Public Registry signed a new MoU to expand the service to purchases and sales of land titles, demolition of property, mortgages and rentals, and notary services.[105]

Table 1.1 Blockchain-Based Land Registry Projects That Are Being Considered or Undertaken in developing Economies

Economy	Description	Progress and challenges in carrying out the projects
Bermuda	January 2018: the premier announced plans to migrate property deeds system to blockchain.[a]	A task force has been established to create an appropriate regulatory environment.
Georgia	April 2016: BitFury and the government of Georgia signed a deal to develop a system for registering land titles using blockchain. The registration of land titles and property transactions, started a slow rollout in April 2016.	The main barrier was reported to be educational rather than technical.[b] As of April 2017, about 100,000 land titles had been registered.[c] As of the mid-2017, about 160,000 registrations had been processed.[b] Moving the process onto the blockchain, the costs to the buyer and the seller are expected to reduce from US$50–200 to the range of US$0.05–0.10.
Ghana	Bitland, a blockchain platform that registers land in Ghana started in January 2016.[d] The pilot project was being carried out with 28 communities in Kumasi, Ghana.	As of early 2017, 500 deeds filed Bitland offers real estate land registration services to citizens companies and farm unions[e]
Honduras	In the mid-2015, the Honduran government and Factom signed a letter of intent to record land title for the city of La Ceiba.[f]	It was reported in December 2015 that the project had "stalled" due to political issues
India	2017: Telangana and Andhra Pradesh states announced plans to use blockchain for land registry. Telangana started a land registry pilot project in the capital city of Hyderabad. In October 2017, the Andhra Pradesh government collaborated with a Swedish startup, ChromaWay, to create a blockchain-based land registry system for the planned city of Amaravati.[g]	It was reported in September 2017 that a complete rollout of the program in Hyderabad and nearby areas would take place within a year.[h]

(Continued)

Economy	Description	Progress and challenges in carrying out the projects
Rwanda	Early 2017: Swiss cybersecurity and IoT solutions company, WISeKey and Microsoft teamed up to launch the Rwandan Blockchain project.[i] The first phase of the project will be in land registry.	The project is a part of the Rwanda's digital transformation master plan.[j]
Ukraine	February 2016: Ukrainian government implemented a blockchain-based eAuction platform in real estate auction April 2017: Ukrainian government and BitFury announced plans to introduce blockchain-based registries for land, businesses and other assets.[b]	Faced resistance from the country's bureaucracy.[b] A pilot project will be carried out before the full implementation.

a Milano, A. 2018. "Bermuda could launch a blockchain land registry." www.coin-desk.com/bermuda-launch-blockchain-land-registry/.
b economist.com. 2017. "Governments may be big backers of the blockchain." www.economist.com/news/business/21722869-anti-establishment-technology-faces-ironic-turn-fortune-governments-may-be-big-backers.
c Snip, I. 2017. "Georgia: Authorities use blockchain technology for developing land registry." *EuroasiaNet*, www.eurasianet.org/node/83286.
d Gharib, M. 2017. "Blockchain could be a force for good. But first you have to understand it." www.npr.org/sections/goatsandsoda/2017/01/11/503159694/blockchain-could-be-a-force-for-good-but-first-you-have-to-understand-it.
e Custodio, M. 2017. "Blockchain land registry Bitland and Foodcoin ecosystem partner." http://blocktribune.com/blockchain-land-registry-bitland-foodcoin-ecosystem-partner/.
f Rizzo, P. 2015. "Blockchain land title project 'Stalls' in Honduras." www.coindesk.com/debate-factom-land-title-honduras/.
g Lawful Editors. 2017. "Leveraging blockchain for the real estate industry," December 4. www.lawfuel.com/blog/leveraging-blockchain-real-estate-industry/.
h CNN. 2017. "Indian state plans to store citizen data on a blockchain." https://tinyurl.com/ydc5fc3b.
i IAFRIKAN NEWS. 2017. "Rwanda government's blockchain project gains momentum." www.iafrikan.com/2017/10/13/rwanda-government-blockchain-project/.
j https://cryptovest.com/news/wisekey-looks-to-put-rwandas-land-titles-on-the-blockchain/.

Blockchain can lead to substantial improvements in costs and speed of property transfer. For instance, to buy or sell land in Georgia, currently the buyer and the seller go to a public registry house and pay US$50–200, which depends on the speed with which they want the transaction to be notarized. Moving this process onto the blockchain, the costs are expected to be in the range US$0.05–0.10.[106]

Many other developing economies are exploring the use of blockchain in property registration and some are already adopting. However, they are not at the level that has been reported in Georgia. In the Indian state of Andhra Pradesh, the government hopes that blockchain-based land registry system would allow people to collateralize property, receive loans from financial institutions, and make investments using that asset.[107] The blockchain company Ateon reported that it was working in Saudi Arabia and other countries in the region on a number of use cases including land registry.[108]

A point to be noted is that the examples in Table 1.1 are still far from a full implementation of the potential of blockchain. For instance, the pilot project in Brazil replicates the existing legal structure of property ownership and transfer. In the future, a full blockchain solution is expected to replace the current centralized siloed system. A blockchain-based system will provide ultimate accuracy and security. Nonetheless, the simple fact that land ownership data are on blockchain means that Brazilian, whose lands are registered on blockchain will not face the problem that many Haitians have experienced following the 2010 earthquakes. In blockchain, there is no single point of failure; records are on many computers or devices that hold identical information.

In several developing economies, policy, regulatory, and administrative frameworks are evolving in order to capitalize upon emerging opportunities created by blockchain to transform property registries. In November 2017, a task force was established Bermuda in order to create an appropriate regulatory environment and to utilize blockchain to attract foreign companies and create new jobs. The government was reported to be working with Ambika Group and the Bermuda Business Development Agency and other organizations to identify possible uses of the technology.[109]

Case Summary

Current centralized systems of property registry are susceptible to manipulation. That is, information is likely to be manipulated and put to inappropriate uses. Blockchain's decentralized access and immutability mean that malicious actions can be detected and prevented. Problems related to distrust and suspicion of government agencies can be effectively addressed by blockchain.

Using blockchain, fraud problems such as those that have plagued Honduran property owner can be solved effectively. Blockchain thus ensures that a comprehensive and robust system exists for property registration. This technology can encourage the participation of small-holder farmers and small business owners in the formal sector and stimulate their investment in productive assets and activities.

Notes

1 Jurney, C. 2017. "The world's largest public companies 2017," 24 May, www.forbes.com/sites/corinnejurney/2017/05/24/the-worlds-largest-public-companies-2017/#63574d4a508d.
2 Newport, F. 2016. "Americans' views of socialism, capitalism are little changed." http://news.gallup.com/poll/191354/americans-views-socialism-capitalism-little-changed.aspx.
3 Nikitina, O. 2004. "Changing times, changing attitudes: What do Russians really think about the transition to capitalism?" *Russ Profile* 1(4), pp. 26–27.
4 Streeter, R. 2010. "Asian entrepreneurs are bullish on the future," 3 August, http://online.wsj.com/article/SB10001424052748704271804575404650983236426.html.
5 Doing Business. 2017. "Doing business 2018 reforming to create jobs," 31 October, www.doingbusiness.org/reports/global-reports/doing-business-2018.
6 World Bank. 2015. "Entrepreneurship is the trend in Latin America." www.worldbank.org/en/news/feature/2015/09/30/emprender-esta-de-moda-en-america-latina.
7 Kovessy, P. 2014. "Survey: Youth startups in Qatar stifled by red tape," 11 February, https://dohanews.co/survey-youth-startups-in-qatar-stifled-by-red-tape/.
8 Sitte, A., & Rheault, M. 2009, "Arab Youth express strong entrepreneurial spirit." *Gallup Poll Briefing*, 9 June, p. 3.
9 AllWorld Network. 2012. "Overview: The Saudi fast growth 100 and Arabia 500." www.allworldlive.com/saudi-arabia-100/overview.
10 Seligson, H. 2010. "Nine Young Chinese entrepreneurs to watch." 28 February, www.forbes.com/2010/02/26/young-chinese-entrepreneurs-to-watch-entrepreneurs-technology-china.html.
11 Baumöl, W. S., Litan, R. E., & Schramm, C. J. 2007. *Good Capitalism, Bad Capitalism, and the Economics of Growth and Prosperity*, New Haven, CT and London: Yale University Press.
12 Morris, R. 2011. "GEM endeavor 2011 high impact entrepreneur entrepreneurship report." http://gemconsortium.org/docs/295/gem-endeavor-2011-high-impact-entrepreneurship-report.
13 Adly, A. I. 2009. "Politically-embedded cronyism: The case of post-liberalization Egypt." *Business and Politics* 11(4). www.bepress.com/bap/vol11/iss4/art3.
14 EMF (Emerging Markets Forum). 2009, 'India 2039: An affluent society in one generation'. www.emergingmarketsforum.org/papers/pdf/2009-EMF-India-Report_Overview.pdf.
15 According to Plato, "oligarchy" is governance by a small group of people. In Plato's approach, oligarchs are different from nobles in terms of legality. Whereas nobles are few but rightful rulers, oligarchs rule in an unlawful way. In the contemporary literature, an oligarch is a large business owner controlling sufficient resources to influence national policy making and/or judiciary to further his/her economic interests.
16 Panahatan, A. 2010. "Entrepreneurship as a compulsory subject in the education of Indonesian," 8 August, http://edukasi.kompasiana.com/2010/08/08/entrepreneurship-as-a-compulsary-subject-in-the-education-of-indonesian/.
17 Cetron, M. J., & Davies, O. 2008. "Trends shaping tomorrow's World." *Futurist* 42(3), pp. 35–50.
18 Frazier, D. 2012. "Indonesia minister: 'We need four million entrepreneurs,'" 14 May. www.forbes.com/sites/donaldfrazier/2012/05/14/indonesian-minister-we-need-four-million-entrepreneurs/.

19 Bosma, N., Jones, K., Autio, E., & Levie, J. 2007. "2007 Executive report, global entrepreneurship monitor."

20 The World Bank. 2018. "Women entrepreneurs finance initiative." www. worldbank.org/en/programs/women-entrepreneurs.

21 World Bank. 2018. "Women, business and the law 2018," 29 March, https:// live.worldbank.org/women-business-and-law-2018-report-launch.

22 Mastercard. 2018. "Women in charge: Mastercard index reveals how countries are progressing to empower women entrepreneurs." https://newsroom.master card.com/press-releases/women-in-charge-mastercard-index-reveals-how-countries-are-progressing-to-empower-women-entrepreneurs/.

23 Mastercard. 2018. "Mastercard Index of Women Entrepreneurs (MIWE)." MASTERCARD. https://newsroom.mastercard.com/wp-content/uploads/2017/03/Report-Mastercard-Index-of-Women-Entrepreneurs-2017-Mar-3.pdf.

24 Muravyev, A., Schaefer, D., & Talavera, O. 2008. "Entrepreneurs' gender and financial constraints: evidence from international data," http://ideas.repec.org/p/kse/dpaper/11.html.

25 Bugshan, F. 2012. "Lack of mentors may hinder Women's entrepreneurship in GCC." *Gallup Poll Briefing* 15, p. 4.

26 Frazier, D. 2012. "Indonesia minister: 'We need four million entrepreneurs.'" www.forbes.com/sites/donaldfrazier/2012/05/14/indonesian-minister-we-need-four-million-entrepreneurs/.

27 Gandhi, G. 2010. "Indian entrepreneurs need a hug: Google's Gandhi." 16 February. http://blogs.wsj.com/india-chief-mentor/2010/02/16/indian-entrepreneurs-need-a-hug-google%E2%80%99s-gandhi/.

28 Blanchflower, D. G., Oswald, A., & Stutzer, A. 2001. "Latent entrepreneurship across nations." *European Economic Review* 45(4–6), p. 680.

29 ECEI (European Commission Enterprise and Industry). 2010a. "Eurobarometer Survey on Entrepreneurship."

30 Ahmad, N., & Hoffmann, A. N. 2008. "A framework for addressing and measuring entrepreneurship." *OECD Statistics Working Paper*, January. www.olis.oecd.org/olis/2008doc.nsf/LinkTo/NT000009FA/$FILE/JT03239191.PDF.

31 Baumol, W. J. 1990. "Entrepreneurship: Productive, unproductive, and destructive." *Journal of Political Economy* 98(5), pp. 893–921.

32 Karabegović, A., & McMahon, F. 2008. "Economic freedom in North America."www.fraserinstitute.org/uploadedFiles/fraser-ca/Content/research-news/research/articles/EconomicFreedominNorthAmerica2008.pdf.

33 New Euorope. 2010. "The change we need." 18 July. Issue: 894. www.neurope.eu/articles/The-Change-We-Need/101952.php.

34 Baumol, W. J. 2008. "Mega entrepreneurs: Active molders and creators of key institutions." mimeo, *Berkley Center for Entrepreneurial Studies*, New York University.

35 Murphy, K. M., Shleifer, A., & Vishny, R. W. 1993. "Why is rent seeking so costly to growth?" *American Economic Review* 83(2), pp. 409–414.

36 Ahmad & Hoffmann. 2008. "A framework for addressing and measuring entrepreneurship."

37 De Backer, K. 2008. "Definition and measurement of high growth enterprises: The OECD – EUROSTAT entrepreneurship indicator programme." INNO-Views Policy Workshop, Brussels. www.proinno-europe.eu/extranet/upload/deliverables/1_1_De_Backer_WS06_Brussels7962.pdf (Accessed 17 November 2008).

38 Audretsch, D. B., & Fritsch, M. 2002. "Growth regimes over time and space." *Regional Studies*, 36, pp. 113–124.
39 Bains, E. 2009. "Qatar tackles region's jobless youth." *MEED: Middle East Economic Digest* 53(26), pp. 26–27.
40 Dyer, P., & Yousef, T. 2007. "Will the current oil boom solve the employment crisis in the middle east." Arab World Competitiveness Report, World Economic Forum, 31, http://belfercenter.ksg.harvard.edu/files/AWCR%203.pdf.
41 Stangler, D., & Litan, R.E. 2009 "Where will the jobs come from?" *Kauffman Foundation Research Series: Firm Foundation and Economic Growth*, November 2009.
42 Reynolds, P. D., Bygrave, W.D., Autio, E., Cox, L., & Hay, M. 2002. *Global entrepreneurship monitor 2002 executive report*. Wellesley, MA and London: Babson College/London Business School.
43 Nickell, S. J., Nicolitsas, D., & Dryden, N. 1997. "What makes firms perform well?" *European Economic Review*, 41, pp. 783–796.
44 Carree, M., & Thurik, A.R. 1998. "Small firms and economic growth in Europe." *Atlantic Economic Journal*, 26(2), pp. 137–146.
45 Country Specific Information, http://lnweb90.worldbank.org/eca/eca.nsf/1f3aa35cab9dea4f85256a77004e4ef4/ae1f227d6ac1b39085256a940073f4eb?OpenDocument.
46 *Economist*. (2009). Reforming through the tough times. 71.
47 Ibid.
48 Casey, M. 2016. Could blockchain technology help the world's poor? 9 March. www.weforum.org/agenda/2016/03/could-blockchain-technology-help-the-worlds-poor?utm_content=buffer913be&utm_medium=social&utm_source=twitter.com&utm_campaign=buffer.
49 Klapper, L., Amit, R., & Guillén, M.F. "Entrepreneurship and firm formation across countries." www.nber.org/chapters/c8220, pp. 129–158.
50 De Soto, H. 2000. *The Mystery of Capital*. New York: Basic Books.
51 Casey, M. 2016. "Could blockchain technology help the world's poor?" www.weforum.org/agenda/2016/03/could-blockchain-technology-help-the-worlds-poor?utm_content=buffer913be&utm_medium=social&utm_source=twitter.com&utm_campaign=buffer.
52 *Economist*. 2009. "Reforming through the tough times."
53 Smith, W. 2005. "Unleashing Entrepreneurship, the Brookings Blum Roundtable: The Private Sector in the Fight against Global Poverty, Session I: Facilitating Entrepreneurship's Contribution to Development," 3 August, www.brookings.edu/global/200508blum_smith.pdf.
54 Ibid.
55 Malhotra, H. B. 2009. "Oligarchic capitalism may take hold in India," 22 September. www.theepochtimes.com/n2/content/view/22829/.
56 Fonseca, R., Michaud, P., & Sopraseuth, T. "Entrepreneurship, wealth, liquidity constraints, and start-up costs." www.law.illinois.edu/publications/cllpj/archive/vol_28/issue_4/fonsecaarticle28-4.pdf.
57 W. Smith. 2005. "Unleashing entrepreneurship, the Brookings Blum roundtable: The private sector in the fight against global poverty, Session I: Facilitating entrepreneurship's contribution to development," 3 August, www.brookings.edu/global/200508blum_smith.pdf.
58 commerce.gov. 2010. "Fact sheet-outreach to muslim-majority countries," 27 April. The U.S. Department of Commerce. www.commerce.gov/news/fact-sheets/2010/04/27/fact-sheet-outreach-to-muslim-majority-countries.
59 *Economist*. 2010. "Making a success of failure," p. 68.

60 *Economist*. 2004. "Measure first, then cut," 11 September, 372 (8392).
61 Molinski, D., & Shirouz, N. 2009. "Venezuela's president threatens Toyota." *GM*. 26 December, http://online.wsj.com/article/SB1000142405274870403 9704574615990386867578.html?mod=WSJ_hpp_MIDDLTopStories.
62 Baumgartner, E. 2001. "Private enterprise." *Business Eastern Europe*, 25 June, p. 4.
63 Basta, V. 2017. "Venture investing in the US and Europe are totally different industries." https://techcrunch.com/2017/06/07/venture-investing-in-the-us-and-europe-are-totally-different-industries/
64 Warner, M., & Daugherty, C. W. 2004. "Promoting the 'civic' in entrepreneurship: the case of rural Slovakia." *Journal of the Community Development Society* 35(1), pp. 117–134.
65 E.T Hall. 1976. *Beyond Culture*. New York: Anchor Press.
66 Silatech, "The Silatech index: Voices of young Arabs." *Gallup*, November 2010), 16, http://sas-origin.onstreammedia.com/origin/gallupinc/media/poll/pdf/Silatech.Report.2010.Nov.pdf.
67 Ohe, T., Honjo, S., Oliva, M. & Macmillan, I.C. 1991. "Entrepreneurs in Japan and silicon valley: A study of perceived differences." *Journal of Business Venturing*, 6 (2), pp. 135–144.
68 Pease, S. L. 2009. *The Golden Age of Jewish Achievement*, First edition, Deucalion.
69 Karlan, D., & Valdivia, M. 2006. Teaching entrepreneurship: Impact of business training on microfinance clients and institutions, Yale University, typescript; Munshi, K. 2007. *From Farming to International Business: The Social Auspices of Entrepreneurship in a Growing Economy*, NBER Working Paper No. 13065.
70 Tozzi, J. 2012. "China's next export: Venture capital," 17 May. www.business week.com/articles/2012-05-17/chinas-next-export-venture-capital.
71 Manchin, A., & Crabtree, S. 2010. "Europeans don't think schools encourage entrepreneurs: Americans, Chinese think their schools do better jobs," 17 August, www.gallup.com/poll/142163/Europeans-Don-Think-Schools-Encourage-Entrepreneurs.aspx.
72 BDC. 2016. *The Scale Up Challenge: How are Canadian Companies Performing?* Toronto: Business Development Bank of Canada.
73 BIS. 2013. *"Small Business Survey 2012: SME Employers,"* A report by BMG Research, UK Department for Business, Innovation and Skills.
74 Coutu, S. 2014. *The Scale-Up Report on UK Economic Growth*. Printed with the permission of the Information Economy Council, a joint industry and Government body, London.
75 *businessweek.com*. 2010. "Mexico's Calderon seeks stronger antitrust law, fines (Update1)." www.businessweek.com/news/2010-04-05/mexico-s-calderon-seeks-stronger-antitrust-law-fines-update1-.html.
76 Canberra Times. 2010. "What the world needs now is definitely not 1011 billionaires," 17 March, p. 11.
77 *Economist*. 2011. "Making the desert bloom," 27 August, 400(8748), pp. 59–61.
78 Hurst, E. Liquidity constraints, household wealth and entrepreneurship. http://faculty.chicagobooth.edu/erik.hurst/research/final_entrepreneurship_JPE_sept2003.pdf.
79 Freedman, P.L., & Click, R.W. 2006. "Banks that don't lend? Unlocking credit to spur growth in developing countries," *Development Policy Review* 24(3), pp. 279–302.
80 Moreno, L. A. 2007. "Extending financial services to Latin America's poor." *McKinsey Quarterly*, Special Edition, pp. 83–91.

81 *Economist.com.* 2011. Let a million flowers bloom, 10 March, www.economist. com/node/18330120.
82 Ibid.
83 Amsden, A. H. (1991). "Diffusion of development: The lateindustrializing model and greater East Asia." *The American Economic Review*, 81(2), pp. 282–289.
84 Acs, Z., Braunerhjelm, P., Audretsch, D., & Carlsson, B. 2009. "The knowledge spillover theory of entrepreneurship." *Small Business Economics*, 32(1), pp. 15–30.
85 Cappelli, P., Singh, H., Singh, J., & Useem, M. 2010. "The India way: Lessons for the U.S." *Academy of Management Perspectives*, 24(2), pp. 6–24.
86 Kaplan, S. 2009. "Faith and fragile states." *Harvard International Review*, 31(1), pp. 22–26.
87 Kitching, J., Smallbone, D., & Athayde, R. 2009. "Ethnic diasporas and Business competitiveness: Minority-owned enterprises in London." *Journal of Ethnic & Migration Studies*, 35(4), pp. 689–705.
88 Clay, J. 2005. Exploring the Links between International Business and Poverty Reduction: A Case Study of Unilever in Indonesia. Oxfam GB, Novib, Oxfam Netherlands, and Unilever. London 2005.
89 United Nation Commission on the Private Sector Development. 2004. *Unleashing entrepreneurship: Making business work for the poor.* New York: Report to the Secretary-General of the United Nations, UNDP.
90 Africa Commission Realising the Potential of Africa's Youth. www.afdb. org/fileadmin/uploads/afdb/Documents/Generic-Documents/Report%20 of%20the%20Africa%20Commission-Realising%20the%20Potential%20 of%20Africa%27s%20Youth.pdf.
91 afdb.org. nd. Africa Commission Realising the Potential of Africa's Youth. www.afdb.org/fileadmin/uploads/afdb/Documents/Generic-Documents/ Report%20of%20the%20Africa%20Commission-Realising%20the%20 Potential%20of%20Africa%27s%20Youth.pdf.
92 afdb.org. nd.
93 Schaefer, P. 2009. "A $9 trillion question: Did the world get Muhammad Yunus wrong?" *Foreign Policy*, 18 August, www.foreignpolicy.com/articles/2009/08/18/a_9_trillion_question_did_the_world_get_muhammad_ yunus_wrong?page=0,0.
94 Shane, S. 2008. *The Illusions of Entrepreneurship: The Costly Myths That Entrepreneurs, Investors, and Policy Makers Live.* New Haven, CT: Yale University Press.
95 Polrot, S., & De Senneville, F. 2017. "Blockchain: The "Trust Machine" that Africa needs?" *Fieldfisher*, www.fieldfisher.com/publications/2017/02/ blockchain-the-trust-machine-that-africa-needs#sthash.fZXGtvj8.vfM MyQrZ.dpbs?utm_source=Mondaq&utm_medium=syndication&utm_ campaign=View-Original.
96 Ogundeji, O. 2016. "Land registry based on blockchain for Africa." www. itwebafrica.com/enterprise-solutions/505-africa/236272-land-registry- based-on-blockchain-for-africa.
97 Jones, A. 2016. "How blockchain is impacting industry," 13 July, http:// internationalbanker.com/finance/blockchain-impacting-industry/.
98 Hanstad, T. 2013. "The case for land reform in India." www.foreignaffairs. com/articles/india/2013-02-19/untitled?cid=soc-twitter-in-snapshots- untitled-022013.
99 Balaji, S. 2017. "India's blockchain revolution goes beyond banks into land records and private firms." www.forbes.com/sites/sindhujabalaji/2017/12/28/ indias-blockchain-revolution-goes-beyond-banks/#216e9b084123.

100 Puiu, T. 2015. "How bitcoin's blockchain could mark an end to corruption," 29 October, www.zmescience.com/research/technology/bitcoin-blockchain-corruption-04232/.
101 Yaga, D., Mell, P., Roby, N., & Scarfone, K. 2018. "Blockchain technology overview." *National Institute of Standards and Technology Internal Report* (NIS-TIR) 8202.
102 Ogundeji, O. 2016. "Land registry based on blockchain for Africa." www.itwebafrica.com/enterprise-solutions/505-africa/236272-land-registry-based-on-blockchain-for-africa.
103 Higgins, S. 2016. "Republic of Georgia to develop blockchain land registry." www.coindesk.com/bitfury-working-with-georgian-government-on-blockchain-land-registry/.
104 Shin, L. 2017. "The first government to secure land titles on the Bitcoin blockchain expands project." www.forbes.com/sites/laurashin/2017/02/07/the-first-government-to-secure-land-titles-on-the-bitcoin-blockchain-expands-project/#38e77bec4dcd.
105 Ibid.
106 Shin, L. 2016. "Republic of Georgia to pilot land titling on blockchain with economist Hernando De Soto, BitFury." www.forbes.com/sites/laurashin/2016/04/21/republic-of-georgia-to-pilot-land-titling-on-blockchain-with-economist-hernando-de-soto-bitfury/#2e38dfb76550.
107 Battacharya, A. 2018. "India's government wants to kill Bitcoin, but it loves blockchain." https://qz.com/1148361/budget-2018-indias-government-wants-to-kill-bitcoin-but-it-loves-blockchain/
108 Writer, S. 2017. "Saudi Arabia is determined to reap the benefits of Blockchain." www.zawya.com/mena/en/story/Saudi_Arabia_is_determined_to_reap_the_benefits_of_Blockchain-SNG_106695786/.
109 Milano, A. 2018. "Bermuda could launch a Blockchain land registry." www.coindesk.com/bermuda-launch-blockchain-land-registry/.

Chapter 2

The Entrepreneurial Ecosystem and Its Components

This chapter's objectives include:

1   To demonstrate an understanding of entrepreneurial activities from an ecosystem perspective.
2   To appraise the relative importance and interrelationships among some of the key elements in an entrepreneurial ecosystem.
3   To describe the roles of the government and other actors in bringing changes in an entrepreneurial ecosystem.
4   To identify various types of flows across different entrepreneurial ecosystems.
5   To analyze the determinants of productivity in an entrepreneurial ecosystem.
6   To identify some ways to change an entrepreneurial ecosystem.
7   To assess the roles of entrepreneurship support programs such as coworking spaces, incubators, accelerators, and scale-up hubs.

Introduction

Entrepreneurship as a whole has much to learn from an understanding of a natural ecosystem. An ecosystem can be defined as a biological environment that consists of living or biotic components (e.g., animals and plants) as well as nonliving or abiotic physical components (e.g., air, soil, water, and sunlight) with which the living organisms interact.[1] The study of an entrepreneurial ecosystem involves complex relationships of entrepreneurial firms with key players, contexts, and ingredients such as government agencies, industry and trade association, consumers, investors, financial institutions, capital markets, national culture as well as natural and geographic factors. Each of these components influences and is influenced by the entrepreneurial ecosystem.

Before turning to the focus of this chapter—key elements of an entrepreneurial ecosystem—it is essential to first discuss the importance of developing a good entrepreneurial ecosystem. A good entrepreneurial ecosystem values creativity, innovation, and excellence; facilitates part-nerships among key players; and enables the development of good ideas and technologies to reach the market. Such an ecosystem can attract latent high-tech entrepreneurs and other types of high-expectation entrepre-neurs because people see a chance to build successful companies. A good entrepreneurial ecosystem also attracts local and foreign investments. All these lead to a noticeable role in promoting economic and social develop-ment locally, regionally, and nationally.

The concept of entrepreneurial ecosystem provides a practical and ho-listic approach to understanding the development of the entrepreneurial climate. For instance, policy makers can take actions to align incentives to foster a productive and successful entrepreneurial ecosystem, which nur-tures entrepreneurial behavior and enhances entrepreneurship productiv-ity. Likewise, entrepreneurial firms, singly and collectively, take measures to create an entrepreneurial environment that allows them to take calcu-lated risks and become successful.

Comparing Natural and Entrepreneurial Ecosystems

Productivity of an Entrepreneurial Ecosystem

Ecosystem productivity provides the most appropriate starting point for the treatment of entrepreneurial activities from the ecosystem perspec-tive. One way to measure productivity in an ecosystem is to look at the rate of synthesis of organic materials (e.g., leaf litter and woody mate-rial),[2] which principally takes place through photosynthesis by primary producers (e.g., trees and sea grass). Ecosystem productivity determines the population size of herbivores, omnivores, carnivores, and other or-ganisms that the ecosystem can support. A related concept is the carrying capacity, which is the maximum population size of a species that can be sustained by the environment given the supply food, water, and other necessities. Put differently, carrying capacity is the environment's max-imal load.[3]

The productivity of an entrepreneurial ecosystem may be measured by the extent to which financial, material, human, and knowledge resources are used to achieve positive entrepreneurial impacts such as job creation, economic growth, and poverty alleviation. An increase in productiv-ity leads to a higher carrying capacity of an entrepreneurial ecosystem, which means more job creation, higher incomes, and higher standards of living.

In the natural ecosystem, the rate of photosynthesis is high in the pres-ence of a proper amount and combination of temperature, carbon dioxide, water, sunlight, and nutrients (e.g., coral reefs and rain forest). A wrong combination of these factors may lead to a low rate of or no photosynthesis (e.g., unavailability of water in deserts, very low temperature on the tundra, and lack of nutrients in the open ocean).[4] This process has a parallel in an entrepreneurial ecosystem. An effective entrepreneurial ecosystem is characterized by the existence of lively and active networks of individuals and organizations to facilitate entrepreneurial activities. For instance, financial institutions provide early stage funding for sensible ventures. Educational institutions provide the required talents. Local government agencies such as the municipality provide supports for entrepreneurs. Entrepreneurship is culturally supported. That is, being an entrepreneur is viewed as a respected career choice. Moreover, business failure is not viewed negatively. There are also a number of entrepreneurial role models and successful entrepreneurs, who provide advice, support, and mentoring to new entrepreneurs.

A common problem with some of the entrepreneurial ecosystem is the lack of the right combination of key ingredients. For instance, many young technology firms with promising ideas lack financial resources to implement their projects. Likewise, as noted in Chapter 1, China reportedly has a large number of venture capitalists interested in funding U.S. startups; they lack skills and experience to manage venture investments.

Diversity in an Entrepreneurial Ecosystem

Diversity has an important role and function in an ecosystem. A diverse ecosystem containing varied terrain (e.g., caves, mountains, forests, and bodies of water) and inhabited by a wide range of native species of flora and fauna is likely to be healthy and has a higher probability of containing species that are likely to have a strong ecosystem effect. Each species, irrespective of their size and type, has an important role to play and thus boosts ecosystem productivity. Diversity can also increase the efficiency of resource use.[5] Species diversity generally enhances the health of an ecosystem, which is less likely to be seriously damaged by calamities and natural disasters such as extreme weather situations.

The health and productivity of an entrepreneurial ecosystem depend on the diversity of entrepreneurial firms. Mature and healthy entrepreneurial ecosystems are characterized by size, product, market, industry, technological, and structural diversity of entrepreneurial firms. Firms of each type are likely to have a niche in the entrepreneurial ecosystem that would help keep the entrepreneurial system healthy, resilient, and productive. Diversity also allows entrepreneurial firms to establish alliances with other firms that could be complementors.

In order to illustrate this phenomenon, we consider South Korea. In the early stage of development, government-sponsored schemes encouraged the growth of "chaebols" (family-owned conglomerates) such as Hyundai and Samsung, which helped transform the economy. The revenue of the biggest chaebol is about 20% of South Korea's GDP.[6] According to Korea Fair Trade Commission, the combined sales of South Korea's 31 largest conglomerates in 2016 was US$1.1 trillion or 84% the country's GDP.[7]

Chaebols have created entrepreneurial opportunities for small- and medium-sized enterprises (SMEs). SMEs make most of the parts for Korean carmakers such as Hyundai, Kia, and Daewoo. The chaebols support SMEs in a variety of ways—direct and indirect, formal and informal. For instance, several of the biggest chaebols have launched in-house lending programs that support financing needs of their SME partners. For instance, in 2017, Samsung announced a plan to launch a US$445 million fund to provide interest-free loan for a year to small businesses in its supply chain.[8]

Chaebols and SMEs have distinct roles in the country's economic growth and job creation. SMEs are major contributors to the country's job creation. SMEs account for 99% of the companies and 88% of the manpower in South Korea.[9] Compared to big firms in the country, South Korean SMEs are, however, inefficient as measured by operating profits as proportions of sales and value added per worker.[10]

Poor-Quality Species and Parasites and Their Effects

In a natural ecosystem, prevalence of poor-quality species is one of the main causes of low productivity and destruction of the ecosystem. This phenomenon has a striking and interesting parallel to the functioning of the entrepreneurial ecosystem. Easy availability of government money, which is distributed without carefully looking at the efficiency, depth, and quality of entrepreneurial ideas, will encourage the formation of many low quality firms. This situation will have a negative impact on the pace and rate of deal flow for private equity investors. That is, venture capitalists or private equity investors on the other hand are less likely to receive business proposals/investment offers. One might cite many examples to illustrate this point. One example is Canada's government sponsored Labor Fund Program started in the 1990s, which was largely unsuccessful. The program was mostly managed by people with little knowledge and experience in venture capital. Investment decisions were driven by political processes rather than merit-based considerations. Moreover, the fund was much bigger in terms of size than the private venture capital market. Consequently, private venture capitalists were intimidated and scared off by the Labor Fund Program.[11]

Another example is Malaysia's BioValley, a US$150 million complex started by the government to attract firms in the biotechnological industry. The proposed cluster lacked the necessary organic development and became a target of criticism and mockery as the "Valley of the BioGhosts."[12] A dilemma was apparent: whether to develop a qualified workforce first, or establish biotech companies.[13] The BioValley was far from completion even a decade after the scheduled completion date of 2005. There were too many biotech graduates but too biotech firms by then.

Other high-profile but unsuccessful government-funded programs include Dubai's entrepreneurial hub, Australia's BITS (Building on Information Technology Strengths) program and the European Union's (EU) European Investment Fund (which was started in 2001 with an endowment of more than €2 billion (about US$2.8 billion)), Japan's Tsukuba Science City, and Egypt's "Silicon Pyramid."[14] In this regard, just like ecosystem productivity can be increased by replacing poor-quality species by nutritious grasses, the quality of an entrepreneurial ecosystem can be improved by encouraging high growth enterprises.

Even worse is the fact that formal and informal institutions in some economies promote the growth of parasitic entrepreneurs. A journalist noted that parasitic entrepreneurs in Egypt produced low quality goods, which were sold to the state and they did not pay taxes.[15] Parasites can bring marked changes in the dynamics of the ecosystem by directly or indirectly modifying the environment of other organisms. Research in natural ecosystem has indicated that parasites' actions lead to increased mortality and reduced fecundity of the host population. In an entrepreneurial ecosystem, resources and opportunities that enable the parasitic entrepreneurs to pursue their economic goals are likely to scare off high-quality challengers.

Feedback Systems

Ecosystems contain feedback mechanisms that function to maintain the various elements of the system in an equilibrium state. The interaction among various elements of the ecosystem exhibits dynamic exchange processes, which are associated with the circulation of energy or materials. A negative feedback loop tends to slow down a production process in an ecosystem, whereas the positive feedback loop tends to accelerate it.

As entrepreneurs participate in developing and learning in the entrepreneurial ecosystem, they develop an understanding of what must be done to succeed in the environment. The nature and quality of entrepreneurial ecosystem determine the feedbacks that potential and actual entrepreneurs receive as well as their actual experiences. Entrepreneurial success stories provide positive feedback in the entrepreneurial ecosystem. Moreover, positive feedback systems tend to have a perpetual cycle, which can lead to a further improvement in entrepreneurial performance. High levels of corruption in the government, the proliferation of low quality entrepreneurial firms and parasitic entrepreneurs, on the other hand, is associated with a negative feedback system, which discourages entry in entrepreneurship and reduces levels of productive entrepreneurial activities.

The Essential Elements of an Entrepreneurial Ecosystem

In this section, we first briefly revisit the three key determinants of entrepreneurship noted in Chapter 1, which constitute key ingredients that affect the quality of an entrepreneurial ecosystem: (a) regulatory framework; (b) values, culture, and skills; (c) and access to finance, market, R&D, and technology. Here are some additional examples that demonstrate how these factors are linked to the entrepreneurial ecosystem.

a   **Regulatory framework**: First, the existence of a legislative framework that is comprehensible, sensible, and stable is the most important prerequisite for the development of a good entrepreneurial ecosystem. A well-developed system of legal and commercial rules and enforcement mechanisms (e.g., commercial code, property law, intellectual property rights protection, bankruptcy legislation, contract law, consumer law) contribute to the development of a high-quality entrepreneurial ecosystem. In top business-friendly countries, starting a business involves only a few steps, which can be completed in a few days and costs little for the entrepreneurs. Especially important for many developing economies are rules and procedures to start a business. For instance, one study indicated that, a ten-day reduction in the time taken to start a business can lead to a 0.4% points increase in GDP growth.

b   **Values, culture, and skills**: As to the values and culture in some parts of the world entrepreneurs are associated with negative images. While entrepreneurs are considered as members of the privileged class in many countries, they are arguably regarded as "déclassé," or ascribed a lower or inferior social status in some economies such as France, Germany, and Sweden.[16] Moreover, observers have noted that in countries such as Sweden and the U.K. a business failure is considered as a family disgrace. At the World Entrepreneur Summit in 2007, an Internet entrepreneur noted: "In the U.K., there is a stigma against business failure among the general public, whereas in the U.S. it's almost a badge of honor."[17]

Likewise, despite the high level of entrepreneurial intentions among Arab youths, entrepreneurs have a negative social identity in Arab culture. A 2009 Gallup Poll found that about half of young Arabs viewed entrepreneurs as individuals who think only about profits. The proportions of youth with such a viewpoint were 82% in Lebanon, 72% in Kuwait, and 72% of Palestine.[18] Arab societies are also described as exhibiting a fairly high degree of hostility toward entrepreneurship education. For instance, when an adviser to the Egyptian Education minister initiated some of the educational reforms measures, traditionalists labeled his attempts as "Westernization" of the curriculum.[19]

There is an observation that needs to be made regarding the possibility that entrepreneurship-related values may change over time. For instance, due primarily to increased media coverage of successful start-ups, the stigma of failure is decreasing in Japan. Consequently, more and more young people are pursuing entrepreneurial opportunities.[20]

Young people in Japan have grown up in a world where new companies such as Airbnb, Uber, and Facebook are acting as innovation powerhouses. This phenomenon is drastically different from that of their parents' generation when large companies such as Sony and Nintendo generated most of the innovations.[21]

An upshot is that entrepreneurs have been able to raise as much as US$100 million privately. This is unprecedented for Japan.[22]

c **Access to finance, market, R&D, and technology**: Availability of capital influences not only the ability of firms to enter new markets, but also the ability to compete with incumbent firms.[23] In many developing countries, financial institutions' unavailability of funds and/or unwillingness to lend to small businesses has led to an unfavorable entrepreneurial ecosystem conditions. For most potential entrepreneurs in these countries, a village loan shark is the only available source of capital, whose interest rate is 200%–300% a year.[24] Well-developed consumer markets bring entrepreneurial opportunities, and help the entrepreneurial ecosystem. In some cases, demanding customers force businesses to be more innovative and thus play a critical role in stimulating entrepreneurial activity. A customer can also make it easier to carry out entrepreneurial and innovative activities by communicating its plans expectations and intentions. New technologies may create richer and more favorable contexts and conditions in which to develop entrepreneurial ventures.

d **Natural and geographic conditions**: In addition to the three factors already mentioned, a fourth factor must be considered: Natural and Geographic Conditions, which are important, not only in the natural ecosystem, but also in entrepreneurial ecosystem. Geographic factors such as climate, distance to coastline, landlockedness, availability and type of natural resources, land features (e.g., terrain and topography, the proportions of arable land and land area in the tropics), accessibility to transportation routes, proximity to attractive customers and suppliers affect the pattern and potential for entrepreneurial ventures.

Iceland's Data Islandia

Some entrepreneurial firms and policy makers have utilized a geographic location as a value proposition. For instance, Data Islandia, an Iceland-based company, wants to develop Iceland as the world's data storage center. Data Islandia is responding to the needs of businesses to archive data to comply with various regulations. The company's unique selling propositions included cool climate, geothermal energy, and secure remoteness.[25] Iceland's average annual temperature is 4°C.[26] Renewable energy sources such as hydroelectric and geothermal power plants are used to meet the project's energy needs. Iceland generates more power per capita than any other countries. Almost entire power supply in the country is generated from hydro and geothermal sources, which provide long-term sustainability.

Although major Silicon Valley technology giants such as Apple and Google haven't opened their data centers in Iceland, the country has been able to attract a number of smaller data operations. As of 2015, Verne Global, a provider of advanced data center solutions, had a 44-acre campus in the city of Keflavik. Verne Global's client included the German automaker BMW.[27]

While Iceland has huge renewable energy reserves, the country's remote island location means that the direct export of these reserves to foreign markets has been difficult and expensive. This means extremely energy intensive processes which can be performed in the country such as aluminum smelting, which involves extracting aluminum from its oxide alumina and data centers are better ways of exporting its energy resources.[28] In addition, the country's cool climate can be considered as an asset given that over a quarter of data centers' operating costs in the U.S. are spent on cooling.[29] In 2017, data centers worldwide used about 7% of the global electricity supply.[30]

Emerald Networks' submarine cable system, which is a 5,200 km, 100 Gbps undersea cable connecting North America and Europe via Iceland, would further facilitate Iceland's efforts to develop itself as the world's data center. In an attempt to encourage investments in data centers and other technology projects, the government has reduced duties on imports of equipment.

In early 2018, the telecommunications and IT firms Opin Kerfi, Vodafone Iceland, *Reiknistofnun Bankanna* (RB) the IT Service Center for the Icelandic Financial Market and Korputorg Real Estate ltd announced a plan to construct a modern and high-tech data center in Reykjavík. The data center's first major customer will be RB, which will make the new facility its primary data center.[31]

Coworking Spaces, Incubators, Accelerators, and Scale-Up Hubs as Key Elements of an Entrepreneurial Ecosystem

Coworking spaces, incubators, and accelerators are among the most important components of an entrepreneurial ecosystem.

Coworking Spaces

New York City-based The Farm Coworking defines a coworking space as "a community of like-minded individuals who work together in the same space to collaborate and grow." A coworking space gives an entrepreneur or a professional *a desk to work* or a dedicated office. It can be rented as and when the entrepreneur needs. A coworking space provides individuals with numerous opportunities to collaborate and interact. Some coworking spaces also offer services, events, and networking sessions to startups.[32] For instance, China's UrWork, which had 100 locations in 30 cities worldwide in 2017, also provides opportunities to meet investors, and classes on a number of topics ranging from business strategy to augmented reality.[33]

Coworking spaces are mushrooming worldwide. One estimate suggested that 14,000 coworking spaces were operating worldwide in 2017.[34] In 2017, there were over 250 coworking spaces in Africa.[35] As of the early 2018, about 200 companies were reported to be offering shared office spaces in India. Most of them were targeted at startups.[36] Some organizations operate in coworking spaces many different locations. As of 2017, U.S.-based WeWork had coworking spaces in 203 locations in 50 cities and London-listed IWG had about 3,000 locations in 1,000 cities.[37]

An estimated 1.6 million people worldwide used coworking spaces in 2017, which is expected to reach about 3.8 million by 2020.[38] In 2017, the average per month cost for coworking spaces ranged from US$45 to over US$1,000. The average cost in the U.S. was about US$350 per month.[39]

A number of benefits have been linked to coworking spaces. In a study, 82% of the users coworking spaces reported that coworking expanded their professional networks, 80% received help or guidance from coworking members and 64% reported that coworking networking was a key source of work and business referrals.[40]

Coworking spaces come in all shapes and sizes. India has many women-friendly or women-only co-working spaces. For instance, Wsquare is a women-only coworking space in Chennai, India. In the last eight months of 2017, more than 150 women used the facility. About 80% of the users were entrepreneurs. Others were students, researchers, freelance professionals, or remote employees working for big companies.[41]

Some are targeting narrower niche audiences. Nigeria's 360 Creative Hub provides coworking space for fashion entrepreneurs, who can work on designs and find specific machines needed for production.[42]

Incubators

Incubators help startups with various aspects of entrepreneurial process. There include developing a business and marketing plan, providing mentoring and training typically by proven entrepreneurial investors, and connecting startups with funding sources, industry experts, relevant authorities, and educational institutions. Incubators also help new ventures develop objectives and strategic positioning, conduct feasibility studies and market research.[43]

Some incubators also provide low-cost locations, where startups gather and work on their ideas. Facilities provided include conference rooms and research labs.[44] A startup can stay in the space as long as it needs to or until the business grow to a scale that require relocating to its own space.[45]

Some well-regarded incubators only accept members that are in the earliest stages of startup. The startup may be required to submit its business plan to apply and also for the interview process.[46]

Some incubators provide their services to startups operating in specific sectors. The Bank of England FinTech Accelerator offers blockchain startups an accelerator/incubator environment if the startups focus on incorporating blockchain technology into the existing technology used by the organization.[47] As another example, Huobi Labs is a blockchain incubator started by the Chinese cryptocurrency exchange Huobi. It offers startups advisory services and funding. As of early 2018, the Huobi Labs incubator had contributed to a number of blockchain platforms such as IOStoken. It does not connect startups with venture capital (VC). It offers startup capital itself.[48]

Scale-up Hubs and Accelerators

Scale-up hubs and accelerators provide expert guidance, education, and mentorship to entrepreneurial firms in order to help them reach the next stage of growth.[49] They usually do so in a cohort-based setting for a fixed period (3–6 months).[50] They help startups develop strong institutional strength, vision, and strategy; develop initial products, identify appropriate customer segments; develop connections; and secure resources such as capital and employees.[51] They may also support early-stage companies through seed money.[52] Scale-up hubs and accelerators perform these functions often in exchange for equity. In this way, they help startups prepare to enter into adulthood.[53]

The founders of a small firm often have specific and limited expertise. Growth, however, requires diverse skill sets and knowledge bases. They include those related to commercial (e.g., marketing new products), human resources (e.g., recruiting and training employees), project management (e.g., logistics and organizations of various events), financial (e.g., capital management) and strategic thinking skills (e.g., developing leadership and taking actions to fulfill new missions and strategies).[54] Small firms often face challenges in developing these skills in-house. These are the gaps that scale-up hubs and accelerators fill through training and support.

The accelerator model was invented in the U.S. Europe is, however, rapidly catching up to U.S. levels. In 2015, 26 startup accelerators opened in Europe. By 2016, there were 113 accelerators in Europe,[55] compared to 111 in the U.S. and Canada. However, North American accelerators tend to make higher investments than in startups than their European counterparts. In 2015, U.S. and Canadian accelerators invested US$90.3 million in 2,968 startups compared to US$41 million in 2,574 startups invested by European accelerators.[56] North America also has a higher number of successful startup exits. In the U.S. and Canada, 193 startups that came through accelerators were acquired or went public in 2015 compared to 33 in Europe.[57]

Research has suggested that accelerators have a positive impact on entrepreneurial ecosystems, especially the financing environment.[58] Accelerators often make relatively small investments in early-stage companies. However, companies receiving such investments are able to raise substantial amounts of capital from other sources from seed and early-stage VC deals.[59] For instance, during 2005 to 2015, 172 U.S.-based accelerators invested in more than 5,000 U.S.-based startups with a median investment of US$100,000. These companies raised US$19.5 billion in funding during this period, or US$3.7 million per company.[60]

Scale-up hubs and accelerators operate in diverse settings. In the U.S., accelerators are often run by private companies. They don't have much affiliation with the government agencies. In Europe, many startup accelerators receive funding from the EU in addition to funds from private and institutional investors.[61] For instance, a substantial portion of the European Commission's annual spending of US$900 million for startups is reported to go to accelerators.[62]

In the Middle East, proportionately higher numbers of accelerator operate as non-profit organizations. Whereas 25%–35% of accelerators are non-profits in other regions, about 50% of all accelerators in the Middle East are non-profit. Nonprofit accelerators do not require equity stakes from startups. They tend to focus on industries with specific public benefit such as health tech and edtech. Nonprofit accelerators also focus on providing opportunities for minority groups.[63]

Some accelerators program involves narrow economic sectors. For instance, Romania's Techcelerator targets startups in the technology sectors such as software, cybersecurity, AI, IT solutions for health, AgTech and FinTech. In the early 2018, it announced that it would provide €25,000 (about US$30,000) funding for 15–20 startups that have a prototype or at the Minimum Viable Product stage. The startups with a high probability of success would have the opportunity to receive a second investment round, which could be up to €75,000 (about US$91,000). The ten-week program was reported to have 60 local and foreign mentors.[64]

The Roles of Policy and Regulation in Enhancing the Quality and Productivity of an Entrepreneurial Ecosystem

The government is considered to be the most powerful institutional actor and thus can become an important force in shaping an entrepreneurial ecosystem. Regulative frameworks not only exert direct influence on entrepreneurial activities, but also affect other determinants of entrepreneurship such as market conditions, infrastructures, human capital, and access to finance.

In the Iceland example, the country has regulations and policy in place to provide strong data security and privacy protections. It has stable political environment. The American property management company Cushman & Wakefield's 2016 Data Center Risk Index identified Iceland as the safest place in the world to host a data center.[65] The rank was based on key factors such as energy cost, average Internet bandwidth, ease of doing business, level of corporate tax and political stability.

Iceland has among the lowest corporate tax rates among the OECD countries (www.iceland.is/iceland-abroad/us/nyc/news-and-events/iceland-is-a-leader-in-low-corporate-taxes/6964/). It was reported that the country's parliament was even considering bring down the tax rate to as low as 15%.[66]

In general, the EU has no restriction on its member countries to move their data to Iceland.[67] This can be contrasted with some economies such as India, which are not considered data secure by the EU. The fact that India has not achieved the status of a data secure country prevents flow of sensitive data, such as patient information to India.

The governments can also play a key role in the development of a better corporate governance system, which is one of the most important mechanisms contributing to entrepreneurial success of an economy. Note that corporate governance entails the systems, principles, rules, laws, and processes by which businesses are operated, regulated, and controlled. The idea here is that good corporate governance plays a key role in the integrity of corporations, financial institutions, and markets. Key elements of good corporate governance practices include high level of transparency, respect for minority shareholders and strong and independent boards of directors. For instance, in some economies, controlling shareholders engage in siphoning off company funds through various means.[68] In countries characterized by poor corporate governance, underdeveloped financial and legal systems and higher corruption, the growth rate of the smallest firms is most adversely affected, and fewer new firms, particularly small firms, are created.[69]

Poor enforcement—rather than absence—of existing regulatory safeguards is one of the main constraints to the development of an effective corporate governance mechanism in India. For instance, following the 1991 Indian liberalization and reform of capital markets, a new regulatory body, Securities Exchange Board of India (SEBI) was established in 1992 in order to protect the interests of investors and promote the development of the securities market. However, the SEBI has been accused of not punishing the guilty.[70]

It should be noted that various determinants of entrepreneurship discussed above, however favorable they may be to entrepreneurship in themselves, may be counteracted in practice by flawed policies and corrupt institutions. In some emerging economies ambiguous wording and frequent changes in tax laws allows tax inspectors to engage in corrupt behavior and increase uncertainty for businesses. Moreover, the processes involved with determining whether an entrepreneur had violated the tax law such as the tax inspector's examination of the tax payments and submission of a report to the authorities for verification lack transparency. There is little, if any, supervision of tax inspectors. The upshot of these tendencies is tax inspectors' lack of accountability and substantial discretionary power to determine whether an entrepreneur violated the tax law. In these economies, there is thus a firmly held belief among entrepreneurs that paying bribes demanded by a tax inspector is the only way to avoid more serious troubles.[71]

Politicians' and bureaucrats' engagement in corrupt behavior has been a major concern in many economies. Corruption is the abuse of public authority for private gain. It is a transaction that takes place usually between government officials or representatives and profit-oriented organizations. Corruption may take various forms. Analysts argue that Russia is trapped in a predatory and corrupt system, which has slowed the growth of an entrepreneurial class.[72] Likewise, a private coal miner in China's Shanxi Province told a journalist that corruption accounted for 20% of his operating costs. The proportion is expected to be higher in illegal mines.[73]

A Systems Approach to Understanding the Entrepreneurial Ecosystem: Moving From Parts to the Whole

To take an "ecosystem approach" means that it is important to pay attention to the whole system at work rather than individual elements. That is, instead of analyzing individual components or aspects of the entrepreneurial processes, such as government policy or R&D, we holistically examine all the components and the interactions among them, all as part of one system.

Non-government actors are sometimes more effective than the government in bringing favorable changes in the entrepreneurial ecosystem. For instance, entrepreneurial success is not socially admired in the Scandinavian (see Jante's Law, Chapter 4). In Sweden, the think tank, Timbro is working to bring a long-term shift in the "public opinion in favor of free markets, entrepreneurship, private property, and an open society."[74] The institute is funded mostly by large Swedish corporations. Likewise, the NGO Injaz al-Arab (www.injazalarab.org/), which was formed in 2004 and operated in 13 countries in the Middle East and North Africa in 2010, sends volunteers to teach work readiness, financial literacy, and entrepreneurship in schools. As of mid-2010, Injaz al-Arab programs engaged 10,000 private-sector volunteers and reached over 500,000 students.[75]

There are also instances of news media and popular press devoting substantial space in promoting entrepreneurship. In an attempt to support and encourage local entrepreneurship, Puerto Rico's largest daily newspaper, El Nuevo Día, devoted a weekly page of startup success stories. The stories promoted new forms of social dialogue and created awareness about the ingredients and effects of entrepreneurship.[76]

Corporate governance mechanisms differ across contexts due to differences in culture and history in addition to local power relations, policies, regulations as discussed earlier. While the U.S. and Western European economies have well-developed corporate governance systems, cross-cultural differences in their corporate governance mechanisms are observed, especially in family business. For instance, U.S. businesses are less likely to give senior positions to non-family members than their European counterparts. This difference can be attributed to the fact that U.S. family businesses can grow by just focusing on the large U.S. market, while European companies are forced to internationalize their business at a much earlier stage due to their small national markets.[77]

While all the above factors are important in role to play in an entrepreneurial ecosystem, different factors may dominate the system under different conditions which shape incentives and challenges in establishing certain types of firms. Consider, for instance, ForShe, which is an all-women-driven taxi services in Mumbai, India. The company was founded in 2007 with nine vehicles. The company's target customers are women, who travel alone and prefer such services. Businesses, hotels, and call centers showed interests in these taxis for their women employees. However, taxi driver *is* a very rare occupation for women in India and other Asian countries. ForShe founder noted that a major challenge for her is to find female drivers that are well versed with the Mumbai city.[78]

Concluding Comments

A favorable entrepreneurial ecosystem is characterized by factors such as entrepreneurship-friendly formal institutions, supportive informal institutions, a strong orientation toward innovation and state-of-the-art technologies, a good geographic location and high-quality infrastructures. These conditions are associated with a high rate of firm creation and help existing entrepreneurial firms to survive, thrive, and grow. These factors also help attract foreign firms, which can stimulate the entrepreneurial ecosystem by contributing considerably to the quality, diversity, and competition.

To take an "ecosystem approach" means that various actors interested in entrepreneurship developments shift their focus from parts to wholes. While the roles of factors such as geography and policy in shaping an entrepreneurial ecosystem are discussed in details above, these factors' synergistic interaction with other elements is what makes the entrepreneurial ecosystem more or less productive. The sustainability, health, and productivity of the entrepreneurial ecosystem and firms can be enhanced by the implementation of a more holistic strategy for assessing, monitoring, and managing the entrepreneurial ecosystems. The above discussion indicates that the government has the most important role to play in this process.

End of Chapter Questions

1   Among the key elements of entrepreneurial ecosystem discussed earlier, which one do you think is the most important in driving entrepreneurial activities?
2   Can the state or non-state actors change an entrepreneurial ecosystem? If so, how?
3   Why are policy related factors important for a good-quality entrepreneurial ecosystem?
4   How does corruption influence entrepreneurship?
5   What types of skills are needed to promote entrepreneurship?
6   Select a developing country and critically examine how key elements of entrepreneurial ecosystem discussed in this chapter have influenced entrepreneurship in the country.
7   Are factors related to the access to market, finance, R&D, and technology more important than policy and culture in promoting entrepreneurship? Why or why not?
8   What are the roles of entrepreneurship support programs such as coworking spaces, incubators, accelerators, and scale-up hubs in enriching an entrepreneurial ecosystem?

End of the Chapter Case: The Colombian Entrepreneurial Ecosystem

Colombia could serve as a good example to illustrate how the government in an economy can improve the quality of the entrepreneurial ecosystem and the nature of the barriers it is likely to face. Despite its deep embroilment for a long time, in a war with guerrilla, paramilitary groups, and drug cartels, Colombia has made drastic improvement in its entrepreneurial performance in recent years.

A high defense spending, family-business-dominated culture, and low level of investments in R&D have, however, severely constrained the efficiency and productivity of the Colombian entrepreneurial ecosystem. Moreover, foreigners' perception of the country as "lawless" and "violent" has been difficult to change.

A complaint that is often heard is that Colombia has most of the key ingredients of entrepreneurship but there is the lack of a high-quality ecosystem that unifies these ingredients.[79] For instance, due to the country's rapid economic growth, potential entrepreneurs have relatively easy access to finance. The country performs well in knowledge, innovation, and talent.[80]

Colombia's entrepreneurial revolution is a result of a number of diverse, contradictory, and conflicting forces. Many paradoxes thus exist in the Colombian entrepreneurial ecosystem as well as its various components and processes. Colombian entrepreneurship-related institutions, for instance, are characterized by a recombination of old institutional elements with the introduction of new elements.

Indicators Related to Entrepreneurial Performance and Impact

Indicators related to entrepreneurial performance and impact are mixed. Colombia has become one of the most dynamic economies in Latin America. In 2017, Six Colombian companies were represented in Forbes' Global 2000 list of the world's biggest companies (www.forbes.com/global2000/list/#country:Colombia).

The country's unemployment reduced from 17.3% in 2002 to 12.1% in 2009.[81] It further reduced to a record low level of 7.30% in of 2015.[82]

A lower corporate taxation is expected to contribute to the growth. The OECD's forecast suggested that the Colombian economy would grow by 3% in 2018 and 2019.[83]

A significant informal economy has been a major challenge faced by the Colombian entrepreneurial ecosystem. One estimate suggested that Colombian informal economy employs about half of the country's working population.[84]

The country also performs poorly with respect to poverty reduction. A Gini coefficient of 50.8 in 2016 puts it among economies with the highest income inequalities between the rich and the poor (https://data.worldbank.org/indicator/SI.POV.GINI).

Externalities Generated by Violence, Insecurity, and the Drug Entrepreneurship

Stereotypes and a negative perception of the country have been nurtured and sustained by many foreign investors. A *Business Week* article notes, "The handful of Wall Street analysts who cover Colombia supply their clients with charts of murder rates and kidnappings."[85] However, entrepreneurship-friendly institutions have emerged and operated in an environment characterized by violence and insecurity.

Regulatory Framework

In the 1990s, defense budget averaged 1.35% of GDP. Since 1995, Colombia's military spending as a proportion of GDP has been the highest in Latin America.[86] In 2016, its military spending was 3.4% of GDP, compared to 3.3% in the U.S. Colombia's efforts and achievements on the security front are being recognized. During 2010–2014, homicide rate fell by 26% and 482 municipalities were free of homicides.[87] While significantly improved, laws and enforcement mechanisms in Colombia are weak due primarily to the fact that defense spending is draining the civilian economy in general and entrepreneurial development in particular. Laws and enforcement mechanisms are, however, often ineffective due to a lack of funding for police forces and civil law enforcement.

According to the World Bank's Doing Business 2018 report (www.doingbusiness.org/data/exploreeconomies/colombia), Colombia ranked No. 59 (No. 3 in Latin America and Caribbean after Mexico and Peru) for the ease of doing business. The country's performance is better than the average for Latin America in terms of time taken, costs, and the number of procedures for starting a business. To start a business, eight procedures are needed to be completed which take 11 days and cost 14% of the country's per capita income. It is the second-best country in the world for getting credit to start a business. Credit bureau covers about 95% of the country's adults.

However, Colombia ranked No. 177 in the world in enforcing contract. For instance, enforcing a contract in the capital city, Bogota takes an average of 1,288 days and costs 46% of the claim value.

The Colombian government made a number of efforts to improve the Colombian entrepreneurial landscape. Table 2.1 presents key regulatory developments affecting the Colombian entrepreneurial landscape.

In 2002, the Colombian government launched *Fondo Emprender*, a seed capital fund that specializes in financing companies formed within Servicio Nacional de Aprendizaje (SENA), which is an educational entity established to promote entrepreneurship among students. Working with other entrepreneurship-related entities, this network established more than 20 business incubators, which helped to launch over 1,500 startups by 2012.[88] By mid-2017, the Fondo Emprender provided more than 450 billion pesos (USD$164 million) in funding to about 6,000 companies, which led to the creation of over 22,000 new jobs.[89]

Regarding Colombia's initiatives to create entrepreneurship-friendly regulatory climate, two pieces of legislation deserve mention. In 2006,

Table 2.1 Key Regulatory Developments in Colombia

Time	Key regulatory developments	Remarks
2002	Fondo Emprender was launched.	By mid-2017: provided more than USD$164 million in funding to about 6,000 companies, which led to the creation of over 22,000 new jobs.
2006	Enactment of Ley 1014 de Fomento a la Cultura del Emprendimiento	It led to the creation of national and regional networks for entrepreneurial development.
2009	The Law 1286 provided a legal framework for Science and Technology and elevated the status of Colciencias as a regulating agency.	It focused on supporting high-tech, high-impact entrepreneurs.
2012	iNNpulsa Colombia was launched.	Its aim is to support and promote tech innovation and new ventures.
May 2013	The OECD launched accession discussions with Colombia	The OECD membership is expected to lead to significant improvement in the country's entrepreneurial climate.
February 2018	Only 20 of the 23 OECD Committees had approved Colombia's OECD accession	At a TUAC meeting, Colombian trade unionists complained about the lack of progress in a number of areas and urged the OECD member governments to pressure Colombia to make progress before inviting it to join the OECD.
May 2018	The OECD agreed to invite Colombia to be a new member.	For the membership to be effective, Colombia would need to take required steps at the national level in order to accede to the OECD Convention.

a legal framework/was created to stimulate entrepreneurship across all industries. The law, Ley 1014 de Fomento a la Cultura del Emprendimiento led to the creation of national and regional networks for entrepreneurial development. Through the new law, the Colombian government took the initiative to stimulate the participation of key actors such as Ministers of Trade, Industry and Tourism, Education, and Social Protection; directors of Servicio Nacional de Aprendizaje (technical training), National Planning Department (DNP), and Colciencias (the science and technology authority); and representatives of professional associations, universities, business incubators, and associations of young entrepreneurs.[90] National and regional networks were created to support entrepreneurship.

In 2009, in an attempt to support high-tech, high-impact entrepreneurs, the Colombian government created a national initiative for science, technology, and innovation, which focused on supporting high-tech, high-impact entrepreneurs.[91] The Law 1286 of 2009 provided a legal framework for Science and Technology and elevated the status of Colciencias as a regulating agency. In addition, an emphasis was placed on using science and technology for the societal benefit.[92]

The government launched iNNpulsa Colombia in 2012 with a budget of US$50 million to support and promote tech innovation and new ventures.[93] In 2013, iNNpulsa awarded three grants of up to US$800,000.[94]

Another government initiative is Ministry of Technology and Communications' Apps.co, which focuses on the technology sector. Headquartered in Bogota, Apps.co is an online learning platform that helps to develop digital business ideas into fully developed commercial enterprises.[95] It provides seed funding, training, and mentorship to digital startups.[96] By 2014, Apps.co awarded US$33 million in funding to accelerators and university partnership programs.[97]

In May 2013, the OECD launched accession discussions with Colombia. As of the early 2018, 20 of the 23 OECD Committees had approved Colombia's OECD accession.[98] For some time, the lack of progress in some key areas gave rise for concern. Especially the OECD's Trade Union Advisory Committee (TUAC) was concerned that the Colombian government failed to protect trade unionists or take actions against perpetrators of violence. The issues were finally resolved and in May 2018, member countries of the OECD agreed to invite Colombia to be a new member of the organization.

Initiatives at the Local Level

Ruta N was established in 2010 as a joint venture between the mayor's office of Medellín, public utilities company, Empresas Públicas de Medellín (EPM) and Unidad de Negocios Estratégicos (UNE). It was created to encourage innovation in the city and create favorable conditions for entrepreneurship. RutaN provides affordable office space for entrepreneurs at as low as US$60 per month.[99] It provided tax incentives and professional training programs to rebrand Colombia as a global technology hub. The first wave of efforts paid off brilliantly. As of 2014, the Colombian technology industry was worth US$6.8 billion with 1,800 software development and IT service companies.[100]

Banking, Financial, and Capital Markets

Colombia's small businesses and people have traditionally lacked access to banking and finance. According to the World Bank's Financial Inclusion Data/Global Findex, only 38% of the adult population had an account at a financial institution in 2014 (http://datatopics.worldbank.org/financial-inclusion/country/colombia). A complaint often voiced by entrepreneurs is that Colombian banks often charge high interest rates, are highly regulated and exhibit a relatively high degree of risk aversion. Most entrepreneurs thus get backing from friends and family.[101]

In recent years, initiatives have been taken by the government and the private sector to increase entrepreneurs' access to finance.

Bank Loans

While banks in many developing countries have adopted too conservative lending policies, Colombian banks have been reasonably well managed. One indicator to look at is the liquidity ratio of bank liquid reserves to bank assets. Banks in most developing countries tend to exhibit a high propensity to maintain high proportions of their assets in liquid forms such as cash, deposits with other banks, central bank debt, and short-term government securities. For instance, the ratio was 20.3% for Latin America and Caribbean (excluding high income) and 20.5% for middle-income countries compared to 6.2% in Colombia in 2016 (https://data.worldbank.org/indicator/FD.RES.LIQU.AS.ZS).

Government-Sponsored Funding

Colombia has implemented some pro-SME policies that are based on direct government support of SMEs. The government has increased the availability of micro credit for small entrepreneurs. In 2014, the Colombian government enacted the law 1731/2014, *Fondo de Microfinanzas Rurales* (Rural Microfinance Fund) ("the *Fondo*"). The law provides various mechanisms to increase access to financial instruments for disadvantaged groups. The Ministry of Agriculture & Rural Development would provide initial injection of capital to the *Fondo*. Subsequently it would be self-funded.[102]

FinTech Startups

As of July 2017, 124 FinTech startups were operating in the country, making it the third largest FinTech ecosystem in Latin America, behind México (238 startups) and Brazil (230 startups).[103] Many of these startups focus on lending and crowdfunding. The FinTech firm Lenddo, which uses big data (BD) in assessing, evaluating and refining the creditworthiness of potential borrowers, operates in Colombia. Lenddo allows its members to use their online social connections in order to build creditworthiness and get access to financial services. A typical Lenddo credit application had over 12,000 data points, which can be used to assess the creditworthiness. In April 2014, Lenddo teamed up with Scotiabank to give 100,000 Colombians access to credit cards based on LenddoScores.

Capital Market

Colombian stock market is small with low market capitalization, has a few listed companies, low volume of transactions and shallow with a few types of funds. As of February 2018, the Bolsa had 69 listed companies with a market capitalization of US$122 billion (www.sseinitiative.org/fact-sheet/colombian-securities-exchange/). According to the World Bank, market capitalization as a proportion of GDP in 2016 was 36.8%, which was about the same level as Brazil's 42.2% and Mexico's 33.5% but much smaller compared to Chile's 86%.[104] The Bolsa was also criticized on the ground that it lacked proactivity, was inward-looking in orientation and failed to go beyond just fulfilling its institutional mandate, contributed very little to economic development. In May 2011, Chile, Peru, and Colombia created a common trading platform—Latin American Integrated Market (Mercado Integrado Latinoamericano, or Mila)—by formally combining operations of their stock markets. This development is expected to contribute to the development of the Colombian equity market by drawing more liquidity.

The underdevelopment of the Colombian stock market can be attributed to the demand and the supply sides. In terms of the structure of corporate Colombia, the largest firms in the country have shown reluctance and resistance to list on the stock market. Being mostly family-owned, they are characterized by a conservative mindset and thus tend to avoid volatility in equity markets. As in Mexico, the Colombian middle classes are much more inclined toward real estate investments than putting their money in the stock market.[105] Due primarily to underdeveloped capital market, Colombia-bound foreign investors do not have a lot of investment choices other than in the property market.

Venture Capital

According to Venture Equity Latin America (VELA), Colombia is highly underrepresented in venture capital transactions. During 2011–2015, VC investment in Colombia was US$68 million with 34 funds.[106]

Remittances

According to the World Bank's Migration and Remittances Data (www.worldbank.org/en/topic/migrationremittancesdiasporaissues/brief/migration-remittances-data), Colombia's foreign remittance was estimated at US$5.5 billion in 2017. This was higher than Brazil's US$2.7 billion.

Foreign Direct Investment

Foreign direct investment (FDI) takes place when a firm invests directly in new facilities to produce and/or market in a foreign country. Foreign multinationals' FDI in Colombia averaged US$9.1 billion a year between 2005 and 2008, which reached US$9.5 billion in 2010[107] and US$13.5 billion in 2016.[108] This surge in FDI can be primarily attributed to an improvement in security. However, the focal points of FDI in have been on extractive industries such as mining and energy projects.[109] The FDIs were market access-seeking types, focusing on national as well as regional market. The city of Bogota, however, is benefitting from investment in modern economic sectors such as extractive industries such as financial services and communications. During 2007–2016, the city received about US$17 billion in FDI, leading the development of the city as one of Latin America's leading business centers.[110]

Access to Market

For many Colombian firms, maximum potential is reached in their home market. The domestic market thus offers little growth opportunity. They have realized that the only way to grow would be to expand in foreign markets, possibly through M&A. Colombia's multinational companies (multilatinas), however, have been less internationalized compared to those from other major nations in the region.[111]

The country reached a free trade agreement with the U.S. in 2011, which has increased market access for its firms. According to the United States International Trade Commission (USITC), as of 2017, Colombia had become among the top three providers of 64 goods to the U.S. For instance, in 2016, the U.S. imported over US$1 billion worth of Colombian coffee and more than US$792 million of flowers.[112]

R&D and Technology

Colombians have an abundance of entrepreneurial curiosity and interest. For instance, the world's top two cities from where per capita Google search for the management thinker "Peter Drucker" originated from were

Bogota and Medellín.[113] An article published in Brand Strategy[114] even goes as far as to say that Colombia's Medellin city has "the most dynamic and professional business culture." Colombia also has an advantage in the development of business process outsourcing. Analysts point out that Colombians speak "clear, unaccented Spanish."

One observation was that Colombia lacks absorptive capacity and has failed to develop its technological capabilities to effectively utilize FDI inflows as well as foreign development assistance. The country spends very little on innovation and technology. According to *Euromonitor International*, Colombia's R&D spending in 2017 was estimated at around 0.2% of GDP.

For many Colombian businesses, local diversification was traditionally the only way to grow due to factors such as protectionism and foreign-exchange restrictions. One upshot of this tendency, as in many other Latin American countries, is that Colombia lacks a mature corporate governance culture. Many industries in Colombia are dominated by premodern traditional patriarchal family-owned businesses, which are characterized by concentrated ownership structures. They tend to have an expectation of family succession. The country's businesses are adopting responsible business practices and codes of conduct.

Case Summary

Various elements of the Colombian entrepreneurial ecosystem have witnessed a dramatic progress in the past few decades. The national and local government agencies in Colombia are taking initiatives to encourage an entrepreneurial culture. Colombia's largest incubators such as INNpulsa in Bogota, RutaN in Medellin and Apps.co are providing a big boost to the country's entrepreneurs.

To some extent, a whole ecosystem developed around drug entrepreneurship has made it challenging to develop productive entrepreneurship. Dismantling the ecosystem is not an easy task. On the plus side, security situation has drastically improved, which is an important precondition for entrepreneurial development. Most potential foreign investors, however, have not yet realized this progress. Policy makers, entrepreneurs, and other institutional actors need to take measures to change the country's image as a lawless, violent, and dangerous place.

Notes

1 Campbell, N.A., Reece, J.B., Taylor, M.R., Simon, J.E., & Dickey, J.L. 2009. *Biology Concepts & Connections*, Sixth Edition. Cummings Benjamin, p. 2, 3.
2 Helms, D.R., Helms, C.W., & Kosinski, R.J. 1997. Biology in the laboratory, Macmillan.

3   Hui, C. 2006. "Carrying capacity, population equilibrium, and environ-
    ment's maximal load," *Ecological Modeling*, 192, pp. 317–320.
4   Helms, D.R., Helms, C.W., & Kosinski, R.J. Biology in the laboratory.
    Macmillan, 1997.
5   Chapin III, S.F., Walker, B.H., Hobbs, R.J., Hooper, D.U., Lawton, J.H.,
    Sala, O.E., & Tilman, D. 1997. "Biotic control over the functioning of eco-
    systems," *Science*, 277(5325), pp. 500–504.
6   aljazeera.com. 2016. South Korea's chaebol: Economy at a crossroads, 19
    November, www.aljazeera.com/programmes/countingthecost/2016/11/south-
    korea-chaebol-economy-crossroads-161119111619759.html.
7   Shiwen, Y. 2017. "Samsung electronics to launch $445m fund targeting South
    Korean SMES," 28 May, www.dealstreetasia.com/stories/samsung-445m-
    south-korean-smes-73601/.
8   Ibid.
9   *Korea Times*. 2010. "Korea times: Korea has competitive support system for
    small firms," June 4.
10 *Economist*. 2011. "What do you do when you reach the top?" 12 November,
    400(8759), pp. 79–81.
11 Dan Richards' interview with Josh Lerner, "Why public funding of ven-
    ture capital has failed," February 1, 2011, http://advisorperspectives.
    com/newsletters11/pdfs/Why_Public_Funding_of_Venture_Capital_Has_
    Failed.pdf.
12 "Fish out of water: Policymakers are turning their minds to the tricky sub-
    ject of promoting entrepreneurship," 29 October 2009, www.economist.
    com/node/14743944.
13 thestar.com. 2014. Malaysia's biotech landscape finally starting to emerge, 13
    November. www.thestar.com.my/lifestyle/features/2014/11/13/malaysias-
    biotech-landscape-finally-starting-to-emerge/.
14 "Prospects bright for UK's 'Silicon Roundabout," 16 December 2010,
    http://blogs.reuters.com/great-debate-uk/2010/12/16/prospects-bright-
    for-uks-silicon-roundabout/.
15 Kaplan, R.D. 1996. "War after peace," *New Republic*, 214(18), pp. 22–23.
16 Isenberg, D.J. 2010a. "Entrepreneurship in Haiti," 18 July, www.huffington
    post.com/daniel-isenberg/entrepreneurship-in-haiti_b_650519.html.
17 Singleton, A. 2008. "The stigma of failure is bad for Britain," 15 January, http://
    blogs.telegraph.co.uk/alex_singleton/blog/2008/01/15/the_stigma_of_
    failure_is_bad_for_britain.
18 Sitte, A., & Rheault, M. 2009. "Arab youth express strong entrepreneurial
    spirit," *Gallup Poll Briefing*, 9 June, p. 3.
19 Theil, S. 2007. "Teaching entrepreneurship in the Arab world," *Newsweek
    International*, 14 August, German Marshall Fund of the United States, www.
    gmfus.org/publications/article.cfm?id=332.
20 Choudhury, S.R. 2018. "Japan is changing its views on entrepreneurship, and
    that could be good for start-ups," www.cnbc.com/2018/03/18/working-in-
    japan-views-on-entrepreneurship-and-start-ups-are-changing.html.
21 Ibid.
22 Ibid.
23 Ho, Y.P., & Wong, P.K. 2007. "Financing, regulatory costs and entrepre-
    neurial propensity," *Small Business Economics*, 28, pp. 187–204.
24 Gross, D. 2008, "Poverty: Cheap loans at insanely high rates? Give us more,"
    Newsweek, 20 September, www.newsweek.com/id/160074.
25 *Economist*. 2008. Computers without border, 25 October.

26　Gudjonsson, H. 2018. The Arctic, where cold storage comes cheap for the digital age, 22 March, www.ft.com/content/779c1102-2d2b-11e8-97ec-4bd3494d5f14.

27　Maria Gallucci. 09/03/15. Iceland lures data center companies with cheap, renewable energy, www.ibtimes.com/iceland-lures-data-center-companies-cheap-renewable-energy-2081695.

28　Icenews. 2008. "Iceland green data centre dream still alive," November 13, 2008, www.icenews.is/2008/11/13/iceland-green-data-centre-dream-still-alive/.

29　Browning, J., & Valdimarsson, O.R. 2012. "Iceland, data-center hub?" March 29, 2012, www.businessweek.com/articles/2012-03-28/iceland-data-center-hub.

30　Gudjonsson. March 22, 2018.

31　February 28, 2018. Reykjavík to open its first large-scale Data Center next year, http://icelandmag.is/article/reykjavik-open-its-first-large-scale-data-center-next-year.

32　Church, G. 2017. "Coworking vs accelerators vs incubators: The ultimate guide for startups," https://allwork.space/2017/08/coworking-vs-accelerators-vs-incubators-the-ultimate-guide-for-startups/.

33　Yang, Y. 2017. "Meet Mao Daqing—China's king of co-working," www.ft.com/content/4ce139f8-a4fd-11e7-b797-b61809486fe2.

34　Foertsch, C. 2017. "More than one million people will work in coworking spaces in 2017," www.deskmag.com/en/the-complete-2017-coworking-forecast-more-than-one-million-people-work-from-14000-coworking-spaces-s.

35　Aransiola, D. 2017. "The rise of coworking spaces in Africa," www.deskmag.com/en/the-rise-of-coworking-spaces-in-africa-958.

36　Khan, T. 2018. "Why the co-working industry is gravitating towards large companies and SMEs," https://economictimes.indiatimes.com/small-biz/sme-sector/why-the-co-working-industry-gravitating-towards-large-companies-and-smes/articleshow/63038041.cms.

37　Evans, J. 2017. "Shared offices gain popularity as companies value the flexibility," www.ft.com/content/84a8f010-7eb0-11e7-ab01-a13271d1ee9c.

38　King, S. 2017. "Coworking is not about workspace—It's about feeling less lonely," https://hbr.org/2017/12/coworking-is-not-about-workspace-its-about-feeling-less-lonely.

39　Ibid.

40　Ibid.

41　Sushma, U.N. 2017. "A coworking space by women, of women, for only women," https://qz.com/1138489/indias-first-women-only-co-working-office-is-the-perfect-place-to-find-work-life-balance/.

42　Aransiola, D. 2017. "The rise of coworking spaces in Africa," www.deskmag.com/en/the-rise-of-coworking-spaces-in-africa-958.

43　Ballout, L. 2017. "The importance of incubators and accelerators," http://news.arabnet.me/the-importance-of-incubators-and-accelerators/.

44　The Chambers. 2018. "Incubators & co-working spaces," www.raleighchamber.org/incubators-and-co-working-space.html.

45　Deeb, G. 2014. "Is a startup incubator or accelerator right for you?" www.forbes.com/sites/georgedeeb/2014/08/28/is-a-startup-incubator-or-accelerator-right-for-you/#6441d5123d7a.

46　Harris, A. 2017. "Coworking space vs. startup incubator vs. accelerator: Which is best?" www.rocketspace.com/tech-startups/coworking-space-vs.-startup-incubator-vs.-accelerator-which-is-best.

47 Town, S. 2018. "The VC juggernaut awakens: Institutional capital, block-chain startups, and you," https://cryptoslate.com/crypto-venture-capital/.
48 Ibid.
49 Webonboarding and webexpenses bring you the Scale-up Hub. 6 July 2017. www.webonboarding.com/2017/webonboarding-and-webexpenses-bring-you-the-scale-up-hub.
50 Hathaway, I. 2016. "Accelerating growth: Startup accelerator programs in the United States," www.brookings.edu/research/accelerating-growth-startup-accelerator-programs-in-the-united-states/.
51 Cohen, Susan L. 2013. "What do accelerators do? Insights from incuba-tors and angels," *Innovations: Technology, Governance, Globalization*, 8(3–4), pp. 19–25.
52 Bates, S. 2017. "What is the difference between accelerators, incubators and co-workingspaces?"www.seedrs.com/learn/blog/accelerators-incubators-co-working-spaces.
53 Pernell. 2012. "Accelerators vs incubators: What's the difference?" www.busi-nessinsider.com/accelerators-vs-incubators-whats-the-difference-2012-12.
54 OECD. 2018. "Enabling SMEs to scale up," Plenary session 1, *The 2018 OECD Ministerial Conference*, 22–23 February 2018, Mexico City.
55 O'Brien,C.2016."Europehasgonecrazyforstartupaccelerators,with26opening in 2015," https://venturebeat.com/2016/06/14/europe-has-gone-crazy-for-startup-accelerators-with-26-opening-in-2015/.
56 Gust. 2015. "Global accelerator report 2015," http://gust.com/global-accelerator-report-2015/.
57 O'Brien, 2016.
58 Fehder, D. C. and Yael, V. 2014. "Accelerators and the Regional Supply of Venture Capital Investment," working paper, http://papers.ssrn.com/sol3/papers.cfm?abstract_id=2518668.
59 Lustig, N. 2017. "A new era for startup investing in Latin America," https://techcrunch.com/2017/05/19/a-new-era-for-startup-investing-in-latin-america/.
60 Hathaway, I. 2016. "Accelerating growth: Startup accelerator programs in the United States," www.brookings.edu/research/accelerating-growth-startup-accelerator-programs-in-the-united-states/.
61 Dam, C. 2017. "The different types of startup accelerators in Europe and USA," https://medium.com/@cindydam/the-different-types-of-startup-accelerators-in-europe-and-usa-1217f045e20a.
62 O'Brien,C.2016."Europehasgonecrazyforstartupaccelerators,with26open-ing in 2015," https://venturebeat.com/2016/06/14/europe-has-gone-crazy-for-startup-accelerators-with-26-opening-in-2015/.
63 Forbes. 2016. "The state of the startup accelerator industry," www.forbes.com/sites/groupthink/2016/06/29/the-state-of-the-startup-accelerator-industry/#5bfd81de7b44.
64 Ro Insider. 2018. "New accelerator in Romania finances tech start-ups," www.romania-insider.com/techcelerator-romania-launch/.
65 Max Smolaks 5 July 2016 Iceland rated as the world's safest location for a data center, www.datacenterdynamics.com/content-tracks/design-build/iceland-rated-as-the-worlds-safest-location-for-a-data-center/96520.fullarticle.
66 Levitan, D. 2014. Is Iceland poised to become a data center paradise? 6 Novem-ber, https://spectrum.ieee.org/energywise/telecom/internet/iceland-data-center-paradise.

67 Hamilton, D. 2010. "Q&A: Verne Global's Lisa Rhodes on Iceland data centers," September 2, 2010, www.thewhir.com/web-hosting-news/qa-verne-globals-lisa-rhodes-on-iceland-data-centers.
68 Bertrand, M., Mehta, P., & Mullainathan, S. 2002. "Ferreting out tunneling: An application to Indian business groups," *Quarterly Journal of Economics* 117(1), pp. 121–148.
69 Beck, T., Demirgüç-Kunt, A., & Maksimovic, V. 2002. "Financial and legal constraints to firm growth: Does size matter?" World Bank Working Paper 2784. Washington, DC.
70 "Ashima goyal regulation and De-regulation of the stock market in India," September 8, 2005, http://papers.ssrn.com/sol3/papers.cfm?abstract_id=609322.
71 "International Consortium for Law and Development, Knowledge in the Service of Democratic Social Change," The Kyrgyz Workshop on Drafting Anti-Corruption Legislation, 22–26 November 2004, www.iclad-law.org/Country%20Projects/KyrgyzAlt.html.
72 Fish, S. 2005. *Democracy Derailed in Russia: The Failure of Open Politics.* New York: Cambridge University Press.
73 Epstein, G. 2009. "The price of corruption," 30 October, www.forbes.com/2009/10/30/china-coal-corruption-communist-party-beijing-dispatch.html.
74 Lehrer, E., & Hildreth, J. 2002. "Scandinavia's surprising turn from Socialism," *The American Enterprise*, 13(8), pp. 42–44.
75 ameinfo.com. 2010. "Injaz Al-Arab Board convenes in Qatar," June 2, 2010, www.ameinfo.com/234264.html.
76 Isenberg, D.J. 2010b. "How to Start an Entrepreneurial Revolution."
77 Cambieri, G. 2011. "Family business challenges differ between the US and Europe," 28 September, www.campdenfb.com/article/family-business-challenges-differ-between-us-and-europe.
78 Chadha, M. 2007. "Mumbai's women-only taxi service," *BBC News*, 8 May, http://news.bbc.co.uk/2/hi/south_asia/6623211.stm.
79 Schipani, A. 2014. "Colombia breaks away from its traditional business mindset," www.ft.com/content/c55cbed0-ed80-11e3-8a1e-00144feabdc0.
80 Schipani, A. 2014. "Colombia breaks away from its traditional business mindset," www.ft.com/content/c55cbed0-ed80-11e3-8a1e-00144feabdc0.
81 DATAMONITOR: Colombia. 2010. *Colombia Country Profile*, 2010, pp. 1–75.
82 tradingeconomics.com. 2018. Colombia Unemployment Rate 2001–2018, https://tradingeconomics.com/colombia/unemployment-rate.
83 oecd.org. 2017. Colombia – Economic forecast summary (November 2017), www.oecd.org/eco/outlook/colombia-economic-forecast-summary.htm.
84 Martínez, L., Short, J.R., & Daniela, E. 2017. "The urban informal economy: Street vendors in Cali, Colombia", *Cities*, 66, pp. 34–43.
85 Farzad, R. 2007. "Extreme investing: Inside Colombia," May 28, 2007, www.businessweek.com/magazine/content/07_22/b4036001.htm.
86 Gonzalez, E. 2017. "Weekly chart: Military spending in Latin America and the Caribbean," 10 May, www.as-coa.org/articles/weekly-chart-military-spending-latin-america-and-caribbean.
87 bogotapost. 2016. "Military spending: The economy of defence," 18 October, https://thebogotapost.com/2016/10/18/military-spending-economy-defence/.

88 Blohm, M., Fernandes, A., & Khalitov, B. 2013. "Entrepreneurship in Colombia: 'Try Fast, Learn Fast, Fail Cheap.'" http://knowledge.wharton.upenn.edu/article/entrepreneurship-in-colombia-try-fast-learn-fast-fail-cheap//.

89 Dueñas, A. 2017. "SENA's Fondo Emprender to provide $12 Million USD in startup funding in Colombia," 11 August, www.financecolombia.com/sena-fondo-emprender-provide-12-million-usd-startup-funding-colombia/.

90 Vesga, R. 2015. "The case of Innpulsa Colombia The evolution of a public policy for the promotion of business hyper-growth." *Public Policy and Productive Transformation Series, N° 19.*

91 Espinosa J.E.A. 2015. "Why Chile and Colombia lead the world for entrepreneurship," www.weforum.org/agenda/2015/01/why-chile-and-colombia-lead-the-world-for-entrepreneurship/.

92 Correa, J.S., Tejada, M., Fallon, E.C., & Ordonez, G. 2014. "Science and technology policy in Colombia: A comparative review," *European Journal of Scientific Research*, 121(3), pp. 267–285.

93 Schipani, A. 2014. "Colombia breaks away from its traditional business mindset," www.ft.com/content/c55cbed0-ed80-11e3-8a1e-00144feabdc0.

94 Egusa, C. 2014. "Colombia is one of Latin America's most promising new tech hubs," https://techcrunch.com/2014/11/22/an-overview-of-colombia-one-of-latin-americas-most-promising-new-tech-hubs/ (Accessed January 29, 2018).

95 Lustig, N. 2017. "The Colombian startup ecosystem: Bogota, Medellin, Cali, and Barranquilla," www.nathanlustig.com/2017/12/19/the-colombian-startup-ecosystem-bogota-medellin-cali-and-barranquilla/.

96 StartupHook. 2015. "Why is mark Zuckerberg investing in Colombia's startup scene?" http://startuphook.com/tech/why-is-mark-zuckerberg-investing-in-colombias-startup-scene/1455/.

97 Egusa, 2014.

98 United States Council for International Business. 2018. Hampl urges high standards in Colombia's OECD Accession, www.uscib.org/hampl-urges-high-standards-in-colombias-oecd-accession/.

99 Campion, A. 2016. "Why Medellín is the favorite tech hub of South America," 29 January, www.colombianlifestyle.com/why-medellin-is-the-favorite-tech-hub-of-south-america/.

100 Egusa, 2014.

101 Moules, J. 2014. "Start-ups rise as murders plummet in Medellín," www.ft.com/content/a52cf2a6-f262-11e3-9e59-00144feabdc0.

102 progresomicrofinanzas.org. 2015. Rural microfinance fund: Decree 1449/2015, 2 July, http://progresomicrofinanzas.org/en/rural-microfinance-fund/.

103 finnovista.com. 2017. Colombia consolidates its position as the third Fintech ecosystem in Latin America after growing 61% in one year, 28 August, www.finnovista.com/fintechradarcolombia-actualizacion-agosto2017/?lang=en.

104 World Bank. 2018. Market capitalization of listed domestic companies (% of GDP), https://datos.bancomundial.org/indicador/CM.MKT.LCAP.GD.ZS?view=chart.

105 Portes, A., & Smith, L. 2008. "Institutions and development in Latin America: A comparative analysis," *Studies in Comparative International Development*, 2008, 43(2), pp. 101–128.

106 LAVCA. 2016. "Latin America venture capital: Five-year trends," https://lavca.org/industry-data/latin-america-venture-capital-five-year-trends/.

107 Markey, P. 2011. "Colombia sees FDI rising to $10 billion in 2011," 31 March, www.reuters.com/article/2011/03/31/us-latam-summit-colombia-trade-idUSTRE72U5EJ20110331.

108 santandertrade.com. 2018. Colombia: Foreign investment, https://en.portal.santandertrade.com/establish-overseas/colombia/investing.

109 Ibid.

110 Ibid.

111 Grupo Éxito becomes South America's largest retailer, August 14, 2015, www.eiu.com/industry/article/1193436103/grupo-exito-becomes-south-americas-largest-retailer/2015-08-14.

112 globaltrademag.com. 2017. Colombia: A top-three supplier to the United States, 14 June, www.globaltrademag.com/global-trade-daily/colombia-top-three-supplier-united-states.

113 Farzad, R. 2007. "Extreme investing: Inside Colombia," May 28, 2007, www.businessweek.com/magazine/content/07_22/b4036001.htm.

114 Clifton, D. 2007, "Mas y mejor for Latino brands," *Brand Strategy*, 217, pp. 54–55.

Chapter 3

Sources of Entrepreneurial Finances and Their Variation across the World

This chapter's objectives include:

1   To demonstrate an understanding of various types of entrepreneurial financing.
2   To analyze international variations and their sources in the availability of funds as well as types of funds to meet financial needs of potential and existing entrepreneurial ventures.
3   To evaluate the impacts of disruptive economic events such as the 2008 global financial crisis and IT bubble burst on the availability of various types of entrepreneurial finances.
4   To assess the effects of microfinance on the entrepreneurial activities of the poorest people in developing economies.
5   To demonstrate an understanding of motivations of investors associated with various forms of entrepreneurial financing.
6   To assess the appropriateness of various sources of financing for entrepreneurs with different levels of needs and different phases of business operations.
7   To demonstrate an understanding of some of the recent innovations in entrepreneurial financing such as crowdfunding.

Introduction

Not everyone who wants to start a business venture is able to do so. A lack of access to capital is often the biggest roadblock for latent entrepreneurs to materialize the goal of starting their own business. This is true even in advanced economies such as the U.S. A 2017 survey found that 90% of small business owners in the U.S. agreed that credit availability for small businesses is a problem. Over 60% thought that it was harder to get a loan in 2017 than it was in 2008.[1]

Economies worldwide vary widely in terms of the availability of funds to meet financial needs of entrepreneurial ventures, types of available funds, and the relative availability of such funds across various phases of ventures. A country's entrepreneurial finance environment is shaped by diverse motivations of various players such as investors, entrepreneurs, regulatory agencies, and nongovernment organizations.

For most potential entrepreneurs, business financing is not a problem in most industrialized countries. In these countries, policies, structures, and strategies are in place in banks to reduce the risk of lending to SMEs. For instance, SMEs in Organization for Economic Co-operation and Development (OECD) countries benefit from the fact that financial markets in these countries are highly competitive. Market-based banking in these economies forces banks to achieve high returns. For many banks, financing SMEs is becoming attractive. They are also developing effective techniques which distinguish high- and low-risk SME borrowers, and identify those likely to expand and survive. Banks in industrialized countries have also come up with new business models and products, which derive an increasing proportion of revenue from fees for services rather than interest on loans. Such models favor lending to SMEs. There are also well-established systems for raising money through capital markets.[2]

SME in developing countries are more likely to be impeded by the lack of financing than those in developed countries. For many commercial banks in these countries, revenues from fees for services are insignificant. Due primarily to the lack of competition, banks in many emerging markets have been laggards in implementing models which provide incentives to lend to SMEs. This shortage of financing has special implications on the size distribution of firms, Compared with developed counties firms in emerging markets tend to be heavily concentrated at the top and the bottom. In many cases, big firms are powerful oligarchs as discussed in Chapter 1 or state owned enterprises, which have access to bank loans. For instance, some Russian oligarchs received huge loans from state banks and invested in big state companies. Many Western banks have also provided loans to Russia's oligarchs. Likewise, in China, a large proportion of loans from large commercial banks that are state-owned go to state-owned enterprises mainly to finance public infrastructure projects.[3]

The characteristics of the banking system in these markets work against SMEs'. Many banks are state-owned and their credit may be allocated on the basis of government guarantees or in line with government targeting to develop specific sectors. Often banks are subject to ceilings on the interest rates they can charge, which would make it difficult to price credit in a way that reflects the risk of lending to SMEs. Lending to SMEs would involve special risks for financial institutions. This means that if banks are earning acceptable returns on other lending, there is no incentive to develop necessary skills to serve SMEs.

For many potential entrepreneurs, the only way to finance their ventures would be to rely on informal sources. As explained in Chapter 1, microenterprises that are funded through informal sources of capital lack growth opportunities. The shortage of SMEs, also known as the "missing middle," is arguably related to the low rate of economic growth.[4] The availability and composition of formal and informal finances explain the phenomenon of the missing middle.

Despite the ease with which SMEs receive bank loans in OECD economies, innovative SMEs which create value through the development of technology and innovation face problems to access finance in these economies. Such SMEs are perceived as more risky than traditional SMEs or large firms. They often do not meet the criteria for traditional bank loans. Moreover, banks have exhibited higher perceptions of risks with regard to financing innovative SMEs following the so-called dot.com bubble which mainly hit the IT and closely related industries between the late 1990s and early 2000s.[5]

It is also important to note the gender dimension in access to entrepreneurial financing. In the developing world, 70% of women-owned formal SMEs lack access to the capital they need.[6] Women in developing economies were 9% points less likely to have a bank account than men.[7]

Availability and Costs of Bank Financing

Many entrepreneurs prefer bank loans over other forms of financing as such loans allow them to have a full control of the firms and thus have more incentives to exert higher levels of efforts. Traditional bank financing is more important to SMEs due to the fact that they have fewer alternative options available compared to large enterprises. For instance, large South Korean firms are increasing using the capital market for financing and have thus dramatically reduced their dependence on bank credit.

As noted earlier, economies worldwide differ widely in terms of the availability and costs of bank loan financing. First, there are significant differences worldwide in the cost of lending (Figure 3.1). A comparison of annual lending rates (ALR) for short- and medium-term financing needs of businesses across countries would help us understand the variability of the costs of entrepreneurial finance. ALR would serve as an indicator to assess how easy or difficult it is to access the financial resources or capital for starting and/or continuing a business.

The high ALRs in some of the economies (Figure 3.1) are a response to the legacies of their hyperinflationary pasts. For instance, during 1980–1994, Brazil went through a hyperinflation with three-to-four-digit annual inflation rates that went.

The real issue for most potential entrepreneurs, however, concerns availability rather than the costs of capital. In this regard, many OECD countries have realized that focused government intervention is necessary

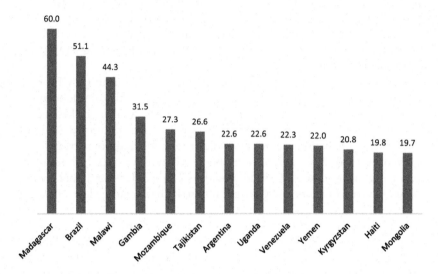

Figure 3.1 **Some Countries with the Highest Annual Lending Rates (2017).**
Source: Euromonitor International.

to improve SMEs' access to finance. They have launched a number of programs to use public funds to facilitate SME lending. One example is European Commission's SME guarantee facility (SMEG) (http://ec.europa. eu/enterprise/policies/finance/cip-financial-instruments/index_en.htm), which encourages banks to make more debt finance available to SMEs such as microcredit and mezzanine finance (which is typically a debt capital that is used to finance existing SMEs' expansion and the lender has the rights to convert to an ownership or equity if the loan is not paid back in time and in full). The SMEG program reduces the banks' risk exposure by providing coguarantees, counterguarantees, or direct guarantees. Consequently, large proportions of SMEs have access to bank financing. For instance, in the EU economies, commercial banks are the main source of finance for 79% of SMEs.[8]

Unavailability of financing is a more critical barrier faced by most entrepreneurs in developing countries. For instance, despite high interest rates, demand for credit exists in most developing economies. According to the World Bank's Global Findex Database 2017, 1.7 billion adults worldwide remain unbanked, who did not have an account at a financial institution or through a mobile money provider.[9] In South Sudan, only 9% of the adults had a bank account.

Part of the problem also lies in the fact that many developing economies are characterized by the lack, or poor performance, of credit rating agencies to provide information about the creditworthiness of SMEs.

A national credit bureau would collect and distribute reliable credit information and hence increase transparency and minimize the banks' lending risks. Many emerging economies lack such an agency and some have a poorly functioning one. This situation puts SMEs in a disadvantaged position in the credit market. This is because SMEs tend to be more informationally opaque than large corporations because the former often lack certified audited financial statements, and thus it is difficult for banks to assess or monitor the financial conditions.

Due to the rapidly increasing internationalization of banking, many foreign banks are active in emerging markets. There is, however, a common accusation that foreign banks "cherry pick" the best borrowers, and lend more to large transparent firms at the expense of SMEs.[10]

Many developing countries also have government-supported programs to help SMEs finance their businesses. For instance, due to the history of high interest rates, Brazil's development bank, the Banco Nacional de Desenvolvimento Econômico e Social (BNDES) dominates long-term debt business. The BNDES provides low-interest loans for longer periods compared to banks or institutional investors. However, due to many bureaucratic and red-tape processes such as notarize signatures for several declarations and certificates lead to significant costs and the process often takes more than 6 months.[11]

The Capital Market

Entrepreneurial firms can also raise money thorough capital markets by issuing debt or equity securities. An initial public offering (IPO), which occurs when a company first sells common shares to the public, is often a major goal for many SMEs. In addition to raising capital to finance growth, a publicly traded company is more likely to gain the trusts of their customers, as it is more closely monitored than private corporations.

Some indicators of capital market development include market capitalization (which is the share price times the number of outstanding shares) of listed companies, number of listed firms, and size of IPO offerings. Economies across the world vary widely in the development of the capital market. For instance, according to the World Bank (http://data.worldbank.org/indicator/CM.MKT.LCAP.GD.ZS), market capitalization as a proportion of GDP in 2016 varied from 7% in Nigeria to 995% in Hong Kong. The worldwide average was 98.2%.

Developing economies such as Nigeria lack appropriate legal and regulatory framework required for the development and functioning of the capital market. These include the lack of effective supervisory and monitoring systems, bankruptcy regulations, and procedures that are hostile to entrepreneurs, the lack of transparent accounting and disclosure standards, and a poor protection of minority shareholders' rights.[12] Moreover, some emerging markets have unfavorable regulations for foreign investors. For instance, in China foreign investors require a license under the qualified foreign institutional investor program to access the financial markets.

In some developing economies, raising money through the capital market represents an undesirable option because of socioeconomic, cultural, and other structural features. For instance, the largest firms in Colombia and some other Latin American countries have shown reluctance and resistance to list on the stock market. Being mostly family-owned, they are characterized by a conservative mindset and thus tend to avoid volatility in equity markets.[13] At the same time, there is also a low degree of willingness of people to invest in the capital market. In Mexico and Colombia, for instance, middle classes are much more inclined toward real estate investments than putting their money in the stock market.[14]

Some emerging economies have, however, experienced strong growth in the capital markets According to Ernst & Young's *Global IPO Trends 2012* report, venture capital-backed firms' strong preference for IPO has been one factor contributing to the rapid growth of IPOs in emerging markets such as China and India. This trend is in contrast with markets such as Israel, Europe and the U.S., where mergers and acquisitions (M&As) account for more than 90% of exits for VC-backed firms.

Venture Capital

Venture capital (VC or Venture) is a form of private equity capital, which is normally provided to immature capital-intensive companies that have high growth potential. The investor may be a person or an investment firm. The investor hopes to generate a return through events such as an IPO or trade sale of the company. In a VC-financed company, the entrepreneur is thus likely to benefit from the VC investor's entrepreneurial experience and managerial input. However, the entrepreneur is required to surrender partial ownership of the venture. In a VC-financed project, there are problems related to adverse selection and two-sided moral hazard. Note that adverse selection (antiselection, or negative selection) arises from information asymmetry between the investor and the entrepreneur. In such a case, one party is unable to determine if the other party is lying. Moral hazard is the problem of not being able to determine if the other party (the entrepreneur or the VC investor in this case) is cheating or acting dishonestly. They cannot verify each other's efforts.

VC is especially attractive for new and innovative companies, which have limited history of operation. They tend to be small to raise capital in the public markets and as noted earlier face difficulty in securing a bank loan. VC funds are important not because a large proportion of entrepreneurs receive them but because they are important funding sources for high-growth firms or SMEs with innovative ideas, products, services or new technologies (innovative SMEs). Indeed, less than 1% of all startups get VC funding, which makes the VC availability irrelevant for most entrepreneurs. In the U.S., for instance, most businesses are created as sole proprietorships and service companies. These businesses tend to be less capital-intensive and thus do not seek or obtain VC funding.

In 2017, global VC funding amounted US$155 billion.[15] The U.S. attracts more VC funding than any other economies (Figure 3.2).

Among the "fastest-growing and most successful companies" in the U.S., about 16% have VC backing.[16] Returns on VC funds to investors in the country have been about 20% annually or twice as much as the average of stocks. In the U.S., public companies with VC backing were estimated to employ 4 million people, account for 20% of market capitalization, and 44% of R&D spending of public companies.[17]

In 2017, five of the world's six largest companies were VC funded.[18] VC investors may sell their investment and exit a company they funded. During 2012–2016, the average U.S. VC exit was about US$200 million compared to US$70 million for Europe. During the period, the number of exits with over US$250 million during was 22 in Europe compared to 166 in the U.S. A reasonably good exit in Europe is US$100 million compared to US$250 million in the U.S.[19] Larger VC funds are becoming common in Europe. About 30% of funds raised in 2016 exceeded €100 million.[20]

Figure 3.2 Venture Capital Investments in Different Geographic Regions in 2017 (US$, billion).

Source: For Asia, Europe, and North America (cbinsights.com. 2018. "Venture capital funding report 2017", www.cbinsights.com/research/report/venture-capital-q4-2017/). For Latin America (www.pehub.com/2018/03/pe-vc-activity-hits-record-latin-america-2017/), For Africa (https://qz.com/1211233/how-much-did-african-startups-raise-in-2017-partech-disrupt-africa).

Business Angels

Business angels or angel investors, who are individuals that provide financial backing through seed money for small startups usually founded by their family members or friends, are becoming increasingly important investors in many countries. Especially, the U.S. has dense networks in which successful entrepreneurs mentor startups and play the roles as "business angels," or general partners of VC firms.

One thing that should be noted is that available data and statistics on the VC industry mainly cover formal private equity investments in the industry, that is, funds raised and investments that circulate through "intermediary" VC companies. While there is the lack or limited availability of hard and reliable data on direct investments made by business angels, such investments are believed to be several times higher than formal VC investment in early stages. In the U.S. alone, business angels are estimated to invest about US$25 billion in 70,000 new companies every year.[21] The global market size angel investment is estimated to exceed $50 billion annually.[22,23]

The VC Industry in Developing Countries

VC and angel investments are a relatively new phenomenon in the developing world. In most of the economies of Middle East and North Africa (MENA), there is the lack of institutional investors that are capable of investing in the VC industry. Likewise, the banks are not interested in being players in the VC industry.[24] Global venture firms, on the other hand, are reluctant to invest in emerging markets due to various challenges such as unfamiliar local laws and accounting standards, stock exchanges that have little experience in technology listings and different negotiating styles. Some developing economies are, however, becoming increasingly attractive destinations for VC.

Accelerators as a New Source of Entrepreneurial Financing

Accelerators are emerging as a key source of entrepreneurial financing (Figure 3.3). The U.S. and Canada account most of such financing. As Figure 3.3 shows, accelerators in the U.S. and Canada invested more than twice as much as those in Europe. Other geographic regions—Latin America, Asia, and Oceania and the Middle East are following close behind. The top five categories invested by accelerators included the Internet of Things (74% of accelerators interested), followed by big data analytics (65%), SaaS (65%), FinTech (64%), and mobile apps (63%).[25]

In 2015, the U.S.-based 500 startups invested more than US$18 million and became the biggest accelerator program in the world in terms of

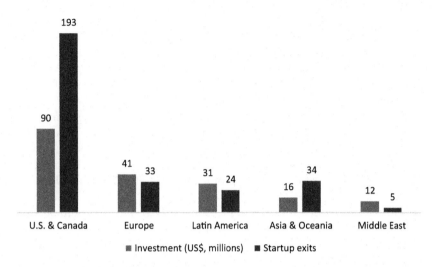

Figure 3.3 Investments and Exits Associated with Accelerator Programs in Different Geographic Regions.
Source: Gust. 2015. "Global accelerator report 2015", http://gust.com/global-accelerator-report-2015/.

investment. Another U.S. accelerator Techstars invested US$17 million in U.S. startups. Other top Seed Accelerators were Start-Up Chile (US$7 million), Latin America's NXTP Labs (US$6 million), Europe's Accelerace (US$4 million), and Canada's Alacrity Foundation (US$3 million).[26]

Startup exits through mergers, acquisitions, and IPOs are considered to be a success indicator of accelerator investment programs. In this regard, again, accelerators in the U.S. and Canada reported the greatest number of startup exits in 2015 (Figure 3.3).[27]

The emergence of accelerator/investment programs has resulted in reduced importance of other sources of entrepreneurial financing such as VC. For instance, VC funding is reported to be declining in Europe. According to Pitchbook analysts, the decline can be attributed to European incubators and accelerators, which may delay the need for VC financing.[28]

Microfinance

Microfinance was started in the 1970s to provide small working capital loans to poor people in the developing world to start a business. A microfinance institution (MFI) typically borrows funds at a low cost and tries to keep loan defaults and overhead expenses very low. Loans are typically made to entrepreneurs without physical collateral.

In 2016, MFIs had 123 million customers, who had borrowed US$102 billion.[29] India had 47 million borrowers with US$15 billion in outstanding loans. Other countries with high number of borrowers were Vietnam, Bangladesh, Peru, and Mexico. Overall, South Asia accounted for 60% of all borrowers in 2016. Latin America and the Caribbean countries had US$42.5 billion in outstanding loans in 2016, compared with US$9.3 billion in Europe and US$8.7 billion in Sub-Saharan Africa.[30] Likewise, in Cambodia, MFIs' loan portfolio US$4 billion in 2017. 1.7 million Cambodians received loans with an MFI in 2017.[31]

The latitude in terms of products offered by microfinance companies has also expanded. Nowadays, microfinance provides low-income people with diverse financial services such as various types of loans (student loans, home loans), savings, money transfer, and insurance. Microfinance is described as one of the highest-profile and most effective examples of an anti-poverty program.[32]

Most microfinance activities are concentrated in the Asia Pacific region (Figure 3.4). India and Bangladesh together account for more than half of all borrowers in the world.

Large multinational banks have also been attracted to the microfinance industry. For instance, Citigroup, Deutsche Bank, and HSBC have separate microfinance divisions. As of 2009, Citibank worked with 85 MFIs in 35 countries.[33] Microfinance has a clear "double bottom line for these multinational banks, social as well as financial, as it allows them to show their corporate social responsibility and to realize attractive returns on investments."[34]

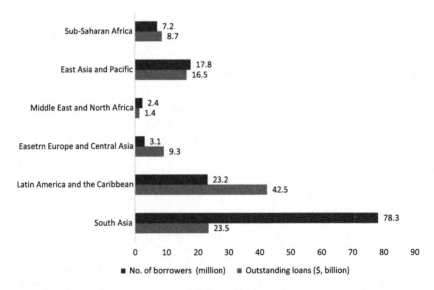

Figure 3.4 **Number of Borrowers Served by MFIs and Outstanding Loans in Various Regions (2016).**

Source: Convergences. 2017. "Is microfinance still working?" Microfinance barometer.

Some countries have relaxed regulations to allow commercial banks to enter into this business. In the Philippines, in 2010, the central bank introduced a policy that allows all banks to lend directly to farmers. Before that, only rural banks that were part of the Micro Enterprises' Access to Banking Services (MABS) program could provide direct loans to farmers.[35]

Interest rates charged by MFIs vary widely and there is no agreement as to what a reasonable rate would be. The average interest rate worldwide is 26%. The Indian MFI, SKS charges 28.3% annual interest rate.[36] Mexico's Compartamos charges interest rates of around 85%.[37] For most poor people who lack access to credit, however, microlenders are a better option than the village loan sharks.

MFIs have demonstrated questionable effectiveness in fighting poverty. Due partly to poor staff management in MFIs, informal intermediaries such as loan sharks still function as a key source of loans for many poor families. Studies have suggested that loan officers at MFIs have an incentive to focus more on the number of loans provided and payback rates. There is little incentive to fund the poorest borrowers. Many loan officers at MFIs know that some borrowers use their loans to lend to poor families. They still provide loans to the informal intermediaries because of potentially higher payback rates.[38] This reinforces the existing socio-economic hierarchies in developing countries.

There is also evidence that microfinance customers borrow money from traditional moneylenders to pay off the debts with an MFI. Proof of that claim is evident in the growth of both microfinance as well as traditional money lending in India. Data from a government survey indicated that in the 1990s, traditional moneylenders' share in the rural Indian household debt increased from 18% to 30%.[39] It is speculated that one reason behind the growth of traditional money lending could be the practice of some microfinance borrowers to borrow money from moneylenders in order to pay their microfinance debt. There is a peer pressure within microfinance groups to pay back loans. A field observation in Andhra Pradesh state of India indicated that women who borrowed from MFIs needed to rotate loans from other sources including local moneylenders to pay to the MFIs.[40]

Crowdfunding

Crowdfunding (CF), which involves raising small amounts of capital from a large number of individuals, is considered to be a major disruption in entrepreneurial financing. Key elements of CF include an online platform, an individual or an entity that needs funding, and a community willing to contribute to the funds.

Equity-based crowdfunding (ECF) is emerging as an increasingly important source of entrepreneurial financing. For instance, "business and entrepreneurship" category accounted for 27.4% of total CF volume in 2012, which increased to 41.3% in 2014.[41] One estimate suggested that the Internet-based ECF market was US$400 million worldwide in 2013, which increased to US$1.1 billion in 2014.[42] In 2014, ECF accounted for 30% of all seed capital in the U.K.[43]

Nonetheless, economies worldwide vary greatly in entrepreneurs' efforts to raise and investors' propensity to invest in ECF. For instance, per capita ECF in 2015 was estimated at US$0.003 in the Latin America and the Caribbean (LAC) region, US$0.23 in Asia Pacific and US$8.32 in the U.S. (Table 3.1).

Table 3.1 The Sizes of ECF Market in Selected Regions and Associated Social and Cultural Factors

Economy	ECF	ECF per capita per year*	Key characteristics of informal institutions from the standpoint of ECF
Asia Pacific region	2015: US$948.3 million.	2015: US$0.23	China: incompatibility of "success-obsessed" culture with failures in startup ventures.[a] India: people care less about social causes and are less likely to offer money if there is no financial return.[b] China, Indonesia, and other countries: less comfortable in trusting a stranger.[c] Lack of trust in online transactions in China, Indonesia, Singapore and other countries.[c] China and other countries: investment culture incompatible with ECF which is associated with an uncertain return, bank lending dominates corporate financing.[d] Investment options more similar to ECF such as VC stock and bond are relatively new.
Canada	2014: US$70 million	2014: US$2	Reliance on banks for investment guidance, a "risk capital investment fatigue" lack of education, success stories and media attention on ECF.[e]

(Continued)

Economy	ECF	ECF per capita per year*	Key characteristics of informal institutions from the standpoint of ECF
LAC	2015: US$2.05 million	2015: US$0.003	Low levels of trust.[f] Trust mainly resides within the "jus sanguinis" ("the right of blood") and not in strangers.[g]
The Netherlands	2015: US$5.04 million	2015: US$0.29	Europe: social stigma attached to bankruptcy. Entrepreneurs going to bankrupt are viewed as "losers".[h]
The Nordic Region (Denmark, Finland, Iceland, Norway, and Sweden)	Mid-2012 to mid-2015: US$7.8 million	2012–2015: US$0.09	
The U.K.	2015 (first 10 months): US$219 million	2015: US$4.10	
The U.S.	2015Q1: US$662 million	2015: US$8.32	Entrepreneurial failure considered to be part of the learning process.[h] Success stories and media attention related to ECF Investment culture that can easily be adapted to the context of ECF.

Source: Adopted from Kshetri, N. 2018. "Informal institutions and Internet-based equity crowdfunding," Journal of International Management 24(1), 33–51.

a ST (SeedInvest Technology), 2016. "Future of crowdfunding in China," www.seed-invest.com/blog/crowdfunding/futureofcrowdfundinginchina.
b Chaudhary, D. 2013. "Crowdfunding gathers momentum in India," 3 April, www.livemint.com/Industry/jmPA6P760o6IUrAU6WAraJ/Crowdfunding gathersmomen-tuminIndia.html.
c Dan, H. 2013. "Trust among Chinese 'drops to record low," 18 February, http://usa.chinadaily.com.cn/china/2013-02/18/content_16230819.htm.
d Liang, Z. 2015. "Crowdfunding in China: Potentials, challenges, risks and solutions," 6 October, at www.crowdfundinsider.com/2015/10/75384-crowdfunding-in-china-potentials-challenges-risks-and-solutions/.
e Conkin, B., & Cormick, A. 2015. "Part two: Is culture killing equity crowdfunding in Canada?" 2 September, http://ncfacanada.org/part-two-is-culture-killing-equity-crowdfunding-in-canada/.
f Canigueral, A. 2015. "Can digital sharing economy platforms pull Latin America's informal sector into the mainstream? Yes. Trade is back!" www.americasquarterly.org/content/can-digital-sharing-economy-platforms-pull-latin-america%E2%80%99s-informal-sector-mainstream-yes.
g Lagos, M. 2001. "How people view democracy: Between stability and crisis in Latin America," Journal of Democracy 12(1), 137–145.
h European Commission. 1998. "Fostering entrepreneurship in Europe: Priorities for the future," Brussels 98, p. 222, final.

In the context of ECF, the first observation is that most economies have not yet enacted ECF legislation. This means that ECF-related formal institutions are not well developed in most countries. For instance, according to a 2015 report of the International Organization of Securities Commissions (IOSCO),[44] which was based on a survey in which 23 member countries participated, only eight—Canada, France, Germany, Italy, Japan, Spain, the U.K., and the U.S.—had "bespoke" ECF regulations. Four—Brazil, South Korea, India, and Mexico—were planning to do so. The remaining economies relied on general securities and financial services laws to govern ECF.[45] The countries participating in the IOSCO survey are big and/or rich. Indeed most small and/or developing nations lack ECF laws. For instance, as of 2015, Malaysia was the only Southeast Asian country to have ECF legislation.

Entrepreneurs are raising ECF even in countries without ECF regulations. For instance, as of September 2016, India lacked ECF laws[46] but had over half-a-dozen equity CF platforms (ECFPs). During the eighteen months leading up to September 2016, Indian ECFPs raised US$52–67 million for about 200 companies.[47] Likewise, as of early 2016, China lacked formal ECF legislation. Nonetheless, ECF is a dominant segment in the Chinese CF landscape.[48] Barriers related to informal institutions are even more pronounced than formal institutions to raise ECF. Whereas the U.S. has an investment culture that can easily be adapted to ECF, China lacks such a culture. For instance, until the early 2000s, bank lending accounted for 90% of corporate financing in China, which reduced to 55% in 2012.[49] Due to the relative newness of individual investments, new channels such as ECF are viewed as high-risk investments.[50]

Initial Coin Offering (ICO)

An ICO is a fundraising tool that allows a startup to trade future cryptocoins in exchange for crypto-currencies of immediate and liquid value such as bitcoin and ethereum.[51] A startup raising money through an ICO can create its own crypto-currency utilizing blockchain protocols such as Ethereum, Counterparty, or Openledger. Roadmap goals and strategies are outlined in a whitepaper. ICO values are set up based on the amount of money a project requires to achieve the stated objectives. Unlike IPOs, token holders do not have ownership rights or asset claims at the company launching the project. Instead, the tokens may act as "bearer instruments" and the users have rights related to a specific project.[52]

According to Fabric Ventures and TokenData, 435 successful projects raised US$5.6 billion in 2017 through ICOs. The 10 largest projects had raised 25% of the amount.[53] However, among 913 ICOs identified, only 48% achieved their funding targets.[54]

Venture capitalists often tend to avoid blockchain companies that have only proof-of-concept or solely white paper-based pre–ICO concepts. They are generally interested only in blockchain projects that have demonstrated significant promise for success.[55] ICOs thus fill an important funding gap for early stage blockchain companies that have not yet developed marketable products.

Token offerings need to be registered in a real-world jurisdiction, which regulates ICO activities. One of the most fascinating aspects of ICOs is a surprisingly high degree of interjurisdictional variation in regulations and policies governing this form of fund raising. For instance, Switzerland is touted as a "cryptocurrency haven."[56] Crypto-ventures in other major economies, on the other hand, have encountered diverse legislative and regulatory obstacles. For instance, the question of when the U.S. government would announce its ICO policy had been anybody's guess for a long time. On July 25, 2017, the U.S. Securities and Exchange Commission (SEC) released its first official public statement on tokens. The SEC report concluded that some coins that were being offered were structured as securities and thus they were required to register with the SEC.[57] In September 2017, the Chinese government issued a blanket ban on ICOs. Business establishments are even banned from offering meeting spaces to crypto-entrepreneurs.

In some economies, considerable revisions have been made in ICO policy. Until 2014, the U.K. stayed away from crypto-currency. In mid-2014, the Financial Conduct Authority (FCA) announced an initiative that would seek to create a favorable environment for crypto-entrepreneurship.[58] This is not unique to the U.K. Russia made a similar U-turn in policy.

International Remittances as a Source of Entrepreneurial Financing

According to the World Bank, international remittances amounted US$429 billion in 2016 (www.worldbank.org/en/topic/migrationremittancesdiasporaissues/brief/migration-and-remittances-publications). International remittances are an important source of financing in many developing countries (Figure 3.5). For instance, a survey of microenterprises in Mexico found that about one-third of the capital invested was associated with migration to the United States. It is argued that economic remittances from diaspora networks play the role of financial intermediaries in the sense that such remittances enable households and microentrepreneurs to overcome credit constraints and imperfections they face in the financial markets in developing countries. Households and microenterprises receiving economic remittances are able to invest in human and physical capital, which is likely to stimulate entrepreneurial activities and contribute to

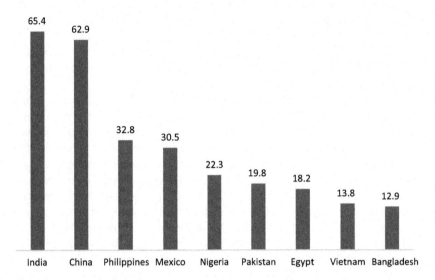

Figure 3.5 Remittance Inflows in Some Developing Countries (2017, US$, billion).
Source: The World Bank.

long-run economic growth of a country.[59] Perhaps even more impressive is that the population at the middle-to-bottom end of the wealth distribution is more likely to benefit from economic remittances.[606162] Note that poor households often face a high degree of credit constraints and thus, have low degree of access to self-employment and entrepreneurship.[63] This issue is rather important because of the fact that poverty reduction has been identified as a key entrepreneurial impact.[64]

While some studies have shown that remittances are mainly used for consumption instead of investment activities, research has also indicated that households receiving international remittances tend to invest more in entrepreneurial activities than those not receiving remittances.[65] Remittances contribute to entrepreneurship by increasing savings and promoting credit mobilization and other forms of investment. Remittance-receiving families often receive funds that are much larger than required for immediate expenditure. They thus deposit the excess funds in the formal banking system, which enhance the banking system liquidity.

Other Important Sources of Entrepreneurial Financing

Many other important sources of entrepreneurial financing exist. We discuss some of them in this section.

Supply Chain Financing

In supply chain financing, companies collaborate with financial institutions to provide financing and other related services such as technical assistance, management, corporate governance, legal compliance to small firms in the company's supply chain. For instance, the Brazilian company, VCP has collaborated with the bank ABN AMRO Real in its Poupança Florestal (Forest Savings Account) program, which provides farmers with financial resources. VCP also provides seedlings and technical assistance to plant eucalyptus and has committed to buying the timber at a fair price after seven years. The Forest Savings Account program is supported by local partnerships with governmental agencies and universities.[66]

Informal Financing Sources

The importance of informal sources is readily understood within the context of the lack of access to formal financing. Informal financing often involves small, short-term loans to borrowers in rural areas. Informal financial institutions often serve the lower end of the market and are complementary to the formal financial system. Two important questions arise: The first question is how informal sources of finance can exist where the formal sources cannot. The second question concerns the financing gap that exists. The answer to the first question involves considering informal investors' superior information about the entrepreneur or enforcement possibilities which reduce problems such as adverse selection and moral hazard. Informal financial institutions rely on relationships and thus have advantages, which enable them to lend, efficiently monitor, and enforce repayment to the entrepreneurs that formal investors such as commercial banks may not trust. The answer to the second question lies in the lack of availability of sufficient funds and relatively high cost of capital. The limited and costly funds constrain growth.[67] Moreover, monitoring and enforcement mechanisms of informal financial institutions are ill equipped and ineffective, which makes them unprepared to scale up investments or to move to the formal sector.[68]

Concluding Comments

A variety of sources exist to meet financial needs of existing and potential entrepreneurs. Financing from accelerators and ICOs are some of the newest sources of entrepreneurial financing.

Availability and affordability of a given source vary across countries, types of ventures, and phases of a business. While there has been a dramatic increase in the availability of different sources of finance for potential entrepreneurs in emerging economies in recent years, the supplies are insufficient to meet financing needs of potential entrepreneurs. Financing

SMEs is a risky proposition for many banks in emerging markets. While largest firms use formal sources of finance (e.g., most bank loans in China go to SOEs), the smallest tend to rely more on informal finance.

Microfinance deserves special attention in the context of emerging economies. In many cases, what seems to be happening, however, is that MFIs are focusing more on increasing repayment rates rather than encouraging productive utilization of micro-credits. Despite the growth of MFIs, predatory lenders are still thriving. When MFIs are poorly managed, they provide entrepreneurial opportunities for "middle men," who take MFI loans and lend to poorer borrowers. As a result, the poorest of the poor microentrepreneurs benefit less. In this regard, one way to increase the success rate of microfinance program is to manage MFIs in a better way. MFIs should also provide trainings that can address the lack of business and entrepreneurial skills of borrowers.

Given the important roles of microcredits and microfinances among the poorest of the poor, such schemes play an important role in developing countries and efforts should be made to boost their effectiveness and diffusion. Many potential entrepreneurs are also unaware of diverse financing options that they may access. In this regard, improving awareness about the various financing options among potential entrepreneurs is also important.

End of Chapter Questions

1   What are some of the potential barriers that MFIs are likely to face in industrialized countries?
2   What are some of the barriers for the development of the VC industry in the developing world?
3   What are some of the key factors that have led to the phenomenon of "missing middle" in developing economies?
4   Do you think that there should be an appropriate interest rate that MFIs can justify charging to potential borrowers? What factors would determine such rates?
5   Do you agree with the following statement: "Microfinance has done more to bolster the status of women and to protect them from abuse than any laws could accomplish"? Why?

End of the Chapter Case: Crowdfunding in Latin America

CF is rapidly taking off in Latin America. Between 2011 and June 2015, Mexican CF campaigns funded 4,081 successful initiatives that raised US$13.13 million from 53,276 investors.[69] There are a number of regional as well as country-specific CF platforms operating in the region (Table 3.2). Just like in Australia and New Zealand, most successful CF

Table 3.2 Some Representative CFPs and Examples of Funded Projects

CFP	Explanation	Examples of funded projects
Idea.Me	• A Latin American CFP, which as of February 2013, funded 180 creative projects and raised over US$1 million.	• Project to create a casual game for iPod, iPhone and iPad which would "become a true vehicle for learning and cultural transfer" in the industry dominated by the Zombie-, ninja-, or pirate-themed game apps.[a] Funding goal of US$5,000 was met • (http://idea.me/projects/30/pewen-collector)
Catarse	• Based in Brazil. • Raised US$1.8 million by 2012.	• US$70,000 was raised from 3,500 people to edit and produce a film about the proposed Belo Monte hydroelectric dam to be built on the Amazon region's Xingu River. In an effort to inform the public of the project's potential impact, the *film captures the views* of diverse stakeholders such as indigenous peoples, environmental scientists, and Brazilian politicians.[b]
CrowdPal (ECF)	• Based in Chile	• RedCapital, a web platform that connects investors with SMEs secured USD $300,000 in commitments on CrowdPal from 11 backers[c]
fondeadora. mx	• Based in Mexico	• Raised about $17,500 to open a center in Iztapalapa to support mom and pop stores by providing basic public services, workshops, and training programs[d]

a Forman, L. 2011. "Chile's first mapuche videogame – Interview with Fernando Rojas for China2Valley", www.leslieforman.com/2011/09/chiles-first-mapuche-videogame-interview-with-fernando-rojas-for-china2valley/.
b Rocha, V.B. 2012. "Crowdfunding's future in Latin America," September 17, www.shareable.net/blog/crowdfundings-future-in-latin-america.
c Crowdpal. 2017. "Chilean based crowdfunding platform successfully closes first campaign," www.prnewswire.com/news-releases/chilean-based-crowdfunding-platform-successfully-closes-first-campaign-300533046.html.
d Carayon, N. 2015. "Tenoli: Power a las tienditas!" https://fondeadora.mx/projects/tenoli/.

campaigns Latin America have been those related to music, dance, theatre and other creative projects.[70]

The region's CF market, however, is less developed compared to most other regions. This is especially the case for ECF. As noted earlier, Latin America and the Caribbean (LAC) region's per capita ECF of US$0.003 in 2015 was much lower than most other geographic regions.[71]

Regulatory Uncertainty

Regulatory uncertainty has had a negative effect in the ECF market. Regulators have special concerns regarding ECF for which regulatory frameworks are not well developed in most economies in the region. In such conditions, it is reasonable to assume that laws and regulations that laid down for a broader scope of activities and purpose (e.g., entrepreneurial activities such as raising finances and investments) may be applied to equity-based CF.

Countries vary widely in the degree of friendliness of the regulatory framework for entrepreneurship. In economies where entrepreneurs face constraints and distortions such as red-tapes and high tax burdens, they may be discouraged from raising ECF. On the other hand, in a country where promoting productive entrepreneurship is a national priority, the legislature and the government may put their support behind ECF even without clear legal rules.

Let us compare Brazil and the U.K. for this purpose, which ranked No. 116 and 10, respectively, in the World Bank's ease of doing business index. In the U.K., generous tax breaks for investing in seed stage favor equity CF.[72] On the other hand, in Brazil, the undeveloped regulatory framework has led to a problematic interpretation of CF. The state bank Caixa Econômica Federal, which is the government department responsible for regulating lotteries and other contests, wanted to classify CF as a contest with prizes. Such interpretation may limit the growth of the CF due to extremely high taxes on payouts.[73]

Low Thin Trust

Online ECF involves fundraising efforts often initiated by a stranger. What is important here is thin trust between strangers rather than thick trust between people that know each other. In Latin America, trust mainly resides within the "jus sanguinis" ("the right of blood"). Latin Americans thus lack trust in unknown people.[74]

One key observation regarding the slow takeoff of ECF in LAC is that the liberalization of markets and economic modernization led to the disbandment of social networks. Whereas these disappearing networks have been replaced by new forms of support systems (e.g., voluntary associations in the U.S.), such systems have not yet emerged in Latin America. Latin American economies thus consist of "lonely populations" who lack social support and links.[75] The trust index of Brazil was 17.5 compared to Norway's 148[76] (Figure 3.6).

As noted earlier, whereas many CF projects promoted by U.S.-based CFPs are product-based and people fund them expecting to receive a product in return, Brazilians tend to be more interested in the project's social benefits. It is also rare in Brazil for a project to be funded at a level higher than asked for by the project creator.[77]

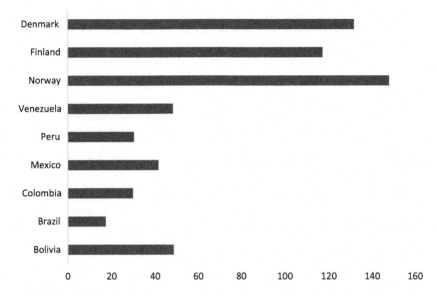

Figure 3.6 A Comparison of Trust Indices of Selected Economies in Latin America with Nordic Countries.
Source: Medrano, J. D., 2016. "Interpersonal trust," www.jdsurvey.net/jds/jdsurveyMaps.jsp?Idioma=%20I&SeccionTexto=0404&NOID=104.

Underdeveloped Payment Mechanisms

Some CFPs in the region have recognized the importance of becoming a global player. Perhaps the greatest barrier a regional player centers on the variation in payment systems across economies in the region. This has been a challenge faced by Idea.Me. A key aspect of Idea.Me's localization involved the use of various payment options acceptable in the LAC region including cash and other methods to account for the region's risk aversion. Crowdfunders can pay with almost all regional currencies such as Argentine and Mexican Pesos, Brazilian Real, and US$. It became the region's first CFP to support Bitcoins. Paypal, MercadoPago (a popular mode of payment for local consumers and businesses in Argentina, Colombia, and Mexico), DineroMail (a mode for local payments in Chile), and Moip (which is used for local payments in Brazil).[78] Idea.Me's websites are in Spanish, Portuguese, and English.

Case Summary

ECF per capita in the LAC is among the lowest in the world. A critical and urgent step for regulators in the region is to enact ECF laws. The case of Idea.Me makes it clear that when entrepreneurs or investors cross borders, they should be aware of local differences in CF-related institutions and do what they can to compensate for these differences. Given the global nature of CF, its growth hinges critically upon the compatibility of the payment mechanisms across countries. International cooperation to harmonize payment systems can stimulate the growth of this industry.

Notes

1 Arensmeyer, J. 2017. "Capital continues to elude small businesses: What can be done?" www.business.com/articles/small-businesses-unable-to-get-bank-loans/.
2 OECD. 2006. "Financing SMEs and entrepreneurs," *Policy Brief*, November, www.oecd.org/cfe/37704120.pdf.
3 Yan, L. 2012. "Development Finance," *Chinese Economy*, 45(1), pp. 8–27.
4 Lee, S., & Persson, P. 2012. Financing from family and friends, *NYU Stern Working Paper FIN-12-007*, 30 August, http://papers.ssrn.com/sol3/papers.cfm?abstract_id=2086625.
5 OECD, 2006.
6 The World Bank. 2018. "Women entrepreneurs finance initiative," www.worldbank.org/en/programs/women-entrepreneurs.
7 Demirgüç-Kunt, A., Klapper, L., Singer, D., & Jake Hess, S.A. 2018. *The Global Findex Database 2017, Measuring Financial Inclusion and the Fintech Revolution*. International Bank for Reconstruction and Development/The World Bank.
8 OECD, 2006.
9 Demirgüç-Kunt et al., 2018.
10 Degryse, H., Havrylchyk, O., Jurzyk, E., & Kozak, S. 2009. "Foreign bank entry and credit allocation in emerging markets," www.imf.org/external/pubs/ft/wp/2009/wp09270.pdf, International Monetary Fund, WP/09/270.
11 7 Challenges SMES face in Brazil, 13 December 2011, http://thebrazilbusiness.com/article/7-challenges-smes-face-in-brazil.
12 de la Torre, A., Gozzi, J., & Schmukler, S. 2007. "Capital market development: Whither Latin America?" Policy Research Working Paper No. 4156, World Bank.
13 Rathbone, J.P. 2010. "Capital markets: Investors require patience more than nimble financial footwork," April 6, 2010, www.ft.com/intl/cms/s/0/53e3395e-4042-11df-8d23-00144feabdc0.html#axzz1VLe1OWo0.
14 Portes, A., & Smith, L. 2008. "Institutions and development in Latin America: A comparative analysis," *Studies in Comparative International Development*, 43(2), pp. 101–128.
15 KPMG. 2018. Venture Pulse Q4 2017 Global analysis of venture funding, KPMG International Cooperative.
16 Kedrosky, P. 2009. "Right-sizing the U.S. venture capital industry," Ewing Marion Kauffman Foundation.
17 Gornall, A., & Strebulaev, I.A. 2015. "The economic impact of venture capital: Evidence from public companies," Stanford University Graduate School of Business Research Paper No. 15–55, https://papers.ssrn.com/sol3/papers.cfm?abstract_id=2681841.
18 Kanies, L. 2017. "Understanding venture capital," https://medium.com/s/understanding-venture-capital/if-you-take-venture-capital-youre-forcing-your-company-to-exit-fc08fcdb32cc.

19 Basta, V. 2017. "Venture investing in the US and Europe are totally different industries," https://techcrunch.com/2017/06/07/venture-investing-in-the-us-and-europe-are-totally-different-industries/.

20 Marovac, N. 2017. "Europe's venture capitalists are closing the gap with Silicon Valley," www.weforum.org/agenda/2017/11/europe-venture-capitalists-silicon-valley/.

21 Hudson, M. 2018. "New Research on Individual Angels Provides Insights for Startup Ecosystem," March 12, genglobal.org/united-states-gban/new-research-individual-angels-provides-insights-startup-ecosystem

22 wbaforum 2017. "World Business Angels Investment Forum Guest Editorial", May 8, www.wbaforum.org/for-potential-business-angels/index.html

23 National Business-angels Association. 2012. "European Business Angel Network Congress," www.ebancongress2012.org/58.html.

24 OECD. 2006. "MENA Investment Policy Brief," Issue 1, April 2006, www.oecd.org/mena/investment/37256468.pdf.

25 Forbes. 2016. "The state of the startup accelerator industry," www.forbes.com/sites/groupthink/2016/06/29/the-state-of-the-startup-accelerator-industry/#5bfd81de7b44.

26 Ibid.

27 Gust. 2015. "Global accelerator report 2015," http://gust.com/global-accelerator-report-2015/.

28 Henry, Z. 2017. "Why Investment in EU Startups Continues to Decline (Hint, It's Not the Reason You Think)," www.inc.com/zoe-henry/eu-startup-funding-2017-brexit.html.

29 Convergences. 2017. "Is microfinance still working?" microfinance barometer.

30 BNP Paribas. 2017. "Microfinance Barometer 2017: Global trends of the sector," https://group.bnpparibas/en/news/microfinance-barometer-2017-global-trends-sector.

31 Chan, S. 2018. "Local bank and MFI sector continue their meteoric rise," www.khmertimeskh.com/50100172/local-bank-mfi-sector-continue-meteoric-rise/.

32 Hubbard, G., & Duggan, W. 2009. *The Aid Trap.* Columbia University Press.

33 Engen, J. 2009. Is microfinance ready for its next big leap?

34 Hermes, N., Lensink, R., & Meesters, A. 2011. "Outreach and efficiency of microfinance institutions," World Development.

35 Remo, M. 2010. "Big banks can now lend directly to farmers," *Philippine Daily Inquirer,* 24 January, http://business.inquirer.net/money/topstories/view/20100124-249251/Big-banks-can-now-lend-directly-to-farmers.

36 Economist.com. 2010. "SKS comes to market: Microfight," 29 July, www.economist.com/node/16702063?story_id=16702063.

37 Evans, J. 2010. "Microfinance's midlife crisis," 1 March, http://online.wsj.com/article/NA_WSJ_PUB:SB10001424052748703315004575073510472268430.html.

38 Arp, F. 2018. "The 34 billion dollar question: Is microfinance the answer to poverty?" www.weforum.org/agenda/2018/01/the-34-billion-dollar-question-is-microfinance-the-answer-to-poverty.

39 Gokhale, K. 2009. "As microfinance grows in India, so do its rivals," *Wall Street Journal – Eastern Edition*, 15 December, pp. A17–A18.

40 Young, S. 2010. "The 'moral hazards' of microfinance: Restructuring rural credit in India," *Antipode*, 42(1), pp. 201–223.

41 Reuters.com. 2015. "Crowdfunding market grows 167% in 2014: Crowdfunding platforms raise $16.2 billion, finds research firm massolution," www.

marketwired.com/press-release/crowdfunding-market-grows-167-2014-crowdfunding-platforms-raise-162-billion-finds-research-2005299.htm.

42 Feit, R. 2015. "Equity crowdfunding by the numbers," 16 November, www.inc.com/ryan-feit/equity-crowdfunding-by-the-numbers.html.

43 Exporter Magazine. 2015. "In with the crowd," 8 July, http://exportermagazine.co.nz/article/crowd.

44 The IOSCO sets standards for the securities sector. Its members are the world's securities regulators.

45 Torris, T. 2016a. "Global crowdfunding & local regulation: From light touch to prescriptive bespoke rules," www.crowdfundinsider.com/2016/05/85762-global-crowdfunding-local-regulation-from-light-touch-to-prescriptive-bespoke-rules/.

46 Crowdfinders. 2016. "International crowdfunding index 2015," London.

47 Menon, S. 2016. "Crowd control: Sebi warning turns off crowdfunding tap for startups," *The Economic Times*, 9 September, http://economictimes.indiatimes.com/small-biz/money/crowd-control-sebi-warning-turns-off-crowdfunding-tap-for-startups/articleshow/54202702.cms.

48 Zhang, M. 2016. "The legislative trends in equity crowdfunding in China," 26 February, http://minnjil.org/the-legislative-trends-in-equity-crowdfunding-in-china/.

49 Walter, C.E., Fraser J., & Howie, T. 2003. "Of China's financial bondage: Beijing discovers another way to repress savings and hide bad debt," 17 January, www.wsj.com/articles/SB100014241278873234686045782472932 07694134.

50 Liang, Z. 2015. "Crowdfunding in China: Potentials, challenges, risks and solutions," 6 October, www.crowdfundinsider.com/2015/10/75384-crowdfunding-in-china-potentials-challenges-risks-and-solutions/.

51 Wilhelm, A. 2017. "WTF is an ICO?" https://techcrunch.com/2017/05/23/wtf-is-an-ico/ (Accessed 7 September 2017).

52 "Are ICOs the new future of start-ups?" 2017. www.mazars.com/Home/News/Latest-News3/Are-ICOs-the-new-future-of-start-ups (Accessed September 7, 2017).

53 Williams-Grut, O. 2018. "Only 48% of ICOs were successful last year—but startups still managed to raise $5.6 billion," January 31, www.businessinsider.com/how-much-raised-icos-2017-tokendata-2017-2018-1?r=UK&IR=T.

54 Town, S. 2018. "The VC juggernaut awakens: Institutional capital, block-chain startups, and you," https://cryptoslate.com/crypto-venture-capital/.

55 Ibid.

56 Lopez. 2017. "An international regulatory shift could tame cryptocurrency market," www.corpcounsel.com/id=1202796983089/An-International-Regulatory-Shift-Could-Tame-Cryptocurrency-Market?mcode=1202617 073467&curindex=1&slreturn=20170802171341.

57 Shin, L. 2017a. "After contact by SEC, protostarr token shuts down post-ICO, will refund investors," www.forbes.com/sites/laurashin/2017/09/01/after-contact-by-sec-protostarr-token-shuts-down-post-ico-will-refund-investors/#7496a499192e.

58 Hajdarbegovic, N. 2014. "UK financial regulator's new initiative encourages Bitcoin innovation," www.coindesk.com/uk-financial-conduct-authority-fca-launches-bitcoin-initiative/.

59 Mundaca, B., & Gabriela, R. 2009. "Financial market development, and economic growth: The case of Latin America and the Caribbean," *Review of Development Economics*, 13(2), pp. 288–303.

60 Lucas, R.E.B. 1987. "Emigration to South Africa's Mines," *American Economic Review*, 77, pp. 313–330.

61 Rozelle, S., Taylor, J.E., & deBrauw, A. 1999. "Migration, remittances and agriculture productivity in China," *American Economic Review*, 89, pp. 287–291.
62 Woodruff, C. & Zenteno, R. 2007. "Migration networks and microenterprises in Mexico," *Journal of Development Economics*, 82, pp. 509–528.
63 Mundaca, & Gabriela. 2009.
64 Ahmad, N., & Hoffmann, A.N. 2008. "A framework for addressing and measuring entrepreneurship," OECD Statistics Working Paper, January.
65 Adams, R.H. Jr. 2006. "International remittances and the household: Analysis and review of global evidence," *Journal of African Economies*, 15(Supplement 2): pp. 396–425.
66 Boechat, C., & Roberta Mokrejs Paro Votorantim Celulose e Papel (VCP) in Brazil: Planting eucalyptus in partnership with the rural poor, http://growing inclusivemarkets.org/media/cases/Brazil_VCP_2008.pdf.
67 Lee, & Persson. 2012.
68 Ayyagari, M., Asli, D., & Maksimovic, V. 2010. "Formal versus informal finance: Evidence from China," *Review of Financial Studies*, 23(8), pp. 3048–3097.
69 Montesinos, D. 2016. "Crowdfunding surge in Mexico opens opportunity for nonprofits and SMEs," https://hipgive.org/crowdfunding-surge-in-mexico-opens-opportunity-for-nonprofits-and-smes/
70 Launcht.com. 2013. "State of international crowdfunding," 6 February, www.launcht.com/blog/2013/02/06/state-of-international-crowdfunding/.
71 Kshetri, N. 2018. "Informal institutions and Internet-based equity crowdfunding," *Journal of International Management*, 24(1), pp. 33–51.
72 MacLellan, K. 2013. "Global crowdfunding volumes rise 81 percent in 2012. Reuters," 8 April, http://news.yahoo.com/global-crowdfunding-volumes-rise-81-125829169.html.
73 flaviogut.com. 2012. "Lack of regulation presents challenges to crowdsourcing in Brazil," 18 June, http://flaviogut.com/post/20133232952/lack-of-regulation-presents-challenges-to-crowdsourcing.
74 Lagos, M. 2001. "How people view democracy: Between stability and crisis in Latin America," *Journal of Democracy*, 12(1), pp. 137–145.
75 Ibid.
76 Medrano, J.D. 2016. "Interpersonal trust," www.jdsurvey.net/jds/jdsurveyMaps.jsp?Idioma=%20I&SeccionTexto=0404&NOID=104.
77 MCS. 2013. "A chat with the Cara from Catarse, my crowdfunding study," 31 January, www.mycrowdfundingstudy.com/2012/01/31/a-chat-with-one-of-the-caras-of-catarse/.
78 Sreeharsha, V. 2012. "Crowdfunding merger points to ambitions in Latin America," 24 August, https://dealbook.nytimes.com/2012/08/24/crowdfunding-merger-points-to-ambitions-in-latin-america/.

Chapter 4

Entrepreneurship in OECD Economies

This chapter's objectives include:

1   To demonstrate an understanding of determinants, performance indicators, and impacts of entrepreneurship in OECD economies.
2   To analyze the variation in the patterns of entrepreneurship across OECD economies.
3   To demonstrate an understanding of various forms of entrepreneurial financing in OECD economies.
4   To understand the causes, contexts, mechanisms, and processes associated with economic and political reform activities undertaken by the newly joined OECD members.

The OECD in Relation to Entrepreneurship

The reasons and motivations underlying the formation of the Organization for Economic Co-operation and Development (OECD) (www.oecd.org/) relate to the development of entrepreneurship and improvement in the entrepreneurial climate in its member as well as nonmember countries that are committed to democracy and the market economy. The organization's missions include supporting sustainable economic growth, improving living standards, boosting employment, maintaining financial stability, assisting nonmember countries' economic development and contributing to the growth in world trade."[1] As of 2018, the OECD had 37 member countries (Table 4.1). The OECD is also strengthening partnership with key nonmember economies such as Brazil, China, India, Indonesia, Russia, and South Africa.

OECD membership is considered to be more symbolic in nature. However, in order to become an OECD member, an economy needs to improve in a number of areas such as democratic freedoms, tax and environment laws, and accounting and statistics rules.[2]

Table 4.1 OECD Member Countries

Australia	France	Latvia	Slovenia
Austria	Germany	Lithuania	Spain
Belgium	Greece	Luxembourg	Sweden
Canada	Hungary	Mexico	Switzerland
Chile	Iceland	The Netherlands	The U.K.
Colombia	Ireland	New Zealand	The U.S.
Czech Republic	Israel	Norway	Turkey
Denmark	Italy	Poland	
Estonia	Japan	Portugal	
Finland	Korea	Slovak Republic	

Variation in Entrepreneurial Performance

OECD member countries show a variation in entrepreneurial performance. For instance, rapid expansion of successful young firms seems to be more of a feature of the U.S. than of other OECD economies.[3] For instance, only 3% of startups in the U.K. become midsized, compared with 6% in the U.S.[4]

There is also substantial heterogeneity across European members of OECD countries in terms of the growth of young firms. In some countries such as Belgium and Sweden, startups continue to grow relatively fast even after five and seven years following entry. In other countries such as Italy and Denmark, flatter growth rates can be seen after the third year.

There are a large number of incubators that cater to companies that have just started. As noted in Chapter 2, Europe has a higher number of accelerators than in North America. However, they should operate more as "scale-up hubs" in a more effective way. Put differently, the quality rather than number of accelerators is likely to have the most pronounced effect on firm growth. That is, what Europe needs is more sophisticated "scale-up hubs" that cater to 100+ employee companies. Such hubs need to provide more advanced mentoring and selective support in order to spread experience and know-how to aspiring CEOs. These hubs would cater to smaller number of CEOs (few dozen instead of a few hundred). A key goal is to fill the experience and mentoring gaps and reduce scale-up and financing risks.[5]

Newly Accessed and Candidate Countries

A review of some of the newly accessed and candidate countries would help illustrate the importance of economic and political climate reforms in order to be qualified for OECD membership. Accession talks to join the OECD had begun with Estonia, Israel, and Slovenia along with Chile and

Russia in May 2007. Their readiness to join the OECD was assessed by the progresses made by these economies in political and economic reform activities, especially in areas such areas as combating corruption, ensuring high standards of corporate governance, and protecting intellectual property rights (IPRs).[6] As explained in Chapters 1 and 2, these factors are critical foundations for entrepreneurial development.

In the discussion below, we look at of the key indicators in these areas for the new members and candidate countries. Economic Freedom Index covers ten components: Business Freedom, Trade Freedom, Fiscal Freedom, Government Spending, Monetary Freedom, Investment Freedom, Financial Freedom, Property Rights, Freedom from Corruption, and Labor Freedom. IPR protection is a component of the Economic Freedom Index. Corruption Perceptions Index measures the perceived levels of public sector corruption. Regulatory Quality Index measures the "perceptions of the ability of the government to formulate and implement sound policies and regulations that permit and promote private sector development."[7] This index can be used to evaluate overall economic and political reforms including the regulatory environment related to corporate governance.

The Newly Accessed Countries

Chile, Slovenia, Israel, and Estonia joined the OECD in 2010. Latvia became an OECD member in 2016. Lithuania's and Colombia's memberships were approved in May 2018. Below we discuss the economic and political reforms undertaken by newly joined members in a number of areas such as combating corruption, enhancement of corporate governance, and IPR protection.

Colombia

As of the early 2018, only 20 of the 23 OECD Committees had approved Colombia's OECD accession.[8] The lack of progress in some key areas was a concern. Especially the OECD's Trade Union Advisory Committee (TUAC) argued that the Colombian government failed to protect trade unionists or take actions perpetrators of violence. According to Human rights groups, there were at least 143 murders of trade union activists during 2012–2017.[9] At a February 2018 TUAC meeting, Colombian trade unionists complained about the lack of progress in a number of areas including tackling informality and improper use of subcontracting and urged the OECD member governments to pressure Colombia to make progress before inviting it to join the OECD.[10]

Another concern is Colombia's illicit mining industry. According to the OECD, illegal armed groups and criminal organizations are playing a key role in gold production in the country. The country's illegal gold mining industry was estimated to generate about $2.5 billion per year.[11] This was three times more than the country's cocaine industry.[12] The OECD also warned that illegal mining in Colombia is associated with serious human rights abuses such as child labor, forced labor, and sex trafficking. There is also significant environmental damage.[13]

Colombia also allegedly failed to control manufacturing and distribution of counterfeit and substandard pharmaceuticals.[14] It was reported that fake pharmaceutical products were imported to Colombia from West African countries. Secret facilities were also reported to exist in the country that manufacture counterfeit drugs.[15]

As mentioned in Chapter 2, the issues were finally resolved and in May 2018, the OECD approved Colombia's membership in the organization. For the membership to be effective, Colombia would need to take required steps at the national level in order to accede to the OECD Convention.

Lithuania

The OECD invited Lithuania to open accession talks in 2015. Lithuania's progress during the accession process was reviewed by 21 OECD Committees. The Committees looked at implementation of substantive OECD legal instruments in Lithuania and the country's policies in relation to OECD best practices. Lithuania introduced a number of reforms and initiatives in key areas such as corporate governance in state-owned enterprises and listed companies, fight against corruption and investment.[16]

On the corporate governance front, Lithuania took initiatives to increase efficiency and transparency of public enterprises. For instance, significant reforms were undertaken in forestry and road maintenance enterprises. It also started depoliticizing SOEs. Likewise, during the accession period, Lithuania amended the Penal Code to increase of fines for corruption related crimes by tenfold.[17] In May 2018, Lithuania was formally invited to become the 36th OECD member.

Latvia

In May 2013, the OECD Council had launched accession discussions with Latvia. Latvia worked closely with 21 OECD Committees that covered diverse issues impacting entrepreneurial performance ranging from investment and corporate governance to trade and export credits. The committees, which were composed of experts from OECD member countries, evaluated Latvia's compliance with OECD standards and best practices.[18] Latvia received positive opinions from each of the 21 committees (www. mfa.gov.lv/en/policy/economic-affairs/oecd/latvia-s-road-to-the-oecd-chronology-of-events). For instance, in the area of corporate governance,

Latvia's framework for listed companies was found to be consistent with the OECD principles. For SOEs, Latvia undertook significant reforms during the OECD accession review process. For instance, it started the process of re-establishing boards of directors, which was abolished in 2009.[19] In the educational sector, it was asked to evaluate and improve the development of skills based on the demands in the labor market and follow best practices in other OECD members.[20]

Latvia hopes that OECD membership will lead to significant improvement in the country's entrepreneurial climate. For instance, it expected improvement in international credit rating which would reduce interest rates related to entrepreneurial financing. Compliance with OECD standards in business operations such as better investment environment and higher degree of investment protection would contribute to higher investor confidence and hence an increase in foreign direct investment.

A further benefit is that Latvia will be included in various policy papers and studies published by the OECD as well as relevant statistics and various databases. A key point here is that surveys and studies conducted by the OECD are viewed by investors and international financial institutions as more credible. An improved legal framework to fight against corruption and stronger enforcement of anticorruption would further improve the entrepreneurial environment.

The country will also gain from deeper economic contacts and increased business and trade cooperation with other OECD member. The OECD membership also provides new opportunities to learn from exemplar OECD countries.[21]

Chile

Following the accession talks, an Accession Roadmap was adopted in November 2007, which set out the terms, conditions, and process for Chile's accession to the OECD. In the Roadmap, the OECD Council requested a number of OECD Committees to provide it with a formal opinion. In light of the formal opinions received from OECD Committees and other relevant information, the OECD Council decided to invite Chile to become an OECD Member in December 2009. After completion of its internal procedures, Chile became an OECD member in May 2010.

While Chileans have shown concerns about massive and endemic corruption in government and state institutions, Chile has seen rapid and phenomenal progress in anticorruption efforts following the end of Augusto Pinochet's dictatorship in 1990.[22] Despite some instances of corruption and criminal activities, the levels are low by the regional standards. A number of high-profile corruption scandals served as a big jolt in bringing the anticorruption efforts. For instance, the Chilean economic development agency (CORFO), the Ministry of Public Works (MOP), the

Central Bank, the Sports and Recreation Department (ChileDeportes), and a number of other state-owned enterprises (SOEs) were embroiled in huge corruption scandals. ChileDeportes' use of state funds for political campaigns in 2006 is the most notable scandal that prompted the Chilean government to introduce a number of regulatory reforms.

Key elements of the new regulatory frameworks include clarification and modernization in the way public employees are paid, new campaign finance legislation, the establishment of a budget commission for monitoring and overseeing government spending, and the establishment of ethical guidelines for public employees. There have also been reforms in the way the MOP awards government contracts. These measures have produced the anticipated effects. In Transparency International's 2017 Corruption Perceptions Index, Chile ranked 26th out of 180 economies.[23]

A concentrated ownership structure with conglomerates and business groups controlling most firms and the capital market's limited liquidity were major challenges facing Chile's corporate governance landscape. Minority shareholders are often vulnerable in such settings due to the controlling shareholders' tendency to engage in irregular practices to extract private benefits. In this regard, Chile has made considerable progress on the corporate governance front, mainly through laws adopted in 2000 on Public Tender Offers and on Corporate Governance, and a Corporate Governance law approved by Congress in 2009.[24] Adequate safeguards are put in place through the new laws to protect minority shareholders which include enhanced transparency standards and restrictive rules regarding the use of privileged information, related party transactions, and conflicts of interest. Major changes have been made to the definition of independent directors as well as their role in reviewing sensitive issues. The 2009 law has also strengthened the governance of Chile's largest SOE, the copper mining company Codelco. The OECD has noted that this is a significant step, which is likely to result in momentum to further reform in the country's other SOEs.

Commercial operations are aided by efficient regulations that support open-market policies.[25] Chile's economic freedom score of 75.2 in 2018 (www.heritage.org/index/ranking) made it the 20th freest economy in the world and the score was the highest in the South and Central America and the Caribbean region. Especially impressive is the country's progress in fiscal health component, in which Chile scored 91.7. Private property is well protected and contracts are secure. Except for some areas such as coastal trade, air transport, and the mass media, there is no restriction of private ownership.[26] The laws provide for compensation in the case of property expropriation. Foreign investors can own up to 100% of a Chilean-based company.

The key to Chile's success on this front is also highly transparent and efficient court administration. For instance, as of 2004, 99% of the courts proceedings were open to the public and out of every 100 crimes reported to law enforcement agencies, 89 cases were closed. In 2004, the average time to process a case varied from 11 to 307 days, which was much quicker compared to the old system.[27]

Israel

The adoption and implementation of the 2000 Companies law and its subsequent upgrades have strengthened Israel's corporate governance. Corporate transactions that are viewed potentially abusive are required to go through stringent approval at the board level and in shareholder meetings. The Israeli authorities are considering to further tighten the rule.[28] Virtually all large companies except for those in public utilities and the military have been privatized and measures to promote a level playing field between public and private enterprises have been introduced.

The Review of Corporate Governance in Israel conducted by the OECD in 2011 made some recommendations for policy changes to further improve the corporate governance quality. A main recommendation was to enhance the autonomy of the Israeli securities regulator, including giving the right to issue secondary regulations and levy fines. The OECD viewed that these measures would provide a better protection to investors than the current system's reliance on legislation and legal enforcement. Other recommendations were to monitor the quality of the auditing of listed companies and to establish specialized courts for hearing commercial cases. The OECD report, however, noted that the country had made progress in several of these areas.

The Israeli court system is independent and bribery as well as other forms of corruption are illegal. In 2008, the offense of bribery to a foreign public official was introduced to the Israeli Penal Law, which prohibits offering or paying a bribe to a foreign public official for the purpose of obtaining business or other advantages.[29] Israel has also launched a campaign to increase awareness of the OECD Convention on Combating Bribery of Foreign Public Officials and the foreign bribery offense. The Inter-Ministerial team on Combating Bribery has coordinated this efforts and the Ministry of Justice (MOJ) has intended to work with the State Comptroller's Office. The MOJ has also established a website, which is dedicated to fighting corruption and international bribery (www.corruption.justice.gov.il).[30]

Protections for property rights and contracts are enforced effectively. Israel's broader efforts specifically aimed at increasing its ability to benefit from an enhanced IPR regime deserve mention. The country has increased the resources of the patent office, upgraded enforcement activities as well as implementing programs to bring ideas funded by government research to the market.[31] In March 2008, the MOJ submitted a statement on IPR in Israel to the Office of the U.S. Trade Representative (USTR) as part of USTR's annual "Special 301" review process. Note that the Special 301 reports identify trade barriers to U.S. companies and products due to the lack of "adequate and effective" IPR protection in other countries. Israel defended its IPR regime as adequate, effective, in conformance with all relevant international obligations, and requested removal of Israel from the "watch list."[32] A 2011 OECD report suggested the importance of improvement in a number of areas including enhancing protection in specific areas of copyright and patent protection and improving administrative efficiency.[33]

Estonia

According to the annual surveys of Transparency International (TI), Estonia has been the least corrupt country in East Europe. In Transparency International's 2017 Corruption Perceptions Index, Estonia ranked 21st.[34]

Indeed, Estonia is cleaner than some of the West European countries, which can be attributed to the proactive measures taken by the country to fight corruption. The Estonian Ministry of Justice invited TI to take a lead role in the drafting of the country's new anticorruption strategy.[35]

The principles of "Honest State" program started in 2004 have been an integral part of the government of Estonia's best practices to fight corruption. The program has a number of components to reduce corruption in the government including auditing local governments, which have been viewed as the greatest source of corruption. The program also requires public servants to file electronic declarations of economic interests. Additional components of the program include the establishment of the National Ethics Council, increase in the number of specialized investigators and prosecutors who focus on corruption, and an anonymous hotline to report corruption cases.[36] Estonia is a signatory to the OECD Convention on Combating Bribery of Foreign Public Officials in International Business Transactions since 2005. As a signatory of the Convention, Estonia is obligated to criminalize bribery of foreign public officials in conducting international business.

Estonia has committed to the development of a superior corporate governance practice. It revised legal frameworks several times based on EU directives. Issues identified earlier such as audit requirements and standards and the lack of institutional arrangements for SOE oversight and monitoring have been addressed. There are voluntary guidelines in issues such as the role of independent directors. These are important because the small size of the market for listed companies and low liquidity mean that market mechanisms are less likely to provide incentives for good corporate governance. Observers have noted that Estonian companies closely follow legal corporate governance requirements.[37]

Estonia's economic freedom score was 78.8 in 2018, which was seventh highest in the world and ahead of many OECD members. Especially impressive is the country's progress in fiscal health component, in which it scored 99.8. Likewise, its investment freedom score was 90.

Only a small number of the country's enterprises in strategic sectors such as main port, the power plants, the postal system, railway, airports, and the national lottery are state-owned. SOEs operate on the same legal bases as private enterprises. Foreign and local investors are treated equally in Estonia. The regulatory frameworks in Estonia have been well developed to adequately protect property rights, including intellectual property such as copyrights, patents, trademarks, industrial design, and trade secrets.

Slovenia

Not long ago Slovenia was plagued with a number of corruption scandals. Some argue that effectiveness of anticorruption institutions is hampered by factors such as the country's small size, a history of close interaction between the public and private sectors, and an important role of personal contacts in business relations. Contrary to these observations, Slovenia has made significant progress on the anticorruption front, as reflected in its position as the least corrupt state in central and southeastern Europe.

As is the case of other transition countries in the region, Slovenia was constantly monitored as part of the process of attaining full membership of international organizations such as the EU, NATO, and the OECD. In response to the Council of Europe's critical report, Slovenia initiated various efforts including the establishment of a coordinating anticorruption commission in 2001. Slovenia has also established specialized law enforcement units to combat serious economic crimes.

A major feature of the Slovenian economy concerns the prevalence of SOEs, both in the listed and in the unlisted sectors. It is thus of paramount important to ensure that there are consistent and transparent ownership policies. Moreover, it is important for the state to act as an informed and responsible shareholder, and make sure that SOE board members possess skills and authority to exercise their functions.[38] In this regard, the accession process led to the country's adoption of key legislation to improve corporate governance framework for SOEs, minority shareholder protection and securities regulation. In April 2010, the Slovenian parliament adopted legislation, which established a central ownership agency to manage all of the State's direct interests in SOEs. In addition, the country is also preparing legislation to define the relationship between the new central ownership agency and two key state institutions overseeing the pension fund (KAD) and restitution fund (SOD).[39]

In Slovenia's Index of Economic Freedom, the property rights component was 60 in 2012, which puts it ahead of many other OECD members.

The country made significant amendments and modifications, particularly during the process of accession to the EU.[40] More specifically, the IPR related regulatory framework underwent several changes between its declaration of independence in 1991 and EU accession in 2004, like most other aspects of regulations. As an EU member, legal standards related to Slovenia's IPR regime are similar to most OECD countries. The country grants protection to copyrights and related rights, trademarks, geographical indications, patents, industrial designs, topographies of integrated circuits, and undisclosed business secrets.[41]

Candidate Countries

In order to provide further insights into the requirements necessary for becoming an OECD member, we describe situations facing some candidate countries. Russia made an official request for OECD membership in 1996. In April 2015, the OECD invited Costa Rica to open formal OECD accession talks.[42]

Russia

While Russia is reported to be made some progress, the overall progress has been lower than required to become an OECD member. Russia lags the newly accessed OECD members in Corruption Perceptions Index, Economic Freedom Index, and Regulatory Quality Index. For instance, in Transparency International's 2017 Corruption Perceptions Index, Russia ranked 135th.[43]

Russia is plagued by bribery and other forms of corruption (Watch the video, "Russia corrupt from top to bottom": www.youtube.com/watch?v=BLTY-dzjlfA). Russian Prime Minister, Dmitry Medvedev claimed that Russia suffers from "legal nihilism" and investors in the country feel unsafe due to concerns regarding law enforcement agencies' ability and willingness to protect them and the legal system's inefficiency. Factors such as weak rule of law, inefficient bureaucracy, and public officials' corrupt practices pose a serious challenge to entrepreneurship in the country.

Russia also suffers from unsatisfactory corporate governance practices, which have created a further barrier to full OECD membership. Investors have complained about instances in which insiders and major shareholders have engaged in frauds such as transfer pricing and asset stripping. They allegedly do so by selling the output, the assets, or the additional securities to another firm they own at below market prices.[44] Russia also adopted a corporate governance code in April 2002. However, the Business and Industry Advisory Committee (BIAC) to the OECD, which consists of the industrial and employers' organizations in the OECD Member countries, are concerned about the lack of respect for and compliance with the code.[45]

In reports submitted to the OECD in 2008 and 2009, BIAC expressed concerns about the lack of strong IPRs protection and inadequate enforcement of IPR in Russia. For 15 consecutive years (1998–2012), Russia has been on the United States Priority Watch List of countries with serious deficiencies in IPR protection. A BIAC report accused that Russia's Internet infrastructure primarily serves as a channel for illegitimate e-commerce involving the distribution of pirated content and software. The report noted that a number of illegal peer-to-peer services and pay-per-download websites hinder the development of the legitimate online market.[46] The BIAC also expressed concerns regarding the law's inadequacy for addressing Internet piracy due to the lack of clear provisions on Internet service provider cooperation and third-party liability, thus failing to provide incentives for intermediaries to assist in curbing piracy.

Despite the above criticisms, Russia has taken a number of positive steps in recent years. In 2011, Russian Parliament passed a law that prohibits Russian companies from bribing foreign officials. Following this, Russia was invited to join the anti-bribery convention in May 2011, which is a step toward an OECD membership for Russia as acceptance into the convention is a requirement for the membership.

Russia has also taken measures to address significant losses by foreign companies due to IPR infringement. It has enacted a law to establish a special court for intellectual property disputes by February 2013. Russia also amended to its criminal code to revise criminal thresholds for copyright piracy. The country's law enforcement authorities have taken criminal and civil actions against some serious copyright infringers.

In 2014, Russia expressed an intention to retaliate against Western sanctions. In response, the OECD stopped talks aimed at allowing Russia to become an OECD member.[47]

Determinants of Entrepreneurship in OECD Economies

While all the economies in Table 4.1 belong to the club of OECD, they differ widely in entrepreneurial performance. This section discusses the key determinants of entrepreneurship in these economies and illustrates key intra-OECD differences in terms of these factors: (a) laws, regulations, and policy; (b) values, culture, and skills; and (c) access to finance, market, R&D, and technology.

Regulatory Framework

The OECD economies differ on various components of regulatory framework. For instance, procedures for starting a business are far more difficult and time consuming in Japan and Chile than in Canada and Australia.

Too many rules and regulations, bureaucracy, and red tape are the primary disadvantages of Chile and Japan. For instance, despite the progress noted above, inefficient and conservative government bureaucracy is widely recognized as a major problem facing Chile.[48] It was suggested that Japan had more than 11,000 rules to regulate businesses in the mid-1990s, which cost the Japanese economy $75–110 billion a year.[49] Among the eight procedures involved in starting a business, the third step, registering at the Legal Affairs Bureau of the MOJ, takes one to three weeks. The authorities can return the filed documents for revisions.

Compared to most other OECD economies, Turkey's regulatory frameworks have been ineffective to drive entrepreneurial outcomes. It is among the OCED countries with the lowest economic freedom. Despite the country's progress in areas such as trade freedom and fiscal freedom, its relatively inefficient judicial system has driven down the overall economic freedom. According to the U.S. State Department's 2010 Human Rights Report (www.state.gov/j/drl/rls/hrrpt/2010/eur/154455.htm), close relationship between judges and prosecutors has been a hindrance to the right to a fair trial.

Another problem concerns long trials. There is also a high rate of infringement of IPRs despite the improvement in the IPR regime. In addition to overburdened and slow court system, the lack of judges with proper training for commercial cases make enforcement of property rights difficult. Inflexible labor regulations have also hindered Turkey's entrepreneurial development. The Turkish labor market is characterized by a high nonsalary cost of employing and difficulty in firing an employee. Turkey also has lengthy and unnecessarily burdensome bankruptcy proceedings.[50] Especially, legal fees associated with bankruptcy proceedings are notoriously high.[51]

In light of the above discussion about Turkey, available data and statistics show that poor regulatory quality, weak rule of law, and corruption are even bigger problems in Mexico. For instance, in Transparency International's 2017 Corruption Perceptions Index, Mexico ranked 135th (tied with Russia).[52] One observation is that excessive regulation in Mexico has been a means of punishing private sector firms. For instance, the local governments are found to use the regulations as a tool to extort and to blackmail the private sector firms. One example to illustrate this point would be regulations in the transport industry prior to 1990, known as regreso vacio or empty return cargo, which prohibited two-way merchandise transportations. That is, private firms the transport industry could transport from the origin to the destination, but not from the destination to the origin. If a firm did not want to make a return trip with an empty truck, it needed to bribe state and federal officials.[53]

Congestion in the law enforcement system caused by drug trafficking and related violence has also led to a decline in the respect for the rule of law in Mexico. For most types of crimes, the rates of arrest and successful prosecution are low. In a few cases, suspects are detained, but they are put to lengthy criminal proceedings and the court is often unable or unwilling to adhere to due process standards, which hampers their trials.[54]

Tax Policy and Entrepreneurship

Among OECD economies, Luxembourg and Switzerland have formulated favorable tax policy to stimulate entrepreneurship. Luxembourg has a low effective corporate tax rate of 21%. Likewise, in 2010, Switzerland's federal corporate tax rate was 8.5%. Even after adding states (known as cantons) and municipal taxes, Switzerland has one of the lowest tax rates in the world.

The average corporate tax rate in Switzerland in 2010 was 21.2%, compared to 30% in Germany and 25.5% in the Netherlands. The top corporate tax rates in country in 2010 varied from 11.8% to 24.2% depending on the location. These rates compare with the U.K.'s 28% and 35% in the U.S. Switzerland had budget surpluses in 2009, while other European countries were severely affected by the global financial crisis and faced debt crises.

These initiatives have paid off brilliantly. According to McKinsey & Co., during 1998–2008, Switzerland attracted regional headquarters of over 180 large foreign companies. Companies such as Kraft Foods, Yahoo, and Google have established European headquarters in Switzerland. As of 2010, over 150 U.S. companies had a presence in Switzerland.

Note too that Switzerland's cantons have more autonomy than states in the U.S. The cantons enjoy autonomy on important issues such as social-security contributions, business and residency permits, and construction codes. The Canton of Zug has been the most attractive location in terms of taxation, which attracted 1,600 new businesses in 2007 alone. Other Cantons are competing with Zug.

Corporate Bankruptcy Laws

It is an overriding reality that most new firms fail during their first five years. For instance, according to the OECD, 62.3% of new firms in the Netherlands and 53.1% of new firms in Hungary that were started in 2007 died within three years. Due to the high potential failure rate of startups, policies that penalize failed entrepreneurs keep most people away from entrepreneurship. On the other hand, a country with regulations that are friendly to failed entrepreneurs and a high tendency to forgive entrepreneurial failure is likely to attract more people in entrepreneurship.

The U.S. has been a global role model for its favorable and lenient corporate bankruptcy law. If an entrepreneurial firm is troubled but potentially viable, Chapter 11 allows entrepreneurs and managers to retain control of the firm, obtain protection from creditors and develop a reorganization plan. The situation is different in Japan, where secured creditors, who, as lenders, hold legally enforceable claim on the company's assets, are given the control rights.[55] The Japanese system is thus more likely to lead to premature liquidation of the firm than the U.S. system. Companies that are "terminally ill," on the other hand, can file for "Chapter 7," which involves liquidation and distribution of available assets among creditors. Debtors filing Chapter 7 bankruptcy can retain certain exempt assets such as household and personal goods, automobiles, and homesteads.

Another important difference is whether or not there is an automatic stay on assets. Among OECD economies, Canada and the U.S. have a provision of an automatic stay on assets, which means that creditors cannot seize the company's assets used as collateral for loans after the bankruptcy proceedings have commenced. In South Korea, on the other hand, regulations do not provide such provisions.

Values, Culture, and Skills

Values and Culture

While OCED economies exhibit a high degree of homogeneity in political institutions, they are culturally heterogeneous. OCED economies differ significantly in entrepreneurs' own view of themselves and preference for entrepreneurship as a career and societal attitudes toward entrepreneurs. According to a survey released by the European Commission, 45% of Europeans would prefer to start their own business instead of working as employees, which compared with 55% in the U.S. In the U.S., 73% view businessmen favorably compared to 49% in Europe. The research also indicated that entrepreneurs in Europe are viewed as exploiters of workers, whereas they are considered as job creators in the U.S.

The lack of respect for entrepreneurs as well as the lack of social appreciation of their work is of especial concern in OECD countries with a socialist past. For instance, according to Global Entrepreneurship Week Policy Survey conducted in 2012, only 28% of entrepreneurs in Hungary thought that people who successfully start new firms have at least the same level of status and respect compared to a manager of a medium-sized company. Hungary ranked 34th out of 34 countries surveyed.[56]

Entrepreneurs regarded as "déclassé" in some OECD countries and are not socially admired in others. Jante's Law, which comes from the Norwegian/Danish author Aksel Sandemose's novel, would help explain the lack of social admiration of entrepreneurial success in the Scandinavian communities. This law is an unspoken code of ethics and explains the pattern of group behaviors observed in these communities. This law is centered around making people act less arrogant and more modest and humble.

Jante's Law teaches people that flaunting their wealth or achievements are unworthy and inappropriate. Commenting on the Danish culture, a report observed that, due to the prevalence of Jante's Law "which condemned the attempt of an individual to do better than others," entrepreneurial success is not socially admired in the country.[57]

That said, in some OECD economies, there has been a drastic change in entrepreneurship-related cultural values. Ireland and Chile are probably two most spectacular examples that have demonstrated how entrepreneurship-related social norms can emerge in a short period. Until the 1980s, Irish youths were attracted to jobs in government and financial services. Defaulting on loans was judged as an immoral practice for businesses. The social norms also stigmatized bankruptcy.[58] The Irish economy produced a number of multimillionaire businessmen in the 1980s. As of 2008, Ireland had over 30,000 euro millionaires and most of them were self-made.[59] Entrepreneurs gradually started treating entrepreneurial failure as a learning opportunity, not as a personal failure or stigma.

Similarly, entrepreneurs in the past had a negative social image as "greedy exploiters" in Chile, which has changed. Until the 1980s, well-educated middle class in the country avoided opportunity-driven entrepreneurship.[60] According to the Chile 2008 GEM Report, 80% of the country's economically active population considered entrepreneurship as a desirable career option. It was estimated that 12.9% of the adult population in Chile consisted of early-stage entrepreneurs. 68% of entrepreneurs were opportunity-based (seeking real opportunities for business and not driven by necessity).[61]

Skills

In terms of education, even in the worst-performing OECD countries, the proportions of tertiary education age cohort enrolled in tertiary institutions are higher than the global average of 26% and sub-Saharan African economies' 6%.[62] However, the real issue is whether students develop entrepreneurship skills in universities. An even more relevant indicator concerns successful entrepreneurs' views regarding the development of entrepreneurial skills and capabilities in colleges and universities. In this regard, entrepreneurs in OECD economies have generally expressed dissatisfaction and frustration with the lack of entrepreneurship-related skills of university graduates. For instance, according to the EU Entrepreneurship Survey, entrepreneurial skills were among most important barriers to entrepreneurship in Denmark. 28% of respondents indicated supply of skills and entrepreneurial capabilities as the main obstacle to entrepreneurship, which was the highest proportion in the EU.[63]

In terms of college and tertiary education entry rates, for example, Australia and Poland perform better than most other OECD economies.

In international comparison, however, university education systems in these two economies do not have a good standing regarding the development of entrepreneurial skills and capabilities. For instance, according to Global Entrepreneurship Week Policy Survey conducted in 2012, only 6% of Australian high-impact entrepreneurs and 8% of Polish high-impact entrepreneurs thought that university-level educational systems in their countries do a good job in teaching entrepreneurial skills.[64] These two countries ranked, respectively, 31st and 29th out of the 34 countries surveyed.

Openness to Immigration and Availability of Entrepreneurial Skills

A country's openness to immigration is tightly linked to entrepreneurial performance, innovation and economic growth.[65] The U.S. is an obvious example of an economy that has benefitted greatly from immigrants' entrepreneurial activities. According to the Kauffman Foundation's annual Index of Startup Activity (www.kauffman.org/kauffman-index), in 2016, immigrants in the U.S. were about twice as likely as the native-born population to start a new business. About 30% of all new U.S. entrepreneurs were immigrants.[66] Likewise, a report of New American Economy found that 40.2% of Fortune 500 firms in 2016 had "at least one founder who either immigrated to the United States or was the child of immigrants."[67]

Access to Finance, Market, R&D, and Technology

Market Access

While most OECD members have well-developed institutions to facilitate market access, some show many clear instances of barriers to market access related to antitrust and unfair competition laws and enforcement. In Chapter 1, we discussed the anticompetitive consequences of barriers to new firms in Mexico. As a further example, there have been many instances of bid-rigging, in which competitors collude so that a competing business can secure a government contract at a predetermined price, which is increased artificially. Most businesses and consumers suffer the consequences of these anti-competitive and illegal practices.

Mexico's Social Security Department spends about US$2.5 billion each year on pharmaceutical products and other goods and services. In order to fight against these anticompetitive acts by improving rules and procedures, and training procurement officers, the Mexican Competition Authority and the Mexican Social Security Institute (IMSS) signed a cooperation agreement with the OECD in 2011 to implement the OECD guidelines. Since then, the OECD and the Mexican Competition Authority have been working with the IMSS to address these issues.[68]

In the OECD's product market regulation index, Japan performed poorly in the "barriers to competition" subcategory, which included areas such as entry barriers and antitrust issues.[69] The real issue is related to the lack of effective enforcement rather than the existence of law. Critics and skeptics have argued that the Japan Fair Trade Commission (JFTC) has not been effective in enforcing the Antimonopoly Act. The JFTC is often viewed as "a watch dog that does not bite."[70] Likewise, notwithstanding the progress France has made on this front, regulatory barriers to entry exist in retail trade, professional services, and other sectors.[71] While some regulations are necessary to protect the consumer, barriers to entry in the country are arguably higher than needed for such purpose in general professions such as accountants, architects, and lawyers; regulated professions such as physiotherapists, veterinarians, pharmacists and hairdressers; and partially substitutable professions such as conventional physicians and practitioners of alternative medicine.[72]

Access to Finance

Compared to less developed economies, OECD economies are characterized by a greater availability and easier access to financial resources for potential entrepreneur. That said, intra–OECD differences can be observed in the availability and affordability of credits. Of the 35 OECD members, 22 belong to the European Union (EU). In this regard, thanks to focused government intervention such as European Commission's SME guarantee facility, large proportions of SMEs in the EU have access to bank financing. A 2014 study of the European Commission found that 62% of SMEs choose bank loans over other forms of financing in order to expand their businesses.[73]

A U.S. Census study found that 70% of SMEs in the country use bank financing to start or acquire a business.[74] In addition, many entrepreneurs such as the founders of Cisco Systems took second mortgages on their homes in order to finance their entrepreneurial venture.[75] Some entrepreneurs also use their credit cards for short-term operating funds.

According to the OECD, the average loan request rejection rate in 2015 was 11% in OECD countries. The highest proportions were 57% for Slovakia and 40.9% South Korea. Finland had the lowest rejection rate of 3% (https://stats.oecd.org/Index.aspx?DataSetCode=SMES_SCOREBOARD).

Due to the substantial size of informal economy in Mexico, potential entrepreneurs are less likely to borrow from formal financing sources. Most informal sector workers are unable to fulfill the requirements necessary to get loans from banks. A taco seller in Mexico City said that he is unable to get a loan from a bank: "The banks have a lot of requirements that I can't meet."[76] Moreover, Mexico's average annual lending rate is highest among the OECD countries (Figure 4.1).

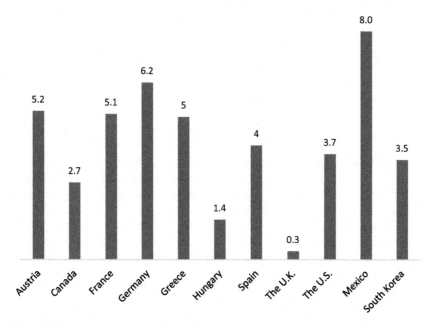

Figure 4.1 Annual Lending Rates in Selected OECD Countries (2017).
Source: Euromonitor International.

VENTURE CAPITAL

Venture capital covers a vanishingly small share of total financing needs in most OECD economies. In most of the OECD countries, VC constitutes a very small percentage of GDP, which is often less than 0.05%. The two major exceptions are Israel and the U.S. where the VC industry is more mature, representing over 0.35% of GDP.[77] Other OECD countries with more developed venture capital markets include Sweden, Switzerland, and the U.K.[78]

MICROFINANCE

Compared to less developed economies, microfinance in the OECD economies has low relative effectiveness vis-à-vis other well-established and well-known sources of financing discussed above. Nonetheless, microfinance obviously holds a tremendous potential in OECD economies if we consider the fact that an estimated 60 million adults (8% of the adult population) do not use formal or semiformal financial services in these economies.[79] Among OECD countries, microfinance institutions (MFIs) especially have a notable presence in Mexico. As of 2016, MFIs in Mexico had 7 million active borrowers with a gross loan portfolio of

US$4.4 billion.[80] Mexico had the world's fifth highest number of borrowers from MFIs.

In the U.S., microcredit is becoming a growing source of credit for small businesses that are unbankable in the conventional credit market. Estimates suggest that the size of the unbanked population in the U.S. is 28 million and about 45 million people have only limited access to the services of financial institutions.[81]

CROWDFUNDING

As discussed in Chapter 3, crowdfunding is becoming increasingly popular in OECD economies. What is more equity-based crowdfunding (ECF) is emerging as an increasingly important source of entrepreneurial financing in these economies. Table 4.2 presents the sizes of ECF market in selected OECD economies. As it is clear from Table 4.2, the U.S. has the world's most developed ECF market. Some compare crowdfunding investors with angel investors and suggest that crowdfunding would create 60 million new angel investors in the U.S. alone.[82]

R&D and Technology

Since R&D is a key driver of a new and innovative product or service, the likelihood of launching a successful product by an entrepreneurial firm, while not guaranteed, is greatly enhanced by the firm's engagement in R&D. R&D activities in an industry would benefit other firms in the same industry as well as in related industry by intra- and interindustry and R&D spillovers, leading to an increase in total factor productivity.

OECD economies differ in their emphasis on R&D. In a March 2018 report released on by KPMG, which was based on its tech innovation survey, the U.S. ranked #1 as the most promising market for technological breakthroughs.[83]

Table 4.2 The Sizes of ECF Market in Selected OECD Economies

Economy	ECF	ECF per capita per year
Canada	2014: US$70 million	2014: US$2
The Netherlands	2015: US$5.04 million	2015: US$0.29
The U.K.	2015 (first 10 months): US$219 million	2015: US$4.10
The U.S.	2015Q1: US$662 million; 2014Q4: US US$483 million	2015: US$8.32 2014: US$6.07

Source: Kshetri (2018).

Israel's civilian R&D per capita is the highest in the world. Israeli government has pursued an effective R&D policy. Attention has been focused on policy toward commercialization of new ideas and technologies. The Office of the Chief Scientist (OCS) (www.matimop.org.il/ocs.html) in the Ministry of Industry, Trade and Labor is a unique government agency for promoting industrial R&D and innovation. It provides a wide range of supports to build and strengthen the innovation ecosystem's links from "idea" to "market." Successful entrepreneurs from private sector are recruited to manage government programs that were launched to support innovation and entrepreneurship.[84]

R&D activities in Israel are also greatly facilitated by the fact that many foreign companies have located their R&D centers in the country. One estimate suggested that by 2010, multinationals such as Alcatel, Deutsche Telecom, Cisco, Google, HP, Merck, Microsoft and IBM had set up 220 R&D centers in the country.[85]

R&D expenditure as a proportion of GDP is among the lowest in Mexico, Turkey, and Greece (Figure 4.2). Comparatively low R&D investments in these economies have led to low productivity per worker. For instance, according to the OECD (http://stats.oecd.org/Index.aspx?Dat/asetCode=LEVEL), the amount of GDP generated per worker in 2011 as a proportion of the U.S. was 29% in Mexico. For instance, while Turkey is making attempts to shift from an economy largely based on low-skilled

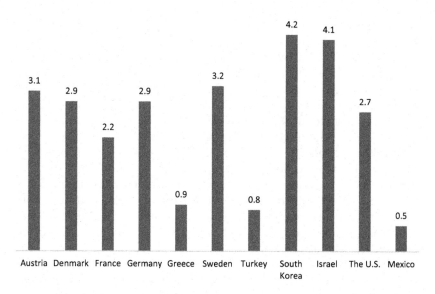

Figure 4.2 Gross Domestic Expenditure on R&D as a Percentage of GDP in Selected OECD Economies (2017).
Source: Euromonitor International.

labor force toward an industrial economy, agriculture accounted for about a quarter of the total employment in 2012.[86] Some problems facing Turkey include business R&D expenditure that is lower than the EU average, and insufficient commercialization of R&D. For instance, according to the OECD Science, Technology and Industry Scoreboard 2011, while the business sector accounts for about 70% of R&D spending in the OECD and 80% in Israel, Turkey is one of the three OECD economies (along with Greece and Poland) in which the business sector's R&D spending is lower than that of the higher education sector.

Concluding Comments

Entrepreneurial performance varies widely across the OECD economies. The heterogeneity across the OECD economies in performance and indicators of entrepreneurship indicates that the local social, cultural, and political contexts constrain the roles that international organizations such as OECD play in modern world affairs.

In response to the intra–OECD regulatory differences, some entrepreneurial firms have engaged in arbitrage among national regulations by moving their activities in order to exploit such differences. For instance, it is reported that an increasing number of Czech companies have moved their headquarters to other OECD and some non–OECD economies with more favorable fiscal environments. By the end of 2009, 4,551 Czech-owned companies were headquartered in the Netherlands. Cyprus and Luxembourg were other top two destinations for Czech companies to house their operations.[87]

In addition to the above differences, OECD economies' entrepreneurial patterns exhibit differences in the relative emphasis on small and big businesses. Countries that are friendliest to small businesses include New Zealand, the U.S., Canada, and Australia.[88] On the other hand, Japan and the Nordic countries have exhibited a tendency to favor big businesses. Some of the world's leading brands such as Ericsson, Ikea, Lego, and Nokia are from the Nordic countries. Likewise, big businesses have driven the Japanese economy.

The OECD accession process has been a catalyst for bringing reforms in the four newly joined countries. Especially for small countries with limited natural resources such as Israel, economic and political reforms are of paramount significance and importance to drive entrepreneurial growth. For Estonia and Slovenia, the reforms required for EU accession also helped them prepare for OECD accession. They had achieved substantial progress on many of the fronts mentioned earlier to join the EU. Especially Chile has overcome significant cultural barriers. While the old system based on patronage, cronyism, and regionalism has hindered the efforts to develop modern reform–oriented institutions in most Latin

American economies such as Brazil and Mexico, Chile has been able to overcome such barriers.

A transparent and stable business climate with no barriers to free trade can create a dynamic environment for entrepreneurs. In this regard, the newly joined OECD members have had more success than countries with longer membership durations in areas such as anticorruption and fight against poor corporate governance, which have encouraged the development of a climate that promotes entrepreneurship. In the Corruption Perceptions Index, for instance, the newly joined members outperform some countries which have been OCED members for longer durations: Hungary (4.6, rank = 54), Czech Republic (4.4, rank = 58), Turkey (4.2, rank = 61), and Mexico (3, rank = 100).

End of Chapter Questions

1   What are some of the reforms needed in Russia to become a full OECD member?
2   Select an OECD economy which has among the lowest per capita incomes and examine the entrepreneurial ecosystems in the economy you selected.
3   Which OECD countries perform the best in terms of major entrepreneurial indicators? What are the main reasons behind their superior performance?
4   During the past three decades, which OECD countries have made the fastest progress in enhancing their entrepreneurial ecosystems?
5   How do the new OECD members differ from the old ones in terms of various determinants of entrepreneurship?

End of the Chapter Case: Israel's Emergence as a Hotbed for Cybersecurity-Related Entrepreneurship

Israel is often referred to as the "startup nation" and is among the world's most sophisticated and vibrant innovation hubs. It has more startups per capita than any other country. A country of only 8 million people, Israel has the third highest number of NASDAQ listed companies behind the U.S. and China.[89] In terms of venture activity, Israel's Tel Aviv is the second largest hub worldwide after San Francisco.[90] Israel attracts as much VC as France and Germany combined.

As an area to illustrate Israel's vibrant innovation system, one can look at the country's cybersecurity startups. In 2014, Israel accounted for 7% of the global cybersecurity market and 13% of new R&D in the sector. These numbers were three times more than the 2010 levels. There was a four-fold increase in cybersecurity-related VC investment in the country during 2010–2014.[91] This is despite export restrictions in the global cybersecurity market. IBM, Cisco, and GE made large acquisitions and investments in Israeli cybersecurity companies in 2013.[92]

In 2017, Israel's cybersecurity firms raised $814.5 million in venture capital and private equity investment. This was 28% higher than in 2016. Israel also accounts for 16% of the world's cybersecurity investment, which puts the country second behind the U.S.[93]

The New York-based data firm CB Insights' Cyber Defenders 2018 report selected 29 cybersecurity startups. Cyber defenders are defined as early- to mid-stage "high-momentum companies" with pioneering technologies that have the potential to transform cybersecurity. With six firms in the CB Insights' 2018 list, Israel ranked #2 after the U.S. in the concentration of cyber defenders.[94]

As mentioned, Israel's cybersecurity market as a proportion of the global cybersecurity market is much bigger that its population, which is 0.1% of the world's population. This can be attributed to strong defense measures of businesses and consumers in the country. The government is also taking measures to strengthen cybersecurity. In September 2014, Israel established a National Authority for Cyber-Defense to strengthen cyber protection for institutes, defense agencies, and citizens. The new authority is described as an 'Air Force' against new cyber-threats.[95]

Firms with Expertise in Diverse Areas of Cybersecurity

Israel-based firms have achieved the depth needed in cyber protection expertise. Some high-profile cybersecurity firms from the country include the financial data security firm Trusteer (acquired by IBM in 2013), CyberArk (specialized in securing and managing privileged passwords and identities), NativeFlow (specialized to manage the Bring Your Own Device (BYOD) problem), Check Point Software Technologies Ltd, Actimize (which provides solutions to global financial institutions to detect fraud, prevent money laundering, and manage risk), and Aorato (which learns and graphs people's network behavior and identifies suspicious activity).[96]

Israel is making attempts to build an image of the country as the center of global CS excellence. The CEO of Israeli cybersecurity company CyberArk put the issue this way: "Everybody understands that you buy Swiss watches from Switzerland and information security from Israel."[97]

Policy Measures

Israel's transparent laws for establishing companies provide favorable and supportive environment to entrepreneurial activities. While foreign investments involving sensitive sectors need prior approval, the country gives equal treatment to domestic and foreign investors in most sectors. Likewise, 80% of the first US$500,000 for every idea identified is funded by the government.[98]

Public–Private Partnership (PPP)

The role of PPP in strengthening Israel's cybersecurity profiles deserves mention. Public and private sector organizations in the country have made a conscious effort to create virtuous circle of entrepreneurship development.

In an effort to foster cooperation and coordination in cybersecurity-related issues among the private sector, academia, cybersecurity experts, and government agencies and to promote long-term research and analysis of cyber-threats, in 2011, Israel created the National Cyber Bureau (NCB).

A strong relationship between military intelligence and the private industry has been a key force in the country's prominence in the world cybersecurity market. The Israeli army's military intelligence and technological units such as Unit 8200 provide much of the training and experience needed for the country's success on the cybersecurity front.[99]

Israel's strong entrepreneurial spirit and top technical universities have been key ingredients of the country's global leadership in cybersecurity. The government has provided favorable tax incentives and subsidies, which have amounted as much as 40% of some companies' staff salaries.[100]

Some Challenges

While it was a welcome addition for the Israeli cybersecurity landscape, the NCB's creation produced internal conflicts and turf wars with the intelligence agency Shabak (also known as ShinBet). The creation of the National Authority for Cyber-Defense, a new cyber-defense authority created in September 2014 to protect civilian networks is expected to resolve the conflict. The new agency reports to the head of the NCB. It is also likely to decrease the influence of Israel's intelligence community in civilian cyber-defense issues.[101]

Case Summary

Many nations worldwide are developing key strengths in a number of cybersecurity areas. Israel has been successful in cashing in on the trend of rapidly rising cybercrime, which has spawned numerous globally competitive cybersecurity firms. The country's success on the cyber-entrepreneurship front can be attributed to the combination of several factors including emergence of cybersecurity sector as a magnet for VC investment, high R&D intensity, the government's initiatives to strengthen the country's cybersecurity and strong PPP.

As noted, the NCB's creation led internal conflicts. This provides an important lesson for policy makers in other countries to adequately prepare for dealing with unexpected problems.

Notes

1 oecd.org. 2010. "OECD work on statistics," www.oecd.org/dataoecd/18/49/44652140.pdf.
2 Dw.com, 2014, "OECD suspends Russia accession talks while Moscow vows 'symmetrical' sanctions," www.dw.com/en/oecd-suspends-russia-accession-talks-while-moscow-vows-symmetrical-sanctions/a-17494773.
3 Calvino, F., Criscuolo, C., & Menon, C. 2016. "No country for young firms? Start-up dynamics and national policies," 29, OECD Science, *Technology and Industry Policy Papers*, Paris: OECD Publishing.
4 Andrew Bounds. 2016. SME lending grows for first time since financial crisis, 1 February, www.ft.com/content/db2a1686-c8e4-11e5-be0b-b7ece4e953a0.
5 Basta, V. 2017. "Venture investing in the US and Europe are totally different industries," https://techcrunch.com/2017/06/07/venture-investing-in-the-us-and-europe-are-totally-different-industries/.
6 OECD. 2010. "Accession: Estonia, Israel and Slovenia invited to join OECD," 5 October, www.oecd.org/document/57/0,3746,en_21571361_44315115_45159737_1_1_1_1,00.html.
7 http://info.worldbank.org/governance/wgi/pdf/rq.pdf.
8 United States Council for International Business. 2018. Hampl Urges High Standards in Colombia's OECD Accession, www.uscib.org/hampl-urges-high-standards-in-colombias-oecd-accession/.
9 Bate, R. 2018. "You down with OECD?" thehill.com/opinion/international/379302-you-down-with-oecd.
10 tuac.org. 2018. "No progress on Trade Union Rights and Safety in Colombia? No OECD Accession" say Colombian Trade Unionists, 22 February, https://tuac.org/news/no-progress-trade-union-rights-safety-colombia-no-oecd-accession/.
11 OECD. 2016. "Due diligence in Colombia's gold supply chain overview."
12 Wyss, J., & Gurney, K. 2018. "Dirty gold is the new cocaine in Colombia—and it's just as bloody," www.miamiherald.com/news/nation-world/world/americas/colombia/article194188034.html.
13 Bate, R. 2018. "You down with OECD?" http://thehill.com/opinion/international/379302-you-down-with-oecd.
14 Bate, R. 2011. "A different kind of drug war with a chance for success," www.realclearmarkets.com/articles/2011/08/06/a_different_kind_of_drug_war_with_a_chance_for_success_99168.html.
15 Moeller IP Advisors, 2017 "Worldwide: How do fake drugs and Chinese counterfeit medicine impact Latin America & its pharmaceutical industry?," www.mondaq.com/Uruguay/x/560082/food+drugs+law/How+Do+Fake+Drugs+And+Chinese+Counterfeit+Medicine+Impact+Latin+America+Its+Pharmaceutical+Industry.
16 OECD. 2018. OECD members agree to formally invite Lithuania as 36th member, 3 May, www.oecd.org/newsroom/oecd-members-agree-to-formally-invite-lithuania-as-36th-member.htm.
17 lrp.lt. 2018. OECD membership finalizes Lithuania's establishment in global organizations, May 30, www.lrp.lt/en/press-centre/press-releases/oecd-membership-finalizes-lithuanias-establishment-in-global-organizations/30093.

18 OECD. 2013. OECD sets out roadmap for Latvia's membership, 16 October, www.oecd.org/newsroom/oecd-sets-out-roadmap-for-latvias-membership.htm.
19 OECD. 2017. "Corporate governance in Latvia," 20 March, www.oecd.org/latvia/corporate-governance-in-latvia-9789264268180-en.htm.
20 Ministry of Foreign Affairs. 2016. "Latvia's accession to the organisation for economic cooperation and development," www.mfa.gov.lv/en/policy/economic-affairs/oecd/latvia-s-accession-to-the-oecd.
21 Ibid.
22 Chapter 4: Business Environment. *Chile Business Forecast Report.* 2011 2nd Quarter, 2, pp. 23–30.
23 transparency.org 2018. Corruption Perceptions Index 2017, 21 February, www.transparency.org/news/feature/corruption_perceptions_index_2017.
24 OECD. 2011. "Corporate governance in Chile," www.oecd.org/dataoecd/21/63/47073155.pdf.
25 Chile, www.heritage.org/index/country/chile.
26 Chapter 4: Business Environment. *Chile Business Forecast Report.* 2010 4th Quarter, pp. 33–40.
27 chile-usa.org. 2005. "Ministry of justice reforms underway," www.chile-usa.org/minjustice.htm.
28 OECD. "Corporate governance in Israel 2011," 10.1787/9789264097698-en, www.keepeek.com/Digital-Asset-Management/oecd/governance/corporate-governance-in-israel-2011_9789264097698-en.
29 "Israel strengthens the battle against bribery and corruption," www.justice.gov.il/MOJEng/Mankal/Corruption/.
30 OECD. 2009.
31 OECD. 2011. "Enhancing Market Openness, Intellectual Property Rights, and Compliance through Regulatory Reform in Israel," www.oecd.org/israel/48262991.pdf.
32 Israel's intellectual property law', 16 Mar 2008, www.mfa.gov.il/MFA/Government/Law/Legal+Issues+and+Rulings/Israel%20intellectual%20property%20law%2016-Mar-2008.
33 OECD. 2011.
34 transparency.org. 2018.
35 "2011 Investment Climate Statement: Estonia, Bureau of Economic," *Energy and Business Affairs*, March 2011, www.state.gov/e/eb/rls/othr/ics/2011/157274.htm.
36 "2011 Investment Climate Statement: Estonia, Bureau of Economic," *Energy and Business Affairs*, March 2011, www.state.gov/e/eb/rls/othr/ics/2011/157274.htm.
37 OECD. 2011. "Corporate governance in Estonia," October 6, www.oecd-ilibrary.org/governance/corporate-governance-in-estonia-2011_9789264119079-en.
38 "Corporate governance in Slovenia 2011", DOI: 10.1787/9789264097704-en, www.keepeek.com/Digital-Asset-Management/oecd/governance/corporate-governance-in-slovenia-2011_9789264097704-en.
39 "Background note: Slovenia's accession to the OECD," www.oecd.org/document/53/0,3746,en_21571361_44315115_45161781_1_1_1_1,00.html.
40 OECD. 2011. "Enhancing market openness, Intellectual property rights, and compliance through regulatory reform in Slovenia," www.oecd.org/slovenia/48263001.pdf.
41 WIPO. 2008d. "Country profile from WIPO guide to intellectual property worldwide," www.wipo.int/about-ip/en/ipworldwide/pdf/si.pdf.
42 OECD. "Members and partners," www.oecd.org/about/membersandpartners/

43 transparency.org. 2018.

44 OECD Observer. 1999, "Corporate governance: getting it right in Russia," www.
oecdobserver.org/news/archivestory.php/aid/21/Corporate_governance:_
getting_it_right_in_Russia.html.

45 BIAC. 2012. "Russia–OECD accession discussions: Improving the Russian
business environment, BIAC Statement to the OECD," 14 May, www.biac.
org/statements/nme/12-06_FIN_BIAC_BIAC_RUSSIA_PAPER_2012.
pdf.

46 "OECD-Russia Accession Discussions: Improving the Russian Business Environment: BIAC Statement to the OECD," 9 March 2011 www.biac.org/
statements/nme/08%2003%202011%20FINAL%20BIAC%20DRAFT%20
BIAC%20RUSSIA%20PAPER%202011.pdf.

47 DW made for minds. 2014. "OECD suspends Russia accession talks while
Moscow vows 'symmetrical' sanctions," www.dw.com/en/oecd-suspends-
russia-accession-talks-while-moscow-vows-symmetrical-sanctions/a-
17494773.

48 Economist. 2012 "Entrepreneurs in Latin America: The lure of Chilecon
Valley, as America shuts out immigrant entrepreneurs, Chile welcomes
them," 13 October, www.economist.com/node/21564589.

49 BusinessWeek. 1995. "Score one more for Japan's Bureaucrats (Int'l Edition),"
2 April, www.businessweek.com/stories/1995-04-02/score-one-more-for-
japans-bureaucrats-intl-edition.

50 heritage.org. 2010b. "Turkey," www.heritage.org/index/country/Turkey.

51 Economist. 2010. "Making a success of failure," p. 68.

52 transparency.org. 2018.

53 Gamboa-Cavazos, M., Garza-Cantu, V., & Salinas, E. 2007. "The organization of corruption: Political horizons and special interests," sitios.itesm.mx/
egap/que_es_egap/inv_pub/EGAP_AP_07_01.pdf.

54 Shirk, D.A. 2011. "Criminal justice reform in Mexico: An overview," Mexican Law Review, info8.juridicas.unam.mx/pdf/mlawrns/cont/6/arc/arc1.
pdf.

55 Franks, J., Nyborg, K., & Torous, W. 1996. "A comparison of US, UK, and
German insolvency codes," Financial Management, 25, pp. 86–101.

56 Global Entrepreneurship Week. 2012. "Global entrepreneurship week policy
survey turns up unexpected results," 14 November, www.unleashingideas.
org/policysurvey.

57 OECD. 2008. "OECD economic surveys: Poland, raising labor supply to
sustain strong potential growth," 10, pp. 19–45.

58 Isenberg, D.J. 2010b. "How to start an entrepreneurial revolution," Harvard
Business Review, 88(6), pp. 40–50.

59 Brown, J.M. 2008. "Lucre of the Irish, prospect," 20 January, 142, www.
prospectmagazine.co.uk/2008/01/lucreoftheirish/.

60 Isenberg, 2010b.

61 Chile. 2008. "GEM Report, 2009. Chileans see entrepreneurship as desirable career option," May 10, 2009, www3.babson.edu/Newsroom/Releases/
Chile-GEM-2009.cfm.

62 Uis. 2010. "Trends in tertiary education: Sub-Saharan Africa," UIS Fact
Sheet, December 2010, No. 10 www.uis.unesco.org/FactSheets/Documents/
fs10-2010-en.pdf.

63 EC (European Commission). 2007. "Entrepreneurship survey of the EU (25
Member States), United States, Iceland and Norway: Analytical Report,"
Eurobarometer.

64 Global Entrepreneurship Week. 2012.

65 Zachary, G.P. 2000. *The Global Me: New Cosmopolitans and the Competitive Edge: Picking Globalism's Winners and Losers.* London: Nicholas Brealey Pub.

66 Furnham. A. 2017. "Why immigrants make great entrepreneurs," 26 November,www.wsj.com/articles/why-immigrants-make-great-entrepreneurs-1511752261.

67 New American Economy Reason for Reform: Entrepreneurship, October, 2016.

68 "Fighting bid rigging in government contracts: Mexico-OECD partnership," www.oecd.org/competition/cartelsandanti-competitiveagreements/fightingbidriggingingovernmentcontractsmexico-oecdpartnership.htm.

69 OECD Economic Surveys: Japan. 2008, "Enhancing the productivity of the service sector in Japan," 4 April, pp. 125–170.

70 Shogo, I. 2001, "Competition in Japan's telecommunications sector: Challenges for the Japan fair commission," 11 October, 1, www.jftc.go.jp/e-page/speech/011011speech.pdf.

71 OECD Economic Surveys: France. 2009. "Strengthening competition to boost efficiency and employment," April, (5), pp. 101–130.

72 Economic Survey of France." 2009. "Strengthening competition to boost efficiency and employment," www.oecd.org/eco/economicsurveyoffrance2009strengtheningcompetitiontoboostefficiencyandemployment.htm.

73 WSBI. 2016. "Not so different: SME financing patterns in Europe and United States," 23 May. www.wsbi-esbg.org/press/latest-news/Pages/Not-so-different-SME-financing-patterns-in-Europe-and-United-States.aspx.

74 Ibid.

75 Schramm, C.J. 2004. "Building entrepreneurial economies," *Foreign Affairs,* 83(4), pp. 104–115.

76 Elinor, C. 2012. "Small banks target lending at Mexico's informal sector," 13 March, www.the-european.eu/story-335/small-banks-target-lending-at-mexicos-informal-sector.html.

77 Entrepreneurship at a Glance 2017. 2017, "Venture capital: Venture capital investments," www.oecd-ilibrary.org/employment/entrepreneurship-at-a-glance-2017/venture-capital-investments_entrepreneur_aag-2017-25-en.

78 *Ernst & Young.* 2002. Globalizing venture capital: Global venture capital insights and trends report 2011, 2 www.ey.com/Publication/vwLUAssets/Globalizing_venture_capital_-_Global_venture_capital_insights_and_trends_report_2011/$FILE/Globalizing_venture_capital_Global_venture_capital_insights_and_trends_report_2011.pdf.

79 Chaia, A., Goland, T., & Schiff, R. 2010, "Counting the world's unbanked."

80 Convergences, 2017. "Is microfinance still working?" Microfinance barometer.

81 Grameen America. 2008, "Grameen America," www.grameenamerica.com/About-Us/Grameen-America.html.

82 Kitchens, R., & Torrence, P. 2012. "The jobs act – Crowdfunding and beyond." *Economic Development Journal,* Fall, 11(4), pp. 42–47.

83 Mostowyk, L. 2018. "US named top global tech innovation leader, China in second spot: KPMG report," https://home.kpmg.com/xx/en/home/media/press-releases/2018/03/us-named-top-global-tech-innovation-leader.html.

84 Murat, S. 2012. "Lessons from a start-up nation," 11 July, http://blogs.worldbank.org/psd/lessons-from-a-start-up-nation.

85 "The Danish enterprise and construction authority profile of Israel: An entrepreneurial country," www.erhvervsstyrelsen.dk/publikationer/ivaerksaettere/Entrepreneurship%20Index%202010/kap05.htm.

86 OECD. 2012. "Science and innovation: Turkey," www.oecd.org/turkey/sti-outlook-2012-turkey.pdf.
87 Heijmans, P. 2010. "EU sets its sights on tax havens," *The Prague Post*, 27 January.
88 Lewis, G. 2007. "Who in the world is entrepreneurial?" *FSB: Fortune Small Business*,17(5), p. 14.
89 Bussgang, J., & Stern, O. 2015. How Israeli startups can scale, 10 September, https://hbr.org/2015/09/how-israeli-startups-can-scale.
90 Dan Richards' interview with Josh Lerner, Why Public Funding of Venture Capital Has Failed, 1 February 2011, http://advisorperspectives.com/news letters11/pdfs/Why_Public_Funding_of_Venture_Capital_Has_Failed.pdf.
91 Cohen, T. 2014. "Israel turns defense capabilities into cyber security tech gold," www.haaretz.com/news/diplomacy-defense/1.617461.
92 Hiner, J. 2014. "UN. How Israel is rewriting the future of cybersecurity and creating the next Silicon Valley," www.techrepublic.com/article/how-israel-is-rewriting-the-future-of-cybersecurity-and-creating-the-next-silicon-valley/.
93 O'Neill, P.H. 2018. "Israel accounts for 16 percent of global cybersecurity investment, second only to U.S." 31 January, www.cyberscoop.com/israel-cybersecurity-venture-funding/.
94 Solomon,S.2018."Israelwinssecond-largestnumberofcybersecuritydealsglobally," 15 April, www.timesofisrael.com/israel-nabs-second-largest-number-of-cybersecurity-deals-globally/.
95 Dvorin, T. 2014. "Israel launches national Cyber-Defense authority," www.israelnationalnews.com/News/News.aspx/185349#.VCm0pVfNJmc.
96 Miller, Z. 2014. "Israeli security companies who could help Putin protect the Sochi Olympics," www.forbes.com/sites/zackmiller/2014/01/29/7-israeli-security-companies-who-could-help-putin-protect-the-sochi-olympics/.
97 Leichman, A.K. 2013. "Israel is the go-to address for cyber-security," www.israel21c.org/technology/israel-is-the-go-to-address-for-cyber-security/.
98 Shah, H.J. 2010a. "Valuate the India opportunity through incubators, demographics and PEG," 9 March, http://blogs.wsj.com/india-chief-mentor/2010/03/09/valuate-the-india-opportunity-through-incubators-demographics-and-peg/.
99 Moskowitz, J. 2014. "Cybersecurity unit drives Israeli Internet economy," www.csmonitor.com/World/Passcode/2014/1205/Cybersecurity-unit-drives-Israeli-Internet-economy.
100 Barnes, J. 2014. "Israel utilises its cyber security expertise," www.ft.com/intl/cms/s/0/8b6e572c-97e7-11e3-8dc3-00144feab7de.html#axzz3EnpyGV6S.
101 Sugarman, E. 2014. "What the United States can learn from Israel about Cybersecurity," www.forbes.com/sites/elisugarman/2014/10/07/what-the-united-states-can-learn-from-israel-about-cybersecurity/.

Chapter 5

Entrepreneurship in Postsocialist Economies in Former Soviet Union and Central and Eastern Europe

This chapter's objectives include:

1   To *demonstrate* an understanding of the natures of entrepreneurial activities in FSU&CEE economies.
2   To *analyze* the drivers of entrepreneurship in FSU&CEE economies.
3   To *evaluate* some of the barriers to transition to market economies in FSU&CEE economies.
4   To *assess* the extent of productive, unproductive, and destructive entrepreneurship in FSU&CEE economies.
5   To *demonstrate* an understanding of the sources of heterogeneity in entrepreneurial activities in FSU&CEE economies.

Introduction

In this chapter, we shift our attention to entrepreneurship in the formerly socialist countries of the Former Soviet Union and Central and Eastern Europe (FSU&CEE). Note that during the socialist economic systems in the past, all these countries were characterized by a pervasive hostility to entrepreneurship. Among the FSU&CEE economies, Czech Republic, Estonia, Hungary, Poland, Slovakia, and Slovenia are OECD members. In Chapter 4, we have discussed at length the importance of economic and political reforms in order to be qualified for OECD membership. Some other FSU&CEE economies, while not yet OECD members, have joined the North Atlantic Treaty Organization (NATO) and the European Union (EU), and thus institutional reforms in these economies were constantly monitored as part of the process of attaining full membership of these international organizations.

In general, there is growing recognition among postsocialist (PS) economies in FSU&CEE that free-market entrepreneurship is essential for ultimately improving their economic future. Even countries that lack membership in any of the above international organizations have demonstrated their commitment and willingness to encourage and promote free-market entrepreneurship. One example to illustrate this point is Russia's Skolkovo project announced by then President Dmitry Medvedev in 2009 to reduce the country's reliance on commodities and develop a globally competitive knowledge-based economy. The plan is to transform 400 hectares farmland near Moscow to Silikonnovaya Dolina or Russia's Silicon Valley. The Skolkovo project includes five "clusters" specializing in IT, energy, nuclear technologies, biomedicine, and space technologies. As of mid-2012, the government had allocated about $4.2 billion for the project.[1] As of February 2012, the project had approved $220 million in grants to 330 startups.[2]

Corporate and personal tax breaks and other incentives are promised for investors and about 200 laws had been amended as of mid-2012 to encourage high-tech investment in Skolkovo. High-level government officials have visited foreign countries to promote the Skolkovo project. In 2010, Medvedev met with a group of U.S. venture fund managers in an attempt to attract venture capital in Silikonnovaya Dolina.[3] Likewise, in February 2012, executive directors of the five clusters of the Skolkovo project visited the U.K. to raise awareness of the opportunities available for researchers and companies and to attract partners and investors. These incentives have already attracted multinationals such as Microsoft, IBM, Siemens, Intel, Cisco, and Nokia. As of early 2013, participant status was granted to over 300 companies. In 2012, Skolkovo announced its intention to open similar innovation city in Vladivostok.

While many examples to promote entrepreneurship in FSU&CEE economies exist, there are various inertia effects that have posed difficulties. One obvious problem concerns the absence of and difficult to construct key ingredients of entrepreneurial ecosystem such as appropriate political, legal, economic, and commercial structures that are needed for a free-market economy. These problems are prevalent even in some FSU&CEE economies that are considered to be successful. For instance, in Poland, which is viewed as among the most successful FSU&CEE economies, small firm size, lack of innovative capacity, limited access to capital, underdeveloped management skills and a lack of experience in conducting businesses in foreign countries have hindered entrepreneurial development.[4] Polish SMEs also complain about the complexity in the legal system, high administrative costs, and high corporate tax rates.[5]

Variation across FSU&CEE Economies in Different Forms of Entrepreneurship

The positive impacts of entrepreneurship are felt across most FSU&CEE economies. For instance, Russia had 27 companies on the 2017 edition of the Forbes Global 2000 list.[6]

Most economies in the region have experienced positive economic growth in recent years. For instance, every country in the CEE region except for Romania experienced a positive GDP growth in 2010. These economies have also made a significant progress in reducing poverty. For instance, according to the Federal State Service for Statistics (Rosstat), absolute poverty in Russia fell from 29% in 2000 to 13.4% in 2007.[7]

Formal and informal institutions needed to support market entrepreneurship have not developed at the same rate across the FSU&CEE economies. There is more variation across FSU&CEE economies' reforms than many analysts predicted. While some FSU&CEE economies have made significant progresses, the reform process has been relatively slow in others. Czech Republic, Estonia, Hungary, and Poland are described as some examples of the successful FSU&CEE economies.

Hungary, a EU member with 10 million people, is described as an example of a post-1989 success. It has one of the most developed venture capital markets among CEE economies. The country has a well-developed entrepreneurial ecosystem consisting of successful serial entrepreneurs, business angels, entrepreneurial infrastructures and services, which provide entrepreneurs with access to skills and expertise.[8] Local governments, local firms development centers such as Hungarian Foundation for Enterprise Development, private firms and professional organizations have teamed up to establish business incubators. Hungary has been successful in producing globally successful firms in leading-edge, technology-intensive sectors. For instance, LogMeln (which allows Internet users to connect remotely), Prezi (a provider of cloud-based software), and Ustream (a provider of a live video streaming service) started from Hungary and globalized their businesses within a few years. As of mid-2012, these three companies had over 110 million users worldwide.[9]

Economies such as Russia and Ukraine, on the other hand, have been slow to develop institutional supports needed to promote productive free-market entrepreneurship. For one thing, political entrepreneurship, in which entrepreneurs use political power, capital, and social networks to maximize economic rewards, is more readily apparent in Russian and some other FSU&CEE economies.[10] Moreover, as is the case of some other developing economies, the ruling elites and their family, friends, and clients have lived a parasitic existence in some FSU&CEE economies. It is argued that Russian economy is a hybrid between Soviet capitalism and feudalism. In the Forbes' 2018 list of 2,208 billionaires (March 2018) 106 were from Russia[11] compared to 62 in 2010.[12]

Russian government officials also engage in predatory behaviors. During 2002–2011, Russia imprisoned about three million entrepreneurs.[13] Many of them were put in prison without trial and unjustly. Some businessmen complained that their commercial rivals paid corrupt police officers to plant evidence against them.

A similar point can be made about many other FSU&CEE economies. It was reported that Kazakh President Nursultan Nazarbayev allegedly transferred at least US$1 billion dollars of oil export revenues to his private accounts.[14] His family members control many key enterprises in the country.

Likewise, an estimate suggested that 13 Ukrainian oligarchs control about 40% of the Ukrainian economy.[15] Three top oligarchs[16] in Ukraine played a key role in supporting the former President Leonid Kuchma's regime. One of the oligarchs, Pinchuk is Kuchma's son-in-law. In 2004, the businessmen's favor gravitated toward the opposition candidate Viktor Yushchenko, who benefited enormously. This shows that governments failing to direct efforts towards buttering up businesses may face severe consequences.

Productive, Unproductive, and Destructive Entrepreneurship in FSU&CEE Economies

Individuals in FSU&CEE economies do not necessarily have a lower propensity to engage in entrepreneurial activities than those in matured market economies. According to International Social Survey Program data set, the proportion saying, "I would prefer to be self-employed" was the largest in Poland—80%.[17] As noted in Chapter 1, people in the FSU&CEE economies have also accepted the idea of free market and capitalism.

The concept of entrepreneurship is, however, quite broad in FSU&CEE economies. Indeed, as noted earlier, entrepreneurs in FSU&CEE economies have come in various forms. One way to classify entrepreneurial activities is in terms of their legalities. There have been an increasing number of businesses within the legal boundary. In rapidly changing environments like those of FSU&CEE economies, however, entrepreneurs find attractive economic niches from outside the current institutional boundaries.[18] A significant proportion of entrepreneurial activities in these economies have been in quasi-legal and extralegal areas.

A related point is that inertia effects of socialism influences entrepreneurial activities in FSU&CEE economies. One scholar noted, "capitalism is built not *on* but *with* the ruins of socialism."[19] Socialism's ruins come in various forms including the influence of MarxLeninism philosophy and the prominence of communist party members and bureaucrats in the entrepreneurship landscape.

Based on the two dimensions discussed above—legality and inertia effects of socialism, we have developed a 2 × 2 typology of entrepreneur types in FSU&CEE economies (Figure 5.1). Our observations above also raise the interesting possibility that institutions in some FSU&CEE economies may do better in promoting entrepreneurship in unproductive and destructive forms than those in matured market economies. Note that free-market

Legality ⇒ Ideology ⇓	Legal	Non-legal/illegal
Socialism dominated	• Collective entrepreneurship	• Elite entrepreneurship • Political entrepreneurship • Red hat entrepreneurship
Capitalism dominated	• Market entrepreneurship	• Institutional entrepreneurship

Figure 5.1 Entrepreneurship in Postsocialist Economies: A Typology.

entrepreneurship, which relies on competition, supply, and demand, is likely to add to the social product and is productive. Some forms of political entrepreneurship are also associated with criminal and quasi-criminal activities,[20] which are inefficient unproductive or even destructive.

Productive Market Entrepreneurship

Market entrepreneurs in FSU&CEE economies depend upon the newly created market institutions. While economic systems in matured market economies are characterized by private enterprise and market entrepreneurship, this form of entrepreneurship is at the early stage of development in most FSU&CEE economies.

Contrary to the stereotypically different expectations that surround FSU&CEE economies, however, market entrepreneurship is growing rapidly in some FSU&CEE economies. A significant proportion of small and self-employed firms in FSU&CEE economies have ingredients of market entrepreneurship in their functioning. For instance, traditional Russian business values have changed gradually and are becoming more and more consistent with free-market entrepreneurship.[21]

Unproductive and Destructive Entrepreneurship

Compared to more matured market economies, unproductive and destructive forms of entrepreneurship tend to be more prevalent in FSU&CEE economies. For one thing, the introduction of market forces in FSU&CEE economy pushed a great deal of economic activity to underground. One scholar notes, "One of every five workers in Eastern and Central Europe labors off the books and receives under-the-table payments."[22] The underground economy as a proportion of GDP is significantly bigger in CEE economies than corresponding figures for EU member countries and sizable proportion of them are also associated with criminal and quasi-criminal activities.[23]

In 1997, Black market accounted for 95% of retail activity In Tajikistan and 50%–60% in Ukraine.[24] According to Goskomstat, Russia's State

Statistics Service, unreported income accounted for 30% of wages paid in the late 1990s in the country. The corresponding figure for Bulgaria is estimated at about one-third.[25] Similarly, according to the Romanian Information Service, the size of unofficial economic activities in the country is about 30%–40% of GDP and in 1998, the size of smuggling was 12% higher than that of official import.[26] Other estimates suggest that the "shadow economy" accounts for about 24% of GDP in Lithuania and 40% in Russia.[27] Formalization of informal economy is a critical practical challenge facing FSU&CEE economies.

Finally, a remarkable example of parasitical existence of entrepreneurs upon the economy is the creation of firms to support criminal activities in some FSU&CEE economies. There are, for instance, companies whose primary purpose is to provide money-laundering services for criminal organizations.[28] Organized crime groups in Russia have been the driving force behind the rapid rise of the global cybercrime industry.

Political Entrepreneurship

One scholar makes an intriguing argument as to how political entrepreneurs emerge in FSU&CEE economies: postsocialist transition is not a transition from *plan* to *market* but from *plan* to *clan*.[29] The essence of the argument is simple: political entrepreneurs take advantage of their positional power to maximize economic rewards. They receive state subsidies and contracts in various forms. This emphasis on the exploitation of positional power is echoed in the political capitalism thesis, which argues that major winners of the PS transformations are the former nomenklatura.[30,31] Political entrepreneurship goes against the idea of capitalism and describes a paradoxical situation of "making capitalism without capitalists."[32]

Russia differs from other transition economies in CEE in several important aspects, inter-alia its vast natural resources, which provides enormous opportunities for rent-seeking.[33] Unsurprisingly, state managers and new entrepreneurs benefitted tremendously through rent seeking in the transition.

While political entrepreneurship also exists in mature market economies, this form of entrepreneurship is more readily apparent in FSU&CEE economies. A central feature of the privatization of state enterprises in CEE economies is that privileged elites converted "limited de facto use and income rights into more de jure alienable rights."[34] In Russia, for instance, following the mass privatization, former nomenklatura appointees accounted for about two-thirds of the top positions in businesses and the government.[35] Likewise, beginning the mid-1980s in Hungary and Poland and in the late 1980s in Romania, political and administrative elites capitalized on their positional power to start their own businesses.

That is not to say that political entrepreneurship is absent in mature market economies such as the U.S. The concept of manifest and latent functions[36] can be very helpful in understanding how the nature of political entrepreneurship differs in FSU&CEE and more matured market economies. Manifest functions are explicitly stated and understood by the participants in the relevant action and the consequences can be observed or expected. Latent functions are those that are not explicitly stated, recognized, or intended by the people involved. In the U.S., for instance, the manifest posture is of private enterprise, but below the surface deeply ingrained are a wide range of firms that are politically dependent. For instance, according to the Center for Responsive Politics, candidates for the U.S. congress and presidency received over $12 million between 1989 and 2000 from the sugar industry.[37] Observers have pointed out the possibility that these political contributions might have an adverse effect on regulatory efforts to revise national nutritional policy. Likewise, large firms in the U.S. textile industry have received institutional favors in various forms such as subsidies and barriers to trade in textile products and thus benefited from political entrepreneurship.[38] In China, on the other hand, the manifest posture is that of the collective enterprise, while the latent reality is privatized enterprise owned by political entrepreneurs.

There are, however, important differences between political entrepreneurship in FSU&CEE economies and matured market economies. Part of the fascinating character of political entrepreneurship in FSU&CEE economies stems from the fact that there is a symbiosis between economic and political elites, where political entrepreneurs take advantage of positional power to maximize economic rewards.[39] In some cases, bureaucrats are also capitalists and possess capability to penetrate into the government apparatus.[40] This situation is similar to economies in the Middle East[41] and is different from more matured market economies, in which economic and political elites tend to be different groups.

Studies conducted in Russia and Eastern European economies have found that the most important barrier to transition to free-market economy centered on Communist Party bureaucrats' resistance. This phenomenon is similar to that in the Middle East, where bureaucrats discourage policies favoring institutional reforms and remain a strong anti-reform force.[42]

Another way of viewing political entrepreneurship is in terms of the entrepreneurs' engagement in central versus peripheral positions. Political entrepreneurs in FSU&CEE economies tend to possess economic and non-economic resources and are central players. In more mature market economies, on the other hand, political entrepreneurs tend to be peripheral players.[43]

A final issue that deserves mention relates to nepotism's influence on political entrepreneurship. As is the case of the Arab world (Chapter 6), such a tendency can be attributed to the culture (e.g., strong kinship ties and obligations to family and friends). While some degree of nepotism is involved everywhere, influences of favoritism, nepotism, and personal connections are more readily apparent in some FSU&CEE economies.

Political Entrepreneurship and Institutional Entrepreneurship

To understand the differences in entrepreneurial activities in FSU&CEE economies and mature market economies, we introduce the concept of institutional entrepreneurship. Actors with key strategic resources or power, who can play an important role in the creation of new institutions related to entrepreneurship, are called institutional entrepreneurs. Institutional entrepreneurs are driven by interests that they value, aware of the possible effects on new institutions they seek to create and calculative.[44] They can change existing models of social or economic orders in the process of starting or expanding businesses.

For the FSU&CEE economies' context, the most relevant issue concerns institutional holes. In many cases, institutional entrepreneurs benefit from such holes, which involve structural gaps between diverse institutional actors, which control complementary resources.[45] In general, such holes tend to be more prevalent in transitional economies such as FSU&CEE economies, than in more matured market economies because institutional rules in the former group are incomplete and ambiguous. In many emerging economies, institutional entrepreneurs' access to political resources facilitates their attempts to create new market institutions.[46]

Institutional entrepreneurship in FSU&CEE economies may entail illegal activities and represent a significant component of political entrepreneurship. An example is *Ex Ante Investment with Ex Post Justification* approach to institutional entrepreneurship.[47] In this form of entrepreneurship, as it happens, an entrepreneur starts or expands a business, which may violate existing laws or regulations. When the business becomes successful and generates social benefits, the entrepreneur reports the business to the government and persuades to change existing laws and regulations. In such cases, access to political resources is critical to succeed.

Determinants of Entrepreneurship in FSU&CEE Economies

Regulatory Framework

One encouraging trend in FSU&CEE economies concerns the governments' shifting basis of legitimacy. In most FSU&CEE economies, governments are moving from coercive control over the state and the legitimacy of MarxLeninism to economic legitimacy based on growth. Unsurprisingly, these economies have undertaken public policies to promote

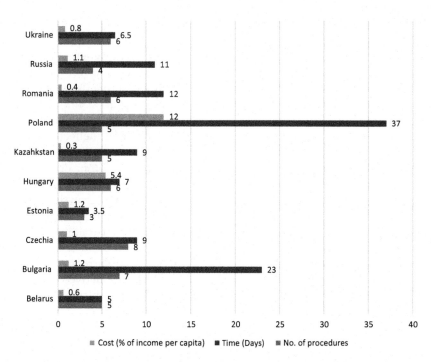

Figure 5.2 Time, Costs, and Procedures Required to Start a New Business in Some FSU&CEE Economies.
Source: The World Bank "Doing Business 2018" (www.doingbusiness.org/rankings).

entrepreneurship as indicated by favorable regulatory climates to start new businesses (Figure 5.2).

According to the World Bank's Ease of Doing Business 2013, Poland was the global top improver in the entrepreneurial climate from June 2011 to May 2012. Of the world's top ten economies that were recognized for making most improvement in the ease of doing business five were FSU&-CEE economies: Poland, Ukraine, Uzbekistan, Serbia, and Kazakhstan.

According to Grant Thornton, 2,372 new laws and decrees entered into force in Poland in 2015.[48] Entrepreneurs in the country are subject to complex and lengthy administrative procedures.[49] For instance, according to the World Bank's Doing Business survey 2018, Polish entrepreneurs need to wait 122 days to get electricity.

The World Bank noted that many regulatory changes had not entered into force. Other laws were available but companies were not aware of them yet.[50] In June 2016, the Ministry of Development announced "100 Changes for Companies."[51] In October 2017, the Polish finance minister noted that 90% of the "100 Changes" were completed.[52] One of the changes, for instance, makes it possible to store employee information in electronic databases instead of the earlier requirement to keep them for 50–100 years.[53]

As noted earlier, an important challenge in promoting entrepreneurship in FSU&CEE economies concerns the deficiency of formal institutions to support the functioning of the market. In overly politicized states, entrepreneurial efforts are diverted away from wealth creation into nonmarket behaviors, which entail securing protection from market forces. In many FSU&CEE economies, because of ineffective legal enforcement of private property rights, entrepreneurs considered it important to acquire political and administrative protection or depend on informal networks for security.[54] The absence of institutions to protect property rights and strong judicial system hinders the growth of private entrepreneurship. In the absence of mechanisms to protect intellectual property and discourage monopolies and unfair trade practices, market entrepreneurship cannot thrive. The existence of appropriate regulative institutions determines whether potential entrepreneurs are likely to engage in new wealth creation through productive entrepreneurship or transfers of existing wealth through unproductive political entrepreneurship.

The government's inability to strengthen the rule of law also raises the interesting possibility that some market entrepreneurs may go underground and many others into political entrepreneurs and rent-seeking activities.[55] Most private actors may be tempted to exploit short-term profit making opportunities under the existing institutional arrangement rather than from engaging in long-term efforts at building new institutions. This is the obvious challenge for promoting market entrepreneurship in most FSU&CEE economies.

As noted above, Russia and Romania were often cited as unsuccessful examples of FSU&CEE economies in promoting market entrepreneurship. Earlier we discussed the roles of supra–national institutions or outside anchor such as the EU and OECD in facilitating the formation of market institution. The significant improvements made by Romania in the past decade further illustrates this point (Figure 5.2). Romania's development was often referred as "stalled" or even "de-development."[56] One expert observed that "the former party bosses are alive and, to the despair of many Romanians, well."[57] In 2000, there were at least 13 institutions involved in the process. It was observed that state officials in Romania lack accountability, it was impossible to sue them and formal complaints have no effects.[58] Barriers to start a business in recent years are less evident in Romania than in some economies that are entrepreneurially more successful. For instance, in terms of the number of procedures, time, and costs, it is much easier to start a business in Romania or Bulgaria than in Poland or Czech Republic (Figure 5.2).

Russia, on the other hand, is not an EU member which may explain less developed market institutions. It is suggested the Russian government arguably acted like a "grabbing hand" and discouraged entrepreneurial activities. The "merchant capitalism" thesis suggested that the dominant direction of change in the former Soviet Union would be "backward" or towards a more primitive merchant capitalism rather than a free-market-based more advanced capitalism.[59]

We can use an example of the Skolkovo project to illustrate barriers facing entrepreneurship in Russia. Progress in the Skolkovo project has been slower than expected. Observers have noted that after Vladimir Putin's return for a third presidential term in 2012, the project has been relegated to a low-priority list.[60] Whereas Medvedev has placed a higher priority on innovation and economic development, Putin's priorities have been in fulfilling his campaign promises such as increasing the availability of emergency housing and public kindergartens.[61] There are also alleged engagements in corruption by government officials.[62] In 2013, criminal cases against two high-ranking officials of the Skolkovo project were filed. The two officials allegedly embezzled $800,000 from the project, which was provided by the government to develop the infrastructure and support local startups.[63]

Values, Culture, and Skills

Entrepreneurial Culture

The battle to promote market entrepreneurship is about more than just creating market friendly political and economic institutions. In this regard, it is important to note that socialism was characterized by a negative social perception of entrepreneurs and market entrepreneurship. Attempts to promote entrepreneurship in some FSU&CEE economies face crucial cultural, social, and cognitive challenges related to skills and psychology. Societal norms and networks that provide support for entrepreneurial risk taking in matured markets are lacking in PS economies. For instance, Russian managers with experience in state-owned enterprises tend to avoid risk.[64] In addition, overcoming institutional inertia such as those related to a lack of accountability, initiative and trust to others has been a problem.[65]

Some have attributed the degree of religious-secular differentiation to explain the heterogeneity in the FSU&CEE economies' entrepreneurial performance. Note that thanks to the communist history, some FSU& CEE economies have large populations of nonpracticing believers and nonbelievers. Among the believers, however, dominant religions in economies in Belarus, Bulgaria, Romania, Russia, and Ukraine are various forms of Orthodox Christianity, which lacked the religious-secular differentiation.[66] On the other hand, Roman Catholic is the dominant religion in Croatia, Czech Republic, Estonia, Hungary, Lithuania, Poland, and

Table 5.1 Some Examples of Barriers to Entrepreneurship in Economies in the Orthodox Group

Country	Institutional barriers to entrepreneurship in CEE economies
Belarus	Businesses are dominated by Soviet-era managers that lack free-market mindsets.
Bulgaria	Bulgarians did not experience the 20th-century capitalist production methods and work habits, risks, and rewards.a After the fall of the communist system in the late 1980s, secret service agents were reported to engage in organized crimes.
Romania	Beginning the late 1980s, political elites started converting their positional power for starting businesses.b
Russia	Following the mass privatization, former nomenklatura appointees accounted for two-thirds of the top positions in businesses and the government. 2002–2011: about 3 million entrepreneurs were imprisoned.
Ukraine	Predatory actions of state officials hinder rural entrepreneurship. Powerful oligarchs have a strong influence on government policies. Businesses are dominated by Soviet-era managers that lack free-market mindsets. The regulatory burden on business takes 14% of a manager's time.

a Spenner, K.I., & Jones, D.C. 1998. "Social economic transformation in Bulgaria: An empirical assessment of the merchant capitalism thesis," *Social Forces*, 76(3), pp. 937–965.
b Stoica, C.A. 2004. "From good communists to even better capitalists? Entrepreneurial pathways in post-socialist Romania," *East European Politics and Societies*, 18(2), pp. 236–277.

Slovakia. It is argued that in the Orthodox countries, informal institutions did not change at the same rate as formal institutions. The Orthodox tradition viewed entrepreneurship negatively and socialism further reinforced the stereotypes. Table 5.1 presents some examples of barriers to entrepreneurship in economies that have Orthodox Christianity as the dominant form of religion.

Entrepreneurial Capabilities

The growth of new enterprise hinges critically upon the availability of entrepreneurial skills to effectively carry out business functions. Some FSU&CEE economies severely lack these skills. Russian managers with experience and training gained under the communist system in state-owned enterprises lack management and business skills needed for free-market entrepreneurship. For instance, observers have noted that the majority of managers who are still running most Russian enterprises have values from the Soviet period as well as values passed on from the previous tsarist era.[67] In general, in CEE economies, while there is no dearth of technology talent, management and marketing skills have been in a short supply. As to the lack of marketing skills, it is important to note that traditionally, a central plan rather than the consumer was the driving force of national production in these economies.

Measures are being taken at various levels to improve entrepreneurial capabilities in most FSU&CEE economies. For instance, by 1995, Poland had 50 business incubators owned by foundations, associations, or local governments, which offered offices for entrepreneurs at lower rents. In order to raise long-term entrepreneurial awareness, Poland's Ministry of Education has introduced an entrepreneurship curriculum at all education levels.[68] The country has also developed policies to attract the diaspora. Poland's new diaspora policy has identified one of the main tasks as to establish a feedback mechanism between Poland and its diaspora living in other countries.[69] These efforts are reflected in Poland's SME-friendly environment. SMEs account for 30% of GDP in Poland compared to 10%–15% in Russia.[70]

Observers have also noted that international practices such as international accounting standards, transparency standards, and corporate governance rules are diffusing rapidly in the region. Likewise, Western professional service providers are operating throughout the region to provide various skills needed for carrying out entrepreneurial activities.

Access to Finance, Market, R&D, and Technology

Access to Market

As noted earlier, institutional reforms in FSU&CEE economies which are members of international organizations such as the OECD, the EU, and the NATO were constantly monitored. Especially the EU members have well-developed competition and antitrust laws in place, which make it easy for a new company to enter the market. Moreover, the EU members also have easy access to the combined population of over 500 million inhabitants in the EU. Entrepreneurial firms in economies that are not EU members, however, face problems related to the access to market.

R&D and Technology

Some FSU&CEE economies have made a significant progress in R&D and technology creation. For instance, many investors think that Russians, Poles, and Romanians outperform the Chinese and the Indian in the creation and operation of high-tech startups needed for breakthrough innovations.[71] CEE economies' superior performance in R&D and IT can be

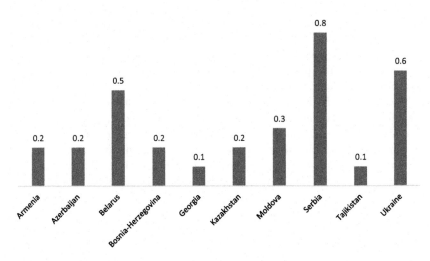

Figure 5.3 Gross Domestic Expenditure on R&D as a Percentage of GDP in Selected FSU&CEE Economies (2017).
Source: Euromonitor International.

attributed to the region's traditional emphasis on science and engineering. Speaking of emphasis on mathematics in Romania, a scientist in Bucharest put the issue this way: "The respect for math is inside every family, even simple families, who are very proud to say their children are good at mathematics."[72]

As Figure 5.3 makes it clear, expenditure on R&D is very low in most of the FSU&CEE economies. However, some of these economies have been heavily engaged in R&D activities in some cutting-edge technologies. One such area is blockchain. As noted in Chapter 1, Georgia has emerged as a global blockchain hub. In 2016, the Swiss startup DECENT Foundation teamed up with local partners in Armenia to establish a Blockchain R&D hub.[73]

Access to Finance

The infrastructures for the financial and capital markets such as banks, stock exchanges, and various sources of venture capital were destroyed in most FSU&CEE economies under communism. Entrepreneurial finance is difficult to obtain and is costly in most of these economies. As Figure 5.4 makes it clear, in most of the FSU&CEE economies, annual lending rates are high.

Nonetheless, most CEE economies have made a significant progress in reforming and developing the financial sector. Due to CEE economies' superior performance in R&D, some VC investors consider the region

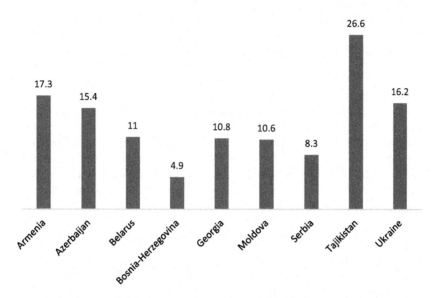

Figure 5.4 Annual Lending Rates in Some FSU&CEE Economies (2017).
Source: Euromonitor International.

more attractive than India and China. This is especially the case for high-tech startups with global potential. By 2007, OpenView Venture Partners, an expansion stage venture capital fund focusing on high-growth technology companies had invested 30% of the company's US$100 million global technology fund in the CEE region. Scott Maxwell, cofounder of the company, noted, "Central and Eastern Europe are already a better play [than China and India]. The technologies are more sophisticated."[74]

According to European Private Equity & Venture Capital Association, CEE economies attracted €645 million (US$900 million) in private equity and venture capital in 2010, which was 60% higher than in 2009. Poland, Czech Republic, Romania, Ukraine, Bulgaria, and Hungary accounted for 94% of the total private equity for the CEE region.[75]

While a weak financial sector and a lack of entrepreneurial skills has hindered the inflow VC and other forms of foreign investments in Russia, there have been many success stories. For instance, as early as in the mid-1990s, Russia had VC-funded companies in the technology sectors that employed high-profile scientists.[76] Domestic venture capital industry is also developing rapidly. In a meeting with U.S. venture capitalists in 2010, Russian President Dmitri Medvedev noted there were about 20 venture funds in the country with combined assets of about $2 billion. Some companies have also raised substantial funds from international IPOs. In May 2011, Yandex NV, also known as "the Russian Google" raised $1.3 billion on NASDAQ.[77]

Concluding Comments

FSU&CEE countries are undergoing a fundamental shift from a centrally planned economy to an entrepreneurial economy. Due to institutional inertia, formal and informal institutions in many FSU&CEE economies are currently less supportive of free-market entrepreneurship than in matured market economies. In many cases, the existing institutions tend to contribute to ineffective entrepreneurial thinking, behavior, and decision making. The issue here thus is not that FSU&CEE economies lack entrepreneurship talents but that a significant proportion of entrepreneurial ventures in these economies lack the characteristics of productive free-market entrepreneurship. The promotion of productive free-market entrepreneurship in FSU&CEE economies requires drastic changes in formal and informal institutions.

Transition from central plan to free market is a complicated process requiring economic, political, and social transformations for FSU&CEE economies. We noted above that FSU&CEE economies vary in terms of the development of free-market entrepreneurship as well as institutions to support private enterprises such as protection of property rights. While some economies have made a quantum leap on that front, institutional changes seem to be more of an upward drift rather than a surge in others' cases. At the same time, there is no clear definition of the type of market economy desired by these economies.

The differences between the entrepreneurially successful and unsuccessful economies, for instance, can be attributed to the entrepreneurial traditions during the communism and precommunism era. For instance, compared with the Czech Republic, Poland, and Hungary, the state was the principal entrepreneur in Russia and private entrepreneurship had a weak tradition even before the revolution. Moreover, during the communism era, while some form of private entrepreneurship was allowed in Hungary and Poland, Russia, and Romania entirely depended on the central planning.[78] Especially Russia spent eight decades under communism, which was longer time than other FSU&CEE economies. The critical elements of the infrastructures of modern capitalism were destructed in the country. It lacks impartial court and secure private property rights. Commercial organizations lack transparency and accountability. Consequently, there has been a higher degree of resistance to construct market institutions.

We also discussed the existence of parasitic entrepreneurs in some FSU&CEE economies. If there is any lesson that biological parasites' actions in environmental ecology teach, it is that the parasitic entrepreneurs adversely affect the host (the state) and may also mediate the influence the state has on other components of the entrepreneurial ecosystem.[79] The presence of these parasitic entrepreneurs may negatively affect health of the economy, economic growth, formation of new firms and their growth, and may increase firm mortality rates.

What conditions can transform the rules of the game so that various forms of unproductive and inefficient forms of entrepreneurship can be converted into productive and efficient free-market entrepreneurship? In most cases, formal institutions are easier to change compared to informal institutions. Deinstitutionalization and reinstitutionalization of social practices, cultural values, and beliefs occur very slowly.[80] A related point is that formal institutions affect and are affected by informal institutions. For instance, entrepreneurship-friendly laws and regulations may erode the hostility to entrepreneurship and profit making at the societal level. Likewise, with the development of skills and expertise needed for free-market entrepreneurship, psychology of risk taking, and social networks to provide support for entrepreneurship, the governments are likely to face pressures to enact new laws and regulations.

One final, but not less important, aspect of informal institutions in FSU&CEE economies that renders it interesting to us is the fact entrepreneurs can take measures to change them in favor of private entrepreneurship. Indeed, as the cases of Chile and Ireland discussed in Chapter 4 suggest, negative social perception of profit making behavior is not a phenomenon observed only in FSU&CEE economies. In this regard, FSU&CEE economies can also borrow a page from Timbro's lesson book (Chapter 2) to change the negative social perception of entrepreneurs and entrepreneurship.

End of Chapter Questions

1   In terms of legality and ideology, what are the different types of entrepreneurial activities in FSU&CEE economies?
2   How are formal and informal institutions affecting entrepreneurial activities in FSU&CEE economies?
3   What are some examples of productive, unproductive, and destructive forms of entrepreneurship in FSU&CEE economies?
4   Give some examples of positive externalities generated by criminal and illegal enterprises?
5   Why do FSU&CEE economies differ in terms of their transition to market economies?
6   Select a FSU&CEE economy. What are the natures of formal and informal institutions for entrepreneurial activities in the economy you selected? How have they changed in recent years?
7   How can productive entrepreneurship be promoted in FSU&CEE Economies?

End of the Chapter Case: Kaspersky Lab—From Russia with Antivirus

Outlining vision and strategy for the company he co-founded in 1997, Eugene Kaspersky, the Moscow-based Kaspersky Lab's (KL) CEO and Chairman, said,

> Our growth strategy bases on several pivotal points, those are: deliver best protection to all our customers, be they consumers or corporate clients and develop best of breed technologies that ensure reliable protection. "Our growth rates prove that it is a good strategy and it will bring us to the leading position on the marketplace."[81]

Headquartered in Russia, KL provides information technology (IT) security software such as antivirus, anti-spam, and network security software to protect computer users against viruses, hackers, and spam. In 2010, KL was the world's fourth biggest IT security company. Due to KL's success in developing innovative products to fight cybercrime, the company was ranked No. 32 in Fast Company's 2011 list of the World's 50 Most Innovative Companies.[82]

The company lagged behind its chief rivals substantially. The two U.S. household names Symantec and McAfee as well as Japan's Trend Micro were much bigger than KL. Symantec and McAfee were described as "an elephant to Kaspersky's mouse" in the global software security market, which was estimated at $16.6 billion in 2010.[83] KL's other top competitors included Finland's F-Secure, Britain' Sophos, Spain's Panda Software and Norway's Norman, Czech Republic's AVG Technologies, Romania's Bit-Defender, Israel's Check Point, and Slovak Republic's ESET.

KL's Inception and the Early Years

Eugene Kaspersky studied in the A.N. Kolmogorov School in Moscow that specializes in physics and mathematics. In 1987, he graduated with a degree in mathematical engineering from Moscow's Institute of Cryptography, Telecommunications and Computer Science. After graduation, he worked for the Russian defense department as a cryptologist and then in KAMI Information Technologies Center. In 1994, Natalya Kaspersky joined him in KAMI, and in 1997 they cofounded an independent company.

Before starting KL, Eugene Kaspersky had developed some antivirus products to pursue his hobby of capturing computer viruses. A complete virus protection package, AntiViral Toolkit Pro was the first product he developed. In a series of independent tests conducted by Germany's Hamburg University, this product won top marks. A virus encyclopedia was among Eugene Kaspersky's early works, which provided analysis and descriptions of tens of thousands of viruses and how they functioned. KL developed many technological standards for the antivirus industry.

KL is Russia's largest software company and the only Russian firm among the world's top 100 software companies. In 2009, the market research firm, IDC's study indicated that KL was the world's 76th biggest Packaged Software Vendors (ranked by 2008 revenue). As of 2011, KL was Europe's largest antivirus company and the world's largest privately held Internet security company.

Tables 5.2 and 5.3 present some indicators related to KL's growth and reputation. While the company performed most of the R&D activities in Russia, its R&D centers were also located in some regional offices—in the U.S. and in China. In 2010, KL got about 84% of its sales outside Russia.[84]

Table 5.2 KL's Workforce and Revenue Growthsa

Year	No. of employees	Revenue (million, US$)	Geographic breakdown of KL revenue	Competitors' performance
2004		24		
2006		67		
2007	900	130	Russia: US$23.4 million, CIS & Baltic countries: US$5 million	Symantec: $2.8 billion from security
2008	1250	274	Russia: US$49.1 million Consumer products: 55%, businesses: 33%.	Symantec: $2.31 billion and McAfee: US$1.13 billion
2009	1787 (631 in R&D).	**391**	Europe: US$188 million, Eastern Europe Middle East Africa (EEMEA): US$97 million, Americas: US$80 million, Asia and Pacific (APAC): US$26 million Consumer: US$255 million, corporate: US$109 million, technology alliances: US$27 million	Symantec: $2.39 billion and McAfee: US$1.19 billion
2010	2,338 (1500 in Russia) 818 in R&D	**538**	Europe: $218 million, Americas region: $134 million, Asia-Pacific region and Japan: $55 million, CIS, Eastern Europe, the Middle East and Africa: $131 million	Symantec: $3.1 billion McAfee: $1.85 billion

(Continued)

Year	No. of employees	Revenue (million, US$)	Geographic breakdown of KL revenue	Competitors' performance
2016		633	Western Europe and the U.S. accounted for $374 million.[b]	
2017	3,900	698[c]	European sales declined by 2% in 2017. It saw strong results in Latin America, as well as Russia and the CIS.[c]	

a Kshetri, N. 2011. "Kaspersky lab: From Russia with anti-virus," *Emerald Emerging Markets Case Studies*, 1(3), pp. 1–10.
b Robertson, J., & Riley, M. 2017. "Kaspersky lab has been working with Russian intelligence," www.bloomberg.com/news/articles/2017-07-11/kaspersky-lab-has-been-working-with-russian-intelligence.
c Reuters. 2018. "Kaspersky Lab 2017 revenue up 8 percent, North America sales fall," www.reuters.com/article/us-russia-kaspersky-lab-results/kaspersky-lab-2017-revenue-up-8-percent-north-america-sales-fall-idUSKBN1F818F.

Table 5.3 Major Events Related to KL's Performance

Time	Event
1994	The AntiViral Toolkit Pro by Eugene Kaspersky was recognized as the best antivirus scanner in the world by Hamburg University test lab.
1997	KL was founded.
2003	KL entered China.
2005	Independent U.S. entity, Kaspersky Lab, Inc. was established.
May 2008	KL had 12 offices worldwide and a partner network of over 500 companies in 100 countries.
October 2008	KL opened an office in Hong Kong.
October 2008	KL opened a Melbourne office (for Oceania) and a Southeast Asia office in Selangor, Malaysia.
Early 2009	KL opened an office in Dubai Internet City.
September 2009	Kaspersky received the National Friendship Award of China.
2009	Kaspersky received the Russian state prize from President Medvedev for improving state security.
2010	KL opened its first Indian office in Hyderabad.
February 2010	KL was named one of the Top 10 Power Brands by PC.com, and voted 'Best Antivirus Software' by the magazine's readers.
April 2010	KL had a direct presence in 29 countries.
April 2010	KL won the Security Brand of the Year award at the Channel Awards.
June 2010	Boston Business Journal's survey found KL as one of the Best Places to Work in Massachusetts.
June 2010	Kaspersky won the Asia Entrepreneur Alliance (AEA) International Distinguished Entrepreneur as CEO of growth and expansion.

Time	Event
November 2010	KL was honored with the Strategic Brand Leadership Award in India.
February 2011	K ranked No. 32 in Fast Company's 2011 list of the World's 50 Most Innovative Companies.
May 2011	90 patent applications related to IT security technologies filed by KL were being processed by in the U.S., Russia, China, and Europe.
2015	KL had 400 million individual users and 270,000 corporate clients.[a]
September 2017	The U.S. banned civilian government agencies from using KL products.

a Menn, J. 2015. "Exclusive: Russian antivirus firm faked malware to harm rivals – Ex-employees," 14 August, www.reuters.com/article/us-kaspersky-rivals/exclusive-russian-antivirus-firm-faked-malware-to-harm-rivals-ex-employees-idUSKCN0Q JICR20150814.

KL had various incentives to attract and retain qualified employees. In 2000, the firm's turnover rate was less than 3%.[85] A survey conducted by The Boston Business Journal in 2010 also named KL as one of the Best Places to Work in Massachusetts. Roger Wilson, KL Vice-President, Marketing noted that the company provided stock options to employees and helped them find housing as well as deal with Russia's bureaucracy to obtain residency permits.[86] This was in stark contrast to most Russian companies, which paid poorly to their employees and payments were unrelated to productivity. Moreover, compensations in most Russian firms rarely included bonuses and stock options in the country.[87]

The Russian Business Environment

Speaking of the barriers in the development of productive entrepreneurship in Russia, Eugene Kaspersky recently put the issue this way: "Russia has a lot of talented software engineers but not a lot of successful businesses. People still have an iron curtain in their minds."[88] When KL was launched, there was no government incentive program in Russia.[89] The lack of proper incentives had also led to a brain drain. According to AmBar, the Russian business association, 30,000–60,000 Russian-speaking professionals worked in the San Francisco Bay Area.[90]

When a KL office was opened in Tianjin, China in 2003, the company benefited from Chinese government's incentives for startups in special economic zone, which included a free office space for a year and a tax holiday.[91] Pointing out the impacts of well-developed infrastructure, tax incentives, and other support networks on the development of the Chinese IT industry, Natalya Kaspersky noted that a similar technology park would stimulate entrepreneurship in Russia.[92]

Since KL relies heavily on intellectual property (IP) for its success, it faced a unique challenge in Russia due to weak IP protection laws and enforcement mechanisms. In most industrialized countries, duties and obligations to one's former employer, confidentiality clauses, and noncompete agreements would prohibit a departing worker from taking valuable information with them. Natalya Kaspersky noted that such agreements were ineffective in Russia.[93] An employee in the Russian Internet advertiser, System.ru, who reportedly took the firm's entire client database to a newly formed rival, was an eye opener for IT firms such as KL.[94]

Trends in the IT Security Industry

The growth of IT security industry is associated with and facilitated by a rapid rise in the cybercrime industry. Some estimates suggest that the global cybercrime industry generated US$1 trillion in 2009.[95] According to IDC, the secure content and threat management sector was worth US$15.1 billion in 2007 and US$21 billion in 2011.

Another important trend was global technology developers' business models based on open innovation and open source. Such models facilitated individuals and enterprises worldwide to develop applications. For instance, Google created an open environment for Android. Developers such as KL could sign up to the Android Marketplace and develop software. The rapidly transforming cybercrime landscape also provided opportunities for Kaspersky Lab and other developing world-based firms to use their technical expertise to expand market. The Romanian IT firm, BitDefender, for instance, was the first to develop a clean-up tool for the Sasser worm in May 2004.[96]

KL, nonetheless, benefitted greatly from the Soviet-era investments in science and engineering. KL considered Russia as an appropriate location to develop IT security products due to the country's skilled workforce and a prevalence of the culture of computer hacking. Eugene Kaspersky noted,

> There are technical universities in every major city and with one million students graduating every year, and there is a big labor market for software engineers. ....Russian engineers are much more expensive than in China or India, who are good if you just want something programmed, but if it's about research, then it has to be Russia.[97]

The Russian environment provides a fertile ground for hackers. Experts say that Russian hackers possess capability to perform sophisticated operations with limited computer power and inexpensive software. 82% of respondents participating in a worldwide poll conducted on a hacker-oriented website indicated that Russia had the world's best computer hackers. Only 5% of the respondents believed that American hackers were the best.[98] In the U.S. National Security Agency-backed "hacking" competition of 2009, among the 4,200 participants, 10 finalists were from Russia, compared to two from the U.S. Noting that the company had no plans to move its R&D in locations such as the Middle East, Eugene Kaspersky noted, "What we really need is the pool of talented engineers and I think Russian software engineers are the best, which is why our core R&D is in Moscow."[99]

KL's Product-Market Strategy and Performance

The company had a stronger competitive position in the consumer market compared to the business market. According to Gartner, KL was the world's third largest vendor of consumer IT security software and fifth largest vendor of Enterprise Endpoint Protection based on 2010 revenues. In addition, dozens of original equipment manufacturers (OEMs) such as Microsoft, IBM, and Cisco used Kaspersky Lab's antivirus engine through licensing.[100]

KL's top consumer products in 2010 were Kaspersky Internet Security and Kaspersky Anti-Virus. In 2009, over 250 million consumers worldwide used KL's products and services (including Technology Alliances) and the company added 50,000 new users every day.[101] As of December 2010, KL's products were used by over 300 million people and about 200,000 organizations.[102] The company had a strong foothold in Russia. The company also occupied strong competitive positions in major emerging markets. In China, KL had 100 million users in 2010.[103] The company's growth markets in Asia also include Thailand, Vietnam, the Philippines, Singapore, and Indonesia.[104]

While KL had an indirect presence through OEM in the U.S. market for some time,[105] the company was a relative late comer in the U.S. market. KL made visible efforts to make up for the late start. In 2006, KL's Internet Suite and Anti-Virus titles began selling through CompUSA, Fry's Electronics, and Office Depot.[106] KL also recruited retailers and distributors such as Best Buy and Staples. In North America (the U.S. and Canada), the number of retail stores selling KL products increased from 200 in 2006 to 15,000 in 2008.[107] KL gave these retailers more attractive profit margins compared to its competitors. KL also provided marketing and technical supports. Jon Oltsik, senior analyst at Enterprise Strategy Group (ESG) commented that KL's approach was based on a "tender, loving care model." The major target market consisted of consumers who were willing to pay extra for a high-quality security programs.[108] Stephen Orenberg, KL's Chief Sales Officer, noted that the company targets "savvier" users interested in results rather than a low price or loyalty to other brands.[109]

IPO Plan Scrapped

The company had an IPO plan, which was postponed due to the 2008 global financial crisis. Regarding the motivations behind an IPO, Eugene Kaspersky commented,

The main reason is not to get money—we have enough—but to raise corporate profile and become more transparent that contribute a lot into company's positions on corporate market, especially in the US and the UK. Gaining market share in corporate segment is one of the key priorities of KL business development.

It is also important to note that KL's two largest competitors McAfee and Symantec are public companies. Symantec was founded in 1982 and went public in 1989. McAfee was founded in 1987 and is a wholly owned subsidiary of Intel Corporation. John Bernstein, General Atlantic managing director and KL board member expected that KL would go for an IPO by 2016. Bernstein said, "We intend to help them with all the steps towards that [IPO]."[110]

In 2012, however, the company announced that it gave up its idea to hold an IPO (www.forbes.com/sites/kenrapoza/2012/02/08/internet-security-co-kaspersky-lab-shelves-ipo-idea-2/#6c07d31e7f69). Kaspersky said that in order to be "as flexible as possible" in making serious decisions, his company would "stay private." He further noted that a public company is "too bureaucratic" which may limit the ability to make decisions in a timely manner (www.ewdn.com/2013/02/06/kaspersky-lab-drops-ipo-plan-to-remain-flexible/)

Alleged Engagement in Espionage Activities

There were reports that Kaspersky antivirus software would furnish Russian intelligence agencies with powerful tools to hijack any computer using the software.[111] Citing internal company emails *Bloomberg Businessweek* reported that KL had maintained a much closer relationship with the Russian intelligence agency, the FSB, than the company had publicly admitted.[112]

In May 2017, six U.S. intelligence and law enforcement agency chiefs were asked in an open Senate hearing whether they would allow their networks to use Kaspersky software. All of them unanimously answered that they would not.[113] The U.S. banned civilian government agencies from using Kaspersky products in September 2017.[114]

In December 2017, the U.S. Congress banned Kaspersky. The ban was the result of the concern that the Russian government might have control over the company's tools, which could be used to steal information from the U.S. government agencies and U.S. companies. As a result of the ban, Kaspersky's U.S. retail sales fell by 61% during the fourth quarter of the FY 2017 compared with the same quarter the year before.[115]

Antivirus products are delicate since they have access to every file on the computers they intend to protect. The software regularly communicates with the antivirus company receive updates, which may provide access to data of sensitive users such as government agencies, banks, and internet companies.[116]

KL's revenue increased 8% in 2017. Sales fell in North America because of the allegations about its link to the Russian government.[117] Eugene Kaspersky responded to the accusation by stressing that its alleged ties to the Kremlin were "unfounded conspiracy theories."[118]

Case Summary

KL is a high-profile example of a successful Russian company that has grown rapidly in the past few decades. The company has been able to gain a dominant position in the antivirus product market in a short period of time.

Kl's alleged engagement in espionage activities *is a big* concern for its growth in the U.S. market. The sensitive nature of product and its Russian origin have played a key role in the recent decline of KL's sales in the U.S. market.

Notes

1 Corcoran, J., & Galouchko, K. 2012. "Russian Silicon Valley plans first IPO as venture capital booms," 20 July, www.bloomberg.com/news/2012-07-20/russian-silicon-valley-plans-first-ipo-as-venture-capital-booms.html.
2 Neate, R. 2012. "Russia reaches for the stars with its own Silicon Valley," *The Observer*, 18 February www.guardian.co.uk/business/2012/feb/19/russia-investment-drive-skolkovo-silicon-valley.
3 Fedynsky, P. 2010. "High risk for venture capital in Russia," 26 May, www.voanews.com/english/news/economy-and-business/High-Risk-for-Venture-Capital-in-Russia-94929299.html.
4 OECD Economic Surveys: Poland 2010, Making the most of globalization. April 2010(8), pp. 95–147.
5 Ibid.
6 Jurney, C. 2017. "The world's largest public companies 2017," 24 May, www.forbes.com/sites/corinnejurney/2017/05/24/the-worlds-largest-public-companies-2017/#63574d4a508d.
7 OECD Economic Surveys. 2009b. Russian Federation, Stabilisation and renewed growth: key challenges, 2009(6), pp. 19–51.
8 Wright, M., Karsai, J., Dudzinski, Z., & Morovic, J. 1999. "Transition and active investors: Venture capital in Hungary, Poland and Slovakia," *Post-Communist Economies*, 11(1), pp. 27–47.
9 Karasz, P. 2012. "Hungarian start-ups defy economic climate," 22 May, www.nytimes.com/2012/05/23/business/global/hungarian-start-ups-defy-economic-climate.html.
10 Stoica, C.A. 2004. "From good communists to even better capitalists? Entrepreneurial pathways in post-socialist Romania," *East European Politics and Societies*, 18(2), pp. 236–277.
11 forbes.com. 2018. "Meet the members of the three-comma club," 6 March, www.forbes.com/billionaires/#1f9d3896251c.
12 Canberra Times. 2010. "What the world needs now is definitely not 1011 billionaires," 17 March, p. 11.

13 Kesby, R. 2012. "Why Russia locks up so many entrepreneurs," 5 July, www.bbc.com/news/magazine-18706597.
14 Kramer, A., & Norris, F. 2005. "Amid growing wealth, nepotism and nationalism in Kazakhstan," *The New York Times*, 23 December.
15 Gorodnichenko, Y., & Grygorenko, Y. 2005. "Are oligarchs productive? Theory and evidence." Mimeo, University of Michigan.
16 According to Plato, "oligarchy" is governance by a small group of people. In Plato's approach, oligarchs are different from nobles in terms of legality. Whereas nobles are few but rightful rulers, oligarchs rule in an unlawful way. In the contemporary literature, an oligarch is a large business owner controlling sufficient resources to influence national policy making and/or judiciary to further his/her economic interests.
17 Blanchflower, D.G., Oswald, A., & Stutzer, A. 2001. "Latent entrepreneurship across nations," *European Economic Review*, 45(4–6), p. 680.
18 Yang, K. 2002. "Double entrepreneurship in China's economic reform: An analytical framework," *Journal of Political and Military Sociology*, 30(1), pp. 134–148; Yang, K. 2004. "Institutional holes and entrepreneurship in China," *Sociological Review*, 52(3), pp. 371–389.
19 Stark, D. 1996. "Recombinant property in East European capitalism," *American Journal of Sociology*, 101, pp. 993–1027.
20 Warner, M., & Daugherty, C.W. 2004. "Promoting the 'Civic' in entrepreneurship: The case of rural Slovakia," *Journal of the Community Development Society*, 35(1), pp. 117–134.
21 McCarthy, D.J., & Puffer, S.M. 2008. "Interpreting the ethicality of corporate governance decisions in Russia: Utilizing integrative social contracts theory to evaluate the relevance of agency theory norms," *Academy of Management Review*, 33(1), pp. 11–31.
22 Williams, C.C. 2009. "The hidden economy in east-central Europe: Lessons from a ten-nation survey," *Problems of Post-Communism*, 56(4), pp. 15–28.
23 Warner & Daugherty. 2004
24 O'Rourke, P.J. 2000. "The godfather decade," *Foreign Policy*, 121, pp. 74–81.
25 Ibid.
26 Szilagyi, G. (u.d.) "Harmonization of regional economic and social policies within the Romanian-Hungarian-Ukrainian border area," www.policy.hu/szilagyi/respaper.htm.
27 O'Rourke. 2000.
28 Kuznetsov, A., McDonald, F., & Kuznetsova, O. 2000. "Entrepreneurial qualities: A case from Russia," *Journal of Small Bus Management*, 38(1), pp. 101–108.
29 Stark. 1996.
30 The nomenklatura were people within the former Soviet Union and other Eastern Bloc countries, who occupied key administrative positions. The communist party of country needed to approve the positions.
31 Hankiss, E. 1990. *East European Alternatives*. Oxford, UK: Clarendon.
32 Eyal, G., Szelényi, I., & Townsley, E. 1998. *Making Capitalism without Capitalists: The New Ruling Elites in Eastern Europe*. London: Verso.
33 Guriev, S., & Rachinsky, A. "The evolution of personal wealth in the former Soviet Union and Central and Eastern Europe," http://siteresources.world bank.org/INTDECINEQ/Resources/Evolution_of_personal_wealth.pdf.
34 Feige, E. 1997. "Underground activity and institutional change: Productive, protective, and predatory behavior in transition economies," In: Nelson, J., Tilly, C., & Walker, L. (eds.), *Transforming Post-Communist Political Economies*, Washington DC: National Academy Press

35 Lazarev, V. 2005. "Economics of one-party state: Promotion incentives and support for the Soviet regime," *Comparative Economic Studies*, 47(2), p. 346.
36 Merton, R. 1968. *Social Theory and Social Structure*. New York: Free Press.
37 Ebbeling, C., Pawlak, D., & Ludwig, D. 2002. "Childhood obesity: public-health crisis, common sense cure," *The Lancet*, 360(9331), pp. 473–482.
38 Rivoli, P. 2005. "The Travels of a T-shirt in the Global Economy: An Economist Examines the Markets, Power, and Politics of World Trade," Hoboken, NJ: John Wiley and Sons.
39 Stoica, C.A. 2004. "From good communists to even better capitalists? Entrepreneurial pathways in post-socialist Romania."
40 Chen, A. 2002. "Capitalist development, entrepreneurial class, and democratization in China," *Political Science Quarterly*, 117(3), pp. 401–422.
41 Kshetri, N., & Ajami, R. 2008. "Institutional reforms in the Gulf Cooperation Council economies: A conceptual framework," *Journal of International Management*, 14(3), pp. 300–318.
42 Atkine, N.B.D. 2006. "Islam, Islamism and terrorism," *Army*, 56(1), pp. 55–62.
43 Greenwood, R., & Suddaby, R. 2006. "Institutional entrepreneurship in mature fields: The big five accounting firms," *Academy of Management Journal*, 49, pp. 27–48.
44 Ibid.
45 Yang, 2004.
46 Groenewegen, J., & van der Steen, M. 2007. "The evolutionary policy maker," *Journal of Economic Issues*, 41(2), pp. 351–358.
47 Daokui Li, D., Feng, J., & Jiang, H. 2006. "Institutional Entrepreneurs," *American Economic Review*, 96(2), pp. 358–362.
48 Polaczek, P. 2016. "Red tape makes economy bleed," http://bpcc.org.pl/contact-magazine/issues/14/categories/63/articles/415.
49 Ibid.
50 The World Bank. 2017. "Poland ranks 27th in World Bank's doing business report," www.worldbank.org/en/news/press-release/2017/10/31/poland-ranks-27th-in-world-bank-doing-business-report.
51 BizNES. 2017. "Falitations for entrepreneurs," www.biznes.gov.pl/en/przedsiebiorcy/biznes-w-polsce/prowadze-firme/ulatwienia-dla-firm-od-2017.
52 Radio Poland. 2017. "Polish FinMin's 100 changes for business plan 90% complete: report," www.thenews.pl/1/12/Artykul/331872,Polish-FinMins-100-changes-for-business-plan-90-complete-report.
53 Polish League against Defamation. 2017. "Government reforms in Poland—The impact so far and future prospects," Part 1—Social Reforms.
54 Yang. 2002b.
55 Alexeev, M. 1999. "The effect of privatization on wealth distribution in Russia," *Economics of Transition*, 7(2), pp. 449–465.
56 Negoita, M. 2006. "The social bases of development: Hungary and Romania in comparative perspective," *Socio-Economic Review*, 4(2), pp. 209–238.
57 Stoica, 2004.
58 OECD. 2002. OECD Economic Surveys: Romania, Paris, Organization for Economic Co-operation and Development, Paris.
59 Burawoy, M., & Krotov, P. 1992. "The Soviet transition from socialism to capitalism: Worker Control and Economic Bargaining in the Wood Industry," *American Sociological Review*, 57, pp. 16–38.
60 France-Presse, A. 2013. "Russian invsestigators search Skolkovo hi-tech hub," 18 April, www.globalpost.com/dispatch/news/afp/130418/russian-invsestigators-search-skolkovo-hi-tech-hub.

61 Barry, E. 2013. "Video shows an angry Putin threatening to dismiss officials," 17 April, www.nytimes.com/2013/04/18/world/europe/video-shows-putin-threatening-to-dismiss-officials.html.
62 RIA Novosti. 2013. *Investigators Search Russian "Silicon Valley,"* 18 April, http://en.ria.ru/crime/20130418/180707737.html.
63 RIA Novosti. 2013.
64 Taylor, T.C., & Kazakov, A.Y. 1997. "Business Ethics and Civil Society in Russia," *International Study of Management of Organization*, 27, pp. 5–18.
65 Ibid.
66 Pipes R. 1992. *Russia under the Old Regime*. New York: Collier Books.
67 Taylor and Kazakov, 1997.
68 OECD Economic Surveys: Poland 2010.
69 isria.com. 2011. "Poland – The Minister of Foreign Affairs on Polish Foreign Policy for 2011", www.isria.com/pages/24_March_2011_18.php.
70 Goldman, M. 2006. "Russia's middle class muddle," *Current History*, 105(693), pp. 321–327; Euro-East. 2000. "Euro-East: Training for enterprise in transition economies," *Euro-East*, 19 December, p. 1.
71 "Where the VCs are flocking now," June 11, 2007, www.businessweek.com/magazine/content/07_24/b4038056.htm.
72 Wylie, I. 2007. "Internet; Romania home base for EBay scammers; the auction website has dispatched its own cyber-sleuth to help police crack fraud rings," *Los Angeles Times*, 26 December, C.1.
73 forbes.ge. 2016. Blockchain R&D Hub of Swiss DECENT launched in Caucasus, http://forbes.ge/news/1703/Blockchain-R%26D-Hub-of-Swiss-DECENT-launched-in-Caucasus.
74 "Where The VCs Are Flocking Now," 2007.
75 "Poland no. 1 in Central & Eastern Europe in private equity and venture capital investment in 2010", 07 August 2011, http://montreal.trade.gov.pl/en/aktualnosci/article/a,18280,.html.
76 Starikov, E.N. 1996. "The social structure of the transitional society (an attempt to "take inventory")," *Russian Social Science Review*, 37(2), p. 17.
77 Kolyandr, A. 2011. "Russian firm holds biggest virtual IPO so far," 3 June, http://blogs.wsj.com/emergingeurope/2011/06/03/russian-firm-holds-biggest-virtual-ipo-so-far/.
78 Stoica. 2004.
79 Wood, C.L., Byers, J.E., Cottingham, K.L., Altman, I., Donahue, M. J., Blakeslee, A. M. H. 2007. "Parasites alter community structure," *Proceedings of the National Academy of Sciences*, www.pnas.org/content/104/22/9335.short.
80 Zweynert, J., & Goldschmidt, N. 2006. The two transitions in central and eastern Europe as processes of institutional transplantation.
81 itpro.co.uk. 2011. Tom Brewster, Q&A: Eugene Kaspersky on taking on the big boys, April 29, 2011, www.itpro.co.uk/633124/q-a-eugene-kaspersky-on-taking-on-the-big-boys.
82 fastcompany.com. 2011. "The world's most innovative companies 2011," www.fastcompany.com/most-innovative-companies/2011/profile/kaspersky-lab.php.
83 Rapooza, K. 2011. "Kaspersky's market share rises as Symantec and McAfee's Falls," *Forbes Blogs*. 13 April. http://blogs.forbes.com/kenrapoza/2011/04/13/kasperskys-market-share-rises-as-symantec-mcafees-falls/.
84 Arnold, 2011.
85 Baumgartner, E. 2001. "Private enterprise, Business Eastern Europe," 25 June, p. 4.

86 Ibid.
87 Ivanenko, V. 2005. "Markets and democracy in Russia," BOFIT Discussion Papers 16, Bank of Finland, Institute for Economies in Transition, www. google.com/url?sa=t&source=web&cd=1&ved=0CBYQFjAA&url=http %3A%2F%2Fwww.bof.fi%2FNR%2Frdonlyres%2FB58974E8-7371-496 D-9405-3B707AC97203%2F0%2Fdp1605.pdf&rct=j&q=+%22stock+ options+in+Russia%22&ei=M_YZTNmyINHyObq9oZwK&usg=AFQjCN FXAkLTGkRXVMt-KeegCG_6r-4Z7g.
88 Kramer, A.E. 2010b. "Russia aims to create a Silicon Valley of its own; Soviet Union built cities to design arms, but now tech business is the goal," *International Herald Tribune*, 12 April, p. 5.
89 Bentley,E.2009. "RussianITcompaniesletdownbyeducation,"26November, www.telegraph.co.uk/sponsored/russianow/business/6661659/Russian-IT-companies-let-down-by-education.html.
90 Kramer, A.E. 2010a. "Innovation, by order of the kremlin," 9 April, www. nytimes.com/2010/04/11/business/global/11russia.html?pagewanted=all.
91 Kramer, A.E. 2010b. Russia aims to create a Silicon Valley of its own; Soviet Union built cities to design arms, but now tech business is the goal.
92 Morris, B. 2010. Russia creates its own Silicon Valley.
93 Baumgartner. 2001.
94 Ibid.
95 Harris, S. 2009. "Digital security in an analog bureaucracy," *National Journal*, 9, 15 June, www.nationaljournal.com/njmagazine/nj_20090613_8035.php.
96 Schenker, J.L. 2004. "Europe's virus fighters are gaining attention; Cyber-security consolidation is expected," *The International Herald Tribune*, 13 May, p. 18.
97 Robinson, G.E. 1998. "Elite cohesion, regime succession and political instability in Syria," *Middle East Policy* 5(4), 159–179.
98 "Russia's Hackers: Notorious or Desperate?" CNN.com. November 20, 2000. www.cnn.com/2000/TECH/computing/11/20/russia.hackers.ap/ index.html (Accessed October 27, 2004).
99 Menon, V. 2010. "Kaspersky Lab eyes No. 3 position in endpoint security," 2 February, www.itp.net/579148-kaspersky-lab-eyes-no-3-position-in-endpoint-security.
100 fastcompany.com. 2011.
101 Luxoft. 2009. "Rapid growth compels leading antivirus software company to identify and streamline operating efficiencies," October 2009, www.luxoft. com/downloads/case_studies/Kaspersky.pdf.
102 Ranger, S. 2010. "Photos: Inside Kaspersky Lab's antivirus HQ," 2 December, www.silicon.com/technology/security/2010/12/02/photos-inside-kaspersky-labs-antivirus-hq-39746674/.
103 McMillan, R. 2010 "Kaspersky: Google hack takes spotlight from Russia," 4 February 2010 www.pcworld.com/businesscenter/article/188590/kaspersky_google_hack_takes_spotlight_from_russia.html.
104 Singh, R. 2009. "Kaspersky banks on SMEs to increase market share," *New Straits Times* (Malaysia), 16 November, p. 8.
105 Claburn, T. 2005. "From Russia with security help," *InformationWeek*, 16 February, www.informationweek.com/news/security/vulnerabilities/show Article.jhtml?articleID=60401340.
106 Olenick, D. 2006. "Kaspersky bows web security SW at retail," *TWICE: This Week in Consumer Electronics*, 22 May, 21(11), pp. 6–5.
107 Swartz, J. 2008. Russian Kaspersky Lab offers antivirus protection in U.S.
108 Ibid.

109 Olenick. 2006.
110 Arnold. 2011.
111 Grotto, A. 2018. "U.S. policy toolkit for Kaspersky labs," https://lawfareblog.com/us-policy-toolkit-kaspersky-labs.
112 Robertson, J., & Riley, M. 2017, "Kaspersky lab has been working with Russian intelligence," www.bloomberg.com/news/articles/2017-07-11/kaspersky-lab-has-been-working-with-russian-intelligence.
113 Ibid.
114 Reuters. 2018. "Kaspersky lab 2017 revenue up 8 percent, North America sales fall," www.reuters.com/article/us-russia-kaspersky-lab-results/kaspersky-lab-2017-revenue-up-8-percent-north-america-sales-fall-idUSKBN1F818F.
115 Marks, J. 2018. "The government filed motions to dismiss two Kaspersky lawsuits Monday, challenging legal and administrative bans," www.nextgov.com/cybersecurity/2018/03/us-seeks-dismiss-kaspersky-suit-against-legislative-ban/146989/.
116 Robertson and Riley. 2017.
117 Reuters. 2018.
118 Robertson and Riley. 2017.

Chapter 6

Entrepreneurship in the Gulf Cooperation Council Economies

Objectives of this chapter

This chapter's objectives include:

1   To *demonstrate* an understanding of the natures of entrepreneurial activities in GCC economies.
2   To *analyze* the facilitators and hindrances of entrepreneurship in GCC economies.
3   To *evaluate* some of the barriers to changes in institutions needed for promoting entrepreneurship in GCC economies.
4   To *assess* the roles of various institutional changes agents in GCC economies in bringing institutional changes related to entrepreneurship.
5   To *demonstrate* an understanding of various sources of finance in GCC economies and their differences with the rest of the world.

Introduction

The six Gulf Cooperation Council (GCC) member states—Bahrain, Kuwait, Oman, Qatar, Saudi Arabia, and the United Arab Emirates (UAE)—have demonstrated an increasingly strong interest in entrepreneurial activities. As noted in Chapter 1, especially young people in the region are reported to have a desire to engage in entrepreneurial activities.

However, entrepreneurship faces various political, social, and cultural challenges in GCC economies. Institutional reforms required to promote productive entrepreneurship have been slow in the region. Although GCC regimes have agreed on the necessity to strengthen the rule of law and move toward free enterprise economy, there have been only superficial reforms. Political and economic liberalizations, which are insignificant in most cases, are responses to crises rather than as the systematic pursuit of stated reform objectives, and reluctantly carried out. The Third Wave of democratization, which started with the fall of the last dictatorships in Western Europe such as Portugal, Greece, and Spain in the mid-1970s and continued in Latin America in the 1980s, has failed to touch the Arab world. There is not a single full-fledged democracy in the GCC region and some new repressive institutions have also emerged.

GCC economies are also characterized by a symbiosis of political and economic elites. Observers refer the 1990s as the "lost" decade for these economies and argue the importance to enhance institutional quality by emphasizing on accountability in government practices, strengthening the rule of law, and controlling bureaucracy and corruption.[1] Experts argue that a genuinely entrepreneurial class, which is lacking in the region, would be the single most important force for change in the region. GCC economies' reform is likely to have far-reaching implications for their own populations as well as those outside the region.

A Survey of Entrepreneurship in the GCC Region

To start with, there is no equivalent word for "entrepreneurship" in Arabic. Unsurprisingly GCC economies lack essential ingredients for the creation of an effective ecosystem for entrepreneurship and innovations. Indeed, the entrepreneurial propensity among the youth is found to be higher in Lebanon and North Africa which are less economically prosperous than the GCC economies.[2]

Probably the biggest challenge facing the region is a low level of involvement of females in economic and entrepreneurial activities. A World Bank survey conducted in the Middle East and North Africa found that a woman is the principal owner of only about 13% of the businesses. This proportion is much lower than in other comparable middle-income economies in East Asia, Latin America and the Caribbean, and Europe and Central Asia.[3] An important benefit that stems from female-owned firms is that such firms in the region tend to hire more women and do so in higher positions than male-owned firms. For instance, female workers accounted for about 25% of the workforce in female-owned firms compared with 22% in male-owned firms. The qualitative differences are even more remarkable as female-owned firms employed a higher proportion of female workers at professional and managerial levels while male-owned firms employed more women in unskilled positions.[4]

In some cases, the direction of change from the perspective of women's participation in entrepreneurial activities has been regressive rather than progressive. A visible example to illustrate institutional change in Saudi Arabia is the Jeddah Economic Forum, which is held annually since 1999 during winter in the Jeddah city. In 1999, women were not allowed at the forum. In 2000, 50 women were allowed to watch the Forum's proceedings. In 2001, there were over 100 women, who were also allowed to ask questions. About 200 women attended the forum in 2002. In 2003, women had their own forum. In 2004, a Saudi businesswoman also delivered the keynote speech. However, in 2004, members of religiously conservative groups vigorously opposed and protested against women's taking center stage at the forum. Consequently, at the 6th Jeddah Economic Forum of 2005, women participants had a separate entry to the hall and were only allowed to ask questions from different room without being seen.

While GCC economies have been able to achieve a sustained economic growth and macroeconomic stability, development of entrepreneurship and job creation have remained a challenge. The public sector has been the main source of employment for their citizens. Some estimates suggest that foreign expatriate workers account for at least 80% of the private sector jobs in these economies.[5] The preference for public sector jobs acts as a barrier to entrepreneurship in the GCC economies. For instance, compared to working in the private sector or be self-employed, public sector jobs are preferred by 60%–73% of youths in the region.[6] Moreover, public sector jobs seriously lack productivity. A Kuwaiti female entrepreneur noted, "... by doing this [becoming an entrepreneur] I'm not working in the public sector where... there's nothing to do. For every 20 people in government, 18 sit around doing nothing."[7]

While some GCC economies have undertaken some successful mega-projects, these economies have failed to promote the development of small- and medium-sized enterprises (SMEs). This is a serious problem since small companies account for most of job creation as well as production and innovation of mature economies, especially in the service sector. Moreover, a significant proportion of small enterprises grow into medium-sized players. SMEs are likely to play a critical role in the region as most GCC economies are experiencing unemployment rates in the double digits, which are higher among young people. In 2011, 39% of Saudis in the 20–24 age group were unemployed.[8] Likewise, in 2009, 27% of the youth in Bahrain were unemployed, which was the highest among the GCC economies.[9] Until recently, GCC governments have not taken serious efforts to create jobs for women or to encourage women entrepreneurship. Women represent a significant pool of qualified human capital.

A significant proportion of SMEs in some GCC economies are owned by foreigners. A manager of Kuwait Small Developments Project Company noted that most small businesses in Kuwait are run by expatriates. The domination of the small business landscape by foreigners has led to a reluctance for the Kuwaiti nationals to launch their own firms. Moreover, there is an easy availability of government employment for Kuwaiti nationals.

GCC economies' oil-fueled prosperity has acted as a barrier to entrepreneurship development. An expert summarized this dynamics: "There is a dominant business class in the Middle East, but it owes its position to oil or to connections to the ruling families. Its wealth is that of feudalism, not capitalism, and its political effects remain feudal as well."[10] Some GCC governments, however, have realized the need to encourage entrepreneurship. For instance, to reduce its reliance on the oil industry, the Kuwaiti government wants to increase the number of Kuwait-run enterprises and broaden the base of the country's economy. Kuwait Small Developments Project Company announced a plan to lend up to 80% of the capital needed for starting a venture. The borrower doesn't need to pay service charges or interest. Potential entrepreneurs are also provided with viability studies and their business plans and ideas are looked at by experts.[11]

Startup Mentoring Programs and Collaborative Workspaces

Startup mentoring programs such as accelerators and incubators and community-based infrastructures such as coworking spaces are rapidly emerging in the region. In 2018, Saudi Badir Accelerator started financing Saudi technology startups. Each selected startup received more than $133,000 in funding.[12] Other benefits provided by the Saudi Badir Accelerator include training, workshops, business offices, strategic guidance, and legal support. Five startup technology companies were selected for the second cohort, which will start on January 1, 2019. The qualified startups were in the areas of blockchain, virtual reality, e-commerce, e-learning, and vehicle services.[13]

Bahrain's Fintech Bay initiative aims to attract fintec companies from across the world, including cryptocurrency-focused operations. It provides them with world-class infrastructure. It the largest coworking space in the region.[14] A 10,000-square-foot space in the capital city Manama's Arcapita building is dedicated for this purpose.[15] It also provides the region's first onshore regulatory sandbox, in which business licences are offered that are tailored specifically for startups.[16] Central Bank of Bahrain (CBB) established fintec regulatory sandbox in June 2017. Under the regulatory sandbox program. Startups and fintec firms can test and experiment with their banking ideas and solutions.[17]

Women and Entrepreneurship

According to Al Masah Capital, SMEs led by women in the GCC countries were estimated to value $385 billion.[18] Al Masah report noted GCC governments have taken several measures on the political, business and educational fronts to stimulate women entrepreneurship. They include regulatory improvements, lower entry and exit barriers, increased representation of women in chambers of commerce, and increased female literacy rates.

Determinants of Entrepreneurship in GCC Economies

Regulatory Framework

As are the cases of most developing countries, GCC states implemented import substitution policies for several decades. In recent years, in most of the GCC economies, the tasks related to starting a business have been vastly simplified and eased compared to what they used to be (Figures 6.1 and 6.2).

A comparison of Figures 6.1 and 6.2 also indicates that women need more procedures and longer time to start a business than men. For instance, in the UAE, the Personal Status law, art. 71 and 72, requires a married woman to seek her husband's consent in order to leave the marital home. This process takes one day to complete (www.doingbusiness.org/data/exploreeconomies/united-arab-emirates#starting-a-business). There are similar laws in other GCC countries.

Economic reform measures' speeds in the GCC economies have, however, been slower than what potential entrepreneurs would like to see. Institutions promoting free enterprise system and free enterprise economy are severely lacking. There is no minimum wage law in most of the GCC economies. Some argue that the introduction of such a law may force firms to be more efficient and the associated jobs are likely to be perceived better. While some GCC economies have recently introduced minimum wage laws, these are only for their nationals. For instance, Oman has

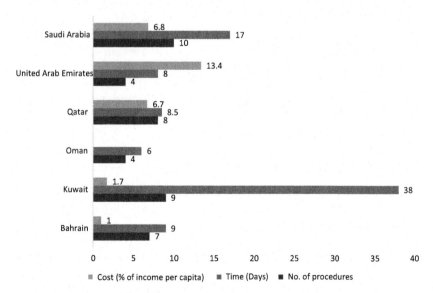

Figure 6.1 Starting a Business in the GCC Economies (men).
Source: The World Bank "Doing Business 2018" (www.doingbusiness.org/rankings).

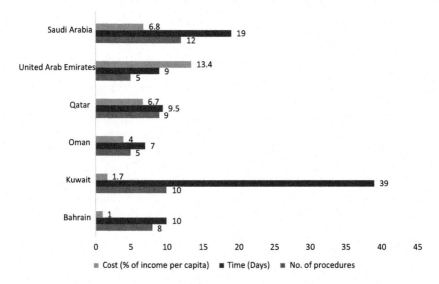

Figure 6.2 Starting a Business in the GCC Economies (women).
Source: The World Bank "Doing Business 2018" (www.doingbusiness.org/rankings).

introduced a regulation that has set a minimum wage for Omani workers in the private sector but not for non-Omanis.[19]

Bahrain is the only the GCC country that offers foreign entrepreneurs same level of benefits as nationals. For example, foreign entrepreneurs can enjoy 100% land and business ownership, even outside of free zones.[20]

Unsurprisingly, GCC economies, and Arab in general, scored the lowest in a comparison of legal reform across the world's regions. Likewise, while business climate in the region was above the world average and it outperformed other emerging markets on indicators related to infrastructure and some institution dimensions, the region stood second last to Africa on market orientation.[21]

Regulatory Uncertainty

Regulatory uncertainty has been a key challenge for investors in the region. In a 2017 anticorruption campaign in Saudi Arabia, hundreds of princes, government ministers and businessmen were detained for three months at the capital city Riyad's luxurious Ritz-Carlton Hotel. Some of the detainees were allegedly abused. The Saudi government said that it collected over $124 billion in "settlements" with businessmen and officials.[22] A main criticism that has been levelled against the anticorruption campaign was the lack of transparency.[23] This has triggered an uncertainty among potential investors. Some analysts think that potential investors are concerned that same thing might happen to them.[24]

Bankruptcy Laws

GCC economies have made progress in bankruptcy-related policy issues. For instance, the UAE's new bankruptcy law enacted in 2016 offers several paths to help companies facing financial difficulties.[25] For instance, insolvency with restructuring allows a company's debts to be restructured with the approval of creditors. The process is overseen by the courts. Likewise, protective composition is a debtor-led, court-sponsored process to rescue a business that is in financial difficulty but not yet insolvent.[26]

Likewise, in March 2018, Bahrain revised bankruptcy law that allows room for entrepreneurial risk and failure.[27] The country was reported to study similar laws in entrepreneurially successful countries such as Singapore, the U.K., and the U.S. as well as neighboring countries to provide more flexibility to business owners in areas related to capital restructuring.

Values, Culture, and Skills

Entrepreneurial Culture

Entrepreneurship development faces various social issues and cultural challenges in the Arab region. First, many of the consumption habits associated with global capitalism are considered to be "antithetical" to Islamic ethical traditions.[28] Observers note that people in the region look down on capitalism. There has also been a widespread negative attitude toward entrepreneurship involving small businesses as well as toward menial and low-paying works. Since private sector jobs in these economies suffer from an image problem, entrepreneurs face barriers to hire qualified employees.

Some concepts related to entrepreneurship are considered to be too Western and face strong resistance. For instance as "angel investors" sounded too Christian for many Arabs, the promoters needed to replace it with a more religion-neutral term—"uncles' network."[29]

Social norms impose restrictions on female employment, which has led to a low rate of female participation in economic activities in general and entrepreneurship in particular (Figure 6.2). Observers have noted that most women in the region do not consult financial advisors.[30] The GCC tradition of family businesses has also been a barrier to entrepreneurship development and economic growth. Experts say that governments in these economies need to do more to broaden entrepreneurship.

While expatriates constitute a significant proportion of population in most GCC economies, their involvement in high quality entrepreneurship is limited. One problem is that GCC economies have viewed immigrants merely as an extra source of labor.[31] Recruiters organize most of the movements of workers on fixed term contracts. In most cases, contract workers are required to depart the receiving country upon completion of the contract.[32] In this regard, compared to the rest of the GCC and the Middle East, the

Dubai Emirate, UAE has pursued more liberal social and economic policies. The emirate has attracted foreigners for more than a century. Dubai thus performs well in the availability of the key ingredients of the entrepreneurial ecosystem such as wealthy investors and skilled workers.[33]

Entrepreneurial Skills and Capabilities

GCC economies are making significant progress in education. Progress in women's education in the region has been especially impressive. Women outnumber men in most of the Arab universities. Gender gaps in literacy rates and enrollment in primary and secondary schools have fallen dramatically since the 1970s. In 2005, the Saudi government announced plans to establish 17 women-only technical colleges that would provide skills needed for the job market.[34]

In order to reduce their dependence on foreign workers, GCC economies are putting more efforts to improve the education levels and skills of that their own nationals. Some measures are being taken by non-government organizations as well. The NGO Injaz al-Arab (www.injazal-arab.org/), which was formed in 2004 and operated in 13 countries in the Middle East and North Africa in 2010, sends volunteers to teach work readiness, financial literacy, and entrepreneurship in schools. As of mid-2010, Injaz al-Arab programs engaged 10,000 private sector volunteers and reached over 500,000 students.[35]

That said, GCC economies are facing major human capital constraints. GCC entrepreneurs are not well versed in supporting skills such as those related to forecasting techniques, market research, and business models.[36] The GCC economies perform poorly in international student-achievement tests. The educational system emphasizes on preparing the citizens for luxury works rather than for productive employment.

If there is a lesson in the entrepreneurship development of mature economies, it is that providing vocational training and adopting strict professional standards would lead to professionalization of blue-collar workers which would lead to a higher level of prestige of their works. Short-term certificate and diploma programs would also help.

Access to Finance, Market, R&D, and Technology

Access to Markets

Some argue that GCC economies political and economic systems resemble and can be accurately described as feudalism rather than capitalism.[37] One upshot of this approach is that big businesses dominate the markets in the region, especially in vital and important productive sectors. Market access barriers continue to pose serious obstacles for the growth of

SMEs and new firms. The antitrust laws in these economies are not well equipped to deal with this problem of the dominance by big businesses. In 2012, a prominent Saudi attorney called for a stronger antitrust law to eliminate business monopolies in the country.[38]

However, entrepreneurial firms in the region are in a favorable position to gain access to major foreign markets. Factors related to natural openness to international trade such as distance with major economies in the world (their location near Europe) and the common language of Arabic, which is spoken by over 160 million people and is the official language of 22 countries, facilitate these economies' entrepreneurial firms' access to foreign market.

R&D and Technology-Related Factors

GCC economies have exhibited a culture of heavy reliance on low-cost and low-skilled imported labor, mainly in the labor-intensive industries such as construction and services. This culture has favored low-quality entrepreneurship in the region by encouraging inefficient production techniques. Due to an easy availability of cheap labor, organizations in the GCC region have also faced little pressure to reform their organizational structures, develop the skills of their workforce, and introduce superior technologies.

R&D is virtually non-existent in the region. Figure 6.3 compares gross domestic expenditure on R&D as a percentage of GDP in some GCC economies with OECD economies. Due to their lack of emphasis on R&D and technology adoption, GCC economies remain in a low-productivity trap.

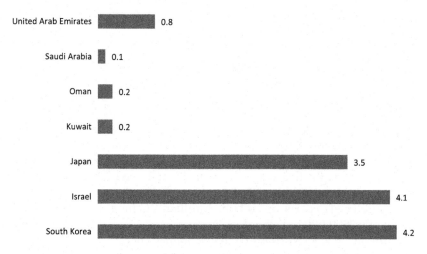

Figure 6.3 Gross Domestic Expenditure on R&D as a Percentage of GDP: A Comparison of Some GCC Economies and OECD Economies (2017).
Source: Euromonitor International.

Access to Finance

Given their prosperity levels, GCC performs poorly in most indicators related to access to finance. In 2016, $889 million was invested in startups in GCC economies.[39]

BANK LOANS

In the GCC economies, banks provide very limited lending to SMEs. For instance, SME lending accounts for only about 4% of total bank lending in the UAE. The proportion in Saudi Arabia, Kuwait, and Oman is 2%. They are even lower in Bahrain and Qatar at 1% and 0.5%, respectively.[40]

In some cases, religious motivation prevents SMEs from accessing the available conventional sources of financing. For instance, some entrepreneurs lack willingness to use banking services that are not Shariah-compliant. In Saudi Arabia, about 90% of SMEs look for Shariah-compliant banking services. In this way, due to their unwillingness to use non-Islamic finance, they are locked out of the lending market.[41]

VENTURE CAPITAL

According to BECO Capital, the GCC region had 115 private players operating in the venture capital (VC) sector.[42] The UAE accounted for 41% of the total VC activity in 2015 recorded in the region in 2015.[43] Bahrain also established a $100 million fund of funds for venture capital.[44]

The establishment of the Gulf Venture Capital Association (GVCA) is a key development. The GVCA was formed by a consortium of institutions and professionals in GCC economies. The GVCA is "committed to supporting the growth of a strong venture capital and private equity industry within the Arabian Gulf."[45] Likewise, in 2011, the Omani Centre for Investment Promotion and Export Development launched a VC fund of US$135 million to be spent by 2020. The goal is to promote investment in science and technology in the GCC region. The fund is expected to attract foreign high-tech firms and R&D facilities to the region. It also expects to support local SMEs in the technology sector. The services provided include finance for five years, access to IT and energy, and mentoring. In 2011, the UAE-based Arab Science and Technology Foundation also announced a plan to set up an US$15 million VC fund. Its plan is to distribute US$500,000 to technology startups.[46]

A unique characteristic of GCC economies concerns a large number of high net worth individuals. An estimate of the Gulf Investment House suggested that the private wealth of the GCC region was US$1.5 trillion in 2007. Experts argue that GCC's high net worth individuals are in a strong position to provide VC financing. In this way, they can play the roles played by institutional investors or banks in the U.S. and Europe.[47]

CAPITAL MARKETS

The capital markets of the region have many contradicting features. The ratio of market capitalization to GDP for the GCC region is similar to those of many matured markets. Nonetheless, the region's stock markets are not well developed in some important aspects. The ratio of traded equity to GDP for the GCC region remains lower than in many emerging economies. The GCC stock markets have also experienced wide fluctuations, which have undermined investor confidence and created difficulties for fund managers at the exit stage.[48] Moreover, exchanges specializing in high growth companies (such as NASDAQ) are lacking in the region.

Formal and Informal Institutions in Relation to Entrepreneurship

This section explores formal and informal institutions in the GCC economies in greater detail. Notwithstanding some institutional reforms in GCC economies, a close look indicates a lack of substantiveness. For instance, in most cases, holding elections is the only measure taken to promote democracy and the elections arguably tend to be merely "rubber-stamp affairs."[49]

Institutional reforms attempts in the region are facing various roadblocks. At the Forum of the Future's 2005 meeting of the intergovernmental initiative for reform in the broader Middle East, three GCC economies—Bahrain, Oman, and Saudi Arabia—supported Egypt's approach to restrict independence of NGOs.[50] In Saudi Arabia, women were allowed for the first time in 1999 to attend sessions of the Shura as observers. The Shura's chairman, however, reminded that Islam denies women's right to public offices. Likewise, in Bahrain, the King emphasized the necessity to resume democracy, but critics doubt whether democratic moves are genuine. Those challenging the rulers to engage in dialogues were banned from public gatherings. In 2005, authorities closed a leading human rights organization. A leader who called on the Prime Minister to resign for human rights violation and failure to restore growth was arrested. Clubs such as Bahrain Centre for Human Rights, General Organization for Youth and Sports, and Al-Uruba are viewed as cultural establishments and barred from political activities. In February 2011, the country's Shi'ite Muslim majority organized a protest on the street seeking more jobs and a greater voice in government. A crackdown and martial law forced to end the protest.

To take yet another example of institutions shifting into reverse gear, consider Kuwait. In the early 2000s, more women were wearing the veil than before and university classes were segregated by gender.[51] While the rulers are in favor of empowering women, there have been oppositions from the Islamic groups. These groups also voted against women's right to vote on social and religious grounds. While Kuwaiti rulers promised a genuine democratization, the progress has been insufficient.

Among GCC rulers, those with Western education or with Western-educated advisors have introduced substantial institutional measures. In Kuwait, Western-educated members, who gained posts in the cabinet, introduced an economic package in 2001 to attract foreign investment.[52] Similarly, Sheik Mohammad, the crown prince of Dubai, who has played a critical role in modernizing the country, has a team of Western-educated economic advisers. GCC regimes are also facing institutional reform pressure from citizens with access to Western-style education. Some notable examples include Kuwait's first open political party formed by Western-educated liberals, protest by Western-educated Kuwaiti women during the 1992 Election and candidacy of 28 women—mostly Western-educated—in the 2006 parliamentary elections, and Saudi intellectuals' petition to the king in 2003 calling for a constitution and bill of rights.

The Governments' Reform Measures

The government is the most powerful institutional actors, and this is in a special position to create market institutions, change the legal rules, and enforce private actors' behavior. In the GCC region, free enterprise economy is far from being fully institutionalized. Even if the governments like to take reform measures, they have to appease actors with disparate purposes and conflicting interests such as bureaucrats, entrepreneurs, financial, corporate and economic elites; intellectuals, opinion makers, religious spokespersons, multinationals, foreign governments, international agencies, interest groups, labor unions, and ordinary citizens.

Institutional Change Agents

It would be erroneous, however, to conclude that government is the only actor associated with institutional changes. More broadly, it may be helpful to consider the roles of institutional change agents or institutional entrepreneurs. Institutional entrepreneurs challenge or disrupt particular models of social or economic orders and construct new institutions. They are effective in identifying opportunities, frame issues and problems, and mobilize various types of resources in an attempt to change societal beliefs, norms, and value systems. They also engage in activities related to deinstitutionalization (dissolution of existing logic or governance structure) as well as institution formation, which entails the birth of a new logic or governance structure.[53]

Institutional entrepreneurs come in many shapes and sizes. In GCC economies, some examples of institutional entrepreneurs include Western-educated professionals, Western-educated liberals who formed Kuwait's first open political party, Kuwaiti women groups who protested during the 1992 Election for their voting right, women candidates in Kuwait's 2006 elections; and Saudi intellectuals, who submitted petition to the king in 2003 calling for a constitution and bill of rights.

Institutional entrepreneurs' subject positions need to be dominant that can allow them to gain wide legitimacy, bridge diverse stakeholders, and compel other actors to change practices.[54] It is important for them to mobilize external and internal constituents, have financial resources, and be able to communicate with other institutional actors in the system so that their initiatives are perceived favorably.[55]

Selective Adaptation

Social, political, and economic contexts can constrain actions that the government and institutional entrepreneurs can undertake. The idea of selective adaptation can be helpful in understanding this dynamics. Selective adaptation entails balancing local needs with pressures of compliance with practices (institutional reforms) imposed from outside. Selective adaptation is typically framed as a process by which exchanges of non-local rules across cultural boundaries are mediated by and interpreted in terms of local practices, conditions, imperatives, and norms.[56]

The nature of selective adaptation is a function of perception, complementarity, and legitimacy. First, the processes and results of selective adaptation depend on how policy makers and other institutional change agents perceive the content and effect of foreign and local institutional arrangements. Complementarity describes a situation in which seemingly contradictory phenomena can be combined so that they reinforce each other effectively and at the same time essential characteristics of each component are preserved. Legitimacy concerns the extent to which local communities support the purposes and consequences of selective adaptation. The effectiveness of selectively adapted legal forms and practices depends to an important degree on local acceptance. Institutional reforms pressures, for instance, may face opposition by actors benefiting from the existing institutional arrangements.

The "Triple Embeddedness" Thesis

The gist of the "triple embeddedness" thesis[57] is that in determining institutional changes, it is important to examine the interaction and interdependence of the economy, polity, and society. To put things in context, elements of political institutions such as democracy and the rule of law and the nature of the civil society are tightly linked with business climate.

Society-related factors include the nature of social organizations—"the holistic order" and "the extended order" and the society's orientation toward the West (e.g., the presence of Western-educated leaders, technocrats, and citizens). Polity-related variables include the government's dependence on businesses and on Western countries. Finally, resource-based economic development is an economy related variable. Table 6.1 presents some factors facilitating or hindering institutional changes in the region.

Table 6.1 Factors Facilitating and Hindering Institutional Reforms in GCC Economies

Factor	Effects on the government's substantiveness of reform measures	Effects on progressive/regressive institutional changes
The "holistic order" of the society	• Economic and political logic for reform may face difficulties. The government may be unwilling to take substantive reform measure.	• Institutional changes processes that are against the "general binding moral prescripts" face resistance.
The presence of Western-educated leaders, technocrats and citizens	• Open to Western-style reforms and can influence policy makers to take substantial measures.	• Support to reform measure. • Externality effects.
The government's dependence on businesses	• Governments that are vulnerable to capital dependence are likely to adopt probusiness policies.	
Bureaucrats' involvement in businesses	• The government may not take substantial reforms that go against bureaucrats' interests.	• Institutional reforms may adversely affect bureaucrats' utility functions. They may be unwilling to direct attention and provide supports and resources to reforms.
Dependence on Western countries	• Pressures to bring institutional reforms.	
Ability to achieve economic development without reforms	• The regimes can hold their citizens at bay by providing some welfare. • Institutional entrepreneurs may face communicating need for change.	

The "Holistic Order" and the "Extended Order"

Institutionalists and historians have argued that institutions' propensity to change can arguably be described with two ideal types of social organizations—the holistic order and the extended/functionally differentiated order. A holistic society is often characterized by an ideology, mostly in the form of a religion, that "claims validity for all spheres of action and thought" and an action's legitimacy is evaluated on the basis of a "general binding moral prescripts imposed by a superior authority" rather than by economic, political or juridical logics.[58] To take an example, conservative Islamist factions such as Islamic Salvation Front view Islam "as a holistic order whose societal organization is perfect and does not allow individual beliefs."[59] In some cases, the ideology concerns the value system such as the Asian values.

As noted above, the government and institutional entrepreneurs engage in selective adaptation of foreign practices. This means that practices incompatible with local conditions and norms are less likely to be introduced or likely to fail if they are introduced. In a holistic society, selectively adapted practices become ineffective because they lack legitimacy or local communities' support. The government's and institutional entrepreneurs' attempts to bring changes may face difficulty going beyond preinstitutionalization.

From the standpoint of institutional reforms in GCC, the most relevant issue concerns the notion of a holistic society. As noted above, conservative version of Islam views Islam "as a holistic order whose societal organization is perfect."[60] This emphasis is echoed in other recent perspectives on Islam. The secular/religious distinction is less likely to exist in Islam. To take one example, whereas Western governments do not provide assistance to religious related charities, there is no such restriction in some Islamic governments. The Islamic mission (da'wa) in Saudi Arabia, for instance, is state-sponsored. Islam has propagated "a holistic conceptualization of life, embracing politics, economics and society."[61] One scholar observes, "Extremists exploit the common misunderstanding of Muslims' holistic view of life; everything is religion and everything is Islam; financial, social, intellectual, theological, military, and political."[62]

The upshot of these tendencies is that institutional changes that go against Islam's logic face resistance. Citizens in these economies think that Islam as inherently democratic and thus perceive no distance between Islam and democracy.[63] They express simultaneous support for democracy and Islam. In these economies, a significant amount of time is devoted to Islamic instruction in educational institutions.[64] Religious and cultural influences make educational reform a sensitive topic. Islam is thus providing a foundation for the politics of GCC economies. In the ideological arena, Islamic world is one of the notable exceptions to the observation that democracy is the "spirit of the times." A scholar put the issue this regarding the influence of Islam's holistic nature on politics[65]:

> The rhetoric of religious movements refuses to recognize the autonomy of politics and instead attempts to put the state under the control of religion. Such religious movements ....leave no room for cultural, intellectual or ideological differences.

Islam's influence is readily apparent in businesses and economics. Islamic economics, which differs from Western capitalism by several measures, claims that Islam provides an "all-encompassing model for social, economic, and political life."[66] Commercial shariah, for instance, differs drastically from Western business laws in several notable respects. It is probably hard to imagine democracy in the GCC region involving English common law, which is likely to bring a disruption in the society.

Islam's holistic order has been a barrier to Western-style institutional reforms and a driving force behind regressive changes in GCC economies. This pattern is powerfully illustrated in Shura's chairman's argument against women's right to public offices in Saudi Arabia, ban from political activities of clubs such as Centre for Human Rights, the General Organization for Youth and Sports and Al-Uruba in Bahrain and Islamic groups' oppositions to empower women in Kuwait. Observers have noted that in some GCC economies such as Oman, Qatar, and Bahrain, on most political issues, the monarchs are arguably more liberal than the societies they rule.[67] For instance, deliberations in the Bahrain parliament focus more on social than political issues.

The absolute monarchies possessing both religious and political power also benefit from the holistic order (Table 6.2). Accordingly, most GCC rulers lack accountability; can survive through repression, cooptations, and manipulation; and maintain control over opponents.[68] Beyond all that, being a "reformist" by complying with the West is an unpopular option for GCC rulers. For instance, in the Arab world, Qatar is perceived as "little more than an American military base."[69]

Western-Educated Leaders, Technocrats, and Citizens

A growing number of studies have suggested that governments controlled by "coalitions with strong internationalist links" tend to carry economic reform measures early and consistently.[70] Evidence consistent with this proposition has emerged from Mexico, Thailand, and Korea in the 1980s; as well as from the Middle East.[71] Such internationalist coalitions are typically dominated by a team of technocrats that have extensive foreign training and experience.

Table 6.2 Political and Religion Landscapes of GCC Economies: Major Highlights

Economy	Political	Religious	Remarks
Bahrain	• Started political liberalization in 2002. In a referendum, the electorate voted to create a parliament and an appointed Majlis al-Shura. • 2005: Closed a leading human rights organization.	• Political Islam moderate; Islamist groups dominate the parliament. • Five women (a Christian, a Jew) are appointed to the Shura Council.	• The least oil reserve among the GCC economies and thus is forced to liberalize the economy.
Kuwait	• Most political power with the ruling Sabah family. • Ahead of most GCC economies on reform.	• Religious fundamentalism is increasing.	• Influence of Saudi Arabia becoming stronger.
Oman	• 1996: "Basic Law"— provided a Bill of Rights, guaranteed freedom of the press, encouraged religious tolerance, insisted on an equality of race and gender.	• Constitution is "grounded" in Islamic tradition. • The Sultan convened a Majlis al-Shura, or Consultative Council.	• Critics claimed that the 1996 initiatives were the results of an attempted coup two years earlier.
Qatar	• 2003: Qataris (including women) voted and approved a new constitution— called for the establishment of a parliament. • First gulf state to permit unrestricted free press.	• Follows strict Wahabi sect of Islam (like Saudi Arabia) but has been more flexible in religious ideology.	• Critics argue that the new constitution institutionalized the absolute power of the emir and his family.
Saudi Arabia	• Shura: king appointed and only representative institution. • Considering letting male citizens elect regional councils.	• The Shura's chairman reminded that Islam denies women right to public office.	• The most conservative GCC country in many aspects.
UAE	• Moderate political culture.	• No religious extremism. • Tolerance for other religions.	• Moderate foreign policy.

Actors with internationalist links exist at various levels of the political and social structure. Leaders and politicians with internationalist links at the highest level of policy making are more likely to take reform measures compared to those without such links.[72] Western-educated leaders such as Morocco's King Mohamed VI and Jordan's King Abdullah seem to be more open to reforms than most Arab leaders.

At the next level, bureaucrats help precipitate institutional changes by directing attention and providing supports and resources. There is growing recognition that internationalist links provide technocratic and educational expertise necessary for reform. Technocrats with extensive foreign training and experience are more open to Western-style reforms.

However, there is another point that is perhaps even more important. Outsiders lack a wide legitimacy and thus can do little to bring changes. Some governments also oppose institutional reform pressures from outside. Morocco's King Mohammed VI put the issue this way: "Self-reform is an internal process. Just as we refrain from giving lessons to others, we will not tolerate being told what to do. No one…shall impose their views on us."[73] A narrow set of attributes that is attractive with only one group of institutional actors is not sufficient to mobilize a wider cooperation needed to bring institutional changes. Western-educated technocrats' subject position allows them to acquire a wide legitimacy and bridge diverse stakeholders. As insiders, institutional reforms supported by them are likely to possess a high face validity. They are thus expected to play a forefront role for changes.

Many old GCC leaders are not open to social, technological, and economic ideas. Western-educated GCC leaders, on the other hand, seem to be bringing institutional reforms. For instance, Western-educated Qatari Emir Sheikh Hamad introduced the country's first popular elections in 1999, which also allowed women to vote and run for office. He has a team of Western-educated advisers. Unlike most Arab rulers, Western-educated GCC rulers or those with Western-educated advisors seem to emphasize more on economic gains than on political order. Such a pattern is powerfully illustrated in Kuwait's introduction of an economic package in 2001 to attract foreign investment and Sheik Mohammad's measurers to modernize Dubai.

Western-educated GCC technocrats are energetic, disciplined, qualified, and competent to carry out reforms. They have become important institutional change agents or institutional entrepreneurs. In 1991, mostly Western-educated Kuwaiti liberals formed the first open political party. In 2003, 104 Saudi intellectuals, many of them Western-educated, presented a petition to the king. The petition, "A Vision for the Present and Future of the Homeland," called for a constitution and bill of rights.[74] It proposed an elected legislature; local and regional elections; an independent judiciary; and a guarantee of "freedom of expression, association, assembly, the right to vote and to participate, as well as human rights." It urged the king to confront corruption, bribery, and power abuse and argued that a constitutional monarchy would help counter Muslim extremism.

Reform also depends on populations with a democratic culture. Citizens with a strong desire of democratic participation are likely to exert pressure for progressive changes. During the 1992 Election in Kuwait, groups of women—mostly Western-educated—protested against their exclusion from voting. Similarly, in the 2006 parliamentary elections, women were allowed to vote and there were 28 women candidates, mostly Western-educated.

Governments' Dependence on Businesses; and Economic and Political Elites' Merger

Political institutions tend to have built-in biases that systematically favor specific classes. In a discussion of the dynamics of class forces and state-level policies, businesses deserve special attention. The capital-dependence theory argues that governments that are constrained by the need to generate private investment face structural pressures to adopt policies favoring businesses.[75] Research indicates that governments with capital dependence are likely to adopt pro-business policies even without businesses' pressures.

Rulers' control over economic decision-making influences the success of a reform. In an economy characterized by a high degree of dependence of the government on domestic businesses, the businesses can exert a strong grip on state policies. What seems to be happening in such economies is businesses regulating the state rather than vice versa. On the other hand, governments ignore interests of businesses with a low economic importance, which lack "veto points."[76] Jordan, which depends on foreign aid and the government is the direct aid recipient, is an example of such an economy. The state allocates investment and employs 50% of the workforce.[77]

Of equal importance in the discussion of the government-businesses nexus is bureaucrats' involvement in businesses. A cohesive reform team involving bureaucrats is a defining feature of a successful reform.[78] Academic research conducted in China, Mexico, Russia, and other Eastern European countries have indicated that the most important barrier to transition to a market economy centered on resistance from the bureaucracy.

Theoretically, the government can control bureaucrats through laws and by specifying the details of implementation. If bureaucrats are taking advantage of positional power to maximize economic rewards, institutional reforms adversely affect their utility function. Moreover, bureaucrats, who are also capitalists, possess power to penetrate into the government appa-ratus.[79] Bureaucrats in such cases are thus against deinstitutionalization of existing institutions or formation of new institutions. One thus would not expect the government to take substantial reform measures that go against bureaucrats' interests.

While some degree of nepotism is involved everywhere, influences of favoritism, nepotism, and personal connections are more readily apparent in GCC. Such a tendency can be attributed to the culture (e.g., strong kinship ties and obligations to family and friends). One scholar goes even further, saying: "In the Arab world nepotism has none of the negative associations it has in the West."[80] Another scholar observes: "Corruption and nepotism [prevails], and the concept of the state [isn't] fully under-stood...as a guardian and representative of individual and community interests."[81]

To understand the infancy of capitalism in the GCC, it may be helpful to consider shared mutual interests between merchant and ruling families. Big businesses play influential roles in political decision-making and re-main a strong antireform force. Note too that management principles of these businesses have a very few elements of Islamic economics.

In Saudi Arabia, the royal family entered in businesses from the 1960s and have benefited from the status quo. Similarly, in Oman, the Sultan received resources to run the state from merchant families and provided them with institutional favor as well as security and protection.[82] For the ruling elites, the arbitrary application of business laws provides an impor-tant access to resources.

There has also been a colossal increase in bureaucrats' involvement in businesses. Bureaucrats thus discourage policies favoring institutional re-forms and outside investments and remain a strong antireform force. An expert noted: "It's just that bureaucracy, corruption and uncertainty make it difficult to build a business bigger than a market stall."[83]

Dependence on Western Countries

As noted above, selective adaptation is a function of how policy makers perceive the "purpose, content and effect" of foreign and local institu-tional arrangements.[84] The content of Western countries' institutional arrangements in administering aid and loan affects developing countries' reforms. Western countries, especially the United States, and international agencies such as the International Monetary Fund and the World Bank have governance criteria[85] in aid and lending decisions.[86] The United States has helped friendly regimes develop into "regional showpieces of globalization" and provided with military support.[87]

In highlighting the role that dependence on aid can play in institu-tional reforms, consider the Middle East. From this standpoint, there are two groups of economies. The countries of the first group (Tunisia, Morocco, Egypt, and Jordan) have benefited from foreign aid and have been consistent in implementing reforms. The countries of the second group (post-1981 Syria, Iran and Sudan, the pre-1994 Algeria, and the pre-2003 Iraq), on the other hand, were hostile to the United States and resisted reforms.[88]

The countries in the first group, which desperately needed aid, met WTO entry requirements in record time. Ironically, it is the aid that remains a major motivation behind reforms. For instance, a main benefit of joining the WTO highlighted by Jordanian officials was the "massive aid" that the country would receive. The United States, the EU, and Japan provided assistance to "ease the pain and political costs" of reform.[89]

Some GCC governments depend on Westerns powers, particularly the United States, for external security as well as on technology and economic fronts. For example, the United States arguably provides Saudi Arabia with defense against external threats. Saudis have used the United States as a "shield" to counter external threats and U.S. troops protect ruling sheikhs' oil fields.[90] The Saudi–U.S. relationship grew to include the exchange of U.S. technology for Saudi cash. While there is some evidence of U.S. influence on societal practices and institutions in Saudi Arabia, the changes are insignificant.

Unsurprisingly, compared to many developing economies, GCC economies are less dependent on the West. GCC regimes' responses with respect to Western powers and foreign multinationals are largely symbolic. Indeed, GCC states face virtually no pressures from OECD countries. For instance, observers have noted that the United States has relied on Saudi Arabia to provide a long-term oil supply and is unwilling to push the Saudi regime for institutional reforms. At the same time, the Saudis are "unbribable and unmaneuverable."[91] One scholar notes:

> Because of its dependency on Middle East gas and oil, Europe's high talk about human rights doesn't apply much to Arab extremists with energy-rich patrons in the Gulf. America is in a war against Islamic fascism, yet treads carefully around Saudi Arabia, despite the kingdom's subsidies to America-hating madrasahs.[92]

Ability to Achieve Economic Development without Reforms

Economic performance is positively related to a regime's legitimacy. The economic performance-legitimacy nexus is stronger for authoritarian regimes than democratic ones. While some view authoritarian regimes' economic performance based legitimacy as superficial, such a strategy is producing results for some rulers. A reform-based growth may produce complementarity for authoritarian regimes as essential characteristics of both authoritarianism and reform exist side by side.

The terms "performance legitimacy" is often used to describe a justification for political repression by governments delivering high growth.[93] Poor economic performance, on the other hand, may result in the loss of legitimacy. Asia provides a robust example to illustrate this form of legitimacy. Most of the past and present authoritarian Asian regimes (e.g., Singapore, Malaysia, and China) acquired legitimacy through high economic growth. In Indonesia, Suharto's legitimacy was based on the country's improved living standards during his rule. In sum, if an economy performs well, institutional entrepreneurs face difficulty in communicating the need for change and value of the proposed changes.

Most GCC governments' ideologies entail different forms of nationalism. Economic failure erodes a government's legitimacy and fosters an ideological vacuum, as old ideologies (e.g., nationalism) are perceived as failures.[94] Falling oil/gas production and growing youth unemployment are among powerful factors pushing reform in GCC economies. Unsurprisingly achieving growth has been a top agenda. In this regard, oil revenue's impact on institutional changes deserves special attention. GCC economies exhibit a high degree of reliance on oil. For instance, in Kuwait, Oil accounts for about 60% of the GDP and 95% of export revenues.[95]

By meeting citizens' economic expectations and providing some welfare GCC regimes have reduced resentment toward them. They have been able to hold their citizens at bay. As it happens, a major reason behind GCC economies' poor performance on the institutional reform front is the region's lack of interest in attracting FDI. They have large current account surpluses and are net capital exporters. While reform is producing complementarity effects for some Asian authoritarian regimes, GCC governments have been able to deliver growth without reform.

Unsurprisingly, political, economic, and financial crises have induced an appetite for reforms. When oil price declined in the 1980s, GCC regimes offered a wider political participation to ensure peace and legitimacy. In 1998, the then Kuwaiti Oil Minister put the issue this way: "The...decline in oil prices may be a blessing in disguise...Although it has been difficult for us to do in the past politically, may be we can search for alternative sources of income."[96] When oil prices were low in the early 1990s, Kuwait and Saudi Arabia moved toward economic reforms. Kuwaiti government discussed about turning the country into a free trade zone while "acknowledging the need to prepare their citizens for painful changes." Then Kuwaiti Oil Minister went on saying: "Every walk of life has been subsidized...We have to see how we're going to work through this."

Kuwait and Saudi Arabia were thus searching for new solutions or were in the pre-institutionalization phase of reform. Broad institutional support rather than economic and technical efficiency is, however, critical to move beyond pre-institutionalization. With increased oil price and the absence of such a support, the whole reform process pretty much stopped right there.

Among GCC economies, per capita oil and gas production is among the lowest for Bahrain, which is arguably the most diversified GCC economy. It has a history as an important financial center. It took substantive measures (e.g., extensive banking sector reform) to attract industries such as ship repair and financial services. It is also worth noting that Bahrain is the only the GCC country that offers foreign entrepreneurs same level of benefits as nationals. For example, foreign entrepreneurs can enjoy 100% land and business ownership, even outside of free zones.[97]

Concluding Comments

While some positive steps have been taken toward increasing investments in education, developing entrepreneurship and capital markets and reforming economic and political institutions, there exists an urgent need to intensify these efforts. Compared to the successful East Asian economies, GCC economies have failed to take a sensible and considered approach to the development of human and physical capital. A heavy reliance on imported labor has led to a negative perception of many jobs as unattractive, due primarily to the fact that they are associated with poor working conditions. At the same time, employers try to gain as much as possible from the expatriate workers.

Institutions arguably have a higher propensity to change when they are characterized by contradictions, which "create conflicting and irreconcilable incentives and motivations."[98] Nowhere is this characteristic more evident than in the GCC region. In this regard, there are some well-founded rationales for and against doing business in the GCC region as well as a number of misinformed and ill guided viewpoints. Many foreign investors, for instance, see the GCC region as a breeding ground for terrorists and underestimate the region's importance despite its GDP of about US$1 trillion.

As is the case in many authoritarian regimes, GCC rulers have been able to acquire "performance legitimacy" by meeting their citizens' economic expectations. Unlike many developing economies, they do not need foreign aids and loans. The oil-based growth has also reduced their dependence on FDI. This means that GCC economies are less dependent on foreign multinationals, Western governments and international agencies. Second, merchant families, royal entrepreneurs and elite entrepreneurs, who have an extremely close and mutually advantageous relationships with the government and are benefitting from the status quo; and government bureaucracies have been a strong antireform force.

A third aspect of GCC is "the holistic order" of the society, which tends to shift power balance toward antireform groups. Institutional change processes that go against Islam's logic face resistance. Islam's influence is readily apparent in politics (e.g., perception of no distance between Islam and democracy) and in business (e.g., commercial shariah). Moreover, Islam has provided credibility and added legitimacy to GCC regimes because of absolute monarchies' possession of religious power.

Despite the above observations, some encouraging signs are emerging. As of 2007, the UAE's eight campuses of the Higher College of Technology required students to take entrepreneurship training. Over 60% of the campuses' engineering students were women.[99] Even in Saudi Arabia, which is considered to be one of the most conservative societies, institutional changes are taking place, which have facilitated females' participation in entrepreneurial endeavors and enhanced their status in the business world. Estimates suggest that women account for 0.8% of total private sector employees.[100] While most women work as teachers, the women workforce is diversifying in other occupations such as doctors, journalists, news anchors, and television presenters. In 2007, the Saudi government announced plans to reserve one-third of all government jobs for women.[101]

The following observations can be made regarding some mechanisms to achieve effective institutional changes and successfully operate in the GCC region.

The Principle of Minimal Dislocation

The above analysis indicates that transition to Western form of capitalism is a big jump from the current institutional arrangements of GCC economies. Progressive institutional changes are sustainable only if there is a "minimal dislocation." Put differently, the incorporation of a new behavior must have a minimally disruptive effect in the community. In this regard, transition of GCC businesses to the principles of Islamic economics is likely to be a more feasible option than to Western form of capitalism.

Bricolage or Complementarity as a Strategy to Operate in GCC Economies

For foreign entrepreneurial firms, combining components from the existing institutional environment and reorganizing them strategically—also known as bricolage[102]—can be an important way to operate in the GCC region. Western financial institutions, for instance, operate in the GCC region according to the principle of Commercial shariah and have helped boost GCC regimes' performance legitimacy by bringing jobs and FDI in the region. This approach can also be viewed as complementarity as two seemingly contradictory phenomena (Western capitalism and Commercial shariah) are combined and essential characteristics of each component are preserved.

Decline in Production/Price of Oil as a Possible Jolt to the Existing Institutions

The interesting question for GCC region is what factors could give a jolt to the existing institutions. Decline in production and/or price of oil is probably the single-most important force that can threaten GCC regimes' performance based legitimacy. As noted earlier, in the early 1990s, Kuwait and Saudi Arabia were at the preinstitutionalization phase but subsequent increased oil prices reduced their incentives to take substantive actions to move toward full institutionalization of reforms. In the current interaction pattern of institutional actors in the GCC context, decline in oil price is likely to shift the power balance in favor of proreform actors such as foreign multinationals and Western governments.

Western-Educated Leaders and Technocrats as Agents of Institution Change

Western-educated leaders and technocrats have introduced and facilitated reform measures. If a GCC economy with an internationalist coalition develops as a reformist showcase economy, other GCC regimes may consider reform as an appropriate arrangement. Note that currently being a "reformist" is an unpopular option in the Arab world.[103]

Need for Proreform Actors to Be Organized and Vocal

Proreform constituents tend to be "generally unorganized, silent, and nearly invisible politically," whereas antireform actors are "frequently organized and vocal."[104] Most obviously, the political process is likely to respond to those with voice. In the GCC region, proreform actors such as political parties, interest groups, and unions need to be more organized and vocal in order to bring more entrepreneurship-friendly institutional changes.

End of Chapter Questions

1   Why are the incentives low for GCC policy makers to take measures to change institutions in favor of entrepreneurship?
2   What are some of the characteristics of GCC rulers that are more open to institutional reforms? Explain with examples.
3   Select a GCC country. Comment on the quality of entrepreneurial ecosystem in the country you selected.

4   Do Western governments differ in terms of their orientation toward institutional reforms in GCC economies compared to other developing countries?

5   What are some of the barriers facing an entrepreneurship promoter in GCC countries?

End of the Chapter Case: Qatar Financial Center Meets Mega-Entrepreneurial Interests

The Qatar Financial Centre Authority (QFC Authority) is a government institution located in Doha, the capital of Qatar. It was established in 2005 to provide legal, regulatory, tax, and business infrastructure and environment for firms in financial services and other related sectors.[105] A key goal of the QFC is to bring global best practices to Qatar and focus on investment opportunities at the local and regional levels.

Special Laws Governing Firms Operating in QFC

The general law is that foreign firms are required to have a local partner that owns at least a 51% of the shares.[106] In 2004, Qatar amended the law to allow foreign investment in the banking and insurance sectors with the approval of the Cabinet of Ministers. Moreover, foreign financial services firms established at the QFC are allowed 100% ownership. In 2009, Qatar amended law to allow foreign investors to hold 100% ownership in certain sectors including business consultancy and technical services, information and communication services, cultural services, sports services, entertainment services, and distribution services. However, in response to complaints by local firms of unfair competition, in 2015 the QFC stopped issuing new licenses to foreign law firms.[107]

The QFC is one of two authorities under which 100% foreign-owned companies are allowed to operate in Qatar. It also allows 100% repatriation of profits. Businesses can trade in any currency. The QFC also has an internationally competitive tax system. The corporate tax rate is 10% on locally generated profits.[108]

While Sharia law is practiced in Qatar, the QFC follows legal structure based on English common law. For instance, the QFC has enacted data protection laws modeled after the European Union's data protection directive to regulate the processing, storage, and transfer of personal data.[109]

Firms Operating in the QFC

As of August 2017, 410 companies in diverse sectors had made direct investment of QR75 billion in the QFC.[110] Some prominent examples include international banks, such as Credit Suisse,[111] research services firms such as Bloomberg *and* Thomson Reuters, valuation services firms such as ValuStrat and Management consulting firms such as PWC and McKinsey.[112]

In June 2017, diplomatic and trade boycott was imposed on Qatar by four Arab countries: Saudi Arabia, the UAE, Egypt, and Bahrain. The country experienced an air, sea, and land blockade. Heightened concern was expressed by the elites that their investments registered in foreign countries could be frozen.[113] The blockade led to an increase in investments in the QFC. Qatar's state-owned companies, rich Qataris, and companies that were mostly owned by Qatari shareholders redirected their investments to the QFC.

Conclusion

The QFC was established to attract international financial services and firms in related sectors. A key aspect of this initiative is that organizations operating within the QFC follow different laws. It has been reasonably successful in attracting high-profile global companies.

Notes

1 Azzam, H.T. 1999. "Arab states urged to liberalize trade, lure investment to bolster growth," *Middle East Newsfile*, 2 September; Reed, O. L. 2001. Law, the rule of law, and property: A foundation for the private market and business study, *American Business Law Journal*, 38(3), pp. 441–473.
2 Bains, E. 2009. "Qatar tackles region's jobless youth", *MEED: Middle East Economic Digest*, 53(26), pp. 26–27.
3 "The environment for women's entrepreneurship in the middle east and north Africa region," http://siteresources.worldbank.org/INTMENA/Resources/Environment_for_Womens_Entrepreneurship_in_MNA_final.pdf.
4 Ibid.
5 Kotilaine, J. 2011. "Comment: Labour reform key to development," 23 March, www.ft.com/cms/s/0/04f08dec-5563-11e0-87fe-00144feab49a.html#axzz1Z2bM9tr6.
6 Bains. 2009.
7 Atkinson, S. 2011. Kuwait hands out cash to bridge small business gulf, 3 July www.bbc.co.uk/news/business-14006885.
8 Arnold, T. 2011. "Oman raises minimum wage for nationals," 17 February, www.thenational.ae/news/worldwide/middle-east/oman-raises-minimum-wage-for-nationals.
9 Bains. 2009.
10 Zakaria, F. 2004. "Islam, democracy, and constitutional liberalism," *Political Science Quarterly*, 119(1), p. 1.
11 Atkinson, 2011.
12 gccstartup.news. 2018. "5 startups qualified for Saudi Badir Accelerator in its second cohort," 20 January, www.gccstartup.news/saudi-arabia/5-startups-qualified-for-saudi-badir-accelerator-in-its-second-cohort/.
13 Ibid.

14 Manalo, K. 2009. "Bahrain's Fintech Bay offers infrastructure to crypto companies," March, https://cryptovest.com/news/bahrains-fintech-bay-offers-infrastructure-to-crypto-companies/.
15 Semcow, K. 2018a. "Bahrain launches major fintech hub", 6 March, www.thenational.ae/business/bahrain-launches-major-fintech-hub-1.710688.
16 Ibid.
17 Ibid.
18 arabianbusiness.com/. 2016. "Gulf SMEs led by women entrepreneurs worth $385bn," www.arabianbusiness.com/gulf-smes-led-by-women-entrepreneurs-worth-385bn-643830.html.
19 The minimum wage including salary and benefits was 140 R.O. (about US$363) per month. 2011 Investment Climate Statement Bureau of Economic, Energy and Business Affairs, March 2011, www.state.gov/e/eeb/rls/othr/ics/2011/157339.htm.
20 Semcow, K. 2018b. "Is Bahrain the region's next innovation hub?" 6 March, www.thenational.ae/business/is-bahrain-the-region-s-next-innovation-hub-1.710682.
21 Egypt Business Forecast Report (EBFR). 2006. Chapter 3: Special Report, 4th Quarter, pp. 26–38.
22 Reuters. 2018. "Saudi Arabia says it has seized more than $124 billion in corruption purge," 30 January, www.abc.net.au/news/2018-01-31/saudi-arabia-seizes-more-than-$124-billion-in-corruption-purge/9377370.
23 Algethami, S., & Narayanan, A. 2018. "Saudi Purge puts investments at risk as uncertainty lingers," 29 January, www.bloomberg.com/news/articles/2018-01-29/saudi-corruption-purge-risks-investments-as-uncertainty-lingers.
24 Northam, J. 2018. "Saudi Prince may have trouble finding U.S. investors after anti-corruption campaign," 16 March, www.npr.org/2018/03/16/594364448/saudi-prince-may-have-trouble-finding-u-s-investors-after-anti-corruption-campai.
25 Gulf Business. 2017. "Unravelling the UAE's bankruptcy law," 22 July, http://gulfbusiness.com/unravelling-uaes-bankruptcy-law/
26 Ibid.
27 Semcow. 2018b.
28 Heftier, R.W. 2006. "Islamic economics and global capitalism," Society, 44(1), pp. 16–22.
29 Theil, S. 2007. "Teaching entrepreneurship in the Arab world," Newsweek International, 14 August, German Marshall Fund of the United States www.gmfus.org/publications/article.cfm?id=332.
30 Maceda, C. 2010. "World of wealthy women," 14 August, http://gulfnews.com/business/your-money/world-of-wealthy-women-1.667819.
31 Simon, G. 1998. "Who goes where?" UNESCO Courier, 51(11): pp. 23–25.
32 Lucas, R.E.B. 2001. "Diaspora and development: Highly skilled migrants from East Asia," Report prepared for the World Bank, http://citeseerx.ist.psu.edu/viewdoc/download?doi=10.1.1.147.6620&rep=rep1&type=pdf.
33 Balasubramanian, A. 2010. "Rebuilding Dubai," Harvard International Review, 31(4), pp. 10–11.
34 Saudi Gazette. 2010. "Saudi women: A major growth driver for the country's diversification policy," 2 August, www.saudigazette.com.sa/index.cfm?method=home.regcon&contentID=2010080379929.
35 ameinfo.com. 2010. "Injaz Al-Arab board convenes in Qatar," 02 June. www.ameinfo.com/234264.html.

36 "Opportunities Mixed with Challenges: Creating Technology That Reso-
    nates in the Arab World," 02 November 2010, http://knowledge.wharton.
    upenn.edu/arabic/article.cfm?articleId=2559.
37 Zakaria. 2004.
38 Arab News. 2012. "Saudi attorney calls for new antitrust law," 13 August.
    http://arabnews.com/economy/saudi-attorney-calls-new-antitrust-law.
39 D'Cunha, S.D. 2017. "Gulf crisis: Qatar startup ecosystem can hold out against
    Arab Embargo," www.forbes.com/sites/suparnadutt/2017/07/14/gulf-crisis-
    qatar-startup-ecosystem-can-hold-out-against-arab-embargo/#151dbc7611b0.
40 Augustine, B.D. 2016. "Venture capitalists come to the rescue of GCC SMEs,"
    31 July, http://gulfnews.com/business/sectors/banking/venture-capitalists-
    come-to-the-rescue-of-gcc-smes-1.1871070.
41 Alam, N. 2015. "Islamic finance: An opportunity for SME Financing,"
    www.ifac.org/global-knowledge-gateway/islamic-finance/discussion/
    islamic-finance-opportunity-sme-financing.
42 Augustine. 2016.
43 Ibid.
44 Semcow. 2018.
45 MENA Investment Policy Brief, Issue 1, April 2006 www.oecd.org/datao-
    ecd/26/54/37256468.pdf.
46 azensys.com. 2011. "Venture capital to boost innovation in Arab world," 25
    July. www.azensys.com/2011/07/25/venture-capital-to-boost-innovation-
    in-arab-world/
47 MENA Investment Policy Brief, Issue 1, April 2006.
48 Ibid.
49 Hudson, M.C. 2002. "Imperial headaches: Managing unruly regions in an
    age of globalization," *Middle East Policy*, 9(4), pp. 61–74; Jamal, A.A. 2006.
    "Reassessing Support for Islam and Democracy in the Arab World? Evidence
    from Egypt and Jordan," *World Affairs*, 169(2), pp. 51–63.
50 Gershman, C., & Allen, M. 2006. "The assault on democracy assistance,"
    Journal of Democracy, 17(2), pp. 36–51.
51 Kristof, N. D. 2003. "Running for the Exits," *New York Times*, 18 April, A. 15.
52 Kuwait Country Review, 2006, Political Overview, pp. 7–31.
53 Scott, B.R. 2001. "The great divide in the global village," *Foreign Affairs*,
    80(1), pp. 160–177.
54 Hoffman, A.J. 1999. "Institutional evolution and change: Environmental-
    ism and the U.S. chemical industry," *Academy of Management Journal*, 42(4),
    pp. 351–371.
55 Groenewegen, J., & van der Steen, M. 2007. "The evolutionary policy
    maker," *Journal of Economic Issues*, 41(2), pp. 351–358.
56 Potter, P.B. 2001. The Chinese Legal System: Globalization and Local Legal
    Culture. London: Routledge.
57 Boettke, P., & Storr, V. 2002. "Post classical political economy," *American
    Journal of Economics & Sociology*, 61, pp. 161–191.
58 Zweynert, J., Goldschmidt, N. 2006. The Two Transitions in Central and
    Eastern Europe as Processes of Institutional Transplantation.
59 Zoubir, Y.H. 1996. "Algerian Islamists' conception of democracy," *Arab
    Studies Quarterly*, 18(3), pp. 65–85.
60 Ibid.
61 Kadir, S. 2004. "Islam, state and society in Singapore," *Inter-Asia Cultural
    Studies*, 5(3), pp. 357–371.

62 Zuhur, S. 2005. "A hundred Osamas: Islamist threats and the future of coun-
    terinsurgency," US Army War College, Strategic Studies Institute, Carlisle
    Barracks, PA. December 2005, p. 26.

63 Jamal, A.A. 2006. "Reassessing support for Islam and democracy in the Arab
    world? Evidence from Egypt and Jordan," *World Affairs*, 169(2), pp. 51–63.

64 In Bahrain and Kuwait, about 10% of total class hours are devoted for Islamic
    instructions. In Saudi Arabia Islamic instruction consumes 32% of class time
    for grades 1–3 and decreases for higher grades (about 15% for grades 10–12).
    The figures for Qatar are 8%–17%.

65 Ergil, D. 2000. "Identity crises and political instability in Turkey," *Journal of
    International Affairs*, 54(1), pp. 43–63.

66 Heftier. 2006.

67 Zakaria. 2004.

68 Hudson. 2002.

69 Kéchichian, J.A. 2004. "Democratization in gulf monarchies: A new chal-
    lenge to the GCC"; Power, C. 2003. "Hillary Clinton stand back," *News-
    week*, 10 November, pp. 31–32.

70 Stallings, B. 1992. International Influence on Economic Policy: Debt, Sta-
    bilization and the Crisis of Import Substitution, in The Politics of Economic
    Adjustment, ed. Stephan Haggard and Robert Kaufman, Princeton, NJ:
    Princeton University Press, p. 75.

71 Marr, P. 2003. "Iraq "the day after": Internal dynamics in post-Saddam
    Iraq," *Naval War College Review*, 56(1), pp. 12–29.

72 Glasser, B.L. 1995. "External capital and political liberalizations: A typology
    of Middle Eastern development in the 1980s and 1990s," *Journal of Interna-
    tional Affairs*, 49(1), pp. 45–73.

73 Fattah, H.M. 2005. "Conference of Arab leaders yields little of significance,"
    New York Times, 24 March, A. 12.

74 Ignatius, D. 2003. "Home-grown Saudi reform." *The Washington Post*, 7
    March, A. 33.

75 Lindblom, C. 1977. *Politics and Markets*. New York: Basic Books.

76 Hicks, A. 1999. *Social Democracy and Welfare Capitalism*. Ithaca, NY: Cornell
    University Press.

77 Reiter, Y. 2004. "The Palestinian-Transjordanian rift: Economic might and
    political power in Jordan," *The Middle East Journal*, 58(1), pp. 72–92.

78 Haggard, S., & Kaufman, R.R. 1995. *The Political Economy of Democratic
    Transitions*. Princeton, NJ: Princeton University Press.

79 Chen, A. 2002. "Capitalist development, entrepreneurial class, and democ-
    ratization in China," *Political Science Quarterly*, 117(3), pp. 401–422.

80 Lewis, R. 1995. "How peace can come to the Middle East," *Management
    Today*, July, pp. 80–81.

81 Khashan, H. 1997. "The new world order and the tempo of militant Islam,"
    British Journal of Middle Eastern Studies, 24(1), pp. 5–24.

82 Al-Haj, A.J. 1996. The politics of participation in the Gulf Cooperation
    Council states: The Omani Consultative Council.

83 Pollock, R.L. 2002. "Mideast peace? Let's start with the rule of law," *Wall
    Street Journal*, 27 November, A.10.

84 Potter, P.B. 2004. "Legal reform in China: institutions, culture, and selec-
    tive adaptation," *Law & Social Inquiry*, 29(2), pp. 465–495.

85 The U.S. has created a Millennium Challenge Account (MCA), which has
    strict standards related to governance and economic reform measures for
    recipients.

86 Krasner, S.D., & Pascual, C. 2005. "Addressing state failure," *Foreign Affairs*, 84(4), p. 153.
87 Economist. 2002a. "Murder, and its consequences: How safe an anti-Iraq Ally is Jordan?" 31 October.
88 El-Said, H., & Harrigan, J. 2006. "Globalization, international finance, and political Islam in the Arab world," *The Middle East Journal*, 60(3), pp. 444–466.
89 Pfeifer, K. 1999. "How Tunisia, Morocco, Jordan and even Egypt became IMF success stories," *The Middle East Report*, 29(210), pp. 23–26.
90 Seznec, J. 2005. "Business as usual," *Harvard International Review*, 26(4), pp. 56–60.
91 Rosner, S. 2007. "Selling arms to the Saudis," www.haaretz.com/hasen/pages/rosnerBlog.jhtml?itemNo=888300&contrassID=25&subContrassID=0&sbSubContrassID=1&listSrc=Y&art=5#article888300.
92 Hanson, V.D. 2006. "How oil lubricates our enemies," *The American Enterprise*. 17(6), p. 44.
93 Acharya, A. 1999. "Realism, institutionalism, and the Asian economic crisis," *Contemporary Southeast Asia*, 21(1), pp. 1–29.
94 Richards, A. 2002. "Socioeconomic roots of Middle East radicalism," *Naval War College Review*, 55(4), pp. 22–38.
95 Bakhsh, S. 2015. "Silicon Desert: Can Kuwait move from oil to entrepreneurs?" 19 November, www.bbc.com/news/business-34798157.
96 Lancaster, J. 1998. "Gulf States hurt by oil-price slump; Kuwaitis, Saudis may face spending cuts in popular programs," *The Washington Post*, 14 June, A.21.
97 Semcow. 2018.
98 Campbell, J.L. 2004. *Institutional Change and Globalization*. Princeton, NJ: Princeton University Press.
99 Theil. 2007.
100 Saudi Gazette. 2010. "Saudi women: A major growth driver for the country's diversification policy," 2 August, www.saudigazette.com.sa/index.cfm?method=home.regcon&contentID=2010080379929.
101 Ibid.
102 Campbell. 2004.
103 Kéchichian. 2004.
104 Kikeri, S., & Nellis, J. 2004. "An assessment of privatization," *The World Bank Research Observer*, 19(1), p. 87.
105 Bloomberg. 2016. "Qatar financial centre authority appoints Haitham Al-Salama as chief economic adviser," 21 August, www.bloomberg.com/research/stocks/private/snapshot.asp?privcapId=22549074.
106 Reuters. 2016. "New Qatar financial city will be open to non-licensed foreign firms," 20 September, www.thenational.ae/business/new-qatar-financial-city-will-be-open-to-non-licensed-foreign-firms-1.207577.
107 U.S. Department of State. 2015. "2015 investment climate statement Qatar," www.state.gov/e/eb/rls/othr/ics/2015/241709.htm.
108 The European. 2017. "Qatar financial centre: A platform for growth," 31 October, www.the-european.eu/story-12529/qatar-financial-centre-a-platform-for-growth.html.
109 Latham & Watkins LLP. 2013, "Data protection and privacy laws in the middle East," 15 October, www.jdsupra.com/legalnews/data-protection-and-privacy-laws-in-the-24928/.
110 Al Raya Newspaper, Qatar Tribune, 2017. "Al Jaida: QFC now has 410 companies with Assets of QR75BN," 27 August, http://portal.www.gov.qa/

wps/portal/media–center/news/news–details/aljaidaqfcnowhasfourhundred
andtencompanieswithassetsofqrseventyfivebn.

111 24/7 Wall St. 2008. "Qatar's $15 Billion Bank Rescue Fund," https://
247wallst.com/banking-finance/2008/02/18/qatars-15-billi/.

112 Mukherjee, A. 2017. "Raising the game: Qatar financial centre authority
CEO Yousuf Mohamed Al-Jaida," 17 February, www.entrepreneur.com/
article/289088.

113 Sayegh, H.A. 2017. "Gulf boycott boosts Qatar as wealth comes home,"
19 December, www.businessinsider.com/r-gulf-boycott-boosts-qatar-as-
wealth-comes-home-2017-12.

Chapter 7

Entrepreneurship in Africa

Objectives of this chapter

This chapter's objectives include:

1   To *demonstrate* an understanding of the natures of entrepreneurial ac-
    tivities in African economies.
2   To *analyze* the facilitators and hindrances of entrepreneurship in
    African economies and compare them with other regions of the world.
3   To *evaluate* some of the successful as well as unsuccessful activities
    related to entrepreneurship in African economies.
4   To *evaluate* the roles of foreign companies in driving entrepreneurship
    development in Africa and their roles to the local economy.
5   To *demonstrate* an understanding of western response to low level of
    entrepreneurial activities in Africa.

Introduction

Africa is arguably the richest continent in terms of the stock of minerals and
natural resources. However, the continent's entrepreneurial performance has
been weak. Although entrepreneurial activities arguably existed in Africa
before colonization, such activities slowed down since the colonial period.[1]
It is argued that Africa's entrepreneurial failure can be attributed to factors
such as the lack of sensitivity of raw agricultural products to international
prices, poor infrastructure, lack of human and financial capital, and government policies that are not entrepreneurship-friendly.[2] According to a Gallup
poll, 59% of Nigerians were unhappy with the filing process for registering
a business.[3] Productive entrepreneurship in African economies has also been
hindered by a lack of quality standards and inappropriate trade policies.

However, there are many successful entrepreneurs in Africa who come
from various demographic, cultural, and educational backgrounds. Studies
have also found the existence of many competitive small businesses in the
region. Some successful businesses in the continent have found creative
ways to overcome economic, social, political, and institutional barriers to

entrepreneurship. For instance, the Rwanda-based fashion label, KEZA was able to overcome various barriers for the company's business model to work in Rwanda. The company trained manufacturing cooperatives in such areas as design, quality control, product consistency, and accounting.[4] It trains Rwandan women in business development and. The company has partnered with Rwandan women to bring their handmade jewelry to the U.S. KEZA has developed a social entrepreneurship-based business model, which is sustainable and is making a profit.

There have also been encouraging initiatives from some government agencies. In March 2018, Commercial banks in Nigeria announced a plan to launch 500,000 agent networks to offer basic financial services across the country in collaboration with the Central Bank of Nigeria (CBN), mobile money operators and super agents.[5] Note that in Nigeria, super agents are businesses or individuals that are licensed by the CBN and contracted by financial service providers to engage in financial market activities. A super agent can identify, train, monitor, and manage other subagents.[6] Super agents are expected to enhance financial inclusion in rural communities.[7]

A Survey of Entrepreneurship in Africa

Observers have noted that while entrepreneurial activities existed in Africa before colonization such activities slowed down since the colonial period.[8] Most African economies have failed to productively utilize their natural and human resources.

A lack of jobs and high prices were major factors that contributed to mass protests, leading to the Arab Spring in 2011, which affected some economies in Africa.[9] South Africa, the most prosperous economy in Sub-Saharan Africa (SSA), is reported to have a youth unemployment rate of about 54%. Likewise, in Ghana, while the official unemployment rate is 5.2%, the underemployment rate is 47%.[10]

According to the World Bank, the share of Africans that are poor declined from 56% in 1990 to 43% in 2012. However, due to population growth, the number of poor people has increased. For instance, about 330 million Africans were estimated to be living in extreme poverty in 2012 compared to 280 million in 1990.[11] The World Bank projects that "the world's extreme poor will be increasingly concentrated in Africa."[12]

Although some African economies are growing fast, because of high-income inequality, the population at the bottom of the economic pyramid has seen virtually no improvement in living standards. Among the world's 10 countries with the highest income inequalities, seven are in Africa.[13] South Africa, Namibia, Botswana, and Central African Republic are among five countries with the most unequal income distribution—based on the Gini index (http://databank.worldbank.org/data/reports.aspx?source=2&series=SI.POV.GINI&country=).

A problem hindering entrepreneurial efforts in Africa is the large size of the region's informal economy. The informal economy represents about 38% of the GDP.[14] In Malawi, only 50,000 people out of a population of 12 million (0.4% of the total population) are estimated to have formal jobs in the private sector.[15] A Gallup survey conducted among Nigerians found that 69% of potential entrepreneurs would not formally register their businesses and only 19% of the respondents said their business would be formally registered.[16]

Positive and Encouraging Signs

There are number of positive and encouraging signs in Africa's entrepreneurial landscape. Some African economies have made significant strides in improving their entrepreneurial climate.

Contrary to the widespread belief that indigenous entrepreneurship is less well represented in Africa, various studies have shown that Africa doesn't lack entrepreneurial talent. The continent has an abundance of entrepreneurs who possess the ability to identify business opportunities and to exploit them, and recent surveys conducted in some African economies have confirmed this view.[17] For instance, a Gallup Poll indicated that 67% of Nigerians have thought of starting a business. The proportion was among the highest rates in West Africa.[18]

Some cities in Africa have rapidly developed a strong startup ecosystem. According to a report from Startup Genome, the local startup ecosystem in Lagos, Nigeria was valued at US$2 billion. According to the report, Lagos was the most valuable city although there were only 400–700 active startups, compared to 1,200 in Cape Town.[19]

Entrepreneurship Support Programs

Entrepreneurship in the continent has access to support programs such as incubators and accelerators. Community-based organizations, such as coworking spaces, are a relatively new phenomenon in Africa. They are, however, diffusing rapidly. In 2017, there were over 250 coworking spaces in Africa, 80% of which were established after 2015.[20]

Some are focusing on the latest technologies such as blockchain. For instance, Nairobi, Kenya-based BitHub Africa is a blockchain accelerator for local startups. It was founded in 2015. BitHub Africa provides consulting services for organizations based in Africa and the Middle East to deploy blockchain-based solutions. It also helps blockchain startups *to* scale up faster. A special focus is on incubating microlending startups. It also engages in lobbying activities in order to bring favorable regulations for ICOs and cryptocurrencies. In Cape Town, South Africa, the Block-chain Academy provides training on cryptocurrencies and blockchain technology to startups and entrepreneurs. It also advises local businesses to use blockchain technology.[21]

Others are targeted to the young population. The Kumasi Business Incubator (KBI) at the Kwame Nkrumah University of Science and Technology (KNUST) helps young entrepreneurs turn business ideas into viable businesses. World Bank's eGhana Project provided partial funding for the KBI to support the government's goal to increase employment through ICT and public private partnerships.[22] It specially focuses on software development and applications. The KBI was established in 2011 in partnership with the National Board for Small Scale Industry (NBSSI).[23]

Some analysts have, however, argued that the incubation model is not working in Africa, at least in some areas such as software. For instance, none of the nine biggest software startups in Nigeria (Konga, Wakanow, Iroko, Paga, DealDey, Jobberman, Cheki, PrivateProperty, Nairabet, Nairaland) were built by an incubator.[24] One reason could be that incubators are attracting the "wrong" kind of founders, that want to be "taught" about building a startup and attend the incubation center regularly to be "incubated." It is suggested that the incubators should focus on finding the best founders.[25]

Entrepreneurial Firms Mobilizing Positive Social and Economic Change

There are also some high-profile examples of African businesses with highly effective entrepreneurial impacts. South Africa is the largest center of entrepreneurial activities in Africa, which has more than half of top 100 companies in the African continent. An example of a South African company, which has been able to build a global brand is South African Breweries Ltd. (SAB). SABMiller, which was created by the merger of SAB and the Miller Brewing Company, holds a prominent place in the global beer market. One of its brands, Castle has been introduced as a premium beer brand across the world.[26] SABMiller has discovered how to tap the local taste for homemade brews, making them with cheap inputs (instead of barley), while adapting modern technology and promoting local economic development.

In Africa, SABMiller buys local crops such as sorghum instead of importing expensive barley. A SABMiller-commissioned study indicated that for every job in SABMiller's breweries in Uganda, the company supported over one hundred other jobs throughout the country. The company has thus contributed to local economic development by stabilizing the prices of local commodity such as sorghum and increasing farmers' incomes.[27]

To take an example, Ekuphileni Poultry and Agricultural Farming Cooperative, a women-owned farm in Utrecht, a town in the foothills of the Balele Mountains in South Africa, was reported to receive a huge investment in March 2018 from SABMiller, the Department of Small Business

Development (DSBD) and the Department of Agriculture and Rural Development.[28] Ekuphileni had received R6.4-million in investment by that time. A total of 11 cooperatives supplied maize to SAB.

Diversification of Entrepreneurial Activities

While many African economies export oil and a few types of natural resources, some, especially non-resource-rich ones such as Kenya, Tanzania, and South Africa, have made a significant progress in diversifying exports. On average, 17 export products of these countries constitute 75% of total exports. African countries' progress has been more impressive in diversifying export markets. While developing countries accounted for only about 25% of African exports in the early 1990s, their share rose to about 50% by 2009.[29]

In some African economies, there is little or no gender gap in entrepreneurship, and men and women are reported to have equal propensity to be entrepreneurs. A Gallup survey, for instance, indicated that in Nigeria, 67% of female respondents and 68% of male respondents liked the idea of starting a business.[30] Women's propensity to engage in entrepreneurial activities in Nigeria compares more favorably with many economies in Arab and Asia. In 2006, for instance, proportions of the adult population (aged 18–64) engaged in entrepreneurial activities in India were 18.9% for men and 13% for women.[31]

Increase in Opportunity-Based Entrepreneurial Activities

More and more entrepreneurial activities in the country are opportunity-based instead of necessity-based. In Nigeria, people with jobs are found to have a higher propensity to start a business than those without a job. For instance, 77% of Nigerians who had a job expressed an interest in starting a business compared to only 53% of those who were unemployed.[32]

Natural Resources and Their Relations to Entrepreneurship

Africa principally remains a source of natural resources, raw materials, and commodities; it is considered to be the most mineral rich continent in the world. One estimate suggests that about two-thirds of the world's cobalt is mined in central Africa.[33] Similarly, the Ivory Coast, Ghana, Nigeria, and Cameroon are the four major West African cocoa producers. The Ivory Coast alone produces about 43% of the world's cocoa. Likewise, Zimbabwe has the second largest reserves of platinum in the world and large quantities of other precious metals such as gold and copper.[34]

African economies carry enormous potential for entrepreneurship in agricultural development because of the continent's abundance in natural resources and labor.[35] Yet, it is also apparent many African countries export agricultural products such as cocoa, coffee, tobacco, and cotton, mainly in raw forms.[36] There has been limited success in their attempts to add value to agricultural products through processing and their use to develop other industrial sectors. Moreover, because of the recent global financial crisis (GFC), some African economies are severely affected by declines in global demand and value for these commodities.[37]

The continent holds 8%–9% of the world's crude oil reserves and provides about 10% of the global production.[38] This is considerably less compared to the Middle East's 62%. However, some industry analysts believe the continent could have much more undiscovered reserves. Indeed, during 2000–2005, 30% of the world's newly discovered oil reserves were from the Gulf of Guinea region of Africa's west coast.[39] More importantly, West Africa's oil reserves are of high quality. For instance, a low sulfur content of West Africa's oil makes it easier and cheaper to refine.[40] Furthermore, West African reserves are easily accessible to Western Europe and the U.S. by sea.

Natural resources have also transformed some African countries' economic orientation. For instance, after the discovery of oil in 1957, Nigeria began transformation from an agriculture-based to an oil-dependent economy. Most African countries have made little progresses in reforming institutions to promote entrepreneurship. Among the African countries that are Arab League members, the depth of institutional reforms is arguably low in Algeria and the region's primary export economies such as Comoros, Djibouti, Mauritania, Sudan, and Yemen. Likewise, although Morocco has encouraged economic liberalization, there has also been a convergence of business and government interests in the country.[41]

Determinants of Entrepreneurship in Africa

Regulatory Framework

Laws, regulations, and policy in most African economies have been major barriers to entrepreneurship development. Factors such as corruption, the quality of the rule of law and the effectiveness of the national legal system in enforcing contracts have acted as barriers hindering the development of entrepreneurship. An upshot is that Africans have a relatively low degree of trust in government agencies. Citizens often tend to have more faith in informal institutions such as religious and traditional leaders compared to formal ones such as the state.

The rule of law in many African economies is weak. For instance, in Tunisia, established business elites have attempted to protect their privileges and benefits from the existing regulations. They have done so through close relations with corrupt politicians and bureaucrats. This has come at the expense of new entrepreneurs from marginalized regions.[42]

According to African Union, corruption has cost Africa about US$150 billion annually, or a quarter of the region's GDP. The World Bank has estimated the figure even higher—US$500 billion to US$1 trillion.[43] Note that these figures are significantly higher than the continent's FDI, which was US$59 billion in 2016 (http://unctad.org/en/pages/PressRelease.aspx?OriginalVersionID=408).

According to Freedom House's *Freedom in the World* 2017 report, only 18% of the SSA countries were in the "free category." 41% were in "partly free" and 41% were in "not free" category.[44] Freedom House referred to Africa as the world's "most politically volatile region" in terms of political rights and civil liberties in 2013. Commenting on elections and superficiality of Africa's donor-driven democracy, an article noted, "While donors make regular electoral contests a condition for aid and debt relief, many African regimes have paid little more than lip-service to reforms, aided by the relative weakness of state institutions which enable the subversion of free elections."[45]

Observers have noted that in many African countries with weak institutions, economic policy is dominated by wealth redistribution instead of wealth creation. One reason most African countries have been unable to attract investments concerns a lack of institutions to protect the long-term security of property rights.

Governments' Involvement in Economies

Most African countries have mixed economies with varying degrees of market economy and state ownership. A number of firms were nationalized in these economies and private and public firms function side by side. Compared to other regions in the world, in most SSA countries, governments control a significantly higher proportion of national resources and in most of them, the government is the largest employer.[46] In some African countries, the nationalization process is still going on and large, economically central firms that are particularly attractive for the national take over. For instance, in 2004, Zimbabwe's ex-president Robert Mugabe announced his government's plan to demand half-ownership of all privately owned mines in the country to stay in control of its natural resources.[47]

In Africa, the commercial class and the national elite have a high degree of complementary characteristics. As noted earlier, African commercial class lacks financial and managerial ability to run "high markets."[48] State elite, on the other hand, see professional and personal rewards in nationalizing such markets.

Capitalism in African Economies

Many African economies are characterized by oligarchic capitalism. Illustrating the existence of oligarchic capitalism and cronyism in Africa, a Boston

Globe article asserts, "African leaders, their cronies, European traders, foreign heads of state, and American middlemen, among others, have reaped billions from the continent's oil resources over the last four decades."[49] The ruling elites and their family, friends and clients have thus lived a parasitic existence in some African economies. According to creditors and *Publish What You Pay*, in 2004, about US$300 million or about one-third of Congo's oil revenues did not show up in the country's budgets.[50]

Ease of Doing Business

African economies are heterogeneous in their policies to promote entrepreneurship. In this regard, African economies vary widely in terms of costs and time required in starting a business (Figure 7.1). It is relatively easy to start a business in some economies such as Morocco and South Africa.

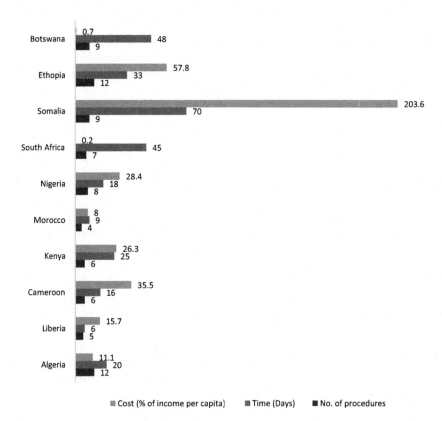

Figure 7.1 Starting a Business in Some Economies in Africa.
Source: The World Bank "Doing Business 2018" (www.doingbusiness.org/rankings).

However, according to the World Bank's Doing Business 2018 report, of the ten least business-friendly countries, six were in Africa: the DRC, Central African Republic, Libya, South Sudan, Eritrea, and Somalia. Regulatory burden, bureaucracy, and the lack of political will have severely affected formal operations of businesses in the continent. In Somalia, which had the world's worst regulatory climate according to the World Bank's Ease of Doing Business 2018, nine procedures are needed to be completed to start a business which take 70 days and cost 204% of the country's per capita income.

Values, Culture, and Skills

Value and Culture

As noted in Chapter 1, in some societies, family and social obligations act as barriers to productive entrepreneurship. Observers have noted the existence of a culture of "forced mutual help" in Africa.[51] That is, wealthy individuals in many African economies have a social obligation to share their wealth with their relatives and members of the extended family that have less wealth.

Entrepreneurial Skills

Among the biggest roadblocks for entrepreneurial performance in the region are the lack of entrepreneurial skills and poor management of human resources. An observation is that African private entrepreneurs lack financial and managerial ability to run large and sophisticated businesses.[52] Estimates suggest that about 60% of Africa's population is younger than 25.

According to a 2018 World Bank report about 50 million children in Africa were out of school.[53] According to the UNDP's Human Development Report 2013, among the 25 and older population, only 23.7% females and 35.1% males had at least secondary education, which compares with the world average of 52.3% and 62.9%, respectively.

Education offered by schools in Africa is reported to be of low quality. Among second-grade students that were assessed on numeracy tests in several Sub-Saharan African countries, three-quarters were unable to count beyond 80. 40% could not do a one-digit addition problem. A large proportion could not read even a single word.[54]

Among the students enrolled in secondary education, only 5% get vocational training. Moreover, business studies are virtually absent and critics point out that most apprenticeships involve child exploitation.[55]

Access to Finance, Market, R&D, and Technology

Access to Finance

HOUSEHOLD SAVING

There are overlapping functions of saving, credit, and insurance. Savings can thus partially substitute for credit and insurance, especially when markets for the latter two are imperfect. Analysts have linked economic under-performance of SSA with a low savings rate.

SSA's saving rate is the lowest across all regions and there has been a declining trend.[56] For instance, according to the South African Reserve Bank (SARB), the household saving rate declined in South Africa during 2000–2016 and reached a record low of −2.7% in 2013.[57]

Saving rates as proportions of disposable incomes in selected African economies are presented in Figure 7.2. Overall, African economies saving rates are substantially lower compared to those of China and India, which had saving rates as proportions of disposable income as 37.5% and 25.5%, respectively, in 2017.

The low savings rate can be attributed to a low-level flow of financing between the informal and formal sectors. Capital flight has worsened the situation. In this regard, household savings are also less prone to capital flight.

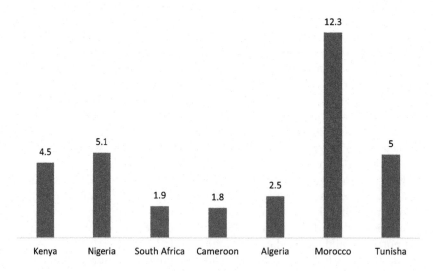

Figure 7.2 Saving as a Percentage of Disposable Income in Selected African Economies (2017).
Source: Euromonitor International.

REMITTANCES

Remittance flows to SSA economies amounted US$33 billion in 2016.[58] Although most money sent home by migrants is spent on consumption, remittances also contribute to entrepreneurial activities because they allow even the very poor to save. Although remittance transfer costs have declined significantly in Latin America and in Asia, they are still high in Africa.

The average cost of sending money in SSA averaged 9.8% which made it the highest-cost region in the world.[59] In some parts of Africa, costs to remit money home can be as high as 25% of the sum to be remitted. Moreover, rural areas account for 30%–40% of remittances to Africa, where the recipients have to travel a long distance to get their cash. Africa has the same number of remittance payout locations as Mexico. Note that Mexico has only one-tenth of Africa's population. Restrictive laws and prohibitively high fees have thus hindered the potential of remittance to contribute to poverty reduction and productive entrepreneurship.

CAPITAL MARKETS

Capital markets are described as the "lifeblood" of entrepreneurial and economic development. Most of Africa's capital markets are small, illiquid and are not properly regulated.[60] As of 2016, there were 29 exchanges in Africa, representing 38 nations' capital markets.[61] The JSE ranked the 19th largest stock exchange in the world by market capitalization. It is the largest exchange in Africa.[62]

In 2017, US$2.8 billion was raised by 28 IPOs and US$10.6 billion by equity follow-on public offer or further offers (FOs). Note that in a follow-on public offer (FPO) a public company listed on a stock market exchange issues shares to investors. During 2013–2017, there were 519 African ECM transactions that raised US$52.7 billion.[63] African equity capital markets (ECM) activity in 2017 was largely driven by the financial sector for FOs, and consumer services sector for IPOs.[64]

Analysts argue that it is important to establish larger regional stock exchanges in Africa to provide the liquidity, security, and ease of access that investors want. The continent's leaders need to work together.[65]

AVAILABILITY AND COSTS OF BANK FINANCING

Availability of bank finances has also been a barrier to entrepreneurial activities. Banking penetration is low in the continent. Banks find it difficult to convert deposits into loans. Many banks were nationalized in the 1970s and have been poorly run. It is observed that politicians tend to treat banks as their "piggy-banks," like coin containers used by children.[66]

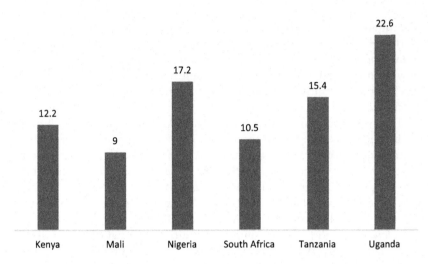

Figure 7.3 Annual Lending Rates in Some African Countries (2017).
Source: Euromonitor International.

According to a Gallup poll, 73% of Nigerians expressed concerns about getting a loan.[67] According an Adviser to the CBN, 60% of Nigerians are "under banked."[68] In order to open a bank account or credit line in Nigeria, birth certificate or passport is required. A survey found that only half of the country's population had one of them.[69]

Studies have found that low interest rates lead to an increase in new business startups. According to the *Euromonitor International*, in 2017, of the world's five countries with the highest annual lending rates (ALR) for short- and medium-term financing needs of businesses, four were from Africa: Madagascar, Malawi, Gambia, and Mozambique (Figure 3.1). In general, all African countries have high ALRs compared to advanced OECD countries (Figure 7.3).

Venture Capital

Venture capital (VC) is a relatively new phenomenon in Africa. According to Partech Ventures, African startups raised US$367 million in VC funding in 2016,[70] which reached US$560 million in 2017.[71] Other estimates suggest that African startups would raise more than US$1 billion VC funding by 2018.[72]

In South Africa, VC investment in 2016 was R872 million (about US$71 million) in 114 deals compared to R372 million (about US$30 million) invested in 93 deal in 2015. The average deal size in 2016 was R7.6 million (about US$616,000) compared to R4 million (about US$324,000) in 2015.[73]

In mature startup ecosystems such as San Francisco, New York, or London, investors tend to specialize by the stage of investment. Investors are confident that if they financed certain stages of growth, the next stages will be covered by others. In new startup communities, the later-stage investors are often missing.[74]

R&D and Technology

The growth of new enterprises depends upon the development of the knowledge base through R&D. R&D investment, technology diffusion, patent system and standards, technological cooperation between firms, broadband access, and university/industry interface affect entrepreneurial performance.

Modern technologies can also help fight against corruption and other social problems. For instance, Ghana's Bitland uses blockchain to store land registrations. As of early 2018, the project had been trialed in 28 communities in Kumasi. By allowing citizens to record land titles in a way that cannot be deleted or changed by a third party, Bitland hopes to reduce illegal displacement and corruption.[75]

As Figure 7.4 makes it clear, expenditure on R&D is very low in African economies. However, there have been some successful R&D efforts in Africa, which are likely to contribute to the continent's entrepreneurial development. Foreign Policy magazine conducted a survey with the

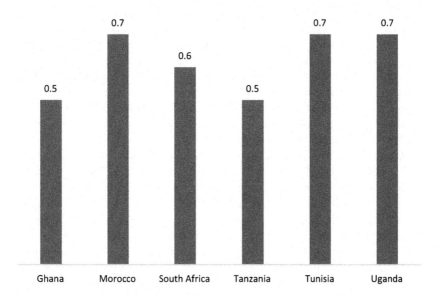

Figure 7.4 Gross Domestic Expenditure on R&D as a Percentage of GDP in Selected African Economies (2017).

world's top Internet experts regarding the Internet-related innovations. 7% of the experts viewed Africa as "the most innovative place for Internet-related technology." The corresponding proportions for other regions and economies were: Europe: 4%, China: 4%, India: 7%, and Pacific Rim: 5%. The experts viewed Africa's Internet-related innovations as "On-the-ground solutions designed by communities for communities."[76]

One of the key features of the Africa's digitization initiative is that innovation in this area is that it is increasingly home grown. Regarding the importance of home grown innovations, the founder of the African Institution of Technology and Chairman of Fasmicro Group, Ndubuisi Ekekwe put the issue this way: "Building the AI [artificial intelligence] models for the African consumer cannot be optimally driven by Silicon Valley vendors; rather, African universities and research institutes who understand the nuances of being an African are better positioned for this task."[77] This is in sharp contrast to other sectors of the African economy, such as mining or agribusiness, in which much of the know-how is imported and the wealth is extracted.[78] In this section, we discuss some information technology-related innovations created in SSA economies.

M-Pesa

M-Pesa (Swahili for mobile money) is operated by Kenya's largest cell phone service provider, Safaricom. M-Pesa allows can be used to send and receive money using cell phones.

M-Pesa is used to make person-to-person transfers (P2PTs), receive mobile phone credits, pay school fees, pay electricity bills, and save money. It can also be used for shopping. Many Kenyans use M-Pesa and other mobile payment systems.[79] As of 2011, Kenya had 10 million households but 14 million M-Pesa accounts, which held 40% of the country's savings.[80] About 70% of the Kenyan adult population used M-Pesa to make five times as many transactions as credit and debit cards combined together.[81] In the 2015 financial year, the value of M-Pesa transactions reached US$50 billion or 79% of the country's GDP.[82]

There were 22.62 million M-Pesa subscribers in June 2017 compared to 17.12 million in mid-2016.[83] In the FY, 2017–2018, 537.2 million transactions were made, which were valued at Shs 1.65 trillion (about US$1.65 billion). M-Pesa's market share was 80.8%.[84]

As of September 2016, M-Pesa was also used in Tanzania, South Africa, Afghanistan, India, Romania, and Albania.[85] In 2014, M-Pesa was launched in Romania by Vodafone, where about 35% of the population lacks access to formal banking. Romanian M-Pesa customers can transfer as little as one new Romanian leu (0.22 euro cents) up to 30,000 lei (€6,715) per day. In 2017, however, Vodafone terminated the service in Romania.[86] In 2016, Vodafone Romania M-Payments lost € 2.5 million.

EpiSurveyor (Magpi)

A team of programmers in Kenya developed the EpiSurveyor system (now known as Magpi).[87] EpiSurveyor is among the most popular and publicized tools involving the cloud and mobile phones for collecting and analyzing data. In the beginning, the team received grants from the World Bank, the United Nation Foundation, and the Vodafone Foundation.[88]

It has been used in improving water supply availability and reliability. The non-profit organization, Aquaya.org employs EpiSurveyor to help operators of rural water systems submit water quality data to their managers.[89] EpiSurveyor has also been used in healthcare, agriculture, business, research, and conservation.[90] In 2008, the World Health Organization (WHO) and Kenyan health ministry used EpiSurveyor to fight against polio. Health workers used EpiSurveyor to track an emergency vaccination campaign, which helped stop a potential polio epidemic.[91]

Nomanini's Lula

The South African startup, Nomanini sells a "business in a box," a cloud-based mobile prepaid airtime machine, to small informal entrepreneurs, which allows them to set up a "mini-business." It is called Lula (meaning "easy" in Zulu language), which is especially useful to provide services to support individuals engaged in small business and informal economic activities such as taxi drivers and "on the go" vendors. Lula generates and prints codes, which people purchase to add minutes to their mobile phones. Lula runs on the Google App Engine, which is the same infrastructure that powers Google's own applications such as Google Calendar, Gmail, and Google Docs. That is, Google provides the framework and storage and manages servers for Lula. Google also provides services to software applications associated with Lula beyond those that are available from the operating system (known as middleware). In addition, Google provides runtime-related services such as supporting the execution of programs required to print vouchers using Lula.

Namibia's Paratus Telecom has diversified its offering by launching a new mobile airtime distribution service called "Katiti." The service runs on Nomanini's cloud-based mobile point of sale platform and is designed to be used by informal traders and budding entrepreneurs. Local vendors are given a brightly colored and virtually indestructible terminal, or "business in a box" from which they can sell prepaid airtime vouchers. The platform is cloud-based, so vendors simply "upload" airtime when they have Internet access.[92]

Local designers of a technology can find an appropriate way so that the observability of the innovation is ensured. For instance, Lula owners wear a lanyard around their necks to carry the device so they are instantly noticed in places such as a busy train stations.[93] Africa's prepaid airtime market was estimated at US$60 billion in 2013 is expected to increase to US$85 billion by 2015.[94] A key reason behind the increasing success and popularity of Lula is that pre-paid minutes can be used as cash or spent in shops in a number of African countries such as Côte d'Ivoire, Egypt, Ghana, Uganda, and Nigeria.[95] In November 2013, Nomanini entered the Kenyan market. The company also announced its plan to enter Zambia, Nigeria, and Tanzania.[96] Many people in Africa, especially in rural areas, use such vouchers to pay for services such as electricity, water, insurance, and airtime for mobile phones. The low penetration rates of computers, Internet and smartphones, and the fact that a large proportion of the population lacks a documented home address make this an attractive option economically and technologically. Mobile prepaid services do not require Internet access or a bank account and can be purchased them in small or large amounts. A further reason for the popularity of such a voucher is that it is difficult to distribute physical vouchers because of theft and fraud risks.

biNu

biNu (www.binu.com/)[97] is a free mobile software platform, which is used to access books. biNu moves much of the processing to the cloud instead of doing it on the phone. In 2013, biNu was reported to have over 4 million monthly users. Worldreader, which describes its mission as: "make digital books available to children and their families in the developing world, so millions of people can improve their lives," uses Amazon's AWS to download books.[98] Worldreader has made thousands of free books available on the cloud. biNu's Worldreader app was released as a beta version in April 2013, which had been installed on about 5 million mobile phones as of 2013-end.[99]

The app is designed to run on a moderately priced and multipurpose phones (feature phones)[100] rather than high-end smartphones. In this way, biNu allows feature phones and low-end smartphones to have a smartphone-like experience through cloud-based apps and services. The books can be accessed through a free mobile software platform biNu. Most of the processing is performed in the cloud's servers instead of on the phone.[101] According to biNu's developers, by moving processing to the cloud, biNu works ten times faster than regular mobile web browsers. It makes graphics and text on the cloud and the data is sent back to the phone as tiny images. An advantage of sending the data as images is that the text can be displayed in any language irrespective of the language a phone is programmed to handle. Each image consists of only one or two packets of data of less than 1 kilobyte (KB) each. Information is not sent twice. The servers remember the information that is sent before and only provides new instructions that are needed to change the content on the screen.[102]

Market Access

By 2060, the continent's middle class is expected to triple to reach over a billion people.[103] However, domestic markets are small in most African economies. Increased access to foreign market is thus important for African entrepreneurs. Some have argued that economic aids tied to regionalization are more likely to be effective in stimulating entrepreneurship in Africa. The Sudanese-British entrepreneur Mo Ibrahim noted, "The World Bank should refuse to fund any project which is not regional. African governments must be pressed to regionalize their economies and stop being 53 little countries, each with their flag, jealously watching each other."[104]

Foreign Companies' Entrepreneurial Activities in Africa

International entrepreneurship involves exploiting capital, labor and other resources across the globe. Africa's abundance of natural resources makes it an attractive destination for resource-seeking investments for foreign businesses. Note that resource-seeking investments are made to establish access to basic material, input factors, and natural-resource such as those in energy, metallic minerals, wood, paper and other raw materials. Most foreign companies have mainly concentrated on accessing the natural resources in the continent. For instance, Western oil companies such as ExxonMobil and Chevron of the U.S., France's Total, and Britain's BP and Shell are planning to invest tens of billions of dollars in SSA.[105]

It is suggested that the U.S. and China are actively competing for access to Africa's oil, gas, and other resources. The U.S. imports 15% of its oil from Africa and the proportion is expected to reach 25% by 2015.[106] It is suggested that by 2017, it will import more oil from Africa than from the Middle East. Nigeria, Africa's biggest oil exporter and the world's 11th largest producer, with a capacity of 2.5 million barrels per day, is the fifth largest oil supplier of the U.S. In 2005, the U.S. imported more oil from the Gulf of Guinea region of Africa's west coast than it did from Saudi Arabia and Kuwait combined.[107]

China's gravitation toward Africa for the acquisition of energy and other natural resources deserves special attention. This is because oil and natural gas production in Asian countries is insufficient to meet the Chinese demand.[108] A large proportion of Middle Eastern exports of oil and gas production goes to the U.S. and Europe. An estimate suggested that Africa accounted for 25% of China's oil imports in 2004, which increased to 33% in 2006.[109]

Africa is not only a strategic source of raw materials but is also becoming an attractive market. Foreign companies have thus increased market-seeking investments in Africa.[110] Partly because of economic liberalization, there has been a greater availability of imported goods. However, it is worth noting that government purchases account for a significant proportion of imports in some African countries. In Ethiopia, government purchases account for 40% of total imports, with loans by international financial institutions such as the World Bank and the African Development Bank.[111]

Arbitrage Strategies

Arbitrage strategies entail exploiting opportunities associated with differences across countries. Foreign companies' potential to benefit from utilizing the region's raw materials and natural resources can be described in terms of economic arbitrage, which entails exploiting specific economic factors. Foreign companies can also benefit from geographic arbitrage, which involves the exploitation of geographic factors such as the region's strategic location.[112] For instance, there is a potential to expand their operations to utilize the continent's labor force to serve international markets, especially the European ones. Likewise, Chinese firms can use Africa's geographical position as proximity to Europe to establish factories in the continent and sell products to the European market. There is also an opportunity to benefit from the cultural arbitrage (e.g., language skills of the workforce). For instance, Indian off-shoring companies can utilize the continents' English-, French-, and Portuguese-speaking populations to provide call center services to Europeans.

For some multinationals, combining components from the existing institutional environment and reorganizing them strategically has been an important way to operate in Africa. For instance, the British bank—Barclays—is strategically utilizing Susu collectors in Ghana, which are among the oldest financial groups in Africa. Susu collectors' main function is to collect savings daily from informal traders. This approach can also be described as an institutional arbitrage, which entails exploiting opportunities associated with differences in formal and informal institutions across countries.

Allegation Regarding the Exploitation of Africa's Resources by Foreign Multinationals

There are many examples and complaints regarding exploitation of these resources by Asian, European, and American multinationals at low costs.[113] For instance, global mining companies are making huge profits by extracting gold, diamonds, copper, and other metals from Africa. Likewise, using fruits, flowers, and vegetables from the continent and paying "starvation wages" to African workers, European grocery retailers produce their own label products.[114]

In recent years, complaints regarding exploitation of Africa's minerals and natural resources are especially directed at China. A Zimbabwean politician, Arthur Mutambara noted, "China comes to Africa and extracts raw materials and goes back to China."[115] China's African involvement has also been criticized by some environmentalists. A July 2005 report of the International Rivers Network and Friends of the Earth accused China's Exim Bank for funding environmental unfriendly projects such as the Merowe Dam in Sudan. Likewise, quoting a primatologist, a huffingtonpost.com article noted, "China's thirst for natural resources, including wood and minerals, is leading to massive deforestation in Africa and the destruction of crucial wildlife habitat."[116]

Global multinationals are using their marketing and branding power to make big profits from Africa's natural and labor resources, raw materials, and commodities[117] With an example of A la Perruche, a brand of cubed sugar sold in New York, a development expert illustrates problems faced by African companies on the branding front: "The carton of 1.1 pounds of pure cane sugar pressed into cubes is imported from France. The back of the box states, 'Product made of Swaziland or Congo sugar packaged in France.' The value of the sugar on the international market is about 12 cents, though the carton, which boasts 'since 1837,' sells for US$5.99. Africans try to earn a living while selling raw sugar on the international market for 11 cents a pound; the French, with their skills in packaging and marketing, pocket the dollars."[118]

Low Degree of Linkages to the Local Economy

A problem facing the continent is a limited impact of foreign firms' entrepreneurial activities to the local economy. For instance, there are reports that the garment manufacturing industry in many parts of Africa is shallow. That is, this industry has few linkages to the domestic economies. In some African economies such as Namibia and Lesotho, even skilled direct employees for this industry are foreigners.[119]

Western Response to Low Level of Entrepreneurial Activities in Africa

The member countries of the Group of Eight (*G8*), which is a forum for the governments of the world's eight wealthiest countries in the West, believed that debt relief and increasing aid to Africa would help promote economic development and entrepreneurship. African economies received US$568 billion in economic aid during 1958–2009.[120] Donor flow accounts for 30%–40% of the budget of some of the poorest African nations such as Guinea-Bissau, Burkina Faso, Togo, Malawi, and Swaziland.[121] In Ethiopia, foreign aid constitutes over 90% of the government budget.[122]

A growing number of observers have noted that efforts to relieve debt and increase aid have been largely unsuccessful in fighting poverty and promoting entrepreneurship in Africa. Some argue that the U.S. has been a supplier of food aid and contraceptives instead of being a provider of development assistance to Africa.[123] Zambian economist Dambisa Moyo believes that foreign aid in Africa has deepened the poverty, led to an economic distortion and fueled corruption and inequality in the continent. Other analysts have also expressed their disappointment with the existing system of aid to stimulate economic development in Africa.

To understand the feelings that accompany these critics' viewpoint against the process of increasing aid, consider one detail: out of US$1 aid given to Africa, about 16 cents was spent to pay to consultants based in donor countries, 26 cents went to emergency aid and relief operations, and 14 cents into debt servicing. African economies pay about US$20 billion in debt repayments annually.[124] Analysts suspect that corrupt officials take a large proportion of the remaining, leaving very little to benefit the poor people who really deserve the aid.

An increasing number of observers have advocated the necessity to increase the private sector's involvement in the economy and help develop a market-based system.[125] Analysts have argued that a reorientation of aid to promote private businesses in poor countries would be more effective. Zambian economist Dambisa Moyo has also advocated alternatives such as encouraging trade and foreign direct investment with the continent and developing microfinancing and capital markets. Note that private businesses have been a cornerstone to economic development in the fast growing developing countries. However, promotion of private business has rarely been the principal focus of development aid.

The emphasis on trade and investment rather than aid is echoed in a journalist's field observation in Liberia:

> It is chock-full of aid groups rushing around in white SUVs doing wonderful work (in Liberia). But it also needs factories to employ people, build skills and pay salaries and taxes. Americans are horrified by sweatshops, but nothing would help Liberia more than if China moved some of its sweatshops there so Liberians could make sandals and T-shirts.[126]

Foreign aids also lack linkages to the local economy. One example to illustrate this situation would be to consider U.S. aid. In 2004, the U.S. had provided African economies with US$1 billion in food aid, 90% of which was spent on foods manufactured in the U.S. Similarly, the plan for AIDS also required use of FDA-approved drugs, which are expensive. Overall, no attention was paid to investing in generic drugs and prevention programs. The poor (the intended beneficiaries), or the NGOs and foundations working with them, receive a small percentage of the total aid and have very little say in how it is used. Aid may benefit the givers and aid administrators as much as or even more than the recipients.[127]

Concluding Comments

Development of a free enterprise economy in Africa with a strong rule of law and property rights is likely to benefit not only the African society but also the global economy. However, Africa's abundant natural and human resources have mainly benefitted American, European and Asian multi-nationals and the continent's dictators and tiny minorities. There has been a failure to bring economic and developmental advantages for the poor people. There has been a vanishingly small stock of FDI outside the oil industry. Optimism about entrepreneurial development in Africa is thus pretty rare.

A common thread runs through corruption and instability in most countries in the continent—connection to natural resources. In some countries such as the DRC and Sierra Leone, mineral resources have been blamed for economic, political, and social problems such as excessive corruption, political instability, and even state collapse.[128] A common-place observation is that Africa's oil or mineral wealth is a curse rather than a blessing, which has led some countries in the continent to economic and political instability, social conflict and environmental degradation (Watch the video "Blood Diamonds – The True Story": www.youtube.com/watch?v=C7lmjjDlzp0). Faced with examples such as these in many resource-rich African countries, some authors have used the term "resources curse" to describe their economic failure.[129] A journalist observed, "because of wars, dictatorships and thieves, Angola and other oil-rich African nations have failed so far to turn their natural wealth into better lives for their citizens."[130]

An uncomfortable reality is that the development of productive entrepreneurship has been slow in most African economies. Some argue that Western aid to Africa may have benefited donor countries and aid administrators rather than the intended recipients in Africa.

Some African economies undergoing market and economic reforms have been able to attract foreign investment. Tunisia, which offers a one-stop shop for foreign investors with all services, including courts and customs, in one building, is one example. As of 2000, Tunisia had the third largest FDI stock in the Middle East, which is a phenomenal success considering its small size and a lack of oil.[131] As noted earlier, democracies and liberalization in some African countries have shifted into reverse gear. However, some countries in the continent have made visible progress toward democracy. According to Freedom in the World 2013, three SSA countries moved from Partly Free to Free: Lesotho, Sierra Leone, and

Senegal. Likewise, Ethiopia recently moved from one-party to multiparty system. Since economic freedom and political freedom are highly correlated, political freedoms may lead to economic liberalization and boost private entrepreneurship. In recent years, Ethiopia has won some of the flower-exporting business away from its neighboring country Kenya.

The above discussion also indicates that African economies need to strengthen linkages of foreign investments to the domestic economies. There is also an urgent need to hasten these efforts to benefit from foreign trades and investments.

The preceding examples also point to the fact that many foreign firms' entrepreneurial activities in Africa may have come at the expense of local entrepreneurs. In recent years, thousands of fishermen on Africa's coast have lost jobs. In this regard, political process in a country has a built-in bias that favors organized groups and industries compared to those that are unorganized.[132] For example, most African countries do not have large and organized local commercial fishing industries to pressure their governments. A lack of domestic entrepreneurs' organized movements can be attributed to such dynamics.

It is also worth mentioning that some African businesses have performed well in the international markets. Some businesses such as SAB and Ecobank have internationalized successfully. Likewise, KEZA helped the Rwandan cooperatives connect to an international market for luxury products. However, cases like these are extreme in the present context.

Third-world MNCs are familiar with the business terrains of other developing countries thanks mainly to economic, cultural, and political proximity, and thus experience a lower degree of foreignness associated with dissimilarity or lack of fit in the operating contexts of these countries. Environment in Africa may thus enable better arbitrage opportunities for multinationals based in developing economies such as China and India than those in industrialized economies.

Multinational enterprises based in Asia, Europe, and North America have allegedly exploited natural and human resources in Africa. Foreign governments and multinational enterprises have employed ecological discourses to establish discursive legitimacy and gain access to the continent's natural resources. For instance, EU officials and other beneficiaries of fishing-rights agreements in Africa have argued that unregulated domestic fishermen are the real problems behind the decline in the continent's fisheries stocks. It is argued most domestic fishermen in Africa tend to fish close to the shore, which offer suitable habitat for fish spawning. EU officials have also made the point that most African countries have performed poorly in managing their fish stocks.[133]

African economies have been hard hit by the GFC. Many economies are facing stiff budget cuts because of low foreign aid and declining remittances from the West. Domestic investment is also severely affected by high interest rates and depreciation of national currencies, thereby affecting the level of entrepreneurship support and resources.

African countries can increase benefits of foreign trade and investments by creating efficient channels for forward and backward linkages, labor mobility, and stimulation of knowledge and technology transfer to local firms.[134] Income growth among the wider population is likely to produce forward linkages leading to a growth of demand for small businesses' outputs.

End of Chapter Questions

1   Which are some of the best performing economies in Africa? Which ones are the least performing economies in the continent?
2   Why are complaints regarding exploitation of Africa's minerals and natural resources are directed at China in recent years?
3   What are some examples to illustrate that global multinationals are using their marketing and branding power to make big profits out of Africa's natural and labor resources, raw materials, and commodities?
4   What are arbitrage strategies? What are some examples of arbitrage strategies pursued by foreign multinationals in their operations in Africa?
5   How effective are the Western approaches of debt relief and economic aid to promote economic development and entrepreneurship in Africa?
6   Do you agree with the observation that Africa's oil or mineral wealth is a curse rather than a blessing? Why?
7   Select an African economy that has among the best entrepreneurial climates in the continent (e.g., Ghana). Select another African economy that has among the worst entrepreneurial climates in the continent (e.g., the Democratic Republic of Congo). Do some research on some determinants of entrepreneurship in these countries and compare them. What conclusions can you draw?

End of the Chapter Case: Kilimo Salama's Weather-Based Index Insurance Enhancing Smallholder Farmers' Entrepreneurial Capacity

The social enterprise Kilimo Salama (KS) (safe agriculture in Swahili) has brought together actuarial science, agronomy, climate science, economics and remote sensing to develop a weather-based index insurance in an attempt to serve a vulnerable market that traditional insurance schemes have ignored. Its micro insurance scheme attempts to protect small farmers in Kenya against poor weather conditions. KS is a partnership between the Syngenta Foundation for Sustainable Agriculture, the Kenyan insurance company, UAP, and Safaricom. It also gets financial assistance from the International Finance Corporation, a sister organization of the World Bank.[135]

KS started a pilot project in 2009, insuring 200 corn farmers in the region of Nanyuki in Kenya and subsequently started also covering wheat, sorghum, cotton, beans, and coffee. By 2011, it insured 22,000 farmers and became the largest insurance project in Africa.[136] As of 2013, KS had insured over 187,000 small farmers in Kenya and Rwanda.[137] The number of farmers insured by KS increased to over 233,000 in Kenya, Tanzania, and Rwanda in 2014.[138] For some farmers the cost of insurance amounts to as little as 1 kg of maize, seed, or fertilizer.[139]

In order to reduce transaction costs and build trust with clients, the index insurance mainly relies on solar-powered weather stations and cellphones. Kenya's weather stations traditionally employed manual rain gauges. KS modernized 32 of them with solar power and computerized gauges. Weather stations are equipped with wireless sim-cards that transmit data on rainfall levels, sun, and temperature every five minutes to a cloud-based server.

The insurance is completely automated. KS uses cellphones for signing up farmers and paying out insurance claims. It does not have to rely on insurance agents. Policies are distributed through dealers, who sell seeds, fertilizers, and chemicals to farmers. The dealers are provided with camera phones to record the purchase. They use an advanced phone application with camera and phone functions to scan and capture policy information through a code. The information is uploaded to Safaricom's mobile cloud-based server, which administers policies. Farmers instantly receive information about their policy and payouts in SMS messages.[140] At the end of the growing season, payouts go electronically to the farmer's cell phone account.[141]

A farmer who buys insurance is linked to the nearest weather station, which is within 20 kilometers. At the end of a season, the data is aggregated and combined with satellite data in order to map out rain patterns. KS works with agronomists to calculate the index and identifies the locations that experienced too much rain, too little rain, or rain at the wrong time. Farmer payouts are calculated based on crops, location, and the amount invested in seeds.[142] If the rainfall is insufficient early in the growing season, or too late in the corn season, farmers in that area get an automatic payout. Farmers are not required to file a claim. In the case of extreme weather that destroys the whole harvest, they get the full amount. No farm visit is necessary.[143] Insurance claims are normally settled within four days.[144]

Farmers can buy the insurance at the beginning of the season for about 10%–20% of the amount they invest in seeds and inputs.[145] However, paying 10% of their costs for insurance is a huge burden for many farmers. KS recruited partners such as Syngenta who cover half the cost of the premium if farmers buy their products. In this way, local firms can facilitate the adoption by creating trust with local communities.

The availability of weather stations and cell phones dramatically lowered the cost of writing policies. Indeed, sending the text message welcoming the new client has been the biggest component of cost associated with providing insurance for KS.[146]

Appropriateness of Index Insurance

Researchers and practitioners have advocated the development and use of index insurance contracts to manage the risks faced by farmers and agricultural producers. Whereas conventional insurance compensates an insurer based on verifiable losses, under an index insurance scheme such as that of KS, payment to an insured farmer depends on the observed value of a specified index.[147] The benefits of index insurance are greater to lending institutions such as agricultural/industrial development banks and microfinance institutions (MFIs) than to borrowers.[148] Historical data on corn and the other crops insured by KS indicated that payouts based on weather-based index are about the same as payouts for crop damage by bad weather.[149]

Benefits to Farmers

The benefits go far beyond the crop damage insurance. KS regularly sends up-to-date climate data to farmers with SMS. Farmers also receive information regarding the ways to increase agricultural productivity, and protect crops in case of bad weather.[150] Another benefit to farmers is that banks and MFIs are more comfortable in giving loans to farmers thanks to the insurance scheme. In this way, access to essential credit is becoming easier for farmers.

Case Summary

The repaid diffusion of cellphones has made it possible for KS to offer insurance to farmers at a low cost. KS has been playing a key role in stimulating entrepreneurial activities of smallholder farmers. Farmers who have insurance have easier access to entrepreneurial finance. The up-to-date climate data that farmers receive from KS on a regular basis also helps to increase their agricultural activities.

Notes

1 Takyi-Asiedu, S. 1993. "Some socio-cultural factors retarding entrepreneurial activity in Sub-Saharan Africa," *Journal of Business Venturing*, 8, pp. 91–98.
2 Robson, P.J.A., & Obeng, B.A. 2008. "The barriers to growth in Ghana," *Small Business Economics*, 30(4), pp. 385–403.

3 Rheault, M., & Tortora, B. 2008. *Nigeria: Drivers and Challenges of Entre-preneurship.* www.gallup.com/poll/106345/nigeria-drivers-challenges-entrepreneurship.aspx.

4 Ruxin, J. 2009. *Fashion, Rwanda and the Power of Social Entrepreneurship,* www.huffingtonpost.com/josh-ruxin/fashion-rwanda-and-the-po_b_397458.html.

5 Chima, O. 2018. "W'Bank reveals improving economic inclusion among women," www.thisdaylive.com/index.php/2018/04/02/wbank-reveals-improving-economic-inclusion-among-women/.

6 EFInA. 2018. "Scoping study on super agents," www.efina.org.ng/assets/ResearchDocuments/OtherResearch/Updated-Jan-2018/EFInA-Super-Agents-Scoping-Study-Aug-2016.pdf.

7 Ogah, D., Okwe, M., & Adeoye, T. 2015. "Agent banking: Penetrating markets, rural communities for financial inclusion," https://guardian.ng/business-services/agent-banking-penetrating-markets-rural-communities-for-financial-inclusion/.

8 Takyi-Asiedu. 1993.

9 Finnan, D. 2018. "PodcastTunisia must increase investment and push through reforms, says OECD," http://en.rfi.fr/africa/20180403-tunisia-must-increase-investment-and-push-through-reforms-says-oecd.

10 Chowdhury, A. 2017. "Nearly half the continent is living in poverty. No won-der they want out of Africa," www.huffingtonpost.com.au/anis-chowdhury/nearly-half-the-continent-is-living-in-poverty-no-wonder-they-want-out-of-africa_a_23120197/.

11 worldbank.org. 2016. "While poverty in Africa has declined, number of poor has increased," March, www.worldbank.org/en/region/afr/publication/poverty-rising-africa-poverty-report.

12 Beegle, K., Christiaensen, L., Dabalen, A., & Gaddis, I. 2016. "Poverty in a rising Africa," Washington, DC: World Bank. © World Bank. https://open knowledge.worldbank.org/handle/10986/22575 License: CC BY 3.0 IGO."

13 worldbank.org. 2016. "While poverty in Africa has declined, number of poor has increased," March. www.worldbank.org/en/region/afr/publication/poverty-rising-africa-poverty-report.

14 Novitske, A. 2017. "Top African tech trends to look out for in 2018," 20 December, https://vc4a.com/blog/2017/12/20/top-african-tech-trends-to-look-out-for-in-2018/.

15 The Economist. 2006a.

16 Rheault, & Tortora. 2008.

17 Elkan, W. 1988. "Entrepreneurs and entrepreneurship in Africa," *World Bank Research Observer*, 3(2), pp. 171–188.

18 Rheault, & Tortora. 2008.

19 Kazeem, Y. 2017. "Africa's most valuable startup ecosystem is also the least lucrative for software engineers," 31 March, https://qz.com/943613/lagos-is-africas-most-valuable-startup-ecosystem/.

20 Aransiola, D. 2017. "The rise of coworking spaces in Africa," 22 March, www.deskmag.com/en/the-rise-of-coworking-spaces-in-africa-958.

21 Charania, N., & Naupari, C. 2018. "Blockchain's big potential in Africa," https://venturebeat.com/2018/04/01/blockchains-big-potential-in-africa/

22 The World Bank. 2016. "Ghana's Young entrepreneurs get a boost to their businesses," www.worldbank.org/en/news/feature/2016/05/11/ghanas-young-entrepreneurs-get-a-boost-to-their-businesses.

23 GNA. 2011. "KNUST sets up Kumasi Business Incubator," www.modern ghana.com/news/319994/1/knust-sets-up-kumasi-business-incubator.html.

24 Essien, M. 2015. "Why startup incubators in Africa just don't work," http://ventureburn.com/2015/11/startup-incubators-africa-just-dont-work/.
25 Essien, 2015.
26 Haigh, D. 2009. Why Africa must nurture home-grown brands. *Managing Intellectual Property*, 193, pp. 82–84.
27 Kapstein, E.B. 2009. "Africa's capitalist revolution," *Foreign Affairs*, 88(4), pp. 119–129.
28 Douglas, B. 2018. "A cooperative in Utrecht received a multi-million Rand investment recently," https://newcastleadvertiser.co.za/147415/huge-investment-for-utrecht-maize-farm/.
29 Chuhan-Pole, P. Korman, V., Angwafo, M., & Buitano, M. 2011. "Africa's Pulse," April, Volume 3 http://siteresources.worldbank.org/INTAFRICA/Resources/Africas-Pulse-brochure_Vol3.pdf.
30 Rheault & Tortora. 2008.
31 Allen, E, Langowitz, N., & Minnitti, M. 2006. *Global Entrepreneurship Monitor: 2006 Report on Women and Entrepreneurship*. Babson Park, MA: Babson College.
32 Rheault & Tortora. 2008.
33 See: "Future causes of conflict," www.ppu.org.uk/war/future_wars.html.
34 Mutasa, H. 2009. "Zimbabwe's "special" relationship," *aljazeera.net*, english. aljazeera.net/focus/ chinabuystheworld/2009/08/200981083259504514.html.
35 Stryker, J.D., & Baird, K.E. 1992. "Trends in African agricultural trade: Causes and prognosis," *Policy Studies Journal*, 20(3), pp. 414–430.
36 Sáez, L., & Gallagher, J. 2009. "Authoritarianism and development in the Third World," *Brown Journal of World Affairs*, 15(2), pp. 87–101.
37 Green, P.L. 2009. "Africa in a squeeze," *Global Finance*, 23(5), pp. 18–22.
38 Bell, G. 2006. "US, China to spur massive Africa oil growth," *Reuters*.
39 Donnelly, J. 2005. "China scooping up deals in Africa as US firms hesitate," *Boston Globe,* Burdens of oil weigh on Nigerians: Ecological harm, corruption hit hard. *Boston Globe*, www.boston.com/news/world/africa/articles/2005/10/03/burdens_of_oil_weigh_on_ nigerians/.
40 Bajpaee, C. 2005. *The eagle, the dragon and African oil*. www.atimes.com/atimes/ China_Business/GJ12Cb01.html.
41 Schlumberger, O. 2000. "Arab political economy and the European Union's Mediterranean policy: What prospects for development?" *New Political Economy*, 5(2), pp. 247–268.
42 Aldouri, S., & Meddeb, H. 2018. "In face of protests, Tunisia needs bold economic reforms," www.chathamhouse.org/expert/comment/face-protests-tunisia-needs-bold-economic-reforms.
43 Global Witness. 2006. "Breaking the links between the exploitation of natural resources, conflict and corruption," UNCTAD Expert Meeting on FDI in natural resources, www.unctad.org/ sections/wcmu/docs/com2em20p0019_en.pdf.
44 Freedom House. 2017. "Populist and autocrats: The dual threat to global democracy," https://freedomhouse.org/report/freedom-world/freedom-world-2017.
45 Sáez & Gallagher. 2009.
46 Mvunganyi, J. 2010. *African Youth Bear Brunt of Global Economic Crisis*. www1.voanews.com/english/news/africa/African-Youth-Bear-Brunt-of-Global-Economic-Crisis-82601422.html.
47 African Times. 2004.
48 Wilson, E.J. 1990. "Strategies of state control of the economy: Nationalization and indigenization in Black Africa," *Comparative Politics*, 22(4), pp. 401–419.

49 Donnelly, J. 2005. "In oil-rich nation, charges of skimming: Congolese officials said to reap profits," Boston Globe.
50 Ibid.
51 Raymond, F. 1951. *Elements of Social Organization*. Boston, MA: Beacon Press.
52 Wilson, E.J. 1990. "Strategies of state control of the economy: Nationalization and indigenization in Black Africa," *Comparative Politics*, 22(4), pp. 401–419.
53 Oyeniran, A. 2018. "Africa's learning crisis may fail to eliminate extreme poverty – World Bank," https://independent.ng/africas-learning-crisis-may-fail-eliminate-extreme-poverty-world-bank/.
54 Ibid.
55 Smith, A.D. 2009. "Trade, not aid, is latest hope: Donors are now focusing less on charity and more on the continent's entrepreneurs," *The Guardian (London) - Final Edition*, 27.
56 Mtomba, V. 2015. "Sub_Saharan Africa has lowest savings rate," www.newsday.co.zw/2015/12/sub-saharan-africa-has-lowest-savings-rate/.
57 Khumalo, K. 2017. "Time to get into the habit of saving," www.iol.co.za/personal-finance/time-to-get-into-the-habit-of-saving-10073466.
58 worldbank.org. 2017. "Remittances to developing countries decline for second consecutive year," 21 April, www.worldbank.org/en/news/press-release/2017/04/21/remittances-to-developing-countries-decline-for-second-consecutive-year.
59 Ibid.
60 The Economist. 2015. "Unblocking the pipes," www.economist.com/news/leaders/21640349-africa-needs-lot-capital-private-equity-offers-lessons-how-get-it-there-unblocking.
61 Nanyang Business School. 2016. "Africa's stock exchanges competitive in the global stock markets," *African Business Insights*, www.ntusbfcas.com/african-business-insights/content/challenges/343-africa-s-stock-exchanges-competitive-in-the-global-stock-markets.
62 Ibid.
63 Apo. 2018. "African capital markets indicate recovery in 2017 with overall increase in value and volume of equity capital market (ECM) transactions," www.cnbcafrica.com/apo/2018/03/06/african-capital-markets-indicate-recovery-in-2017-with-overall-increase-in-value-and-volume-of-equity-capital-market-ecm-transactions/.
64 PWC. 2017. "2017 Africa Capital markets to watch," www.pwc.com/ng/en/publications/africa-capital-markets-watch.html.
65 The Economist. 2015. "Unblocking the pipes," www.economist.com/news/leaders/21640349-africa-needs-lot-capital-private-equity-offers-lessons-how-get-it-there-unblocking.
66 Ibid.
67 Rheault & Tortora 2008.
68 Awhotu, E. 2010. 60% of Nigerians don't have access to bank. *CBN Adviser*, leadershipnigeria.com/index.php/news/headlines/11222-60-of-nigerians-dont-have-access-to-bank--cbn-adviser.
69 MasterCard. 2017. "Informal cash savings groups are driving female entrepreneurship in Nigeria," https://qz.com/566627/informal-cash-savings-groups-are-driving-female-entrepreneurship-in-nigeria/.
70 Diallo, A. 2017. "Africa is the next frontier for VCs," https://venturebeat.com/2017/04/01/africa-is-the-next-frontier-for-vcs/.

71 Kazeem, Y. 2018. "Startup venture funding jumped more than 50% in Africa last year to a record high," 21 February, https://qz.com/1211233/how-much-did-african-startups-raise-in-2017-partech-disrupt-africa/.
72 Barrica, A. 2016. "Next, final frontier: lessons learned investing in West & South Africa," https://500.co/next-final-frontier-lessons-learned-investing-in-west-south-africa/.
73 ventureburn.com. 2017. "Here are eight facts you should know about venture capital in South Africa," http://ventureburn.com/2017/11/venture-capital-south-africa/.
74 Virani, S. 2016. "Here's why it's so tough for African startups to raise funding internationally," https://qz.com/780118/heres-why-its-so-tough-for-african-startups-to-raise-funding-internationally/.
75 Charania, N., & Naupari, C. 2018. "Blockchain's big potential in Africa," https://venturebeat.com/2018/04/01/blockchains-big-potential-in-africa/.
76 Foreign Policy. 2011. "The FP Survey: The Internet", September/October 2011, (188), pp. 1–9.
77 Ekekwe, N. 2015. "The challenges facing e-commerce start-ups in Africa," https://hbr.org/2015/03/the-challenges-facing-e-commerce-start-ups-in-africa (Accessed February 5, 2018).
78 Kelly, T. 2014. "Tech hubs across Africa: Which will be the legacy makers?" http://blogs.worldbank.org/ic4d/tech-hubs-across-africa-which-will-be-legacy-makers.
79 Talbot, D. 2011. "Chasing the African cloud," www.technologyreview.com/news/425922/chasing-the-african-cloud/ (Accessed July 9, 2016).
80 Rosenberg, T. 2011. "Doing more than praying for rain," http://opinionator.blogs.nytimes.com/2011/05/09/doing-more-than-praying-for-rain/?_r=0 (Accessed October 9, 2016.
81 Aglionby J. 2016. "New payments service to launch in Kenya," http://www.ft.com/cms/s/0/fa4acc9c-7c9d-11e5-98fb-5a6d4728f74e.html.
82 Ibid.
83 Kivuva, E. 2018. "M-Pesa maintains top slot of mobile money space," www.the-star.co.ke/news/2018/03/23/m-pesa-maintains-top-slot-of-mobile-money-space_c1734019.
84 StandardReporter.2018."SafaricomrewardsM-Pesacustomerswithdata,voice, SMS package," www.standardmedia.co.ke/business/article/2001273107/how-safaricom-rewards-m-pesa-customers-with-data-voice-sms-package.
85 The Star. 2016. "Letter from Berlin – From politics to the Olympics to M-health: The brotherly competition between Kenya and Ghana". www.the-star.co.ke/news/2016/09/01/letter-from-berlin-from-politics-to-the-olympics-to-m-health-the_c1411336 (Accessed July 9, 2016).
86 Romania Insider. 2017. "Vodafone closes its money transfer service in Romania," www.romania-insider.com/vodafone-m-pesa-romania/.
87 Goldstein, S. 2012. "Mobile data collection: A leapfrog technology for health improvement,"www.k4health.org/blog/post/mobile-data-collection-leapfrog-technology-health-improvement.
88 Clozel, L. 2014. "How two health aid workers created an app before the age of apps existed." http://technical.ly/dc/2014/10/14/two-health-aid-workers-created-app-apps-existed/.
89 Kanyi, M. 2012. "Case studies: Who uses Magpi (formerly EpiSurveyor)," https://datadyne.zendesk.com/entries/21282536-Case-Studies-Who-Uses-Magpi-formerly-E.
90 Goldstein, 2012.

91 mhealthinfo.org. 2010. "EpiSurveyor mobile health data collection," www.
    mhealthinfo.org/project/episurveyor-mobile-health-data-collection.
92 allafrica.com. 2014. "Namibia: 'Katiti' mobile airtime distribution service
    launched in Namibia." http://allafrica.com/stories/201411041022.html.
93 acceptingpayments.quora.com. 2010. "This orange box you've never seen
    before is changing payments," http://acceptingpayments.quora.com/This-
    Orange-Box-You%E2%80%99ve-Never-Seen-Before-Is-Changing-
    Payments.
94 Douglas, K. 2013. "How Nomanini wants to replace airtime scratch cards 5,"
    www.howwemadeitinafrica.com/how-nomanini-wants-to-replace-airtime-
    scratch-cards/28794/.
95 economist.com. 2013. "Giant reality-check four of the world's biggest
    lenders must face some nasty truths," www.economist.com/news/finance-
    and-economics/21584331-four-worlds-biggest-lenders-must-face-some-
    nasty-truths-giant-reality-check.
96 nomanini.com. Nomanini. 2014. http://nomanini.com/news/2013/11/19/
    nomanini-expands-operations-east-africa (Accessed October 9, 2016)
97 binu.com. 2013. "Help" http://m.binu.com/help.php.
98 Hardy, Q. 2012. "Active in cloud, Amazon reshapes computing," www.
    nytimes.com/2012/08/28/technology/active-in-cloud-amazon-reshapes-
    computing.html?_r=0.
99 Ruz, C. 2013. "Cloud computing key to improving literacy in Africa,"
    https://sciencenode.org/feature/cloud-computing-key-improving-literacy-
    africa.php.
100 Compared to a basic mobile phone, which can only be used for voice calling
    and text messaging, a feature phone has additional functions but not as many
    as in a smart phone.
101 Ruz. 2013.
102 Ibid.
103 The Economist. 2015. "Unblocking the pipes," at www.economist.com/
    news/leaders/21640349-africa-needs-lot-capital-private-equity-offers-
    lessons-how-get-it-there-unblocking.
104 Smith, A.D. 2009. Trade, not aid, is latest hope: Donors are now focusing
    less on charity and more on the continent's entrepreneurs. *The Guardian
    (London) - Final Edition*, 27.
105 Thompson, C. 2007. "The scramble for Africa's Oil, new statesman," www.
    globalpolicy.org/component/content/article/154/25931.html.
106 Donnelly. 2005.
107 Thompson. 2007.
108 Brookes, P., & Shin, J.H. 2006. *China's Influence in Africa: Implications for
    the United States*. The Heritage Foundation: www.heritage.org/Research/
    AsiaandthePacific/bg1916.cfm.
109 Hanson, S. 2008. *China, Africa, and Oil*. www.cfr.org/publication/9557.
110 Pritchard, C. 1997. "Into Africa," *Marketing Magazine*, 102(38), p. 12.
111 See: "Ethiopia Chapter 1. General Overview," http://ieo.ae/ethiopia_go.htm.
112 Ghemawat, P. 2003. "The forgotten strategy," *Harvard Business Review*,
    81(11), pp. 76–84.
113 Haigh, D. 2009. "Why Africa must nurture home-grown brands," *Managing
    Intellectual Property*, 193, pp. 82–84.
114 Ibid.
115 Newstime Africa. 2009.
116 huffingtonpost.com.

117 Haigh. 2009.
118 Colburn, F.D. 2006. "Good-bye to the 'Third World,'" *Dissent*, 53(2), pp. 38–41.
119 Rasiah, R., & Ofreneo, R.E. 2009. "Introduction: The dynamics of textile and garment manufacturing in Asia," *Journal of Contemporary Asia*, November, 39(4), pp. 501–511.
120 Vassiliou, P. 2010. *A Hand Up, Not a Hand Out*. www.forbes.com/2010/01/12/africa-india-poverty-legatum-tech-opinions-contributors-philip-vassiliou.html.
121 Green. 2009.
122 Moyo, D. 2009. "Why foreign aid is hurting Africa," *Wall Street Journal*, (Eastern edition), 21 March, W.1.
123 Awori, A. 2009. "An African perspective on environment and development," *Voices from Africa*, Number 5, Sustainable Development Part 1, www.un-ngls.org/orf/documents/publications.en/voices.africa/number5/vfa5.04.htm.
124 Moyo. 2009.
125 Prahalad, C.K. 2005. "Aid is not the answer," *Wall Street Journal* (Eastern edition), A.8.
126 Kristof, N.D. 2009. "How can we help?" *New York Times Book Review*, p. 27.
127 Prahalad, C.K. 2005. "Aid is not the answer," *Wall Street Journal* (Eastern edition), A.8.
128 Sáez & Gallagher. 2009.
129 Auty, R. 1998. *Resource Abundance and Economic Development*. World Institute for Development Economics Research, Helsinki.
130 Donnelly, J. 2005c. Oil wealth helping few of Angola's poor: Vast reserves cannot undo legacy of war, corruption. *Boston Globe*, www.boston.com/news/world/africa/articles/2005/12/11/oil_ wealth_helping_few_of_angolas_poor/.
131 Foroohar, R. 2003. "A country that works; smart policies and soft dictatorship make Tunisia something unique: A successful Arab economy," *Newsweek*, p. 32.
132 Mitra, D. 1999. "Endogenous lobby formation and endogenous protection: A long-run model of trade policy determination," *American Economic Review*, 89(5), pp. 1116–1134.
133 illegal-fishing.info. 2007.
134 Markusen, J.R., & Venables, A.J. 1999. "Foreign direct investment as a catalyst for industrial development," *European Economic Review*, 43(2), pp. 335–356.
135 Rosenberg, T. 2011. "Doing more than praying for rain," http://opinionator.blogs.nytimes.com/2011/05/09/doing-more-than-praying-for-rain/?_r=0 (Accessed October 9, 2016).
136 Ibid.
137 IFC. 2016. "International Finance Corporation. Agriculture and Climate Risk Enterprise (ACRE)," www.ifc.org/wps/wcm/connect/industry_ext_content/ifc_external_corporate_site/industries/financial+markets/retail+finance/insurance/agriculture+and+climate+risk+enterprise.
138 businessGreen.com. 2016. "Microinsurance and the new market for climate equity," www.businessgreen.com/bg/feature/2441996/microinsurance-and-the-new-market-for-climate-equity.
139 un.org. 2014. "Africa wired," www.un.org/africarenewal/magazine/special-edition-agriculture-2014/africa-wired.
140 Schneider, S. 2013. "Five ways cell phones are changing agriculture in Africa," http://foodtank.com/news/2013/04/five-ways-cell-phones-are-changing-agriculture-in-africa.

141 Rosenberg, T. 2011. "Doing more than praying for rain," http://opinionator.
    blogs.nytimes.com/2011/05/09/doing-more-than-praying-for-rain/?_r=0
    (Accessed October 9, 2016).
142 Kalan, J. 2013. "Tech fix for Africa's big farming challenge," www.bbc.com/
    future/story/20130408-tech-taps-africas-farm-potential (Accessed October
    9, 2016).
143 Rosenberg. 2011.
144 Gulati, A. 2015. "Drones & doves," http://indianexpress.com/article/
    opinion/columns/drones-and-doves/ (Accessed October 9, 2016).
145 Kalan, J. 2013. "Tech fix for Africa's big farming challenge," www.bbc.com/
    future/story/20130408-tech-taps-africas-farm-potential (Accessed October
    9, 2016).
146 Rosenberg. 2011.
147 Miranda, M.J., & Gonzalez-Vega, C. 2011. "Systemic risk, index insurance,
    and optimal management of agricultural loan portfolios in developing coun-
    tries," *American Journal of Agricultural Economics*, 93(2), pp. 399–406.
148 Skees, J.R., & Barnett, B.J. 2006. "Enhancing microfinance using index-based
    risk-transfer products," *Agricultural Finance Review*, 66, pp. 235–250.
149 Rosenberg. 2011.
150 Omolayo, O. 2015. "These 10 apps will boost agriculture in Africa,"
    http://venturesafrica.com/these-10-apps-will-boost-agriculture-in-africa/
    (Accessed October 9, 2016).

Chapter 8

Entrepreneurship in China

This chapter's objectives include:

1 To demonstrate an understanding of the nature of transformation undergoing in entrepreneurship in China.
2 To analyze the drivers of entrepreneurship in China.
3 To assess the nature of institutional changes related to entrepreneurship in China.
4 To evaluate some of the barriers to institutional changes related to entrepreneurship in China.
5 To demonstrate an understanding of the impacts of entrepreneurship in China.

Introduction

Entrepreneurship is undergoing a significant transformation in China. In 2015 alone, 4.4 million new businesses were registered in the country with an investment of US$5 trillion.[1]

During the Mao era, for instance, private entrepreneurship was virtually eradicated and was a political taboo. Entrepreneurs were shunned and disgraced in the country as late as the 1980s and the entrepreneur as an occupation was often considered for individuals that were not able to find other jobs such as those with criminal records.[2] Entrepreneurship in China thus was an oxymoron and paradox before the country started political and economic reforms in 1978.

In recent years, China has earned a reputation as one of the world's most entrepreneur-friendly county. According to the 2009 GEM report, China has a higher rate of nascent entrepreneurship than the U.S. China also outperforms the U.S. in the rate of ownership of new businesses as well as the rate of ownership of established businesses.[3] Moreover, China also performs better than many countries including the U.S. in the rates of new business growth. According to the 2009 GEM Report, China has the world's highest rate of high-expectation entrepreneurship. Over 4%

of the Chinese working-age population was engaged in high-growth-expectation entrepreneurship during 2004–2009 compared to less than 1.5% in the U.S.[4]

The Chinese Communist Party (CCP) leaders have publicly acknowledged the benefit that entrepreneurs and capitalists can bring to the economy. They have especially encouraged the growth of high technology entrepreneurship. The CCP has welcomed entrepreneurs in the inner circle and upper echelons of the party. There has been a transformation of state-owned enterprises (SOEs) and inward foreign direct investment (FDI) has provided learning opportunities for Chinese firms. Whereas China's so-called "red hat entrepreneurs" were a form of political entrepreneurs, new entrepreneurs increasingly resemble market entrepreneurs and are moving away from depending on political connection.[5]

Entrepreneurs are increasing their dominance in the Chinese political arena and are gaining more respect in the society. A recent survey conducted among Chinese found that 70% of the respondents thought entrepreneurship was a good career choice.[6] The Chinese society has rapidly embraced the idea of entrepreneurship. Entrepreneurial role models in China encourage people to start their own businesses and networks of family members and relatives support entrepreneurs.

A Survey of Entrepreneurship in China

Chinese political leaders have set economic growth as a top priority. There has been a shift in the base of regime legitimacy from MarxLeninism to economic growth. Following the 1978 reforms, China moved away from many of the Marxist approaches such as price controls and state ownership.[7]

Analysts disagree as to the effects of Chinese environment in shaping the entrepreneurship landscape. Some argue that China has "inbuilt" and "government-fostered" mechanisms,[8] which have helped unleash the entrepreneurial spirit of the Chinese. In a poll conducted among Americans by Zogby International and 463 Communications, 49% of the respondents said that China or Japan provide the "creative and entrepreneurial milieu required to form the world's next technological innovator."[9] Only 21% said that the next Bill Gates will be from the U.S. China began a new campaign to support entrepreneurship in 2014. By March 2016, it had opened 1,600 high-tech incubators for startups.[10]

The opposite view is that close state control has led to the failure of apparently abundant Chinese entrepreneurship. Others maintain that Chinese politics was arguably the most liberal in the 1980s. The 1989 Tiananmen events, which ended with a bloody military crackdown, impeded China's entrepreneurial progress. It is also noted that, in the 1990s, China reversed the gradualist political reforms started since 1978.

There are still communal principles such as the existence of communal property. Likewise, despite the substantial decline in state ownership, the state still accounts for a significant proportion of national GDP.[11] The rule of law and other market-supporting institutions, such as private property protection, are weak, as there is no independent judiciary.[12]

The development and growth of the private sector is often mentioned as an afterthought and a result instead of a cause of the country's economic success.[13] For instance, in September 2017, the CCP defined its role in business. In addition, the government's official definition of "entrepreneurship" was offered. According to the new definition, patriotism and professionalism are the most important responsibilities of entrepreneurs. Other responsibilities included observing discipline, complying with laws, innovation, and serving society. The statement did not mention profits. However, the statement assured that entrepreneurs' property would be protected.[14]

Some Macroeconomic Indicators

Entrepreneurialism is booming in China. The evolution of entrepreneur-friendly institutions and China's quantum leap on the entrepreneurship front are reflected in the macro-level economic data and Chinese companies' global performance, outreach, and expansion.

China's annual GDP per capita growth rate during 1978–2017 was around 9%.[15] The phenomenal economic progress of China during the past four decade is a success story for the developing world. This phenomenon is often referred to as the "China paradox," because the country has grown well despite not having a well-developed set of institutions.[16]

According to China Macro Finance, during 2000–2009, the number of registered private businesses in China grew by over 30% annually. One estimate suggested that there were 43 million companies in China in 2010, of which 93% were private companies, which employed 92% of the country's workers.[17] Small- and medium-sized enterprises (SMEs) account for 99.8% of the total number of enterprises, 60% of the total industrial output value, and 57% of the total sales revenue.[18] Firms in the private sector are playing increasingly important roles in the Chinese economy. The private sector in China accounts for more than 60% of the GDP, about 50% of tax revenues, and more than 80% of jobs.[19]

According to the OECD, China's rate of self-employment was 51.2% in 2009 compared to 7.2% in the U.S. Moreover, the China-U.S. gap in self-employment has not changed significantly since 2001, when the data first became available.[20] According to the 2009 study of the GEM, only 7% of the U.S. population in the 18–64 age group that did not have a business intended to start one in the future. In China, the proportion was 23%.[21] Nationwide SMEs account for 75% of new jobs.[22]

Emergence of World-Class Entrepreneurial Firms and Global Brands

In 2014, only 14% of unicorns were China-based, which increased to 35% in April 2018. The number of U.S.-based unicorns has fell from 61% to 41% of the global total during the same period.[23] China and Hong Kong had 263 companies represented in the 2017 Forbes Global 2000 list.[24] Likewise, 24 private corporations were on the 2017 list of the Fortune Global 500 companies compared to 15 in 2016.[25] In addition, three state-owned Chinese enterprises were top five on the list.

China is the home to many world-class entrepreneurial firms that have championed technology and innovation and performed at high levels of productivity and quality. For instance, two Chinese companies made to the Fast Company's 2013 list of "The World's 50 Most Innovative Companies": Tencent (No. 16) and Landwasher (No. 38) (www.fastcompany. com/most-innovative-companies/2013/full-list). *Tencent*, China's most innovative company according to Fast Company's 2013 list, launched WeChat (or Weixin) in 2011, which is a suite of social networking plug-ins that is less expensive, clearer, and faster than calling on phone. WeChat had over 300 million users in less than two years after its launch. Due to its popularity among a large number of Chinese expatriates in the U.S., WeChat was also a top 20 free social networking app in Apple's Store in the U.S.

Inequalities in Income and Wealth

Inequalities in income and wealth in China have accelerated at a phenomenally unprecedented pace. According to an ADB study of 22 Asian developing countries, China was the region's second most unequal country, only behind Nepal. During the early 1990s to early 2000s, China's increase in inequality was also the second highest, only behind Nepal.[26] It is also worth noting that over 90% of China's richest 20,000 people are related to senior government officials or senior members of the CCP.[27]

Informal Economy

As noted in Chapter 1, one way to measure the impacts of entrepreneurship would be to look at the informal economy. There is no systematic data on the size of the Chinese informal economy. The number of workers employed outside the formal sector was estimated to increase from 15,000 in 1978 to 168 million (59.4% of the total number of workers) in 2006.[28]

One estimate suggested that formal salary and wage employment as a proportion total compensation is 15% in China compared to 40% in

Indonesia, the Philippines, and Thailand and 90% in G-7 nations.[29] Other estimates suggest that the size of the shadow economy a proportion of official GDP increased from 10.2% in 1994/1995 to 13.4% in 2000/2001.[30]

Motivation of Chinese Entrepreneurs

According to the 2009 GEM report, proportionately more Chinese entrepreneurs than those in the U.S. are motivated by the desire to make money. The GEM study found that fewer than 40% of Chinese entrepreneurs started businesses to have more independence, and more than 60% of them did so to increase their income. On the contrary, in the U.S., only about 40% of entrepreneurs start businesses to increase income, while almost 60% do so to gain more independence.[31] Keming Yang, author of the book *Entrepreneurship in China*, noted, "The Chinese people have a very strong desire, perhaps the strongest among all nations in the world, to lead an enviable material life. It is a life-long struggle as they constantly compare their standard of material life with that of others around them."[32]

Institutional Changes and Entrepreneurship

From the perspective of entrepreneurship, formal institutions such as legal frameworks and rules, macroeconomic policies and political regimes as well as informal institutions such as cultures, social norms, customs, practices, conventions, and traditions have changed dramatically in the past 50 years. These changes which have facilitated entrepreneurship in China deserve a closer look. Table 8.1 presents some examples of such changes.

Three institutional change mechanisms include institution formation, deinstitutionalization, and reinstitutionalization.[33] Institution formation entails the birth of a new logic or governance structure. In the Chinese entrepreneurship terrain, for instance, Deng Xiaoping's famous statement provides a new logic for entrepreneurship: "To be rich is to be glorious." Similarly, entrepreneurs' entry into the CCP's inner circle and upper echelons and new laws to protect private property and intellectual property rights (IPR) are changing institutions related to entrepreneurship by providing a new governance structure.

In deinstitutionalization, an existing logic or governance structure is dissolved. Deinstitutionalization is related to delegitimation. For instance, the widespread view that only people with criminal records become entrepreneurs has been dissolved in recent years.

Finally, reinstitutionalization involves an existing logic or governance structure replaced by a new logic or governance structure. The old logic among CCP leaders was that private entrepreneurship was associated with

Table 8.1 Understanding Institutional Changes Influencing
Entrepreneurship in China

Institutional component	Institutions in the past	Institutions today
Formal	Entrepreneurial ventures perceived as potential threats to the CCP regime. Weak laws related to private property and entrepreneurship and poor enforcement mechanisms.	Marriage between entrepreneurship and party membership. China has enacted many new laws and enforcement mechanisms are strengthened.
Informal	Chinese societies had highly negative perception of entrepreneurs. Entrepreneurs were sensitive to the communist regime and the society, which resist ownership of private property.	Entrepreneurs are gaining more respect in the society. Society's attitude toward business increasingly favoring entrepreneurship, especially related to high technologies.
	Entrepreneurs had to fulfill social obligations.	Social obligations are not expected.
	Culture of complacency, conformity, and risk aversion. VC funds were related to the Chinese government, which cannot accept the Western level of risk taking.	Overseas Chinese with educations and entrepreneurship experience in the industrialized world are more similar to managers from the Western world. Inflow of foreign VC thanks to dense networks of overseas Chinese.
	Entrepreneurship as an occupation was often considered for individuals not able to find other jobs (e.g., those with criminal records).	Attitude toward entrepreneurship is rapidly shifting.

rising income gap and social unrest, which would lead to negative image of the party. In recent years, there is growing recognition among CCP leaders that a richer economy increases respect for the party.

Changes in Formal Institutions

China's poor performance in transparency, official accountability, and the rule of law is widely recognized. Corruption in the courts has been an issue of big concern. The CCP's Political-Legal Committee, local party committees, and local governments control personnel and funding in the courts.[34]

Formal institutions, which obstructed the growth of entrepreneurship in China, are undergoing fundamental and extraordinary shifts. This has been true for attitudes of rulemaking bodies such as the CCP as well as laws and rules influencing entrepreneurship. Richard L King, a venture partner at GRP Venture Partners, observed, "Despite the flaws of the Chinese system, the Chinese people are not unhappy with it. They may be unhappy with corrupted officials, and corruption remains a major problem."[35] He further explained how prospective leaders in China are "groomed" and have many years to prove their capability and competence. Thomas Friedman of the *New York Times* echoes with King: "One-party autocracy certainly has its drawbacks. But when it is led by a reasonably enlightened group of people, as China is today, it can also have great advantages."[36]

The CCP's Orientation toward Entrepreneurship

The conservative faction in the CCP considers entrepreneurial ventures as potential threats to the party's dominance, ideology, administrative authority, and moral standards. Leaders of this faction perceive improved legal institutions as potential challenges for the CCP's legitimacy and have employed rising income gap and social unrest to justify measures against entrepreneurship.[37] Some analysts argued that the delay in granting full rights to entrepreneurs was due to an institutional inertia.

Chinese legal institutions related to entrepreneurship had been victims of political ideology. Following the 1989 Tiananmen events, the conservative faction's actions severely impacted entrepreneurship. Estimates suggest that the number of private enterprises reduced by 50% that year.[38]

While Russia and Eastern Europe followed Western prescriptions, China has successfully blended nationalism with Marxism. The CCP expects that a richer economy might help burnish China's image worldwide and increase respect for it. For that reason, Chinese government encourages entrepreneurship. In general, China has failed to reform its political institutions but has been successful in constructing economic and market institutions needed to encourage innovation and entrepreneurship.[39]

Institutional actors bringing regressive changes in Chinese entrepreneurship are likely to weaken over time. Why might this be the case? First, as noted above, although some Chinese policymakers consider China's integration with the global market associated with significant socioeconomic costs, they cannot openly reject global integration.[40] To gain legitimacy from international institutions such as the WTO, China is required to respect private entrepreneurship and ownership of private property.

Second, entrepreneurs are being openly accepted into the CCP's inner circle. The CCP's policies and formal legal institutions encourage entrepreneurship. The CCP in 2002 changed its bylaws to allow entrepreneurs to become members. In a 2001 speech during celebrations of the party's 80th anniversary, then President Jiang Zemin acknowledged the benefit that capitalists bring to the economy. He also handed party membership to a capitalist and founder of one of China's most respected private companies and the first private company to list on a foreign stock exchange. In another instance, in January 2003, the CCP appointed one of China's wealthiest private entrepreneurs as deputy chairman of an advisory body to the government of Chongqing municipality. He was the first private businessman in China to be awarded such a high position. By 2017, 79 of the 2,158 members of the Chinese People's Political Consultative Conference (CPPCC), which is the most powerful political advisory body, were on the "Hurun China Rich List," of the Hurun Research Institute.[41] Especially more tech entrepreneurs have been selected as the members of the CPPCC in recent years.

Although some analysts argue that the seemingly impressive position carried "no real power," optimists argue that these entrepreneurs will give the private sector a more powerful voice in policymaking. These activities have undoubtedly bolstered legitimacy to entrepreneurs.

The CCP's legitimacy seeking process (logic) and governance structure are thus changing from the standpoint of entrepreneurship. First, the old logic that entrepreneurial ventures threaten the CCP's dominance, ideology, administrative authority, and moral standards is losing ground in relation to competing institutions. The new logic is that a richer economy helps burnish the CCP's image worldwide. There has thus been reinstitutionalization. Second, as entrepreneurs exert a strong grip to the CCP, one can expect the formation of new institutions through a new governance structure. The legitimacy seeking process requires appeasing multiple institutions that are conflicting and inconsistent. The Chinese government, for instance, has to take measures to satisfy both the conservative faction in the CCP and entrepreneurs. As entrepreneurs strengthen their positions in the CCP, Chinese policy makers are expected to take substantive measures to appease them.

Strong Rules of Laws and Enforcement Mechanisms

There has been a rapid shift in formal institutions related to entrepreneurship. Following the 1978 economic and political reforms, China enacted thousands of new laws to protect private property and IP, and abolished or amended many laws in these areas to comply with the WTO obligations. The formation of new institutions and governance structure is thus likely to promote entrepreneurship.

Under new laws, buyers of pirated goods can be fined five to ten times the value of the goods and manufacturers face jail time and equipment confiscation.[42] The government has provided a significant empowerment to regulatory agencies involved in IPR issues such as the State Administration of Industry and Commerce, the State Administration of Press and Publications, the intellectual property rights office and the State Pharmaceutical Administration.[43] Similarly, China announced its plans to open special centers in 50 cities by 2006 to handle IPR infringement complaints as well as to provide consulting services.[44]

Entrepreneurs as Institutional Change Agents

In China's context, researchers have identified four approaches institutional entrepreneurs employ to create market-oriented institutions by breaking regulative barriers: open advocacy, private persuasion, making a case for exceptions and ex ante investment with ex post justification.[45] First, open advocacy works only if the government is "tolerant enough for opinions that may criticize existing policies, regulations or laws" and the advocated changes are perceived to be beneficial to the general public. Second, entrepreneurs may persuade policy makers privately. Third, an entrepreneur may argue for a special case that is an exception to the existing laws and regulations. Finally, if a business formed or expanded by breaking existing laws generates jobs, tax revenues and other forms of social benefits, the entrepreneur reports to the government and persuades policy makers to bring changes in existing laws and regulations.

In addition to entrepreneurs' roles in bringing changes in existing rules and laws, entrepreneurs may also engage in strengthening enforcement mechanisms. Consider China's IPR laws. With increase in local firms' IP creation, these firms are forcing the government to take substantive measures to strengthen the country's IP regime. According to the Chinese Supreme Court, in 2005, over 16,000 civil cases and 3,500 criminal cases related to IPR violations were handled by Chinese courts and more than 2,900 people were jailed.[46] The number of cases involving IPR protection including patents, trade secrets and counterfeit goods increased by 21% in 2005.[47] It is also important to note that 95% of China's IPR cases in 2005 were brought by Chinese companies.[48]

The Chinese nanotechnology industry provides another visible example to illustrate how local entrepreneurs are taking more aggressive actions in trying to alter the trajectories of institutions related to entrepreneurship. The Nanometer Technology Center established in Beijing is actively involved in protecting IPR.

Shift from Double Entrepreneurship to Legal Entrepreneurship

Institutional boundaries for economic activities are not well defined in China. Exploitation of the regulative uncertainty and the weak rules of laws has arguably become an important form of entrepreneurship in China. This phenomenon is also known as double entrepreneurship which entails maximizing economic rewards and minimizing sociopolitical risks. Entrepreneurs find attractive economic niches from outside the current institutional boundaries. For instance, entrepreneurs depend on relations with government bureaucrats to obtain a business license. At the same time, because of ineffective enforcement of property rights, they have to acquire political and administrative protection or depend on informal norms.

In many developing countries, starting a business entails overcoming a significant amount of red tape. In China, one way to overcome bureaucratic red tape has been to be close to the CCP in order to gain advantages and preferential treatments. A membership in CCP would give an entrepreneur easier access to loans and official protection and discourages the entry of new players. Entrepreneurs also spend time and energy in forming guanxi and cultivating ties with officials. In sum, whereas entrepreneurship in the West is about identifying profitable opportunities, in China, an alliance with those who control financial, physical or human resources is critical to succeed.[49]

Improvement in market-supporting institutions or transformation of a socialist economy into a market economy can thus be an important force in converting double entrepreneurship into legal entrepreneurship.[50] In recent years, Chinese regulative landscape has undergone significant improvement in rule setting and monitoring activities. Consequently, the institutional actors' values are entrepreneurship friendly and progressive.

Changes in Informal Institutions

Societal Perception of Entrepreneurs

The perception of entrepreneurship in China was drastically different from that in market economies. Mao arguably developed a fierce critique of capitalism, private property, income and wealth inequality and material interest. During the Mao era, private entrepreneurship was virtually non-existent and was a political and social taboo.[51] Entrepreneurship was shunned even in the 1980s. Thanks to mindsets that were reminiscent of the Chinese Communist Public Goods Regime, as late as the 1990s, Chinese societies had highly negative perception of those trying to build their own company.

Faced with such societal perceptions, some Chinese entrepreneurs are still sensitive to the society and the communist party that resist ideas related to the ownership of private property. Accumulating a huge amount of wealth is thus a delicate subject. Some people in China still consider entrepreneurs as selfish people who think and act only in regard to their own interests.[52]

That is not to say that the institutional environment has not changed. Indeed, attitude toward businesses and private entrepreneurship is becoming more positive. Chinese leaders have also provided societal validity to entrepreneurship. With the new institutional logic associated with Deng Xiaoping's statement "To be rich is to be glorious," entrepreneurs are gaining more respect in the society.

Societies' Expectation from Entrepreneurs

Some still consider entrepreneurs as members of the working class striving for China's development. Some entrepreneurs are understood as "cadres" and were judged by their ability to provide socialist benefits. From the social standpoint, the road to entrepreneurship is beginning to look like a little smother. Especially, educated entrepreneurs running high-tech businesses are seen as highly respected good businesspeople. There is thus the deinstitutionalization of the logic that entrepreneurs need to fulfill social obligations.

Chinese culture and entrepreneurship

Overseas Chinese with educations and entrepreneurship experience in the industrialized world are likely to possess knowledge and ability to make adaptation in the Chinese context. "Social remittances" associated with immigrants (e.g., ideas, behaviors, and identities) play critical roles in promoting entrepreneurship.[53]

Overseas Chinese returnees are influencing institutions related to the Chinese entrepreneurship landscape through a number of mechanisms. Overseas Chinese, for instance, control assets worth trillions of dollars and have developed complex and dense social organizations and institutions. In recent years, Chinese returnees have developed such institutions in China, which have promoted innovation and risk taking and stimulated interaction among various ingredients of entrepreneurship. This trend is especially evident in industrial and high-tech parks of the country. Overseas Chinese have also contributed in producing synergies and in thickening existing institutions.[54] Successful entrepreneurial spin-offs from Chinese returnees have promoted risk-taking behavior among Chinese.

Cognitive Assessment of Entrepreneurship as an Occupation

While lifelong working for big enterprises is viewed as an ideal job in Japan, employment in big SOEs used to be the most desired career for Chinese. One observation is that people who spent most of their life in such careers dislike entrepreneurship.

Traditionally entrepreneurship was not the most desired occupation for China's best and brightest and was considered for people with criminal records that found it difficult to find other jobs. The situation is changing. A recent survey conducted among Chinese found that 70% of the respondents thought entrepreneurship was a good career choice and 32% expected to start a business in the next three years.[55]

Determinants of Entrepreneurship in China

Regulative Framework

We noted a moment ago that there has been a rapid shift in formal institutions related to entrepreneurship. Traditionally regulative institutions such as insecurity of property rights and close state control hindered entrepreneurship. Private entrepreneurs lacked legal protection. The situation is, however, changing. China is making a shift from top-down, state-directed policies to flexible and market-oriented approaches.

There are many examples to illustrate this trend. The story related to state-run China Telecom's complaint against two entrepreneurs offering callback services in Fujian deserves mention.[56] Their offerings challenged China Telecom's monopoly and high charges. The courts weren't convinced the brothers had violated any laws and ruled against China Telecom. To take another example, Pfizer successfully went against a major Chinese ministry-level government agency to defend its Viagra patent. Across these two examples, we see evidence of deinstitutionalization or diluting control and power of state-owned monopolies and government agencies.

Despite the above advances, China has a long way to go in the pursuit of its entrepreneurship-related goals. Starting a business involves time-consuming and lengthy steps. According to the World Bank's Ease of Doing Business 2018 (www.doingbusiness.org/data/exploreeconomies/china), China ranked 78 out of the 190 economies considered in terms of the regulatory climate. To start a business, seven procedures are needed to be completed which take 22 days and cost 0.6% of the country's per capita income.

Values, Culture, and Skills

Entrepreneurial Culture

While some argue that Chinese culture is entrepreneurship friendly, others suggest that Chinese, in general, tend to lack characteristics needed to be a successful entrepreneur such as independent thinking, risk taking, innovations, and self-determination. It is also suggested that entrepreneurship as discovery and exploitation of market opportunities are incompatible with China's culture of complacency, conformity, and adherence to standard rules and procedures.[57] That said, it would be erroneous, however, to claim the existence of a generic Chinese culture. As discussed earlier, there is a major difference between the social organization and risk taking behavior of Chinese staying in China and Overseas Chinese.

Finally, fatalistic orientation of Chinese people works against entrepreneurship. Compared to people in the West, Chinese arguably believe more in fate and thus tend to rely on opportunism over long-term entrepreneurial strategy.[58]

Entrepreneurial Skills and Capabilities

Intel ex-CEO Craig Barrett argued that the Chinese are "capable of doing any engineering, any software job, any managerial job that people in the United States are capable of."[59] Indeed, more scientists and engineers are staying in or returning to China with graduate degrees from foreign countries to perform R&D work for foreign affiliates or local firms or to start their own businesses. By 2005, 170,000 Chinese with graduate degrees overseas had returned to China. According to the Chinese Ministry of Education, in 2009 and 2010, 108,300 and 134,800 Chinese respectively returned to the country after completing their studies in foreign countries. The number increased to 432,500 in 2016 (http://monitor.icef. com/2018/02/increasing-numbers-chinese-graduates-returning-home-overseas/). MNCs are capitalizing on the huge and growing Chinese research pool to launch products that would help them compete globally.

Following the post-1978 reforms, Chinese firms gradually started importing western management techniques. Traditionally, the import was concentrated on the tangible and quantitative approach. Soft concepts of management, such as marketing and consumer behavior, are relatively less integrated into the Chinese way of thinking. Such concepts were perceived by the CCP as a threat to the communist ideology. Chinese entrepreneurial firms are taking measures to overcome these weaknesses. Some Chinese firms are seeking to overcome weaknesses in the areas of branding, sales, marketing, and technology through M&A.

In a process known as "brain circulation," Chinese engineers and entrepreneurs with work experience in the Silicon Valley are contributing to entrepreneurial development in their home countries.[60] They initially enjoyed home-country advantage by tapping the low-cost skill base and subsequently moved into a higher gear and engaged in the localized processes.

Access to Finance, Market, R&D, and Technology

R&D and Innovations

According to Euromonitor International, China's gross domestic expenditure on R&D as a proportion of GDP was 2% in 2017. In a 2018 report released on by KPMG, which was based on its tech innovation survey, China ranked #2 as the most promising market for technological breakthroughs.[61] Technology industry leaders who participated in the survey were asked about three cities outside Silicon Valley, that will be the leading technology innovation hubs over the next four years. Shanghai ranked #1 and Beijing ranked #7.

Overall China lags behind the West in terms of the state of technology, organizational, and managerial ability. That being said, it is also the case that Chinese companies, thanks to their accelerated pace of technological and scientific advances have developed strong prowess to compete globally in some technology sectors. Some visible examples of such technologies include blockchain, nanotechnology, open source software, cloning technology, and cellular telecommunications.

China's increasing R&D and innovations profile is reflected in the emergence of globally competitive Chinese technology firms. Patents are an important proxy for innovations. In 2017, the Chinese technology giant Huawei filed more patens than any other companies at the European Patent Office in 2017.[62]

In 2009, China increased its patent filings under World Intellectual Property Organization (WIPO) Patent Cooperation Treaty (PCT) by 29.7%. It overtook France to become the fifth largest patent filer to the PCT that year. In 2010, China ranked fourth among the PCT filing countries, only behind the U.S., Japan, and Germany. In 2010, China filed 12,337 patents under the PCT compared to 7,900 in 2009. Among companies, China's Huawei Technologies had the second highest number of patents (only behind Japan's Panasonic) in 2009. In 2008, Huawei had the world's highest number of patents.

In 2009, China's SIPO was the third largest patent office in the world. According to the WIPO's World Intellectual Property Indicators 2012, the SIPO became the world's largest patent office in 2011 by overtaking the United States Patent and Trademark Office (USPTO). It overtook the Japan Patent Office (JPO) in 2010 in terms of the number of patents registered.

In 2017, Chinese companies registered over 1.3 million patents, which was 14.2% higher than in 2016. According to a 2018 WIPO report, China's intellectual property rights office received 43% of global patent applications. This dominance is especially striking in recent technologies and high-growth sectors such as blockchain. According to the WIPO, of the

406 blockchain-related patent applications worldwide in 2017, more than half were from China.[63]

Market Conditions

The huge domestic market has helped Chinese entrepreneurial firms to compete successfully in foreign markets. Among prominent examples are dams projects undertaken by Chinese companies in developing countries. Chinese hydropower companies gained international experience in small dams in small developing countries such as Albania, Algeria, Burma, and Nepal. For instance, in the early 2010, Chinese companies were building about 40% of the 34 planned hydropower projects in Laos and all the 20 plants in Burma.

The economies of scale in the home country and their ability to adapt Western technology to the needs of developing countries at a low cost helped these companies slip into a higher gear. In power projects, Chinese companies' per kilowatt costs are in the US$700–800 range, while developed world-based firms tend to price at about US$ 1,000.

PHYSICAL INFRASTRUCTURES

The development of modern highways, ports, and telecommunications infrastructure has provided the foundation for entrepreneurial development. A comparison with India can be helpful in understanding the development of physical infrastructures in China. It is important to note that every year following the 1978 political and economic reform, China built more modern highways than India had done in the whole period since it achieved independence in 1947.[64]

As of 2016, China had over 67,000 kilometers of railway track (https://data.worldbank.org/indicator/IS.RRS.TOTL.KM?view=chart). In 2017, the country had 25,000 km high-speed rail tracks, which accounted for two-thirds of the world's total. China's high-speed rail tracks is expected to reach 38,000 km by 2025.[65]

The investment and infrastructure spending in the rail network has been a key factor in China's economic recovery. In December 2009, China launched world's fastest long distance passenger train, overtaking western countries and its Asian neighbors. The Harmony express raced 1,100 km in less than three hours travelling from Guangzhou to Wuhan. The journey used to take over 11 hours. The Harmony express reached a top speed of 394 km/hour in pre-launch trials and averaged 350 km/hour on its debut. This compared with a maximum service speed of 300 km/hour for Japan's Shinkansen bullet trains and France's TGV service. In the U.S., Amtrak's Acela "Express" service takes 3.5 hours to travel between Boston and New York, a distance of 300 km. The Chinese government spent US$17 billion on the Harmony express line's construction over 4.5 years. The country has used the recent global financial crisis (GFC) as an opportunity to modernize its economy.

Access to finance

DOMESTIC SAVINGS

Domestic savings have been an important source of investment. China's saving rate as proportions of disposable income was 25.5% in 2017.

One argument is that, as is the case of other Asian economies, the high savings rates in China can be attributed to income insecurity associated with mostly informal jobs. The high saving rates thus may not automatically translate to a higher investment rates. The size of the informal capital market in China, however, indicates that the high domestic saving rate is playing an important role to promote entrepreneurial activities in the country. According to the 2009 GEM report, about 6% of the Chinese in the 18–64 age group made an informal investment in the past three years, compared with less than 4% in the U.S. Informal investment was 11.3% of China's GDP in 2009, compared with only 1.5% in the U.S.[66]

To finance their ventures, many entrepreneurs depend on the informal banking systems, which are formed by pooling household saving and charge annual interest rates of as high as 70%. Estimates suggest that China's informal banking system was a US$630 billion industry in 2011.[67] Due to the GFC-led credit crunch, inflation and rise in the prices of raw materials, an increasing number of entrepreneurs are in the verge of bankruptcy. It was reported that in Wenzhou city many private entrepreneurs went into hiding, fled to foreign countries, or committed suicides.

VENTURE CAPITAL

The Chinese venture capital (VC) landscape is changing rapidly. China represents one of the fastest growing markets for VC investing in the world. In 2017, VC investment in China exceeded US$40 billion, compared to US$35 billion in 2016.[68] In 2017, Chinese telecoms and internet companies accounted for half of the top 10 largest VC deals globally.[69] Didi Chuxing received US$5.5 billion VC financing in April, 2017, which arguably was the biggest VC-backed deal during 2007–2017. The majority of Chinese VC in recent years is raised domestically.[70]

According to the consultancy Zero2IPO Group, Chinese government-backed VC funds raised about US$231 billion in 2015, which tripled the amount under management that year to US$339 billion. According to London-based consultancy Preqin Ltd, this amount was almost five times the sum raised by all other VC firms globally in 2015.[71] By early 2016, there were 780 such funds in China. Most of the capital comes from tax revenue or state-backed loans. Chinese VC companies experimenting with many different approaches and VC models are still evolving.[72]

In the past, a significant proportion of VC funds was linked to the government, which could be considered as a loan.[73] An incubator that lost the government owned VC also became a target of official criticism. Chinese government VC funds could not accept the Western level of risk taking. This situation is likely to change with the maturity of the VC market. Chinese returnees may also change other components of Chinese institutions such as the Chinese VC landscape.

BANK LOANS

Big state banks have dominated the Chinese financial market with huge networks of branches across the country. For instance, in 2015, ABC had about 24,000 branches, ICBC had about 18,000, China Construction Bank (CCB) had about 13,000 and BOC had about 11,000.[74] Lending, however, is disproportionately oriented toward powerful economic and political interests such as state-controlled companies. These banks often find SMEs as unattractive borrowers. It was reported that 89% of SMEs in China face difficulty in satisfying banks' requirements in order to get loans.[75] Small borrowers often tend to lack sufficient collateral, which is required by most traditional Chinese banks.[76]

INITIAL COIN OFFERINGS

In September 2017, the Chinese government issued a blanket ban on initial coin offerings (ICOs). Business establishments are even banned from offering meeting spaces to crypto-entrepreneurs. China's central bank, the People's Bank of China (PBoC) was reported to have reached a conclusion that many ICOs were "covers" for illicit activity. A PBoC report noted, "More than 90% ICO projects could be violating illegal fundraising or fund fraud laws. The percent of project that is actually raising funds for investments is less than 1%."[77] An economist at a state-affiliated think tank noted that the ban was driven by the CCP's fear that cryptocurrencies' "free" nature could evade the CCP's control.[78]

Concluding Comments

A constellation of factors linked to China's global integration is pushing through a fundamental changes in institutions related to Chinese entrepreneurship. China's successful blend of capitalism, nationalism, and Marxism has provided impetus to entrepreneurship and investment. Most CCP leaders have realized that entrepreneurs' contribution to the ambitious economic agenda outweigh the costs related to the challenges to the CCP's legitimacy. For this reason, they are wholeheartedly promoting and facilitating entrepreneurial thinking and practices. The preceding examples also point to an emerging trend in thickened entrepreneurial institutions.

Changing Profiles of Entrepreneurs

Institutional changes discussed earlier are likely to lead to alter the profiles of successful entrepreneurs. In the Chinese entrepreneurship landscape, there are a few commonly accepted rules and norms to govern relationships. This results in greater institutional and social uncertainties where personal relationships are important resources. The institutional entrepreneurs, which depend on government officials for their success, face risks in a market economy. Strengthened rule of law and a higher level of regulative certainty are likely to encourage legal entrepreneurship instead of double entrepreneurship.

Western Influence on Chinese Entrepreneurship Patterns

We discussed a number of mechanisms associated with Western influence on Chinese entrepreneurship culture. For instance, the arrival of an increasing number of overseas Chinese, some with significant entrepreneurial experience, is set to transform the Chinese entrepreneurship landscape. These returnees are likely to be more similar to western entrepreneurs in terms of habits of thought and behaviors related to entrepreneurship. Successful entrepreneurial spin-offs from Chinese returnees may further promote risk-taking behavior among Chinese. Likewise, inflow of VC from the Western world is rapidly growing in China. Recall that Western VC differs drastically from most domestic VC funds that are linked to the government. With China's growing global integration, further influence of Western entrepreneurship culture can be observed.

The Weakest Link in the Chinese Entrepreneurial Landscape

The adoption rate of values promoting entrepreneurship has been very slow among some critical institutional actors such as incubators, state-owned banks, local cadres, tax officers, and government officials. After decades of socialism, the idea of respecting constitutional rights of entrepreneurs has been slow to diffuse among some institutional actors. Chinese incubators, for instance, lack proper cognitive mindsets in assisting entrepreneurs. Private enterprises often complain about difficulties in dealing with state-owned banks and other agencies as well as harassment and extortion by local cadres, tax officers and government officials.[79] These actors have thus been the weakest link in China's entrepreneurship landscape. Measures are needed to accelerate the diffusion of entrepreneurship related progressive changes among these actors.

End of Chapter Questions

1   Compare China and the U.S. in terms of various indicators related to entrepreneurship. What are some of the indicators that would indicate that China's entrepreneurial progress may be faster than in the U.S.?
2   Give some examples of China-originated, world-class entrepreneurial firms and global brands.
3   Has entrepreneurship helped to narrow down inequalities in income and wealth in China?
4   Have the institutional changes taking place in China promoted entrepreneurship?
5   Thomas Friedman noted: "One-party autocracy certainly has its drawbacks. But when it is led by a reasonably enlightened group of people, as China is today, it can also have great advantages." Do you agree with Friedman? Elaborate your response.
6   How should industrialized countries such as the U.S. respond to China's entrepreneurial progress?
7   Intel ex-CEO Craig Barrett argued that the Chinese are "capable of doing any engineering, any software job, any managerial job that people in the United States are capable of." Do you agree or disagree? Why?

End of the Chapter Case: Xiaomi's global ambition

Xiaomi was founded in 2010 by a serial entrepreneur Lei Jun.[80] This budget smartphone and consumer electronics company is also referred to as Apple of China. Within four years after it was founded, the company was valued at more than US$45 billion.[81]

Its core business is based on smartphones, for which the Mi User Interface (MIUI) software (also known as firmware) is a key part. As of December 2017, MIUI had over 300 million activated users globally.[82]

Xiaomi's Smartphone Business

By 2014, Xiaomi became the world's sixth largest smartphone vendor. 97% of its shipments by then were in China.[83] The company's smartphones competes with the latest offerings from global smartphone giants, such as Samsung, and Apple. In March 2018, Xiaomi announced that its s new Android-powered phone Mi MIX 2S would be priced at US$527 in China, compared to the iPhone X's US$1,355. Mi MIX 2S would be equipped with the same hardware products that were used in Samsung's Galaxy S9 and S9+.[84]

International Expansion

Xiaomi entered the Indian market in the third quarter (Q3) of 2014. It followed the same strategy in India as in its home market. By 2015 Q3, it had sold over 1 million phones to Indian consumers. By then, it became #1 one online brand (Kelleher, 2016)[85] and accounted for 30% market share in the online segment.[86] Xiaomi became the No. 1 smartphone seller in India in 2017Q4 overtaking Samsung Electronics, which had held the position for many years.[87]

It also established a second manufacturing plant in India.[88] This meant that 95% of phones sold in India were manufactured in India.

Innovative Business Model

The keys to Xiaomi's success are its innovations in software and hardware and innovative business model. It overall ranked #2 (#1 among technology companies) on the MIT Technology Review's 2015 list for 50 Smartest Companies.[89] Xiaomi creates most of its products with the help of Mi fans by incorporating their feedback into a wide range of products. Xiaomi has been recognized as a company that launches innovative features in its products that consumers haven't seen before. It maintains software updates, and provides spare parts and other services for customers longer than most other companies.

Xiaomi's primary focus is on acquiring Internet users rather than selling phones. It mainly focuses on young users and offers them a variety of services to generate revenues. As of early 2016, it shipped about 50 apps on phones in China, each of which had at least 10 million monthly active users each. Moreover, over 20 apps had over 10 million daily users.[90]

Xiaomi seeks to provide high quality technology products at a low price. It has identified a number of different strategies to reduce costs. It does not advertise. It relies on word-of-mouth through social media. It does not sell products in stores. It continues to sell older devices at reduced prices even after releasing newer models.

In order to offer low prices, it also relies on a small portfolio of products and longer average selling time per device. Hugo Barra, the ex-VP of International put the issue this way: "The more focused the portfolio, the more efficient we can be at managing those costs too" Most of its products stay on the shelf for 18–24 months. They often go through price cuts at least three or four times. It allows the company to secure better deals with its suppliers of components.[91]

Development of New Products

In order to enter into the IoT realm, Xiaomi expanded its capabilities by acquiring, investing and forming partnerships with over 30 companies in a range of industries such as wearable devices, home appliances, online video content, and streaming sites. Xiaomi's acquisition and partnership activities have been centered around the MIUI software.[92] Smartphones have played a key role in the IoT revolution involving a range of connected devices.[93] In this way, the IoT is not completely unrelated to the company's core business activities.

Expanding into the IoT Arena

Chinese innovation ecosystems often involve the codevelopment of collaborative environment and creation of network effects around the core. By engaging in collaborative activities, the core company can overcome the capability gaps and exploit new opportunities in adjacent industries.[94] Xiaomi has expanded from its base in smartphones into the IoT using MIUI.

As of mid-2015, Xiaomi had over ten connected devices based on the IoT such as wristbands, air purifiers and blood pressure monitors and smart TV.[95] The company has also created and sold products related to its Mi Smart Home system. In March 2016, Mi Air Purifier was offered for sale in Singapore.[96]

The IoT has a significant link to the company's core business operations. The IoT has been integrated into their core business activities in such a way that it positively affects their performance and its competitiveness by enhancing the value delivery process. Xiaomi is generating a variety of IoT-related innovations and applications focusing on new areas.

Eying for IPO

It is expected go for IPO in the second half of 2018. Its IPO is likely to be among the biggest of the year. There were reports that the company could seek a valuation in the range of US$80 billion to US$100 billion.[97]

Some Challenges

Chinese firms' activities in India are viewed with suspicion and there is a fear that activities of some of them are against India's national security interest. It was reported that, Xiaomi Redmi Note, the cellphone model developed by the Chinese firm Xiaomi, secretly sent Indian users' data to a China-based server.[98] In October 2014, due to CS concerns, India warned its military against using devices manufactured by Xiaomi. Xiaomi announced plans to open a data canter in India.[99] Xiaomi is currently being investigated by Hong Kong's privacy authority for allegedly sending information to servers in mainland China without user consent.[100] Among the alleged information receivers were China Unicom, and two Chinese internet companies.[101]

Case Summary

As is the case of other successful, China's Internet companies, Xiaomi has flexible and lean organizational structure and business strategies. For instance, it uses online-only marketing. A key to its success is also the management of components and supply chain partnerships. In recent years, it is playing a central role in the creation of IoT-related products and services.

Notes

1 Alois, J.D. 2016. "China is So Huge: 4.4 Million New Businesses Registered in 2015," 2 May, www.crowdfundinsider.com/2016/05/85036-china-is-so-huge-4-4-million-new-businesses-registered-in-2015/.
2 Nair, S.R. 1996. Doing business in China: It's far from easy.
3 Bosma, N., & Levie, J. 2009. "2009 Global Report, Global Entrepreneurship monitor," www.gemconsortium.org/about.aspx?page=pub_gem_global_reports.
4 Shane, S., & Venkataraman, S. 2000. "The promise of entrepreneurship as a field of research," *Academy of Management Review*, 25(1), pp. 217–226.
5 Richter, F. 2000. "China's entry into the WTO and the impact on Western firms," *China Economic Review*, 11(4), pp. 423–427.
6 Gangemi, J. 2007. "Study: U.S. startup activity down slightly in '06," *Business Week Online*, January 11.
7 Hornby, L. 2017. "Communist party asserts control over China Inc," www.ft.com/content/29ee1750-a42a-11e7-9e4f-7f5e6a7c98a2.
8 Monro, A. 2007. "Mysteries of the east," *New Statesman*, 136(4826), pp. 58–59.
9 America. 2007. "The Next Bill Gates," January 15, 196(2), p. 4.
10 Oster, S., & Chen, L.Y. 2016. "Inside China's Historic $338 billion tech startup experiment," www.bloomberg.com/news/articles/2016-03-08/china-state-backed-venture-funds-tripled-to-338-billion-in-2015.
11 Yueh, L. 2018. "Will China ever get rich? Only if it tackles state ownership and strengthens its legal system," www.scmp.com/comment/insight-opinion/article/2137279/will-china-ever-get-rich-only-if-it-tackles-state-ownership.
12 Xiangwei, W. 2017. "Entrepreneurship in China: Strong or dispirited?" www.scmp.com/week-asia/opinion/article/2113446/entrepreneurship-china-strong-or-dispirited.
13 Xiangwei. 2017.
14 Hornby. 2017.
15 Pham, P. 2018. "Is there a secret growth hormone added to China's economy?" 6 March, www.forbes.com/sites/peterpham/2018/03/06/is-there-a-secret-growth-hormone-added-to-chinas-economy/#27e1d2503f13.
16 Yueh. 2018.

17 economist.com. Let a million flowers bloom, March 10, 2011, www.economist.com/node/18330120.

18 China Knowledge. 2010. "China's SMEs need efficient financing channels," 19 February, www.chinaknowledge.com/Newswires/News_Detail.aspx?type=1&NewsID=31452.

19 Xiangwei. 2017.

20 OECD Economic Surveys. 2009b. "Russian Federation, stabilisation and renewed growth: Key challenges," July, 2009(6), pp. 19–51.

21 Shane, S. 2010. "If you want to see entrepreneurs, go to China." 12 March, www.businessweek.com/smallbiz/content/mar2010/sb20100311_996919_page_2.htm.

22 Loyalka, M., & Dammon, A. 2006. "Chinese Welcome for Entrepreneurs," *Business Week Online*, 6 January, p. 1.

23 Loizos, C. 2018. "Startup ecosystem report: China is rising while the US is waning," 20 April, https://techcrunch.com/2018/04/20/startup-ecosystem-report-china-is-rising-while-the-u-s-is-waning/.

24 Jurney, C. 2017. "The World's Largest Public Companies 2017," 24 May, www.forbes.com/sites/corinnejurney/2017/05/24/the-worlds-largest-public-companies-2017/#63574d4a508d.

25 The Japan Times. 2017. "A clash brewing between the CCP and China's entrepreneurs?" www.japantimes.co.jp/opinion/2017/11/27/commentary/world-commentary/clash-brewing-ccp-chinas-entrepreneurs/#.Ws0xmcpDIU.

26 ADB (Asian Development Bank). 2007. "Key indicators of developing Asian and Pacific countries 2007." Manila. www.adb.org/Documents/Periodicals/ADR/ADR-Vol25-1-2.pdf.

27 Kwong, K.K., Yau, O.H.M., Lee, J.S.Y., Sin, L.Y M., & Tse, A.C.B. 2003. "The effects of attitudinal and demographic factors on intention to buy pirated CDs: The case of Chinese consumers," *Journal of Business Ethics*, 47(3), pp. 223–235.

28 Huang, P.C.C. 2009. "China's neglected informal economy," *Modern China*, 35(4), pp. 405–438.

29 Klein, B.P., & Cukier, K.N. 2009. "Tamed Tigers, Distressed Dragon," *Foreign Affairs*, 88(4), pp. 8–16.

30 Bajada, C., & Schneider, F. 2005. "The shadow economies of the Asia-Pacific," *Pacific Economic Review*, 10(3), pp. 379–401.

31 Bosma, N., Jones, K., Autio, E., & Levie, J. 2007. 2007 Executive Report, Global Entrepreneurship monitor.

32 Shane, S. 2010. "If you want to see entrepreneurs, go to China," 12 March, www.businessweek.com/smallbiz/content/mar2010/sb20100311_996919_page_2.htm.

33 Scott, B.R. 2001. "The great divide in the global village," *Foreign Affairs*, 80(1), pp. 160–177.

34 Liu, D. 2006. The transplant effect of the Chinese patent law.

35 King, R. 2010. "A journey home," *Chinese American Forum*, 25(3), pp. 22–25.

36 Mufson, S. 2009. "Asian nations could outpace U.S. in developing clean energy; American markets' slump feeds worry," *The Washington Post*, 16 July, Suburban Edition, A.14.

37 Kahn, J. 2006. "A sharp debate erupts in china over ideologies," *New York Times*, 12 March, p. 1.

38 Ling, Z. 1998. "Chenfu: 1989–1997 Zhongguo Jingji Gaige Beiwanglu (Ups and downs: Memorandum of China's economic reform during 1989–1997)," Tongfang Chuban Zhongxin, Shanghai.

39 Nee, V. 1992. "Organizational dynamics of market transition: Hybrid forms, property rights, and mixed economy in China."

40 Heer, P. 2000. "A house divided." *Foreign Affairs*, 79, pp. 18–24.

41 Wu, Y. 2018. "Tech entrepreneurs a growing force at China's communist party meeting," www.chinamoneynetwork.com/2018/03/05/tech-entrepreneurs-growing-force-chinas-communist-party-meeting.

42 Kanellos, M. 2002. "Software comes of age: Piracy crackdown pays off," *CNET News.com*, Retrieved July 11, 2009, http://news.com.com/2009-1001-940335.html.

43 Yang, D.M. 2002a. "Can the Chinese state meet its WTO obligations? Government reforms, regulatory capacity, and WTO membership," *American Asian Review*, 20(2), pp. 191–121.

44 MacLeod, C. 2006. "China grows more aggressive in thwarting counterfeiters," *USA Today*, 21 April, 4B.

45 Daokui Li, D., Feng, J., & Jiang, H. 2006. "Institutional entrepreneurs," *American Economic Review*, 96(2), pp. 358–362.

46 Culpan, T. 2006. "Industry awaits IP court in China," *Billboard* (22 April), 118(16), p. 14.

47 AFX News Limited. 2006. "Louis Vuitton sues Carrefour in China – report," *AFX.COM*, 20 April.

48 Ibid.

49 Krug, B. 2004. China's Rational Entrepreneurs: The Development of the New Private Business sector. London: Routledge Curzon.

50 Yang, K. 2002b. Double entrepreneurship in China's economic reform: An analytical framework.

51 Peng, Y. 2004. Kinship Networks and Entrepreneurs in China's Transitional Economy.

52 Hsu, C. 2006. "Cadres, Getihu, and good businesspeople: Making sense of entrepreneurs in early post-socialist China," *Urban Anthropology & Studies of Cultural Systems & World Economic Development* (Spring), 35(1), pp. 1–38.

53 Levitt, P. 1998. "Social remittances: Migration driven local-level forms of cultural diffusion," *The International Migration Review*, 32(4), pp. 926–948.

54 Amin, A., & Thrift, N. 1995. 'Globalisation, institutional thickness and the local economy," In *Managing Cities: The New Urban Context*, P. Healey, S. Cameron, I S. Davoui, S. (eds.).

55 Gangemi, J. 2007. "Study: U.S. startup activity down slightly in '06," *Business Week Online*, 11 January.

56 Sender, H. 2000. "China's future: Entrepreneurs," *Far Eastern Economic Review*, 27 January, p. 73.

57 Mourdoukoutas, P. 2004. "China's Challenge," *Barron's*, February 16, 84(7), p. 37.

58 Liao, D., & Sohmen, P. 2001. "The development of modern entrepreneurship in China."

59 Segal, A. 2004. "Is America losing its edge?" *Foreign Affairs*, November/ December, 83(6), p. 2.

60 Saxenian, A. 2005. "From brain drain to brain circulation: Transnational communities and regional upgrading in India and China," *Studies in Comparative International Development*, 40(2), p. 35.

61 Mostowyk, L. 2018. "US named top global tech innovation leader, China in second spot: KPMG report," https://home.kpmg.com/xx/en/home/media/press-releases/2018/03/us-named-top-global-tech-innovation-leader.html.

62 Thiruchelvam, S. 2018. "How China became a leader in intellectual property," 20 April, www.raconteur.net/business/how-china-became-leader-intellectual-property.

63 Ibid.

64 Overholt, W.H. 2009/2010. "China in the global financial crisis: rising influence, rising challenges," *Washington Quarterly*, 33(1), pp. 21–34.

65 Hui, L. 2018. "China's high-speed rail tracks to hit 38,000 km by 2025," 2 January, www.xinhuanet.com/english/2018-01/02/c_136867206.htm.

66 Shane, S. 2010. "If you want to see entrepreneurs, go to China," 12 March, www.businessweek.com/smallbiz/content/mar2010/sb20100311_996919_page_2.htm.

67 Barboza, D. 2011. "China rattled as business owners flee," *International Herald Tribune*, 12 October.

68 KPMG. 2018. "China VC investment hits new heights with USD40 billion in 2017, finds KPMG analysis", https://home.kpmg.com/cn/en/home/news-media/press-releases/2018/01/china-vc-investment-hits-new-heights-in-2017.html.

69 Lee, G. 2018. "Chinese companies account for half of top 10 biggest venture capital financing deals in 2017," www.scmp.com/business/article/2127624/chinese-companies-account-half-top-10-biggest-venture-capital-financing.

70 Allen, D. 2017. "China's red-hot venture capital tech scene," www.eastwestbank.com/ReachFurther/News/Article/China-s-Red-Hot-Venture-Capital-Tech-Scene.

71 Oster and Chen. 2016.

72 Ibid.

73 Harwit, E. 2002. "High-technology incubators: Fuel for China's new entrepreneurship?" *The China Business Review*, 29(4), pp. 26–29.

74 Hongyong, L. 2017. "Why China is cracking down on cryptocurrencies," Again. www.sixthtone.com/news/1000849/why-china-is-cracking-down-on-cryptocurrencies%2C-again (Accessed 18 September 2017).

75 Jing, M. 2014. "Amazon brings its cloud computing to China," www.chinadaily.com.cn/business/2014-01/02/content_17209279.htm (Accessed 5 February 2018).

76 Wildau, G. 2015, "Alibaba's finance arm launches credit scoring service," www.ft.com/intl/cms/s/0/34e77fe8-a6a3-11e4-9bd3-00144feab7de.html.

77 Tian, C. 2017. "Report: China's regulators close to taking action against ICOs," www.coindesk.com/report-chinas-regulators-close-taking-action-icos/ (Accessed September 6, 2017).

78 The Japan Times. 2017. "A clash brewing between the CCP and China's entrepreneurs?" www.japantimes.co.jp/opinion/2017/11/27/commentary/world-commentary/clash-brewing-ccp-chinas-entrepreneurs/#.Ws0xm-cpDIU.

79 Economist. 2002. Not in the club; China's private sector; Yang, D.M. 2002a. Can the Chinese state meet its WTO obligations?

80 XGC. 2017. "About Xiaomi global community," https://xiaomi-mi.com/company/about/.

81 Osawa, J. 2014 China's Xiaomi valued at more than $45 billion, 20 December, www.wsj.com/articles/chinas-xiaomi-raises-over-1-billion-in-investment-round-1419093589.

82 Vincent. 2017. "[Xiaomi] MIUI Has More than 300 Million Activated Users Globally!" en.miui.com/thread-1262032-1-1.html.

83 Kharpal, A. 2014 'China's Apple' lays down challenge to iPhone, Samsung, 22 July, www.cnbc.com/2014/07/22/chinas-apple-lays-down-challenge-to-iphone-samsung.html.

84 Delventhal, S., 2018. "Xiaomi Unveils iPhone X Rival at Half the Cost," at www.investopedia.com/news/xiaomi-unveils-iphone-x-rival-half-cost/.

85 Kelleher, K. 2016. "Xiaomi Exec: 'We're playing a completely different game," http://time.com/4273853/xiaomi-apple-china/.

86 Singal, N. 2017, "Xiaomi sets up its second manufacturing unit in India," www.businesstoday.in/current/deals/xiaomi-sets-up-its-second-manufacturing-unit-in-india/story/248367.html.

87 South China Morning Post. 2018. "China's Oppo embraces Xiaomi's flash sale gambit to grow Indian smartphone sales," www.scmp.com/tech/article/2139021/chinas-oppo-embraces-xiaomis-flash-sale-gambit-grow-indian-smartphone-sales.

88 Singal, N. 2017. "Xiaomi sets up its second manufacturing unit in India," www.businesstoday.in/current/deals/xiaomi-sets-up-its-second-manufacturing-unit-in-india/story/248367.html.

89 technologyreview.com. 2015. "50 Smartest Companies 2015," www.technologyreview.com/lists/companies/2015/.

90 Kelleher, K. 2016. "Xiaomi Exec: 'We're playing a completely different game," http://time.com/4273853/xiaomi-apple-china/.

91 Russel, J. 2015. "This is how Xiaomi keeps the cost of its smartphones so low," https://techcrunch.com/2015/01/19/xiaomi-secret-sauce/.

92 Hendrichs, M. 2015. "Why Alipay is more than just the Chinese equivalent of PayPal," www.techinasia.com/talk/online-payment-provider-alipay-chinese-equivalent-paypal/.

93 Schwartz, H.E. 2015. "Can Apple's IoT efforts keep up with its Chinese rival, Xiaomi?" http://dcinno.streetwise.co/2015/05/27/apple-aapl-vs-chinese-xiaomi-for-the-internet-of-things/.

94 Hendrichs 2015.

95 Griffiths, J., 2015, "Tencent unveils smartphone and 'internet of things' OS in challenge to Xiaomi," *Alibaba*. www.scmp.com/tech/enterprises/article/1779923/tencent-unveils-smartphone-and-internet-things-os-challenge-xiaomi.

96 Millward, S. 2016. "Xiaomi's smart home gadgets are about to go global," www.techinasia.com/xiaomi-smart-home-gadgets-start-global-expansion.

97 Trefis Team. 2018. "How Xiaomi could justify an $80 billion valuation," www.forbes.com/sites/greatspeculations/2018/03/20/how-xiaomi-could-justify-an-80-billion-valuation/#9e540b466faf.

98 gadgets.ndtv.com. 2014. "Xiaomi Redmi 1s and Redmi Note to launch soon in India; prices revealed," http://gadgets.ndtv.com/mobiles/news/xiaomi-launches-redmi-1s-and-redmi-note-in-india-1-558833.

99 bbc.com. 2014. "Xiaomi to open India data centre to allay privacy fears," www.bbc.com/news/technology-29786324.

100 Liu, J.Y. 2014. "Xiaomi under investigation for sending user info back to China," www.zdnet.com/article/xiaomi-under-investigation-for-sending-user-info-back-to-china/.

101 hk.apple.nextmedia.com. 2014. "資料傳北京Apps疑被做手腳", http://hk.apple.nextmedia.com/news/art/20140908/18859462

Chapter 9

Entrepreneurship in India

This chapter's objectives include:

1   To *demonstrate* an understanding of the changes undergoing in the Indian entrepreneurship landscape.
2   To *analyze* the facilitators and inhibitors of entrepreneurship in India.
3   To *assess* the nature of entrepreneurial activities in the Indian IT and offshoring sector and their impacts on the Indian economy.
4   To *evaluate* the impacts of entrepreneurial activities in India on poverty reduction.
5   To *demonstrate* an understanding of the nature and availability of various forms of entrepreneurial finance in India.

Introduction

Because of India's improving entrepreneurial performance, some analysts consider the country as the next Asian miracle.[1] The State's domination over the economy is gradually declining and there are some signs that the country is moving toward a market-oriented system. India has also set explicit policy and objective to become a leading business-friendly economy.[2] In a number of important areas, institutional reform has gained a higher momentum in India than in China. India also outperforms China in many of the World Bank's governance indicators such as rule of law and voice and accountability. India was also among the ten top improvers in 2016/2017 in areas that are tracked by the World Bank in its *Doing Business* report.[3] Some observers have noted that India is shedding its legacy of entrepreneurship unfriendly rules and regulations and Indian politics is becoming open and accountable.

Most impressive of all, in 2016, the Indian government launched the "Start-up India" program. The program seeks to provide a number of policy measures, initiatives, and incentives in order to foster startups in the country. Tax exemption for startups for three years, a US$1.5 billion *corpus fund* to support startups, exemption of capital gains tax for venture capital investments, 80% reduction in patent registration fees and ensuring a 90-day window for startups to close businesses are among the top incentives the Indian government plans to offer to stimulate startups in the country.[4]

Despite the earlier-noted positive trends, entrepreneurial activities are hindered by business–unfriendly labor laws, adverse corporate bankruptcy regulations and the lack of clear property rights.[5] Red tape, bureaucracy and corruptions in the country, both at the national and state levels, lead to longer time, higher costs, and reduced speed and flexibility for entrepreneurs.[6]

Moreover, many Indian entrepreneurs still struggle with a culture that looks down on capitalism and is indifferent to hard work, improvement, and innovations.[7] Other challenges include a big entrepreneurial financing gap[8] and the country's poor R&D and innovation performance.[9]

While some influential entrepreneurs are in a position to take advantage of institutional holes, SMEs tend to be more adversely affected by the dysfunctional institutions. Some observe that reform inertia has been an obstacle for India to outperform China. Observers also often note the most Indian multinational companies are in a primitive or an embryonic stage.[10]

India also suffers from a lack of basic infrastructures and services required for carrying out entrepreneurial activities. According to the Country's Planning Commission, inefficient power supply has hindered entrepreneurial activities, employment creation, and poverty reduction.[11] As of 2016, 15.5% of India's population lacked access to electricity (https://data.worldbank.org/indicator/EG.ELC.ACCS.ZS).

A Survey of Entrepreneurship in India

We begin this section by considering India's economic reform initiatives. India started relaxing industrial regulation in the early 1970s. Trade liberalization began in the late 1970s and the pace of reform picked up significantly in the mid-1980s. Indian entrepreneurship, however, got a big boost following the 1991 economic liberalization, which transformed India's entrepreneurial landscape. Many large and inefficient firms could not survive the competition created by the 1991 liberalization. For instance, of the largest 20 private firms listed on the Indian stock market in 1990, only five were in the top 20 list in 2011.[12]

Startups and SMEs have played a key role in the Indian economy. India has the world's third largest number of startups.[13] According to the National Association of Software and Services Companies, the number of new companies launched in India grew by 40% in 2015.[14] Likewise, as of mid-2016, India was estimated to have more than 45 million SMEs, which accounted for about 40% of the country's GDP.[15]

Various indicators point to an improved entrepreneurial performance of India. Fifty-eight Indian companies were included in the 2017 Forbes' Global 2000 list of the world's biggest companies compared to 47 in 2009.[16]

In a March 2018 report released on by Klynveld Peat Marwick Goerdeler (KPMG), which was based on its tech innovation survey, India ranked #3 as the most promising market for technological breakthroughs.[17] However, no Indian city made to the top ten list. In Startupblink's global ranking of 125 countries and 900 cities, Indian startup ecosystem ranked number 37.[18]

The country has also achieved positive societal changes. For instance, Indian divisions of some leading financial institutions such as HSBC, JP-Morgan Chase, Royal Bank of Scotland, UBS, and Fidelity International were headed by women. Women also accounted for about half of the deputy governors at the Reserve Bank of India.[19] Likewise, in 2018, women led about 25% of social enterprises.[20]

Entrepreneurship in the Indian IT and Offshoring Sector

The story of India's entrepreneurial performance is incomplete without a reference to its offshoring sector. India has been a global capital of the offshore information technology (IT) and business process (BP) offshore outsourcing. According to a study, six of the world's ten leading cities for offshoring are in India.[21]

India's offshoring industry started from back office works, which moved to business process and is gradually shifting toward high-end functions such as R&D. To illustrate this point one may think of the drug industry. Many U.S.-based drug companies are outsourcing drug development processes to India. One estimate suggested that developing a drug in India in the average costs about US$100 million compared with over US$1 billion in the U.S.[22]

India's business and technology services companies' revenues increased from US$4 billion in 1998 to US$167 billion in 2017 (https://economictimes.indiatimes.com/tech/ites/indian-software-services-sector-to-grow-7-9-in-fy19-nasscom/articleshow/62995685.cms). India's entrepreneurial IT firms are heavily export-oriented. The industry exports US$3.75 for every dollar earned in India. For the leading IT company, Infosys, the domestic market accounts for only 1.2% of revenue.[23] According to NASSCOM, the export portion of the sector in 2011 was 26% of India's exports and 11% of services revenue.[24]

This unprecedented growth of this sector has generated opportunities for employment for millions of Indians and vastly improved their living standards. Direct employment created by this industry was estimated at 2.2 million in 2012.[25] The offshoring industry's indirect job creation was estimated to be eight million in 2009.[26] By 2025, this industry is expected to employ seven million people directly and addition ten million indirectly.[27]

In addition to economic impacts, entrepreneurial activities in the offshoring sector have brought some positive societal changes. For instance, women have entered into new status hierarchies. In the offshoring industry, women account for 65% of the workforce and 85% of them work on night shifts. Call centers are breaking the societal taboos as men and women work together in nights to meet daylight needs of Westerners. In the Rajasthan state, the law forbidding *women* to work after sunset was changed at the request of the outsourcing company, Genpact.[28]

Low Overall Entrepreneurial Performance

Despite all the hype surrounding entrepreneurship in India's IT and offshoring sector, a closer look at the overall economy paint a different picture. The country falls behind many other developing economies on important indicators related to entrepreneurial activities. For instance, in terms of high-expectation business launchers per capita, India underperforms Brazil.[29]

The informal economy is substantial and increasing. The size of the informal and shadow economy as a proportion of official GDP was estimated to increase from 18.1% in 1988/1989 to 22.8% in 2000/2001.[30] According to ILO India Labor Market Update (2016) over 90% of the workers in the agricultural sector and 70% in the nonagricultural sector were employed in the informal category.[31]

Consider another indicator related to impacts of entrepreneurship– poverty reduction. According to the UNDP's Human Development Report 2013, during 2002–2011, 32.7% of the population in the country lived on less than US$1.25 a day. The traditional economic sectors are disadvantaged and there is thus very little progress in poverty reduction. While the Indian offshoring sector has been a vibrant and prosper economy with a rapidly rising income driven by highly skilled human resources fostering high productivity and innovation, the rest of the economy mainly consists of poverty stricken, unemployed and deprived masses of people.

Lack of Trickledown Effect and Signs of Oligarchic Capitalism

The benefits of the economic growth are highly concentrated and disproportionately distributed to the wealthiest individuals, a handful of large companies and have failed to trickle down to the poor.[32] About ten families are estimated to control more than 80% of the stock in the country's largest corporations.[33] According to the Asian Development Bank (ADB), large Indian companies have won most of lucrative government contracts, hold power over the country's natural resources, and have "privileged access to land." In a 2007 government survey of about 200,000 services firms in the formal and informal sectors, the top 0.2% accounted for about 40% of output.[34] Likewise, in 2011, the Bombay Stock Exchange (BSE) 100 index of the largest firms accounted for about 70% of Indian stock market value.[35]

The geographic concentration of entrepreneurial activities also deserves mention. The 2007 government survey noted above also found that companies in two states—Maharashtra and Karnataka—accounted for about 50% of output.[36]

India obviously has some elements of a market economy and political democracy. The country, however, lacks a true democratic market system. A report from the ADB suggested that Indian economy has many characteristics of oligarchic capitalism and there is a possibility that this form of capitalism would further consolidate in the country, which can slow long-term development of the country.[37] As it happens in oligarchic capitalism, India has shown signs of adverse impact on incentives required for structural changes as well as the state's reduced autonomy.[38]

Most Indian billionaires have built their wealth by using their economic power to secure policies favoring them. One commentator noted, "While many Indian publicists and economists hail the 'Indian miracle' and classify India as an 'emerging world power' because of the high growth rates of the past five years, what really has transpired is the conversion of India into a billionaire's paradise."[39]

Determinants of Entrepreneurship

Regulatory Framework

Entrepreneurial firms are likely to thrive and act in socially responsible ways if there are strong and well-enforced legislation and regulations in place to ensure such behavior. In this regard, notwithstanding the existence of some essential elements of a democracy, the Indian political system has become inherently "unaccountable, corrupt, and unhinged from the normal bench marks voters use to assess their leaders." One scholar noted, "Corrupted as they are by the party system, India's institutions are incapable of enforcing accountability. India's elites tolerate a level of poor governance and abuse of power that has led to the collapse of democracy elsewhere."

Beyond all that, in India, there are groups with disposition to support traditional values, norms, and institutions, which hamper entrepreneurial practices. Notwithstanding their supports to modern values, the Indian government and court system are forced to settle for compromise, which means a slower progress than they would like to see.

Indian court systems are overburdened and are characterized by procedural delays, and red tape. The Bureau of Democracy, Human Rights and Labor's report, 'Supporting Human Rights and Democracy: The U.S. Record 2004–2005 noted, "poor enforcement of laws, especially at the local level, and the severely overburdened court system weaken the delivery of justice." According to the South Asia Human Rights Documentation Center, there was a backlog of 23.5 million cases in 2002. The court system is decentralized and is largely administered by states. National labor laws are administered at the state level.[40] Due to budget problems, the states have failed to comply with federal directives to upgrade legal infrastructures and court facilities.

Moving to the specific context of entrepreneurship, weak laws and inappropriate regulatory processes hinder efficient entrepreneurial behaviors. For instance, it is argued that corruption is likely to make state subsidies to entrepreneurship such as the Israeli government's incentive to provide 80% of the first US$500,000 for every idea identified, highly ineffective in India. It is speculated that such a model "will lead to favoritism, cronyism and corruption" in the country.[41]

According to the World Bank's Ease of Doing Business 2018 Report (www.doingbusiness.org/rankings?region=south-asia), India ranked No. 100 out of the 190 economies considered in terms of the regulatory climate for entrepreneurship. To start a business, 12 procedures are needed to be completed which take 20.5 days and cost 17.6% of the country's per capita income.

According to the World Bank, it takes seven years to close a business in India compared to the OECD average of 1.7 years. Likewise, the average time to register property in South Asia is 106 days compared to the OECD average of 25 days.

Entrepreneurial and marketing activities are hindered by complex regulations. In the retail sector, for instance, there are barriers such as anti-hoarding laws and signboard licenses. *Competition laws have not* yet been introduced in some sectors of the Indian economy. For instance, in the Indian retail sector, the existing laws work against retailers and favor small mom and pop stores.[42]

Labor regulations

Indian labor market is governed by about 250 labor rules at the central and state levels, which make the country's labor laws are less flexible and less business-friendly than those of China. These laws arguably are restrictive in nature, hinder investments in the manufacturing sector, and discourage firms from introducing new technology that might require reducing the workforce.[43] These labor regulations thus limit businesses' capacity to grow and compete in the global economy. Moreover, companies with over 100 employees require government permission to dismiss workers.[44]

Property rights

Clear property rights would allow entrepreneurs to use the assets as collateral and thus increase their access to capital. Problems related to property rights are key challenges facing entrepreneurial development in India. Some argue that the lack of land ownership remains among the most important barriers to entrepreneurship and economic development in India. One estimate suggested that over 20 million rural families in India did not own land and millions more lacked legal ownership to the land where they built their houses, lived on, and worked.[45]

Indeed landlessness is arguably a more powerful predictor of poverty in India than caste or illiteracy.[46] This issue is important because poverty reduction is considered to be one of the key impacts of entrepreneurship, especially in the context of developing countries such as India.

Especially for entrepreneurial firms that rely heavily on intellectual property (IP), they face a unique challenge in economies with weak IP protection laws and enforcement mechanisms. According to the Global Intellectual Property Center's International IP Index 2016, India ranked 37 out of the 38 countries. Only Venezuela's IP index was worse than that of India.[47] *India is characterized by ineffective IP rights laws* and enforcement mechanisms. A complaint among multinational drug companies is that Indian generics drug makers manufacture counterfeits of patented drugs and sell them for a long time. Due to the Indian *court system's slow* and often ineffective response, multinational drug companies' legal attempts to stop the counterfeiters often take many years.[48]

Values, Culture, and Skills

Entrepreneurial Culture

Societal norms that "permit variability in the choice of paths of life" are likely to promote entrepreneurial behavior.[49] A society's religions *strongly* dictate such a possibility. According to the 2001 census, Hinduism accounted for 80.5% of the Indian population. Islam is the second largest religion, practiced by 13.4% of the population. Hinduism and Islam have many similarities from the standpoint of entrepreneurship. Both promote fatalism and orientation toward the present or the past than the future.

The distinguishing mark of Hinduism, the most popular religion in India, is that it is centered around dharma (duty) and karma (a Sanskrit word that means "actions" or "deeds"). Furthermore, each individual's dharma and moral codes are specific to his/her caste of birth, which often lead to conflicting, confusing, misleading, and often contradictory social and ethical values.[50] More importantly, many beliefs and values run counter to capitalism and entrepreneurship.[51]

Accepting one's destiny rather than trying to control life can be viewed as a central core of traditional cultural values in India. *Reincarnation is an essential tenet of Hinduism, which maintains that if nothing wrong is done in this life, there would a prospect for a better life next time.*[52]

A distinguishing feature of Hinduism is its social structure based on the caste system, which has acted as a major barrier to entrepreneurship.[53] The studies of many researchers over the past few decades have indicated that various obligations associated with the Indian caste system make it more compelling and convenient to follow the family occupation instead of launching a new venture. The caste system has thus hindered class mobility. Unsurprisingly, the Vaishya (the caste of merchants) and non-Hindu communities (e.g., Jains and Parsis) historically dominated Indian businesses community.

Entrepreneurship thrives in a society that places a high value on work and innovation. It is argued that work is not valued in itself in India. Observers also suggest that people in the country work primarily because of emotional attachment with the workplace *or* as a favor to the supervisor or to the employer.

Indian culture also places relatively less value on innovation and gradual improvements. For example, a belief among many people in India is that for the inner soul and mind, being passive and satisfied with the status quo is healthier than trying to improve the situation.[54] Moreover, Hinduism considers work as the performance of duty instead of an ambition to innovate or improve.[55]

Women entrepreneurs in India face additional obstacles. For instance, young female entrepreneurs face higher obstacles compared to their male counterparts in accessing financial resources from their families. While parents of affluent families are comfortable providing capital to their sons to start business ventures. Young women, however, reported that their parents would prefer to fund their wedding than their business ventures.[56]

According to a study of Grant Thornton and Assocham, 9% of the founders of Indian startups are women.[57] Women are estimated to run 14% of Indian businesses.[58] Access to finance has been a key challenge for women entrepreneurs. 79% of women-run enterprises are self-financed and only 4.4% had borrowed money from a formal financial institution or received financial assistance from the government.[59]

India ranked 52nd out of 57 nations on the 2018 Mastercard Index for Women Entrepreneurs (MIWE). The report considered factors such as female entrepreneurs' ability to take advantage of the opportunities related to various supporting conditions.[60] Only five countries—Iran, Saudi Arabia, Algeria, Egypt, and Bangladesh—performed worse than India.

Some communities in the country think that a respectable girl should not expose herself to outside influences. In traditional sectors, it is a taboo and probably hard to imagine for young women to work during nights. Traditionally, *women* were not allowed to work after sunset.

It is also argued that Hinduism has contributed to the promotion of corruption and hindered the country's anti-corruption efforts. First, it is suggested that Hinduism has a forgiving tendency and Hindus are too lenient toward offenders. Second, fatalistic orientation of Hindus is associated with the belief that the status quo cannot be changed, which hinders fight against corruptions.

Some argue that India has a negative attitude toward entrepreneurship. Not long ago, an entrepreneur was viewed as someone that was unemployed and unemployable. Such a social stigma about an entrepreneur led to a preference for jobs in multinationals or the government sector. An observation is that the stigma of being an entrepreneur is gradually disappearing.[61]

Stigma, however, is especially salient in entrepreneurial failure. An executive of Google India noted,

> And don't even think about what will happen if you fail as an entrepreneur. Socially, you will have lost your eligibility for marriage until you get a job. Financially, you'll be saddled with loads of debt, and politically, good luck on somebody acknowledging your entrepreneurial endeavor as real work experience. With all these challenges, one wonders why anyone bothers trying to become an entrepreneur in India?

Entrepreneurial Capabilities

Human development in the country has been slow. According to the UNDP's Human Development Report 2013 (http://hdr.undp.org/hdr4press/press/report/index.html), among the 25 and older population, only 26.6% females and 50.4% males had at least secondary education. India's rank was 136th in the human development index. Labor force participation rate was only 29% for females compared to 80.7% for males.

Although English is an official language in India, only a small proportion of graduates meet the standard required to interact with foreigners. This goes contrary to the widely held belief that India's huge English-speaking population will give it an edge over China and other rising nations in doing business with Western corporations.[62] Customers' complaints regarding difficulties to understand the operators forced some companies to relocate call centers from India to the Philippines.[63]

While India has some professionally run global companies such as Wipro, Infosys, and TCS, there are exceptions rather than the norm. Overall, the country's management style is highly traditional. Characteristics such as willingness to follow logical processes and orientation to details are virtually absent in the Indian work culture.[64] In the same vein, whereas Western countries have the time-is-money culture, Indians have more flexible approach to deadlines.[65] Experts argue that the country needs to go far before a culture of modern and professional management emerges. Similarly, most businesses in the country perform poorly in terms of product quality, reliability, and on-time delivery. Addressing this challenge may be no small feat.

That said, some Indian firms have made significant progress in adopting the culture of modern management. This is especially noticeable in the offshoring sector. In an attempt to address their clients' fear that customer data will be stolen and even sold to criminals, firms have enhanced security mechanisms. For instance, call center employees have to undergo security checks, although such checks are considered to be "undignified".[66] Firms have established biometric authentication controls for workers and banned cell phones, pens, paper, and Internet/e-mail access for employees. Similarly, computer terminals at most offshoring firms lack hard drives, e-mail, CD-ROM drives, or other ways to store, copy, or forward data. In general, Indian outsourcing firms extensively monitor and analyze employee logs.[67]

The lack of entrepreneurial education and training has been a matter of concern for the development of a startup ecosystem in India. About a third of the Indian population was estimated to be illiterate in 2016.[68] An upshot of this is that Indian startups lack skills and experience to build scales and do sales, marketing, and product management.[69] In a survey by Accenture among Indian enterprises, 53% of the respondents cited the lack of talent to be a key challenge in the deployment modern technologies such as big data and cloud computing. Mckinsey estimated that India will need 200,000 data scientists in the near future.[70] India's *No. 2 e-commerce* site, Snapdeal.com said that the company has not been able to find the coders and other big data manpower it needs. The company has recognized the need for worldwide recruitment for experienced programmers dealing with big data, cloud computing and the software for interacting with customers and suppliers. In 2015, it hired a cloud specialist from a Silicon Valley startup. The company was expecting to hire 12 more. Snapdeal was also reported to be considering to establish a software development center in the U.S. and buying firms there in order to capture the needed manpower.[71]

Due to the lack of entrepreneurial education in India, the country's successful companies invest heavily in employees through extensive training and development in firm-specific skills. One study found that firms in the country's IT industry provide 60 days of formal training to newly hired employees and they are paid during the period. Some firms go even further. For instance, Tata Consultancy Services is reported to have a seven-month training program for science graduates in order to convert them into business consultants, and every employee in the company gets 14 days of formal training annually.[72] Infosys has its own internal college to educate new employees, which trained 80,000 employees in "design thinking" as of mid-2016. The goal is to make sure that its employees can advise on the design of IT systems rather than just taking instructions.[73]

Entrepreneurship Support Mechanisms

New organizational mechanisms such as incubators have helped startups *to* grow and bring innovative products and services into the market. As early as in 2010, it was reported that India had around 40 incubators, which mentored between 4 and 20 startups each.[74] One such incubator, Villgro (www.villgro.org/) reported that as of mid-2016, it mentored 119 startups. It also invested US$2.2 million seed money in these startups and *helped them to raise investments* of more than US$19 million.

According to National Association of Software and Services Companies (NASSCOM) and Zinnov Consulting, India, in 2017 had the third highest number of startup incubators and accelerators in the world after China and the U.S. By that year, India has 140 incubators and accelerators. India surpassed Israel, which had 130 incubators and accelerators. China and the U.S. had over 2,400 and 1,500 incubators and accelerators, respectively.[75]

However, a high degree of urban bias has been found in the concentration of incubators and accelerators. In 2017, Bangalore, Mumbai, and Delhi accounted for 40% of all incubators and accelerators.[76]

Access to Finance, Market, R&D, and Technology

Market Conditions

As noted earlier, Indian economy has many characteristics of oligarchic capitalism, which have hindered SMEs' market access. Research has indicated that the 1991 reforms have had little or no effect in promoting SMEs and their development. A small number of well-connected industrialists have dominated the Indian economy and protected themselves from outside competition.[77]

It is also the case that various regulations hinder the access to the domestic market in India. For instance, there are taxes for bringing goods into a state, for taking them out of a state as well as for moving them within a state.[78]

Perhaps the greatest advantage offered by India's big domestic market is that it has helped some Indian entrepreneurial firms to compete successfully in other developing markets. Indian companies are in a position to reconfigure their resources and adapt the business models used in the domestic market to successfully operate in other developing economies.[79] It is argued that Indian firms' capability to deliver value for money in the domestic market has been an important source of competitive advantage to operate in Africa and other developing countries. Nonetheless there a number of market access barriers faced by SMEs and startups.

PHYSICAL INFRASTRUCTURES

A lack of well-developed physical infrastructures has been a barrier to market access. Most roads are narrow. In 2007, there were only 1,500 trucks and one-third of produces were reported to be rotted before reaching the end customers.[80] The global financial crisis further hindered India's infrastructure development. In the late 2008, reports indicated that about half of India's planned highway-improvement projects, which were valued at over US$6 billion, could be delayed by two years.

On the plus side, among other measures, a key component of the "Start-up India" program is US$ 32 billion infrastructure spending in fiscal year 2016–2017 to build 10,000 km of national highways and upgrade additional 50,000 km. The goal is to help SMEs' access to the huge India market.

Access to Finance

Access to finance has been a major barrier facing many potential entrepreneurs in India. An executive of *Google India* notes,

> A bank loan or angel investment is not impossible to get but extremely unlikely. Getting funding is even harder if, like most aspiring entrepreneurs, you are not from a top-tier university and don't have a family with deep-pockets. There are countless 'micro-entrepreneurs' in Indian society who finance their own small businesses as a means to survival but don't have access to the capital necessary to grow them.[81]

Below we describe the situation regarding the common forms of entrepreneurial financing.

BANK LOANS

Indian banks traditionally served rich people. Many Indians that are poor and less educated feel too intimidated to go formal banks. Major banks in the country haven't yet focused on poor and rural populations, which are seen as unprofitable segments.[82]

Observers have noted that potential entrepreneurs in India, who have graduated from a less well-known university or those who belong to a poor family face difficulties in getting funding.[83] The state banks have done little to promote productive entrepreneurship in India. A complaint often heard is that business merits play a little role in loan disbursements. Lending is disproportionately oriented toward powerful economic and political interests such as influential family-owned groups.

According to a study conducted by research firm KPMG and Snapdeal, about 41% of SMEs in India lacked access to bank loans or other financial products offered by banks and other formal financial institutions. The study found that a financing gap of over US$43.5 billion existed in the Indian entrepreneurial landscape.[84]

THE CAPITAL MARKET

According to Ernst & Young's *Global IPO Trends 2012* report, there were 40 IPO deals in the country in 2011, which raised US$1.2 billion and accounted for 3.3% of the global IPO. In 2017, 36 companies went for IPO, which raised US$10.3 billion.[85] Market capitalization of listed Indian companies was US$2.3 trillion in 2017, which is expected to reach US$6.1 trillion by 2027.[86]

In 2012, the BSE and the National Stock Exchange (NSE) launched SME platforms, which has increased SMEs' access to capital market. In the first two months of 2016, 21 SMEs filed documents with BSE and NSE to raise a total of US$27 million crore through IPOs.

In recent years, poor returns have made IPO relatively unattractive for many Indian companies. One study indicated that stocks of 70% of companies that launched IPOs in 2010 were trading below their price in June 2011.[87]

Institutional investors such as pension funds and life insurance companies which pool huge large sums of money and invest those in securities, property and other assets account for about one-eighth of Indian stock market profits compared to over half in Western economies. State-backed firms are estimated to account 40% of stock market profits in the country.[88]

VC INVESTMENTS

Indian VC industry is at a nascent stage of development. In 2017, VC investment in India amounted US$1.3 billion, which was 18.7% lower than in 2016.[89] A large proportion of VC funding in recent years has been in companies operating in online marketplaces.[90]

There are a number of difficulties that stand in the way of VC financing in India.[91] Indian bureaucracy and regulations act as barriers to VC investments. Prior researchers have emphasized the importance of improving the environments related to tax, currency exchange, and other policies in order to attract VC firms.

Observers have noted that Indian entrepreneurs often fail to understand the reality that not all VC-funded companies are likely to achieve an IPO. While there is a greater likelihood of a VC-funded company exiting through an M&A than an IPO in the U.S., Indian entrepreneurs are less prepared for the M&A option.[92]

THE MICROFINANCE INDUSTRY

According to Sa-Dhan, an association of microfinance institutions (MFIs), the Indian microfinance industry was US$9 billion in the FY 2015–2016, which is expected to reach to US$20 billion by 2019. In the FY 2015–2016, the rural area accounted for 28% of the total loans disbursed by MFIs.

At the same time, some negative experiences related to microcredit have been reported. As of early 2010, over 15 million borrowers in India owed microfinance debts of US$2.3 billion.[93] The average Indian household's debt to microfinance banks increased fivefold during 2005–2010. It was also reported that some borrowers used loans intended for business purposes to buy luxury items such as TV and refrigerator.

In Chapter 3, we discussed abusive behaviors of microlenders and their engagement in activities that violated borrowers' human rights. In 2010, the government of the Andhra Pradesh state accused that the microfinance industry's aggressive collection tactics forced many borrowers to commit suicide. The government issued new rules for the functioning of the microfinance industry and almost all issued loans in the state were written off. This led to a strong decline of the microfinance industry. In recent years, the industry is reported to be gradually reviving. It is estimated that the microfinance industry's outstanding loans in the early 2013 were US$2 billion to 3 billion, which was significantly lower than the peak value of around US$5 billion a few years before.[94]

REMITTANCES INFLOW

India receives more remittances than any other country. As noted in Chapter 3, remittance inflow in India exceeded US$65 billion in

2017. Remittances have led to the establishment of new businesses and social service organizations such as nursing homes and educational institutions.

DOMESTIC SAVINGS AND INFORMAL INVESTMENTS

Finally, domestic savings have also been an important source of investment. India's saving rate as proportions of disposable income was 37.5% in 2017. As is the case of China and other Asian economies, the high saving rates in India can be attributed to income insecurity associated with mostly informal jobs. The high saving rates thus may not automatically translate to a higher investment rates.

As mentioned, the formal financial market remains largely inaccessible to startups and SMEs. According to McKinsey, 43% of SMEs in India borrow from informal sources. They do so partly because of the lack of collateral and working-capital lines.[95]

CROWDFUNDING

While crowdfunding is in infancy in India, it is becoming an increasingly important source of external finance for some Indian startups. One estimate suggested that there were 30 crowdfunding platforms (CFPs) in India as of 2016. As of June 2016, the Indian seed capital and angel investment platform, LetsVenture helped 70 companies raise US$27 million. The average deal size was about US$370,000 and the highest amount raised was US$1.33 million.[96]

SUPPLY CHAIN FINANCING

In recent years, large players in the e-commerce sector are taking initiatives to improve the access of this form of financing to SMEs. In 2015, India's largest ecommerce website, Snapdeal announced plans to disburse loans of around US$150 million to SMEs by March 2016 under its seller-financing platform, Capital Assist. It was reported that the firm has teamed up with banks and non-banking finance companies for this purpose.[97] Flipkart has similar lending schemes. In early 2016, Amazon India announced its plans to offer loans to key vendors selling on its portal. The sellers can apply for short-term working capital loans in order to buy more inventory and increase sales on Amazon.in.[98]

R&D and Technology-Related Factors

India's ICT adoption and usage rates have been relatively lower compared to most countries. According to a study released by Google India in

254 Entrepreneurship in India

mid-2011, only two million out of the country's 35 million SMEs were online.[99]

In the World Economic Forum's 2016 Global Information Technology Report, India's overall rank was 91.[100] While India ranked 8th in affordability of ICTs, only 15% of Indian households had Internet access and mobile broadband subscriptions per 100 people was just 5.5.

Nonetheless, there have been some highly visible instances of ICT usage in promoting entrepreneurial activities. As a high-profile example, in October 2010, Intel announced an agreement with an alliance of 70 companies including BSE and CtrlS to develop hardware and software for an open and interoperable cloud. The Open Data Center Alliance (ODCA) works to address security, energy efficiency, and interoperability. The BSE expects that the new trading platforms supported by mobile telephony and clouds would broaden participation by allowing real-time and seamless access to data across phones, laptops, and other devices. This approach would also deepen and *widen asset classes traded*. The new platforms will increase participation of younger Indians in *pension funds*, insurance and mutual funds and others. Especially the popularity of mobile-based cloud applications is promising. Only 80 million Indians were online in early 2011, but more than 670 million used cellphones.

India's overall innovation and R&D profile is weak. According to Euromonitor International, India's gross domestic expenditure on R&D as a proportion of GDP in 2017 was 0.8% compared to 4.2% in South Korea, 4.1% in Israel, and 2% in China. Little of the business in India consists of core R&D needed for cutting-edge products. India lags behind industrialized countries and its neighbor China in terms of various indicators related to R&D and innovations. Due to India's poor R&D and innovation performance, some liken entrepreneurial activities in the Indian IT and offshoring industry to a "hollow ring." An Economist article notes, "India makes drugs, but copies almost all of the compounds; it writes software, but rarely owns the result. ... [it has] flourished, but mostly on the back of other countries' technology."[101]

Concluding Comments

The 1991 economic reform facilitated and stimulated entrepreneurship in India. *The impact on the broad* economy is, however, barely noticeable. While billionaires, oligarchs, and state-owned companies are benefiting from privileges, the playing field is not level for SMEs and new venture startups, which face a host of barriers. Inappropriate regulatory elements and legal bottlenecks have severely hampered productive entrepreneurial activities. Severe and widespread poverty persists in the country while there is great and rising affluence among people working in the outsourcing sector. In sum, we cannot really take the existence of a few entrepreneurial firms in the Indian IT sector the as proof positive that India provides a conducive environment for entrepreneurship. In fact, it is possible to draw the opposite conclusion on the basis of the fact that very little entrepreneurial impact is felt by the mass of the population. Moreover, many Indian entrepreneurs still struggle with a culture that looks down on capitalism and is indifferent to hard work, improvement, and innovations.

To some extent, the structural inertia of the Indian economy has acted as a barrier to foster modern entrepreneurship. India's heavy reliance on agriculture, for instance, has resulted in constraints in resources for entrepreneurial development. For instance, industry and agriculture compete in the allocation of water between states, which has created inter-state rivalries and tensions.

End of Chapter Questions

1 What is the current state of the Indian microfinance industry? What are some of the negative effects of this industry?
2 Comment on the ADB observation that the Indian economy has many characteristics of oligarchic capitalism.
3 Why do some observers argue that Israel model of government funding for start (note that 80% of the first US$500,000 for every idea identified is funded by the government in Israel) would be ineffective in India?
4 How would you rate India's R&D and innovations profile?
5 Compare China and India in terms of various indicators related to entrepreneurship. Which country is better prepared to embrace the global movement toward entrepreneurship? Why?
6 Compare and contrast Hinduism and Islam (see Chapter 6) from the standpoint of entrepreneurship development.

End of the Chapter Case: Flipkart's Search of e-Commerce Opportunities in Rural India

Flipkart is an Indian online shopping destination founded in 2007[102] by two Amazon employees who quit their jobs to *pursue their entrepreneurial ambitions*. It was opened as an online bookstore.

As of 2017, Flipkart was India's largest e-commerce portal.[103] According to Forrester Research's report "Online Retail Forecast (2017–2022) Asia Pacific," Flipkart's gross merchandise value (GMV) market share was 31.9% in 2017 compared to Amazon's 31.1%.[104]

Table 9.1 Flipkart's Evolutions: A Timeline.

Time	Events	Valuation of the company
2007	The company was started with US$6,000 initial capital.	
2009	**The VC firm** Accel India provided US$1 million. Tiger Global Management provided US$10 million.	About US$50 million.
2012	It received US$150 million funding led by South Africa's Naspers. It raised US$150 million from Accel, IDG, IndoUS and Tiger Global.[105]	US$1 billion.
2013	Raised US$200 million from existing investors and US$160 million more from Morgan Stanley, Sofina, Vulcan Capital, and Dragoneer.	
2014	Acquire Myntra Raised US$210 million from DST Global. US$1 billion funding round from GIC Singapore and existing backers. raised a US$700 million fund from hedge funds like Greenoaks, Steadview Capital, sovereign wealth fund Qatar Investment Authority, mutual fund T Rowe Price.	More than US$11 billion.
2015	Raised US$700 million from existing investors.	US$15.5 billion.
2016	2016: loss amounted to US$338.2 million.[106] *The company dramatically lost its value*	US$5.6 billion.
2017	Received US$1.4 billion VC investment from Tencent Holdings, Microsoft and eBay.[107] Japan's SoftBank Group Corp's Vision Fund bought roughly a fifth of the firm for US$2.5 billion.[108]	About US$7.9 billion in November[109]

Lack of Sustainable e-Commerce Business Models

Like other major Indian e-commerce companies, Flipkart has received substantial VC investments. These firms arguably use investors' cash to subsidize and fund discounts in order to attract more customers.[110] In one way, Flipkart and other e-commerce players operating in India have implemented unsustainable business models and practices. For instance, strong sales growth has been recorded among India's large e-commerce firms. Quoting the consultancy firm RedSeer, an Economist article published in April 2017 suggested that in 2015, about 20%–30% of all e-commerce sales went to middlemen at heavily discounted prices. The middlemen then sold the items almost at full prices. It is argued that the

Indian e-commerce industry is struggling to break the "unhealthy cycle" that has perpetuated.[111]

An upshot is that major Indian e-commerce websites are making losses. For instance, in the fiscal year (FY) 2016, Flipkart's loss amounted to US$338.2 million.[112] In that FY, combined net losses of India's three biggest e-commerce firms, Flipkart, Snapdeal, and Amazon in India amounted US$1.4 billion.[113]

Focusing on Rural Areas

Amazon strengthened its position as metropolitan Indian consumers' preferred e-retailer.[114] Forrester Research's survey of 2,000 respondents in nine cities in 2017 found that 80% had shopped on Amazon and only 65% had shopped on Flipkart.[115]

In mid-2017, about one-third of total visits Flipkart's websites came from tier-II and -III. About 60% of mobile internet purchases were from these cities. Moreover, 50% of new customers acquired were through mobile Internet.[116] As of 2017, about 65% of new shoppers of Flipkart were estimated to be from nonmetro areas.[117]

There is, however, a challenge in developing e-commerce market in India's rural areas. According to Deloitte India's report released in January 2018, rural India had only 17% Internet penetration.[118]

Deployment of Advanced Technologies

Flipkart.com uses big data and the cloud to provide e-commerce offerings to benefit from the country's rapidly expanding e-commerce market.[119] For instance, as of 2015, Flipkart was reported to analyze 25 million rows of inventory data every day in order to make data-driven decision.[120] Its cloud infrastructure is built on Dell PowerEdge servers.

Flipkart's machine learning algorithms analyze customers' online activities such as sites visited, information searched, products viewed, and purchased to understand their demographic profiles, behavior, location and product attributes they look for. An analysis of online activities with machine learning algorithms can also help predict customers' trust level with reviews and ratings, delivery expectations and their similarities and differences with other customers. Consequently, it is possible to make personalized product recommendations.[121]

It wants to use drones to deliver goods to rural areas. Such technologies facilitate faster and cheaper delivery of products bought online. For instance, the Chinese e-commerce company, JD.com's delivery costs were reduced by 80% with the deployment of drones and delivery speed improved significantly.[122] However, as of 2018, civilian drones were not allowed in India.[123]

Case Summary

Flipkart hold a strong competitive position in India's huge and rapidly growing e-commerce market. The company, however, is losing its position vis-à-vis its major competitor. Success in maintaining its leadership position hinges on having a robust business model to serve customers and low tier cities and rural areas.

Notes

1 Huang, Y. 2008. "The next Asian miracle," *Foreign Policy* (167), pp. 32–40.
2 World Bank. 2008a. Doing business 2008: India, Bhutan, and Sri Lanka Lead South Asia's jump in reform.
3 DoingBusiness. 2017. "Doing business 2018 reforming to create jobs," October 31, www.doingbusiness.org/reports/global-reports/doing-business-2018.
4 hehindu.com. 2016. "Top 10 takeaways from Modi's speech at Start-up India launch," www.thehindu.com/business/top-10-takeaways-from-modis-speech-at-startup-india-launch/article8114318.ece.
5 Global Intellectual Property Center. 2016. "U.S. Chamber International IP Index U.S. Chamber of Commerce," Washington, DC, www.theglobalip center.com/gipcindex/.
6 Majumdar, S.K. 2004. "The hidden hand and the license raj to an evaluation of the relationship between age and the growth of firms in India," *Journal of Business Venturing*, 19, pp. 107–125.
7 Kshetri, N. 2011. "The Indian Environment for Entrepreneurship and Small Business Development," *Studia Negotia*, 56(LVI), 4, pp. 35–52.
8 economictimes.indiatimes.com. 2015. "Etailers like Snapdeal seek RBI approval to offer loans to SMEs," 16 October 2015, http://economictimes.indiatimes.com/news/economy/policy/etailers-like-snapdeal-seek-rbi-approval-to-offer-loans-to-smes/articleshow/49395754.cms.
9 Economist. 2007. "Imitate or die; Technology in China and India," 385(8554), p. 9.
10 Kumar, N., Mohapatra, P. K., Chandrasekhar, S. 2009. Challenges for Indian Multinationals--The Global Future, HBS Press Chapter, October 26, http://harvardbusinessonline.hbsp.harvard.edu/b02/en/common/item_detail.jhtml;jsessionid=D5WRHOBIDCOVMAKRGWDR5VQBKE0YI ISW?id=6745BC&_requestid=50809.
11 UNDP. 2008. Human Development Report 2007/2008: Fighting climate change: Human solidarity in a divided world, United Nations Development Program (UNDP). Retrieved 15 March 2010, http://hdr.undp.org/en/media/HDR_20072008_EN_Complete.pdf.
12 Foulis, Patrick. 2011. Adventures in capitalism: Indian businesses are rewriting the rules of capitalism in a distinctive and unexpected way, 22 October 2011, www.economist.com/node/21532448.
13 economictimes.indiatimes.com. 2016b. "Startup: Over 400 entrepreneurs queue up for tax benefits," http://economictimes.indiatimes.com/small-biz/startups/startup-over-400-entrepreneurs-queue-up-for-tax-benefits/articleshow/52781886.cms.
14 Fortune.com. 2016. "India's Modi launches $1.5 billion fund for startups," 16 January, http://fortune.com/2016/01/16/modi-india-startup-fund/.

15 economictimes.indiatimes.com. 2016b. "Startup: Over 400 entrepreneurs queue up for tax benefits," http://economictimes.indiatimes.com/small-biz/startups/startup-over-400-entrepreneurs-queue-up-for-tax-benefits/articleshow/52781886.cms.

16 DeCarlo, S. 2009. The World's Biggest Companies. www.forbes.com/lists/2009/18/global-09_The-Global-2000_Rank.html (April 8, 2009).

17 Mostowyk, L. 2018. "US Named Top Global Tech Innovation Leader, China in second spot: KPMG report," https://home.kpmg.com/xx/en/home/media/press-releases/2018/03/us-named-top-global-tech-innovation-leader.html.

18 Startup Blink. 2017. "Countries Global Ranking of Startup Ecosystem (10/2017)," at www.startupblink.com/?leaderboards&countries.

19 Wadhwa, V. 2010a Addressing the Dearth of Female Entrepreneurs. BusinessWeek Online 12.

20 Salovaara, I., & Wade, J. 2018, "How to Support Women Social Entrepreneurs in India," https://ssir.org/articles/entry/how_to_support_women_social_entrepreneurs_in_india.

21 economist.com. On the turn, 19 January 2013, www.economist.com/news/special-report/21569571-india-no-longer-automatic-choice-it-services-and-back-office-work-turn.

22 worldbank.org. 2009. Data Factoids: China and India. http://web.worldbank.org/WBSITE/EXTERNAL/EXTDEC/EXTRESEARCH/EXTCHIINDGLOECO/0,,contentMDK:21189627~menuPK:3349623~pagePK:64168445~piPK:64168309~theSitePK:28.

23 Economist. 2009. Reforming through the tough times, September 12, p. 71.

24 The Hindu Business Line 2011. India's low-cost BPO tag helps draw global investors: E&Y, June 6, www.thehindubusinessline.com/industry-and-economy/info-tech/article2082418.ece?homepage=true.

25 washingtonpost.com. US immigration bill's new visa rules could slow Indian outsourcing juggernaut, April 23. www.washingtonpost.com/business/us-immigration-bills-new-visa-rules-could-slow-indian-outsourcing-juggernaut/2013/04/23/d5a76360-abf7-11e2-9493-2ff3bf26c4b4_story.html.

26 NASSCOM. 2009. Nasscom Strategic Review 2009: Executive Summary. November 25, at www.nasscom.org/upload/60452/Executive_summary.pdf.

27 Chandrasekaran, N. 2017, IT industry to have 7 million direct and 10 million indirect jobs by 2025, May 29, https://blogs.economictimes.indiatimes.com/et-commentary/it-industry-to-have-7-million-direct-jobs-and-10-million-indirect-jobs-by-2025-n-chandrasekaran/.

28 Wadhwa, V. 2009. Lessons from a New Industry Cluster in India. BusinessWeek Online 7-7.

29 Lewis, G. 2007. "Who in the world is entrepreneurial?" FSB: Fortune Small Business 17(5), p. 14.

30 Bajada, C., & Schneider, F. 2005. "The shadow economies of the Asia-Pacific," Pacific Economic Review, 10(3), pp. 379–401.

31 Kumar, G.R. 2017. "An analysis on the role of India's informal economy," www.thehansindia.com/posts/index/Young-Hans/2017-07-14/An-analysis-on-the-role-of-Indias-informal-economy/312388.

32 UNDP. 2008. Human Development Report 2007/2008: Fighting climate change: Human solidarity in a divided world, United Nations Development Program (UNDP). Retrieved March 15, 2010, http://hdr.undp.org/en/media/HDR_20072008_EN_Complete.pdf.

33 Malhotra, H. B. 2009. Oligarchic Capitalism May Take Hold in India. www.theepochtimes.com/n2/content/view/22829/ (Accessed September 22, 2009).

34 Foulis, P. 2011. Adventures in capitalism: Indian businesses are rewriting the rules of capitalism in a distinctive and unexpected way, October 22, www.economist.com/node/21532448.

35 Ibid.

36 Ibid.

37 Malhotra, H. B. 2009. Oligarchic Capitalism May Take Hold in India. Retrieved September 22, 2009, at www.theepochtimes.com/n2/content/view/22829/.

38 EMF (Emerging Markets Forum). 2009. India 2039: An affluent society in one generation. www.emergingmarketsforum.org/papers/pdf/2009-EMF-India-Report_Overview.pdf.

39 Petras, J. 2008. Global ruling class: Billionaires and how they "make it." *Journal of Contemporary Asia* 38(2), 319–329.

40 Deloitte. 2006. *China and India: The Reality Beyond the Hype.* Deloitte Development LLC.

41 Shah, H. J. 2010. "Valuate the India opportunity through incubators, demographics and PEG," 9 March, http://blogs.wsj.com/india-chief-mentor/2010/03/09/valuate-the-india-opportunity-through-incubators-demographics-and-peg/.

42 Economist. 2008. "Business: Unshackling the chain stores," 387(8582), p. 80.

43 economywatch.com, 2014, "India's restrictive labor laws challenge investors," www.economywatch.com/features/Indias-Restrictive-Labor-Laws-Challenge-Investors.11-12-14.html.

44 Deloitte. 2006.

45 Hanstad, T. 2013. "The case for land reform in India," www.foreignaffairs.com/articles/india/2013-02-19/untitled?cid=soc-twitter-in-snapshots-untitled-022013.

46 Ibid.

47 Global Intellectual Property Center. 2016. "U.S. Chamber International IP index U.S. Chamber of commerce," Washington, DC, www.theglobalipcenter.com/gipcindex/.

48 Bhattacharya, S., 2015, "India plans to streamline intellectual property rights process," www.wsj.com/articles/india-plans-to-streamline-intellectual-property-rights-process-1449834245.

49 Hoselitz, B.F. 1960. *Sociological Aspects of Economic Growth.* The Free Press, New York.

50 Elliot, J. 1998. "Held back by Hindu gods?" *New Statesman*, 127(414), p. 28.

51 Dana, L.P. 2000. "Creating entrepreneurs in India," *Journal of Small Business Management* 38(1), pp. 86–91.

52 Elliot, 1998.

53 Dana, 2000.

54 Ibid.

55 Elliot, 1998.

56 Salovaara & Wade. 2018.

57 Dasgupta, B. 2018. "Co-working spaces go the extra mile to guide woman entrepreneurs," https://economictimes.indiatimes.com/jobs/co-working-spaces-go-the-extra-mile-to-guide-woman-entrepreneurs/articleshow/63275583.cms.

58 Saha, D. 2016. "Women run 14% of Indian businesses, most self-financed", https://thewire.in/gender/women-run-14-of-indian-businesses-most-self-financed.

59 Ibid.
60 Mastercard. 2018. "Women in charge: Mastercard Index reveals how countries are progressing to empower women entrepreneurs," https://newsroom.mastercard.com/press-releases/women-in-charge-mastercard-index-reveals-how-countries-are-progressing-to-empower-women-entrepreneurs/.
61 Ganesh, K., 2016. "A serial entrepreneur on why starting up is tough but every bit worth it," Jun 26, http://economictimes.indiatimes.com/smallbiz/startups/a-serial-entrepreneur-on-why-starting-up-is-tough-but-every-bit-worth-it/articleshow/52919870.cms.
62 Mehta, S. N. 2005. "India on the march," *Fortune* 152(2), pp. 191–193.
63 Fairell, D., Kaka, N., & Stürze, S. 2005. Ensuring India's offshoring future.
64 Piramal, G. 2004. "In depth offshoring: In my opinion," *European Business Forum* 19, pp. 40–41.
65 Slater, J. 2003. "India's nifty number-crunchers," *Far Eastern Economic Review*, 2 October, p. 7.
66 Economist. 2005b. "Business: busy signals; Indian call centres," 10 September, 376(8443), p. 66.
67 Fest, G. 2005. "Offshoring: Feds take fresh look at India BPOs; Major theft has raised more than a few eyebrows," *Bank Technology News*, 18(9), p. 1.
68 World Economic Forum. 2016. "The Global Information Technology Report 2016: Innovating in the digital economy."
69 Rai, S. 2014. "India emerges as a hotbed of software product entrepreneurship," www.techrepublic.com/article/matchmaking-at-intech50-indian-software-product-startups-pitch-to-50-cios/.
70 fractalanalytics.com. 201. "Big data talent shortage: How to bridge the gap?" 2 June, www.fractalanalytics.com/news/big-data-talent-shortage-how-bridge-gap.
71 Thoppil, D.A. 2015. "India's Snapdeal says the country doesn't have the programmers it needs," 28 May, http://blogs.wsj.com/indiarealtime/2015/05/28/snapdeal-says-india-doesnt-have-the-programmers-it-needs/.
72 Cappelli, P., Singh, H., Singh, J. & Useem, M. 2010. "The India way: lessons for the U.S," *Academy of Management Perspectives*, 24(2), pp. 6–24.
73 Mundy, S. 2016. "Indian IT services groups adjust to cloud and big data: Wipro, Infosys and Tata under pressure to adapt or be left behind," https://next.ft.com/content/9ad3b946-3d26-11e6-8716-a4a71e8140b0.
74 Chaudhary, D. 2010. "Start-ups in fund trouble, even as incubators hike early-stage funding," www.livemint.com/2010/01/25215034/Startups-in-fund-trouble-eve.html.
75 Sharma, D. 2017. "India now ranks third globally in number of incubators, accelerators: Report," www.vccircle.com/india-now-ranks-third-globally-in-number-of-incubators-accelerators-report/.
76 Ibid.
77 Weitzman, H., & Fontanella-Khan, J. 2011. "US and India: the squeeze on small business," 31 May, www.ft.com/cms/s/0/33de9812-8b8f-11e0-8c09-00144feab49a.html#axzz1PgAoaEbA.
78 Economist. 2008d. "Business: Unshackling the chain stores," 387(8582), p. 80.
79 Harvard Business Review. 2009. "The new frontiers," 87(7), pp. 130–137.
80 Hamm, S., & Lakshman, N. 2007. "Widening aisles for Indian shoppers," *Business Week*, 30 April 2007, pp. 44.
81 Gandhi, G. 2010. "Indian entrepreneurs need a hug: Google's Gandhi," 16 February, http://blogs.wsj.com/india-chief-mentor/2010/02/16/indian-entrepreneurs-need-a-hug-google%E2%80%99s-gandhi/.

82 Bergen, M. 2014. "Will bank accounts catch on in India?" 11 February, www.newyorker.com/business/currency/will-bank-accounts-catch-on-in-india.

83 Gandhi, 2010.

84 economictimes.indiatimes.com. 2015. "Etailers like Snapdeal seek RBI approval to offer loans to SMEs," http://economictimes.indiatimes.com/news/economy/policy/etailers-like-snapdeal-seek-rbi-approval-to-offer-loans-to-smes/articleshow/49395754.cms.

85 asia.nikkei.com. 2018. "Indian IPO fervor cools as volatility pinpoints fundamentals," March 28, https://asia.nikkei.com/Business/Markets/Equities/Indian-IPO-fervor-cools-as-volatility-pinpoints-fundamentals.

86 Wadhwa, P. 2018. "India's equity market-cap to hit $6.1 trillion by 2027: Morgan Stanley," 12 March, www.business-standard.com/article/markets/india-s-equity-market-cap-to-hit-6-1-trillion-by-2027-morgan-stanley-118031200437_1.html.

87 Kohli, D. 2011. "Some investors keeping away from IPOs in Indian market," June 20, 2011, www.channelnewsasia.com/stories/marketnews/view/1136181/1/.html.

88 economist.com. 2011. "Building India Inc: A weak state has given rise to a new kind of economy. Without reform, it will hit limits," October 22, 2011, www.economist.com/node/21533396.

89 Sengupta, S. 2018, "Five venture capital dealmakers to watch in 2018," www.livemint.com/Opinion/MecRmBTOLZNt3JO4Zn2XTL/Five-venture-capital-dealmakers-to-watch-in-2018.html.

90 Velayanikal, M. 2015, "What are the hottest sectors for venture capital in India this year?" www.techinasia.com/hottest-sectors-venture-capital-india-infographic.

91 Dossani, R., & Kenney, M. 2002. "Creating an environment for venture capital in India," *World Development*, 30(2), pp. 227–253.

92 Tagare, P. 2011. "India's entrepreneurs need to see beyond IPOs," 7 June, http://online.wsj.com/article/SB10001424052702304432304576370803985701380.html?mod=googlenews_wsj.

93 Kalesh, B. 2010. "SKS Microfinance gets venture capitalists as promoters for IPO," 10 March, www.livemint.com/2010/03/10205245/SKS-Microfinance-gets-venture.html.

94 economist.com. "Road to redemption," January 12, 2013. www.economist.com/news/finance-and-economics/21569447-industry-starting-revive-road-redemption.

95 Mukherjee, A. 2016. "A WhatsApp moment for Asia's banks," 3 July, www.bloomberg.com/gadfly/articles/2016-07-03/a-whatsapp-moment-for-banks-in-asia.

96 Babu, V. 2016. "Herd mentality: Crowdfunding platforms are proliferating. And very different models are being tried out by different players," www.businesstoday.in/magazine/corporate/crowdfunding-platforms-are-proliferating-with-models/story/232543.html.

97 economictimes.indiatimes.com. 2015. "Etailers like Snapdeal seek RBI approval to offer loans to SMEs," http://economictimes.indiatimes.com/news/economy/policy/etailers-like-snapdeal-seek-rbi-approval-to-offer-loans-to-smes/articleshow/49395754.cms.

98 Maheshwari, R. 2016. "Amazon plans to offer loans to Indian sellers," http://articles.economictimes.indiatimes.com/2016-02-10/news/70509905_1_amazon-india-collateral-free-loans-amazon-in.

99 Narasimhan, T.E. 2011. "57% of SMEs use internet as sales channel, finds survey," 21 June, www.business-standard.com/india/news/57smes-use-internet-as-sales-channel-finds-survey/439821/.

100 World Economic Forum. 2016. "The global information technology report 2016: Innovating in the digital economy."

101 Economist. 2007a. "Imitate or die; technology in China and India," 385(8554), p. 9.

102 Bansal, B., & Bansal, S. 2007. "Flipkart is an online shopping destination for electronics, books, music, and movies in India," www.crunchbase.com/organization/flipkart#section-overview.

103 Chakraborty, S. 2017. "The Flipkart story: A timeline of funding from 2007 to 2017," www.financialexpress.com/industry/technology/the-flipkart-story-a-timeline-of-funding-from-2007-to-2017/595740/.

104 Khatri, B. 2018. "Amazon India closes in on Flipkart's dominance in ecommerce market: Forrester report," https://inc42.com/buzz/amazon-india-closes-in-on-flipkarts-dominance-in-ecommerce-market-forrester-report/.

105 Fannin, R. 2017, "Flipkart's $2.5 Billion Deal from Softbank Signals New Era for Indian Startups," at www.forbes.com/sites/rebeccafannin/2017/08/13/flipkarts-2-5-billion-deal-from-softbank-signals-new-era-for-indian-startups/#25af7ba4ed71 (Accessed February 5, 2018).

106 Nikkei Asian Review. 2017a. "India Flipkart taps venture capitalist as CEO," https://asia.nikkei.com/Business/Companies/India-Flipkart-taps-venture-capitalist-as-CEO (Accessed February 5, 2018).

107 Pymnts.com. 2017. "India's Flipkart Raises $1.4B From Big Players," from www.pymnts.com/news/mobile-commerce/2017/indias-flipkart-raises-1-4-billion-from-three-major-players-funding-ebay-microsoft-tencent-ecommerce/ (Accessed February 5, 2018).

108 Gibson, G., 2018. "Amazon finishes higher despite Trump's new threat on shipping rates," at www.reuters.com/article/us-amazon-com-trump/amazon-finishes-higher-despite-trumps-new-threat-on-shipping-rates-idUSKCN1HA1RR

109 Sen, A., 2017. "Valic trims Flipkart valuation to $7.9 billion," at www.livemint.com/Companies/EJw97b4x13Yd1D0hBw52NN/Valic-trims-Flipkart-valuation-to-79-billion.html.

110 Punit, I.S. 2016. "Amazon and Flipkart are speechless after India announces new foreign investment rules," 29 March, https://qz.com/649873/amazon-and-flipkart-are-speechless-after-india-announces-new-foreign-investment-rules/.

111 The Economist. 2017. "Growth at Indian internet consumer firms has stalled," 6 April www.economist.com/news/business/21720330-they-must-fend-amazon-amid-doubts-about-their-business-models-growth-indian-internet.

112 Nikkei Asian Review. 2017a. "India Flipkart taps venture capitalist as CEO," https://asia.nikkei.com/Business/Companies/India-Flipkart-taps-venture-capitalist-as-CEO (Accessed February 5, 2018).

113 Stacey, K., Massoudi, A. & Inagaki, K. 2017. "SoftBank pushes for merger of India's Snapdeal and Flipkart," 9 April, www.ft.com/content/ea144fda-1d21-11e7-a454-ab04428977f9.

114 Khatri. 2018.

115 Ibid.

116 Vignesh, J. 2017. "For Flipkart, this app makes rural connect," https://economictimes.indiatimes.com/small-biz/startups/for-flipkart-this-app-makes-rural-connect/articleshow/59676188.cms.

117 IDG Asia. 2017. "Amazon and Flipkart to fight for rural markets in India," https://retailanalysis.igd.com/news/news-article/t/amazon-and-flipkart-to-fight-for-rural-markets-in-india/i/16523.

118 Krishna, V., 2018. "Internet penetration may be rising, but the urban-rural digital divide remains a reality in India," https://yourstory.com/2018/03/internet-penetration-may-rising-urban-rural-digital-divide-remains-reality-india/.

119 Mathur, S., 2014. "Cloud Computing Is A Force Multiplier For Emerging Markets," www.forbes.com/sites/oracle/2014/01/09/cloud-computing-is-a-force-multiplier-for-emerging-markets/2/ (Accessed February 5, 2018).

120 Murgai, C. 2015. "Why Big Data is a Game Changer for the Indian eCommerce Industry March 23," www.dqindia.com/why-big-data-is-a-game-changer-for-the-indian-ecommerce-industry/.

121 Lakshminarayanan, A. 2017. "Big Data Insights: The game changer for Indian E-commerce − Ettech," https://tech.economictimes.indiatimes.com/news/technology/big-data-insights-the-game-changer-for-indian-e-commerce/60083471 (Accessed February 5, 2018).

122 Huang, R., 2012. Relaxing crowdfunding rules could help Asia startups, June 18, at www.zdnet.com/relaxing-crowdfunding-rules-could-help-asia-startups-2062305148/.

123 Madhavan, N., 2015, "Flipkart plans drones for rural delivery, wants to persuade govt," www.hindustantimes.com/business/flipkart-plans-drones-for-rural-delivery-wants-to-persuade-govt/story-EZZighpDgU27uwKit VEiNN.html.

Chapter 10

Entrepreneurship in Latin America

This chapter's objectives include:

1   To *demonstrate* an understanding of the entrepreneurship landscape in Latin American economies.
2   To *analyze* the facilitators and inhibitors of entrepreneurship in Latin American economies.
3   To *assess* the regulatory environments related to entrepreneurship in Latin American economies.
4   To *evaluate* major aspects Latin American culture from the standpoint of entrepreneurial activities.
5   To *demonstrate* an understanding of the attractiveness of entrepreneurial activities in some of the key economic sectors.
6   To *evaluate* some major sources of entrepreneurial financing in Latin American economies.
7   To *assess* the environments for technology adoption, innovations, and R&D activities in Latin American economies.

Introduction

Entrepreneurship is flourishing in Latin America, which is home to 626 million people with a GDP (PPP) of US$7.5 trillion in 2015. As noted in Chapter 1, 40% of Latin American youth have reported a desire to become an entrepreneur.[1]

The region is home to a number of dynamic, creative, and innovative companies and entrepreneurs. For instance, Argentina-based Mercado-Libre, which is incorporated in the U.S., is Latin America's biggest e-commerce and online payments platform. Founded in 1999, it is considered to be a combination of the region's Amazon, eBay, and PayPal. In *MIT Technology Review*'s list of 50 Smartest Companies in 2017 MercadoLibre ranked #26.[2] MercadoLibre also ranked #71 in Forbes List of Innovative Growth Companies in 2017.[3]

As another success story, the Argentinian AI customer service startup *Aivo* develops artificial intelligence solutions, which are transforming the way companies interact with customers. *Aivo* is the leader in Latin American virtual assistants markets. Founded in 2012, Aivo's virtual artificial intelligence customer service agents served over one million customers in 2015.[4] As of 2017, it was present in 10 countries. In 2016, it handled over 100 million interactions in English, Spanish, and Portuguese.[5] Aivo was the winner of the 2016 Latin American Frost & Sullivan Award for Product Leadership.[6]

As a final example in this section, the Brazilian mobile app Strider was selected in the Forbes' 2017 list of the "25 Most Innovative Ag-Tech Startups." Strider's pest monitoring application allows farmers to monitor and make decision in treating infestations.[7] For an annual fee, Strider's app converts pests-related data into color-coded "heat maps." Its decision support software tells the location and time for spraying or harvesting. Farmers using Strider's app are reported to save 10%–15% on pesticides.[8]

Some governments in the region have helped develop favorable political and regulatory conditions for entrepreneurship development. In the World Bank's Doing Business 2018 report, half of the 32 economies in Latin America implemented at least one reform in 2017. The region implemented about 400 reforms during 2003–2017.[9]

It is also noted that a culture of innovation has emerged in the region. Governments in the region and the private sector have promoted programs such as accelerators and coworking spaces that are dedicated to promote entrepreneurship.[10] Global startup organizations such as 500 startups and StartupBootcamp have also made inroad into the continent.[11]

A Survey of Entrepreneurship in Latin America

Due to the region's unique culture, history, political structures, and natural heritage, one can observe interesting patterns in entrepreneurship development. There is also a wide regional variation in the entrepreneurship landscape. Examples exist of both successful and unsuccessful efforts to develop an entrepreneurial ecosystem.

Chile can be considered to be an example of an entrepreneurially successful economy in the region. A study of the World Economic Forum of 44 countries identified Chile as a country that has been able to avoid a trap that is common in entrepreneurial impact. Here is how the trap works: in a less-competitive economy, there is a higher tendency among the population to start businesses, most of which are informal. The entrepreneurs, however, are rarely innovative and thus fail to create many jobs. However, as the economy becomes more competitive, the tendency to start businesses among the population decreases, but those who do tend to be more innovative or ambitious. In both of these cases, the conditions lack for achieving full entrepreneurial potential.[12]

On the opposite continuum is Venezuela. One estimate suggested that Venezuela's per capita income reduced by 40% during 2013–2017.[13] The country's unemployment rate was over 20% in 2018. The country's saving rate as proportions of disposable income was −6.5% in 2017. According to a 2016 Venezuelan national survey, 93% of the population was unable to afford food.[14] The Venezuelan government diverted a majority of its resources to build the oil industry. Other industries such as food production have received very little government attention.[15]

In November 2017, Swiss startup StartupBlink released a report that ranked "startup ecosystem strength" of 954 cities and 125 countries.[16] Among the major criteria used in the ranking included the number and quality of startups and supporting organizations, success rates of startups (e.g., the number of unicorns[17]), and business environment (e.g., infrastructure, red tape, and the ease of launching a business). The report included ranks for both cities and countries. In the country rankings, the best performing economies in the region Mexico and Chile ranked 30th and 33rd, respectively.[18]

In some countries, there is a large geographical disparity in entrepreneurial activities. For instance, in Chile, 80% of startups have been registered in the capital, Santiago.[19]

Informality is perhaps among the most notable features of the Latin American entrepreneurial landscape. Indeed, informality is considered to be a principal barrier facing entrepreneurial firms from growing and creating more jobs.[20] One estimate suggested that Latin America had 47–57 million SMEs, of which only three to four million were formal.[21]

Over half of all workers in Latin America are employed in the informal economy.[22] The proportion of informally employed workers is much higher in some economies. In Guatemala, more than 70% of the workforce is employed in the informal economy.[23]

As is the case of other parts of the world, informally employed workers are less productive and would earn less. For instance, informal economy employs 60% of the workforce in Mexico but accounts for only 26% of GDP.[24]

Various factors contribute to the region's informal economy. In Brazil, many firms decide to operate in the informal economy due to the country's unfavorable business environment such as complex regulations, a high tax rate, corruption, red tape, and difficult customs system. These factors make it hard for businesses to keep their products' prices low. High prices in the formal sector also push consumers into buying products from the informal economy such as smuggled and counterfeit goods.[25]

In some countries, high informality can be partly attributed to high minimum wages. For instance, in 2017, Colombia raised minimum wage by 7%. The new minimum wage increased to US$1.18 per hour or US$246 per month.[26] It is argued that due to the high minimum wage certain disadvantaged groups such as low-skilled workers, youth, and old-age workers are less likely to be employed in the formal sector. This is especially the case in less developed regions of the country where productivity is lower.[27]

A concern is that economic benefits of entrepreneurship are accruing mainly to the rich. For instance, by several accounts, Chile is among the most entrepreneurially successful countries in the region. For instance, among the Organization for Economic Co-operation and Development (OECD) countries, Chile has the highest and Mexico has the second highest Gini index.[28] This means that there is a high degree of inequality in the distribution of income and wealth in these countries. This highlights the need to promote financial inclusion.[29]

In the rest of this section, we will discuss some examples of entrepreneurial activities in two important economic sectors: e-commerce and FinTech.

E-commerce

According to Worldpay's 2017 Global Payments Report, the Latin American e-commerce was US$59 billion in 2017, which will increase to US$118 billion in 2021.[30] The region is expected to experience the biggest growth during this period. MercadoLibre is an example of a company that is taking advantage of this entrepreneurial opportunity by offering a number of e-commerce solutions.

MercadoLibre, together with its Portuguese version, MercadoLivre (for Brazil) operated in 19 Latin American economies by 2017 and had 182 million registered users.[31] Using MercadoLibre platform, consumers can buy, sell, and pay. Sellers also use the platform to collect and generate leads in order to initiate consumer interest or enquiry into products or services.[32] In 2016, the company's revenue exceeded US$650 million.[33]

As of 2017, Mexico was the only market where both MercadoLibre and Amazon competed. MercadoLibre bet Amazon to become the leader in Mexico's e-commerce market in 2016.[34] One key factor that differentiated MercadoLibre from its competitors was that it allowed consumers to buy online by paying cash at Oxxo convenience stores.[35] Oxxo is Mexico's largest convenience store chain, which had over 15,000 locations across Latin America.[36]

FinTech

According to the World Bank's "Global Findex Database," 49% of adults Latin America and Caribbean did not have bank accounts as of 2014.[37]

According to the World Bank, 61% of Mexican adults did not have a bank account. There are 14 bank branches per 100,000 inhabitants in Mexico, compared to 33 in the U.S.[38] The problem is further compounded by Mexico's under-developed transport infrastructure. The government's National Survey for Financial Inclusion carried out in 2015 found that the average travel time to a bank branch was 42 minutes in rural areas and 22 minutes in urban settings.[39]

Thus strong business opportunities exist for providing financial services to fulfill the banking and financial needs of the unbanked population. As of mid-2017, Brazil had 244 FinTech companies.[40] About 158 FinTech companies operated in Mexico that year.[41]

The Mexican FinTech company Kueski A high-profile example of an entrepreneurial firm forcing on this sector. As of 2017, Kueski employed 80 people and served over 60,000 clients mostly small businessmen. Most loans are less than US$300, which cover unexpected expenses. By that year, Kueski had made over 250,000 loans worth US$30 million.[42]

Acquiring new customers has become difficult for traditional banks due to their heavy dependence on human resources. The cost of serving a customer through technology is much smaller compared to a bank.[43] Peer-to-peer lending platforms have helped match savers with borrowers and penetrate areas where financing is expensive.[44] Finnovista estimated that these platforms could capture up to 30% of Mexico's banking market by 2027.[45]

Mexico is described as a regional hub for FinTech startups, especially those focusing on financial inclusion. According to the FinTech startup accelerator, Finnovista Mexico accounts for more than a third of FinTech companies in Latin America that target at the underbanked or unbanked populations.

Unsurprisingly the region's FinTech sector is gaining traction as a venture capital (VC) magnet. According to the Latin America Venture Capital Association (LAVCA), startups in the FinTech sector received more investment in 2015 than any other sector. FinTech accounted for about 30% of the IT sector's investment in 2015.[46] The LAVCA's study also found that the region's FinTech industry attracted US$186 million in VC in 2016.[47]

Some regulations have been introduced to control FinTech companies. In December 2017, Mexico's Senate approved a bill that would regulate FinTech sector, including crowdfunding and cryptocurrency firms.[48] The regulation requires crowdfunding companies to assess users' creditworthiness. Crowdfunding companies may also need to submit credit information from a bureau and communicate the methodology used to determine borrowers' risk to the National Banking and Securities Commission (CNBV). All FinTech firms are required to have adequate infrastructure to prevent money laundering and protect against cybersecurity risks.[49] Some FinTech entrepreneurs have expressed concerns that the law significantly increase compliance costs and discourage investment in the industry.[50]

Determinants of Entrepreneurship

Regulatory Framework

Colombia, Mexico, and Peru are among the top-performing economies in the region (Figure 10.1). In Chapter 2, we discussed a number of efforts made by the Colombian government to improve the country's entrepreneurial landscape.

New regulatory approaches have been evolving in the region to promote entrepreneurship.

In 2017, in an attempt to better promote entrepreneurship, Argentina passed its Ley de Emprendedores, which was supported by the Association of Entrepreneurs in Argentina (ASEA) and Argentina Association of Private Equity, Venture and Seed Capital (ARCAP). The law provides tax incentives, a fast-track process to register a company and support for accelerators. Under the new law, new business can be set up in 24 hours and all the processes can be completed online.[51] There is also the provision of public funds to co-invest with private investors in entrepreneurial ventures.[52]

Likewise, Startup Peru was launched by the Peruvian Ministry of Production in 2012. The objective was to stimulate startups and innovative products. In 2017, 837 projects applied with Startup Peru for seed capital from. A total of 106 of them received the equivalent of US$5,000, US$46,000, and US$153,000 in funding.[53] A number of ambitious plans have been considered for enhancing innovation profiles. StartUp Perú plans to provide funding to more than 350 local startups by the end of 2018.[54]

Below we discuss the key elements of regulatory frameworks in two major economies in the region: Brazil and Venezuela. These two are among the economies that are most difficult to start a business (Figure 10.1).

Brazil

Bureaucracy, red tape, and inefficiency in the public sector are among of the most important issues facing Brazilian entrepreneurial firms. According to the World Bank, an average business in Brazil spent 1958 hours on filing taxes in 2017.[55] This was three times higher than in Venezuela and fifteen times more than in European Union countries.[56]

A problem is that Brazil is polarized by politics and weak judicial institutions. The country's bureaucracy is characterized by inefficiency and excessive red tape. In order to get things done quickly, there is a tendency among business and individuals to pay bribes to government officials.[57]

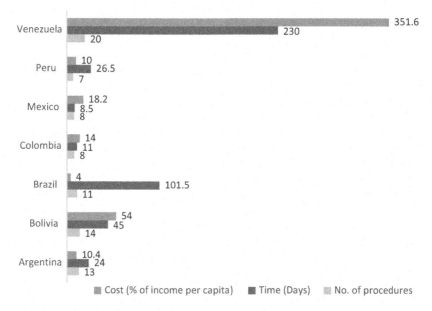

Figure 10.1 Indicators Related to Starting a Business in Selected Latin American Economies.
Source: The World Bank "Doing Business 2018" (www.doingbusiness.org/rankings).

Some encouraging efforts have nevertheless been made in recent years at the national as well as local levels. The Brazilian government has dedicated an online portal to facilitate entrepreneurship among black families and other socially and ethnically disadvantaged groups.[58]

Some local governments have digitized the activities associated with starting a business, which has streamlined the business registration the processes. The São Paulo city government launched a program called *Empreenda Fácil*, or "Easy Business" in May 2017. The goal was to reduce the time taken to start a business to seven days. Potential entrepreneurs can visit an online portal, which integrates all the processes needed by agencies at the federal, state, and municipal levels. Within about a month after the program was launched, about *Empreenda Fácil* received about 18,000 applications. In the first phase, the program processes only applications from businesses that do not require specific licensing. Such businesses are reported to make up about 80% of enterprises in São Paulo. The second phase is expected to include businesses that require higher levels of scrutiny and approval such as hospitals. The third phase of the program will focus on speeding up the process for closing businesses. The long-term goal is to reduce the time taken to start a business to two days or less.[59] This approach is also likely to reduce corruption.

Venezuela

Venezuela is among the world's most difficult place to start a business. The country ranked No. 190 in the environment to start a business. An entrepreneur is required to spend 351.6% of per capita income to start a business in the country compared to 37.5% in Latin America and Caribbean 3.1% in OECD high-income countries.

Venezuela's Fair Prices Law gives The Superintendencia Nacional para la Defensa de los Derechos Socioeconómicos the broad power to regulate the price of a product. The price can be controlled in any stage of the production chain based on the product's strategic importance and social benefit.[60] If a government bureaucrat without thinking seriously and analysis decides that the price of a product is unfair, the business owner may face prison time or expropriation.[61] Price controls have been used to maintain essential goods' prices at affordable levels.

Price controls have been used to achieve various political goals of the ruling elite. In recent years, price controls have reportedly expanded to a wide variety of products such as food, medicines and medical services, car batteries, deodorant, diapers, and toilet paper. The stated goal of these programs was to control inflation and keep products affordable for the poor.[62]

In many cases, however, such a system forces firms to set prices below production costs. Consequently, products disappear from the market.[63] In order to deal with this shortage of basic goods, the government started importing goods and selling them at subsidized prices.[64]

Values, Culture, and Skills

In Chapter 3, we discussed some of the key cultural and sociopolitical features of Latin American economies from the standpoint of entrepreneurship, especially in the context of ECF. This section covers other key elements of values, culture, and skills that have an influence on the region's entrepreneurial landscape.

Cultural Orientation toward Entrepreneurs and Entrepreneurial Failure

One key challenge is that the region's culture has little respect for entrepreneurs and innovators. Some close observers of the regions have noted that whereas soccer stars are role models for millions of children, relatively few young people think that it is "cool" to be a scientist, or a successful entrepreneur.

Entrepreneurial activity is negatively correlated with the stigma of failure. Observers have noted that there is also the lack of social tolerance of failure in the region.[65] Some have noted that people are uncomfortable to talk about failure.[66] Many entrepreneurs believe that to fail in a business is to let down the family.[67]

Gender and Entrepreneurship

Like most other parts of the world, women are underrepresented in the region's entrepreneurial landscape. For instance, only 15% of Latin America and the Caribbean (LAC) region's high-growth entrepreneurs are women.[68] According to Startup Chile, woman account for only 1 out of every 10 team members in startups in the accelerator.[69] In recent years, however, there is some sign that a culture is emerging in which women increasingly participate in entrepreneurial ventures. A study of Global Entrepreneurship Monitor (GEM) found that women led 35% of the country's six million micro and small businesses. They, however, represent 50% of the leadership in newly started businesses.[70] According to Ernst & Young G20 Entrepreneurship Barometer of 2013, half of all new businesses in Brazil were owned by women.

A final observation about gender and entrepreneurship in the region is that women are more likely to be employed than men in the informal sector. 54% of women in Latin America and the Caribbean in nonagricultural jobs are in the regional informal employment (UN women).[71] The proportion is much higher in some economies. For instance, in Peru, 76% of women are reported to work in the informal sector.[72]

Entrepreneurship Skills and Talent

There is a severe shortage of entrepreneurship-related skills in Latin America. Only a small proportion of Latin American college students go into science or engineering. According to the World Bank, in 2015, Chile had 455 researchers in R&D per million inhabitants compared to 7,087 in South Korea.[73]

According to staffing firm ManpowerGroup's 2015 Talent Shortage Survey, about 50% of formal Latin American firms were unable to find candidates with the skills they need, compared to 36% of firms in OECD countries.[74] This was reported to be a particularly pressing issue in Peru and Brazil.[75] 68% of employers in Peru and 61% of Brazil were struggling to fill jobs.

Some educational institutions are offering course and programs that are directed at improving students' mindset and skills in entrepreneurship. For instance, the Universidad de Ingeniería y Tecnología (UTEC) in Peru created business accelerator, UTEC Ventures in 2014. As of 2018, UTEC Ventures had more than 50 companies in its portfolio. It educates and informs students, startups and the public about startups and innovation by organizing events regularly.[76]

Access to Finance, Market, R&D, and Technology

Market Access

In order to understand the market access situation in Latin American economies, it is important to look at these economies' antitrust laws or competition laws, which are designed to ensure that free and fair competition exists in an open-market environment.[77] Broadly speaking, antitrust laws in many Latin American countries and the U.S. have similar elements. However, such laws in the U.S. have a much longer history compared to Latin American countries. For instance, the Sherman Antitrust Act in the U.S. was passed in 1890. Since then the Act has been expanded and amended. On the contrary, antitrust laws in most Latin American countries are relatively new. Most major Latin American countries adopted antitrust laws in the 1990s.[78] Such laws are rapidly changing and evolving.[79] An upshot of the newness is that meaning of the law is unclear and there is less predictability in the enforcement.

Access to Finance

As is the case of most developing economies, general consumer and business finance companies have had limited success in serving the needs of economically active low-income families and microenterprises cost-effectively and sustainably in Latin American economies. One problem is that low-income families and small businesses in these economies often have poor or no credit histories.[80] About a third of companies in the region identified lack of credit as a major constraint.[81]

Small enterprises in the region find it difficult to get access to financing from the bank. For instance, SMEs represent over 90% all enterprises in the region. They generate over half of all jobs and a quarter of the region's GDP.[82] However, only 12% of total credit in the region goes to SMEs.[83] In Mexico, micro-, small-, and medium-sized firms account for more than 99.8% of enterprises in 2014, but they received only 11.1% of total bank credit for businesses.[84]

In some economies, banks and other financial institutions charge extremely high interest rates. For instance, consumers in Brazil are reported to pay an annual average interest rate of 190% for unsecured overdraft, credit card, and consumer loans.[85]

In recent years, entrepreneurial financing situation in the region is improving. Various alternative funding sources are rapidly evolving.

BANK LOAN

Unavailability of bank loans and high interest rates of available loans are major barriers to access in entrepreneurial financing in the region. In general, Latin American countries have high annual lending rates (ALRs) compared to advanced OECD countries (Figure 10.2).

A main obstacle for potential borrowers is the lack of collateral. Banks in the region generally prefer using assets such as land and buildings as

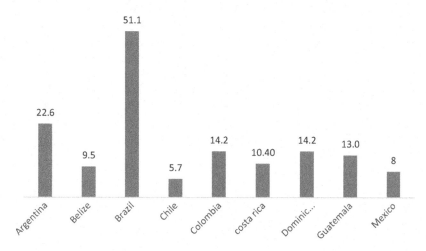

Figure 10.2 Annual Lending Rates in Some Latin American Countries (2017).
Source: Euromonitor International.

guarantees for loans. However, in many developing economies, movable assets such as machinery, equipment, livestock, or crops account for over three quarters of a firm's capital.

There have been some encouraging policy and institutional reforms in order to increase SMEs' access to financing. In order to enable banks to lend to small entrepreneurs that have only movable assets as security, the International Finance Corporation (IFC) worked with governments and banks in Latin American economies to introduce the concept of collateral registries and to implement secured-transaction laws.[86] As of 2016, the IFC had worked with governments in more than 30 countries to establish the legal and institutional frameworks which would make it possible to use movable assets to guarantee loans.[87]

The registry was launched in Colombia in March 2014. By November 2016, over one million registrations were recorded, which were valued at more than US$ 93 billion.[88] By 2016, in Colombia, over 100 financial institutions, including some of the country's largest banks, had participated in the registry as lenders.[89] The joint efforts of the Colombian government, the Association of Chambers of Commerce, and IFC led to the required legislative reforms.

Mexico has also implemented an electronic movable-collateral registry. It was reported that 97% of the registrations support loans to SMEs. Likewise, in mid-2015, a new secured-transactions system came into effect in Costa Rica. By 2016, over 4,500 SMEs in the country received loans that were secured by movable assets.[90]

Government-Sponsored Funding

In order to promote entrepreneurial spirit and practices, some governments in the region such as those of Argentina, Brazil, and Chile are offering equity free funding for startups from all over the world with breakthrough ideas. In Argentina, a city government seed fund program IncuBAte offers startups up to US$30,000 in funding. National and international entrepreneurs with high-impact ideas can apply for the program. The selected startups also receive free office space for a year and mentoring.[91]

CROWDFUNDING

As noted in Chapter 3, the region's crowdfunding market is less developed compared to most other regions. For instance, per capita ECF in the U.S. in 2015 was about 28,000 times that of the LAC regions. However, as discussed in Chapter 3, a number of CFPs in the region are attempting to harness the power of crowdfunding by making it easier for entrepreneurs to raise money through the Internet.

Venture capital   In 2016, VC investments in Latin America reached US$500 million in 197 transactions.[92] VC firms such as Andreessen Horowitz, Sequoia Capital, QED Investors, and Accel Partners have started investing in economies in the region such as Mexico, Brazil, and Colombia.[93] According to the Latin American Private Equity & Venture Capital Association, in 2016, Mexican startups received VC investments of US$130 million in 73 deals.[94] Brazil attracted US$279 million VC investments in 64 deals. VC investment in Brazil rose to over US$575 million in 2017.[95]

In 2016, the Silicon Valley-based VC firm Andreessen Horowitz made its first Latin American investment in Rappi, a Colombian grocery delivery service.[96] As of December 2018, Rappi offered more than 15,000 products such as groceries, food, alcohol, pharmacy products, apparel, and electronics from its partner companies for home delivery.[97] Rappi also offers a courier services, pay bills and deliver cash.[98] Rappi's cofounder and CEO, Simon Borrero noted that Latin America provides strong market opportunities for on-demand delivery services due to a growing middle and upper class.[99]

PRIVATE ACCELERATORS

Private accelerators in the region also play a significant role in improving access to finance for promising startups. Telefonica launched a corporate accelerator Wayra Peru to support digital ventures with potential for international expansion. It provides up to US$50,000 in funding and access to an accelerator program in the capital city of Lima. The startup selected by Wayra Peru also have access to a network of global partners, mentors, and experts.[100] Through Wayra Peru, Peruvian startups received more than US$1.8 million in 2016 from foreign investors.[101]

SUPPLY CHAIN FINANCING

Some companies have developed supply chain financing system. In 2017, Mercado Libre started providing working-capital loans to entrepreneurs in Argentina. Online sellers using Mercado Libre and its Mercado Pago payment platform can get loans, which can be as much as their two months' sales.[102] MercadoLibre also announced plans to launch the service in Brazil and Mexico.

R&D and Technology

RESEARCH AND DEVELOPMENT

Compared to industrialized countries, Latin America economies make lower investment in R&D activities (Figure 10.3). Investment in R&D of economies in the region increased from 0.63% of GDP in 2009 to

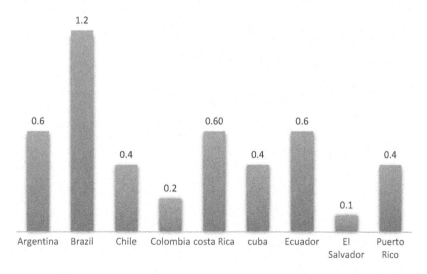

Figure 10.3 Gross Domestic Expenditure on R&D as a Percentage of GDP in Selected Latin American Economies (2017).
Source: Euromonitor International.

0.74% in 2014. This proportion in significantly lower than most other regions and groups of economies such as the OECD's 2.55%, North America's 2.79%, lower- and middle-income country's 1.49% and upper-middle-income country's 1.66%. Most Latin American economies even trail behind South Asia, which spent 0.58% of GDP in R&D in 2015.[103]

One problem is the private sector's limited spending on R&D. For instance, in Colombia, the public sector accounts for 57% of all R&D investments.[104] In the OECD countries, on the other hand, government-financed research and development (R&D) was only 27% of total R&D expenditures in 2014.[105]

Consequently, Latin America performs poorly in measures of innovation, such as patent statistics. The number of patent applications in the region is growing at a slower rate than most other geographic regions. For instance during 2006–2016, the annual growth of number of patent applications in Latin America and the Caribbean was 1.3% compared to Asia's 8.5%. As Figure 10.4 presents, the region's share of the world total in patent applications reduced from 3% in 2006 to 2% in 2016.

Some economies in the region, however, have ambitious plans to increase R&D investment. For instance, the Peruvian Ministry of Production has announced a plan to increase investment in innovation by tenfold by 2027.[106]

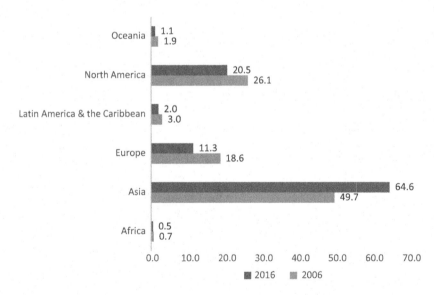

Figure 10.4 Patent Applications by Region: Share of the World Total (%).
Source: WIPO Statistics Database, September 2017. "Patents," www.wipo.int/edocs/pubdocs/en/wipo_pub_941_2017-chapter2.pdf.

ICT USE

Some Latin American countries have taken progressive steps toward the use of ICTs over the past decade. For instance, in order to establish broadband Internet access throughout the country, Colombia's Ministry of Information and Communication Technology a launched US$2.5 billion project Live Digital Plan (Vive Digital) in 2010.[107] The plan is to have the Internet in in remote jungles areas near the borders with Venezuela, Peru, and Brazil with 27 million people (63% of the population) connected to the Internet by 2018.[108] Yet, despite these efforts and successes, Colombia has made a relatively slower progress vis-à-vis many other major economies toward. Among the 128 economies considered in the Speedtest Global Index, In January 2018, Colombia ranked #79 in terms of the mobile broadband download speed and #100 in terms of the mobile broadband download speed.[109]

In general, there remains a large gap in ICT use between Latin American countries and other advanced countries. Internet connection speed in the region is slow compared to other advanced economies. Figure 10.5 presents mobile and fixed broadband speeds in some Latin American economies with fastest broadband speeds and two globally leading countries in broadband speed. Broadband speeds in Latin American economies are significantly below the global average mobile broadband download speed of 22.2 Mbps and average fixed broadband download speed of 41.9 Mbps. Among the 128 economies considered in the Speedtest Global Index, Mexico ranked #52 in terms of the mobile broadband download speed, which had the fastest speed in the region.

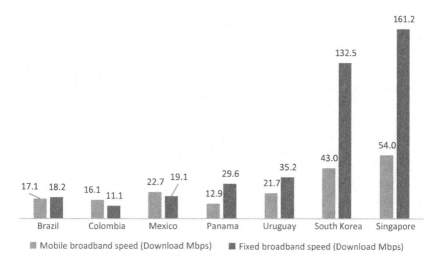

Figure 10.5 Mobile and Fixed Broadband Speed in Some Latin American Economies and Global Leaders (Download Mbps).

Source: Speedtest Global Index, December 2017, www.speedtest.net/global-index.

Concluding Comments

Compared to most OECD countries, Latin America performs poorly in terms of key ingredients of entrepreneurship such as R&D, innovation, and access to finance. In some economies such as Venezuela, market distortion has resulted from the governments' actions. Informality is more prevalent in Latin America compared to most other regions. Some deep-seated psychological and cultural barriers in the region cannot be easily overcome. For instance, most young people in the region often lack a mindset that considers successful entrepreneurs or scientists as role models. A related point is that entrepreneurial failure is likely to evoke shame in the family.

Nonetheless, entrepreneurship is thriving in most of the Latin American economies. In general, entrepreneurship in most major economies is getting a big boost in the region thanks to encouraging policy and institutional reforms. Some economies in the region have taken measures to streamline the process to start new business ventures. Some governments have provided funding for promising business ideas. The favorable regulatory and policy frameworks for entrepreneurs may increase incentives for business formalization and may encourage informal businesses to move out of the informal market.

Innovative startups such as Kueski and Rappi have launched business models to address unique, region-specific challenges. For instance, many FinTech ventures have addressed gaps that exist in traditional bank's practices.

End of Chapter Questions

1   What are some of the recent regulatory and legislative changes in Latin American countries that are likely to change the entrepreneurial landscape?
2   What are some of the unique aspects of cultural issues Latin American countries from the entrepreneurial perspective?
3   How does the common trap in entrepreneurial impact work? How has Chile avoided such a trap?
4   Why are some Silicon Valley-based VC companies finding Latin American countries attractive?
5   What is the current situation of R&D and innovation performance of Latin American countries? How do they compare with other major economies?
6   How do Latin American countries compare with the U.S. in terms of antitrust laws?

End of the Chapter Case: Start-Up Chile in the Chilecon Valley

Start-Up Chile was launched in 2010 in the capital city Santiago's Providencia neighborhood. The goal of this initiative was to create one of the biggest startup communities in the world.[110] It an entirely government-funded initiative and is among about 15 accelerators in the country.[111]

The idea of a government-funded startup incubator is not necessarily a new one. What is unique and striking about Start-Up Chile is that entrepreneurs get equity-free funding. Its "Seed" program was launched in 2010. It is an acceleration program for startups that have a functional product and early validation (Seed).[112] When the program was launched, it offered US$40,000 grants to successful participants. In the subsequent years, the Chilean government lowered the amount to US$30,000. For the 2018 application round, the amount was again increased to the original level of US$40,000.[113] The startups selected by the program also receive office space, as well as opportunities for mentoring and coaching.[114]

Chile has become a role model in this type of accelerator program. As of 2017, the program was replicated in more than 50 countries around the world.[115]

Start-Up Chile also offers two additional program:

a "S Factory" is a preacceleration program for female entrepreneurs, who receive 10 million Chilean pesos (about US$14,000 based on 2017 exchange rates). Female founders selected in the program from around the world can get a one-year working visa to move to Chile to develop their ideas and prototypes.[116] For the March 2017 application cycle, for the "fifth generation" of the program, it announced a plan to accept 20–30 startups in this category.

b "Scale" was launched in early 2015 as a follow-on support for startups, who receive 60 million pesos (US$100,000).[117] To be eligible, the business must be incorporate in Chile. Moreover, it must be run from the country.[118] Companies selected in this category are also required to have tested their solutions and demonstrated the soundness of their business models.[119]

Encouraging Response from Entrepreneurs Worldwide

Every year as many as 3,000 startups are reported to apply to enroll in Start-Up Chile's accelerator program. About 250 are selected for a six-month program. Around three-quarters of the selected startups are from foreign countries.[120]

Start-Up Chile's success in attracting promising startups can also be attributed to other unforeseen circumstances. When Start-Up Chile was started in 2010, Europe had not yet recovered from the 2008 global financial crisis.[121] U.S. businesses were facing difficulty in hiring highly skilled foreign workers.[122] Due to these events in other parts of the world, Chile's open-arms approach became attractive for companies and entrepreneurs worldwide.

Major Goals of the Program

In launching the Start-Up Chile program, the Chilean government has pursued two major goals. First, the Chilean government wants to revitalize country's economy by attracting new tech startups and reduce the country's dependence on commodities such as copper and minerals.[123]

Second, the Chilean government wants the local communities to be more enterprising, growth- oriented, and innovation-driven. Along this line, another major goal of Start-Up Chile is to utilize the global entrepreneurial talent to bring a change in the Chilean business culture.[124] In return for the free seed capital from the government, the selected startups are expected to take part in various events and activities to promote entrepreneurship awareness among the local population. The startups are required to earn 4,000 "social capital points." These points can be earned in a number of different ways such as hosting entrepreneurship-related workshops, mentoring and coaching local entrepreneurs, teaching classes and organizing hackathon.[125] The idea is to engage the local population in activities related to entrepreneurship, technology, and innovation.

An active and Innovative Accelerator

According to New York-based Gust and Fundacity, Start-Up Chile (with 250 startups) was the world's third most active accelerator after the U.K.-based Entrepreneurial Spark (660 startups), and Silicon Valley, the U.S.-based Plug and Play Tech Center (403 startups).[126] In 2017, *Fast Company* Chose Start-Up Chile as the most Innovative Startup accelerator in Latin America.[127]

Favorable Regulatory and Political Climate

Chile has also created favorable regulatory and policy frameworks for entrepreneurs. In 2013, Chile passed the "Law of Businesses in One Day." A new business can be established in a day, which is one of the fastest in the world.[128] It is possible to complete all the paperwork and registration requirements online. The Chilean Association of Entrepreneurs (ASECH) played a pivotal role in passing the law.[129]

A main concern was Chile's punitive bankruptcy law. A positive development in this respect is a new insolvency law approved by the Chilean Congress in 2013. The law became effective in October 2014. The new law has provisions that allow reorganization of businesses that are in financial trouble. The old law mainly focused on the liquidation of debtors' assets. Under the new law, insolvency proceedings fall under the jurisdiction of specialized insolvency courts for insolvency proceedings. Before the law was enacted, randomly selected civil tribunals were responsible for insolvency cases.[130]

Foreign entrepreneurs selected for Start-Up Chile's accelerator program also receive a one year temporary visa.[131] In recent years, Chile has started offering easier and faster visa processing for individuals with high-technology skills and entrepreneurs. A visa is granted in 15 days for qualified foreigners.[132]

Social and Economic Impact

Start-Up Chile has had a favorable impact on the Chilean economy. For instance, by 2016, more than 1,300 startups had gone through Start-Up Chile program,[133] which helped over 3,000 entrepreneurs.[134]

More than 30% of the startups that have been through the Start-Up Chile program were reported to raise additional capital.[135] By mid-2015, the startups had raised US$135 million, which was more than four times the investment of the Chilean government.[136] Most of that came from the U.S.[137]

As of 2016, the Chilean government had invested US$40 million in startups enrolled in Start-Up Chile.[138] By then these startups' were estimated to have a total value of US$1.4 billion.[139] As of the summer of 2016, companies enrolled in Start-Up Chile's accelerator program had created about 1,600 jobs in Chile.[140]

The entrepreneurial activities in Start-Up Chile have also led significant social and cultural changes. As of 2017, entrepreneurs from 79 countries had participated in the Start-Up Chile program, which makes it among the most diverse startup programs in the world.[141] Observers have noted that a robust and vibrant entrepreneurial culture has been the main outcome of this initiative.[142] Not long ago Chile excessively relied on extractive industries. This means that local businesses engaged in low value-added activities.[143] The creation of Start-Up Chile has been a turning point that significantly increased the local population's engagement in high-value added entrepreneurial companies.

Indeed social impacts and cultural changes can be clearly seen among the local population. For instance, only 10% of the applicants to Startup Chile were Chileans when the program started in 2010. By 2014, the proportion increased to 29%.[144]

Key Barriers Facing Entrepreneurial Firms Enrolled in the Program

There are a number of challenges that entrepreneurs need to consider to locate their businesses in Santiago. For one thing, with a population of only 18 million, Chile's domestic market is small.

The country's private VC is also small.[145] For instance, during 2011–2015, VC Investments in Chile was US$85 million with 52 funds.[146]

As many as 80% of Start-Up Chile participants leave Santiago after the six-month program.[147] More than a third of them were reported to move to the U.S.

Another concern is Chile's low investment in R&D (Figure 10.3). In 2016, out of more than 62,000 patents registered in the region, Chile registered only 3,274.[148]

Chile is also facing competition from other economies in the region. As noted earlier, Argentina's IncuBAte is modeled after the Start-Up Chile program. Likewise, Start-Up Brasil was launched in 2013.[149] Startups selected to participate in the program receive investments up to about US$100,000 over the course of a year in the form of monthly grants.[150] The goals are to attract foreign entrepreneurs to the local consumer market and bring positive changes in the local entrepreneurial culture. The program was backed by US$78 million from the government.[151]

There are also allegations of misuse of the funds by some of the startups selected to participate at the program. It was reported that some young entrepreneurs used the Chilean government grants for leisure instead of developing their business plans.[152]

Case Summary

Some critics have questioned the sensibility of offering as much as US$40,000 grants to startups for free. Others think that it would be wiser and more appropriate for the government to invest money in the startups in return for equity. These viewpoints, however, fail to recognize the importance of social and cultural changes that have occurred since the inception of the Start-Up Chile program. As noted above, one key contribution of Start-Up Chile initiative is bringing a dramatic change in the country's entrepreneurial culture. These effects, however, are difficult to measure in monetary terms.

Notes

1 World Bank. 2015. "Entrepreneurship is the trend in Latin America," www.worldbank.org/en/news/feature/2015/09/30/emprender-esta-de-moda-en-america-latina.
2 Technology Review. 2017. "50 smartest companies 2017," www.technology review.com/lists/companies/2017/intro/#dji.
3 Forbes. 2017. "Mercadolibre," www.forbes.com/companies/mercadolibre/
4 Pena, I. 2015. "Startups like to Tango," 21 April, www.huffingtonpost.com/ignacio-peaa/startups-like-to-tango_b_6710884.html.
5 Crunchbase, "Aivo," www.crunchbase.com/organization/aivo.
6 Frost & Sullivan. 2016. "Frost & Sullivan acknowledges the innovation behind Aivo's development of AgentBot, its Intuitive Virtual Agent Software," 3 May, www.przoom.com/news/158632/Frost-and-Sullivan-Acknowledges-the-Innovation-behind-Aivos-Development-of-AgentBot-its-Intuitive-Virtual-Agent-Software/.

7 Sorvino, C. 2017. "The 25 Most innovative Ag-Tech startups," 28 June, www.forbes.com/sites/maggiemcgrath/2017/06/28/the-25-most-innovative-ag-tech-startups/#6561893d4883.

8 Jaggi, M. 2016. "Start-up Brazil: Belo Horizonte is emerging as a leading centre for entrepreneurs," www.ft.com/content/69bd9ea8-abdf-11e6-ba7d-76378e4fef24.

9 Haar, J. 2018. "Latin America is poised for a turnaround in 2018," www.miamiherald.com/opinion/op-ed/article194310244.html.

10 finnovista.com. 2017. "Interview Julie Ruvolo. 2017 Trend Watch: Latin American Venture Capital," www.finnovista.com/interview-julie-ruvolo-2017-trend-watch-latin-american-venture-capital/?lang=en.

11 Egusa, C. 2018. "More than EL Dorado: 3 less obvious benefits of launching in Latin America," https://thenextweb.com/contributors/2018/01/16/el-dorado-3-less-obvious-benefits-launching-latin-america/

12 Drexler, M., & Amoros, J.E. 2015. "Guest post: How Chile and Colombia eluded the entrepreneur trap" www.ft.com/content/9a3b67c1-4215-3fd8-b85a-12624ed2569c.

13 MacDonald, S. 2018. "Is Venezuela on the brink of economic and social collapse," http://nationalinterest.org/feature/venezuela-the-brink-economic-social-collapse-24247.

14 Aloi, B. 2018. "How hunger breeds hatred: Venezuela's shortage crisis," www.mironline.ca/how-hunger-breeds-hatred-venezuelas-shortage-crisis.

15 Landaeta-Jimenez, M., Cuenca, M.H., & Vasquez, G.R. 2016. "Encuesta sobre Condiciones de Vida Venezuela 2016," www.fundacionbengoa.org/noticias/2017/encovi-2016.asp.

16 Imagor, T. 2017. "Startup ecosystem rankings report 2017 startup blink," 20 October, www.startupblink.com/blog/startup-ecosystem-rankings-startupblink/.

17 "A startup company that is valued at over $1 billion is referred as a unicorn," www.investopedia.com/terms/u/unicorn.asp.

18 Galang, J. 2018. "Report ranks Canada third in top 10 startup ecosystems worldwide," https://betakit.com/report-ranks-canada-third-in-top-10-startup-ecosystems-worldwide/.

19 OECD. 2016. "Start-up Latin America 2016: Building an innovative future, development centre studies," *Development Centre Studios.*

20 International Labour Conference. 2015. "Small and medium-sized enterprises and decent and productive employment creation." *International Labor conference.* 104th Session.

21 IFC. 2010. "IFC: Scaling-up SME access to financial services in the developing world," www.ifc.org/wps/wcm/connect/bd1b060049585ef29e5ab-f19583b6d16/ScalingUp.pdf?MOD=AJPERES.

22 The Economist. 2016. "Casual Mondays to Fridays: The high cost of joining the formal sector," www.economist.com/news/americas/21709073-high-cost-joining-formal-sector-casual-mondays-fridays.

23 Telesur. 2015. "UN: Guatemala's informal economy stands at 70%," www.telesurtv.net/english/news/UN-Guatemalas-Informal-Economy-Stands-at-70-20151216-0016.html.

24 Peter, V. 2015. "Top 10 things to know about the Mexican economy," www.weforum.org/agenda/2015/05/top-10-things-to-know-about-the-mexican-economy/.

25 Hodgson, A. 2015. "Top 3 challenges in reaching the Brazilian consumer," https://blog.euromonitor.com/2015/11/top-3-challenges-in-reaching-the-brazilian-consumer.html.

26 Alsema, A. 2017. "Colombia raises minimum wage with 7% to $1.18/hour," https://colombiareports.com/colombia-raises-minimum-wage-7-1-18-hour/.

27 de la Maisonneuve, C. 2017, "Towards more inclusive growth in Colombia," *OECD Economics Department Working Papers*, No. 1423, OECD Publishing, Paris, http://dx.doi.org/10.1787/334902e0-en.

28 Peter. 2015.

29 Multilateral Investment Fund. 2015. "Creating a Crowdfunding ecosystem in Chile," Washington, DC.

30 Contify Retail News. 2018. "Connecting the World's inventories: eBay and PideloRapido partner to provide increased access to Latin American shoppers," www.marketwatch.com/story/connecting-the-worlds-inventories-ebay-and-pidelorapido-partner-to-provide-increased-access-to-latin-american-shoppers-2018-02-09.

31 Technology Review. 2017.

32 Forbes. 2017.

33 Carlen, J. 2017. "Lessons from three little-known entrepreneurs shaping our world | Expert column," https://pilotonline.com/inside-business/news/columns/article_789539a6-0031-5a0f-bf13-8ead23e004c0.html.

34 Technology Review. 2017.

35 Israel, S. 2018. "VIVA e-MEXICO: Amazon, Alibaba and Walmart are investing heavily south of the border," http://dailycaller.com/2018/01/01/viva-e-mexico-amazon-alibaba-and-walmart-are-investing-heavily-south-of-the-border/.

36 Asmann, P. 2017. "Insecurity leads Mexico convenience store chain to close stores," www.insightcrime.org/news/brief/rising-insecurity-regional-closures-mexico-largest-convenience-store-chain/

37 The World Bank. 2014. "World Bank "Global Findex Database," http://datatopics.worldbank.org/financialinclusion/.

38 Woodman, S. 2017. "Fintechs could take 30% of Mexican banking market," www.ft.com/content/5e092fb8-3bb9-11e7-ac89-b01cc67cfeec.

39 Ibid.

40 Rodrigues, R. 2017. "Brazil's fintech boom offers new vertical opportunities for investors," May13, https://techcrunch.com/2017/05/13/brazils-fintech-boom-offers-new-vertical-opportunities-for-investors/.

41 Woodman. 2017.

42 Guthrie, A. 2017. "'Closet entrepreneurs' boost Mexican start-up funding," https://www.ft.com/content/bd32a2dc-3bc1-11e7-ac89-b01cc67cfeec.

43 Woodman. 2017.

44 Ibid.

45 Ibid.

46 Lustig, N. 2017. "A new era for startup investing in Latin America," 19 May, https://techcrunch.com/2017/05/19/a-new-era-for-startup-investing-in-latin-america/.

47 Mergermarket. 2017. "Fintech startups attract capital in Latin America," www.forbes.com/sites/mergermarket/2017/09/19/fintech-startups-attract-capital-in-latin-america/#595f3b7d4eeb.

48 Sheky, E. 2017. "Mexican Senate passes fintech law," 6 October, www.reuters.com/article/us-mexico-finance/mexican-senate-passes-fintech-law-idUSKBN1E00HX.

49 Press Release. 2018. "Pablo Soria de Lachica comments on recent moves to regulate Mexico's Fintech sector," www.digitaljournal.com/pr/3635963.

50 Woodman. 2017.
51 Cruz, M. 2017. "Argentina's government is wooing entrepreneurs with a new law," https://techcrunch.com/2017/06/21/argentinas-government-is-wooing-entrepreneurs-with-a-new-law/.
52 Egusa, C. 2017. "Argentina: A look into Latin America's most global tech hub," https://thenextweb.com/contributors/2017/07/04/argentina-a-look-into-latin-americas-most-global-tech-hub/.
53 Stunt, V. 2017, "Peru is on a bid to catch up with its American neighbors," 10 August, https://techcrunch.com/2017/08/10/peru-is-on-a-bid-to-catch-up-with-its-innovative-latin-american-neighbors/.
54 Egusa, C. 2018. "Tech Ceviche: Why Peru has all the ingredients for a healthy startup ecosystem," https://thenextweb.com/contributors/2018/02/01/tech-ceviche-peru-ingredients-healthy-startup-ecosystem/.
55 "Time to prepare and pay taxes." 2017, 29 January 2018, https://data.worldbank.org/indicator/IC.TAX.DURS.
56 Flueckiger, L. 2015. "Brazil cost' bureaucracy continues to hinder business," *The Rio Times | Brazil News*, http://riotimesonline.com/brazil-news/rio-business/brazilian-companies-need-15-times-more-to-pay-taxes-with-bureaucracy/.
57 Guillian, M. 2016. "This is what could really fix brazil's corruption crisis," http://fortune.com/2016/04/07/dilma-rousseff-brazil-corruption/
58 Coetzee, J. 2014. "The Brazilian entrepreneurial landscape according to Ernst & Young – Ventureburn," http://ventureburn.com/2014/01/the-brazilian-entrepreneurial-landscape-according-to-ernst-young/.
59 Kaiser, A.J. 2017. "How a new program is cutting the brazil cost for entrepreneurs," 19 June, www.americasquarterly.org/content/how-new-program-cutting-brazil-cost-sao-paulos-entrepreneurs.
60 Beneke, F. 2015. "How does competition policy in Venezuela look like?," December, https://developingworldantitrust.com/2015/12/28/how-does-competition-policy-in-venezuela-look-like/.
61 Chacon, A. 2015. "Venezuelan entrepreneurs are the country's true heroes," https://panampost.com/valerie-marsman/2015/11/04/venezuelan-entrepreneurs-are-the-countrys-true-heroes/.
62 Toro, M. N. 2016. "Venezuela is falling apart," www.theatlantic.com/international/archive/2016/05/venezuela-is-falling-apart/481755/.
63 Ibid.
64 Benzaquen, M. 2017. "How food in Venezuela went from subsidized to scarce," www.nytimes.com/interactive/2017/07/16/world/americas/venezuela-shortages.html.
65 Oppenheimer, A. 2014. "Latin America's economic challenge: Innovate or die," www.miamiherald.com/news/nation-world/world/americas/article3925884.html.
66 Heim, A. 2011. "Startup failure in Brazil: A taboo to break," https://thenextweb.com/la/2011/09/18/startup-failure-in-brazil-a-taboo-to-break/
67 Montealegre, O. 2012. "Santiago: Chile's silicon valley," www.diplomaticourier.com/santiago-chile-s-silicon-valley/.
68 Citizen Today. 2015. "Women entrepreneurs leading the way in Latin America," www.ey.com/gl/en/industries/government---public-sector/ey-dynamics-public-private-partnerships.
69 Panniagua, M.R. 2012, "In Latin America, women are breaking barriers to entrepreneurship," https://techcrunch.com/2012/12/22/latin-american-women-work-to-break-barrier-to-entry-in-tech/.

70 women2.com. 2014. "What's next for entrepreneurship in Brazil?," 24 October, www.women2.com/2014/10/24/whats-next-entrepreneurship-brazil/
71 UN Women, "Women in informal economy," www.unwomen.org/en/news/in-focus/csw/women-in-informal-economy#notes.
72 IUCN. 2014. "Peru commits to mainstream gender equality into climate policy," www.iucn.org/content/peru-commits-mainstream-gender-equality-climate-policy.
73 "Researchers in R&D (per million people)," https://data.worldbank.org/indicator/SP.POP.SCIE.RD.P6.
74 Prising, J. 2015. "2015 talent shortage survey," http://manpowergroup.com/talent-shortage-2015/talent+shortage+results.
75 Melguizo, A., and C. Pages-Serra. 2017. "In Latin America, companies still can't find the skilled workers they need," www.weforum.org/agenda/2017/03/in-latin-america-companies-still-can-t-find-the-skilled-workers-they-need/
76 Egusa. 2018.
77 Bynum, J. 2018. "What is an antitust law?" www.investopedia.com/ask/answers/09/antitrust-law.asp.
78 fcpamericas.com. 2015. "Antitrust enforcement trends in Latin America," http://fcpamericas.com/english/brazil/antitrust-enforcement-trends-latin-america/#.
79 Ames, A. N. 2014. "Antitrust Laws are rapidly changing in Latin America," www.natlawreview.com/article/antitrust-laws-are-rapidly-changing-latin-america.
80 Espejo, S. 2018. "Leveraging big data, Mercado Libre offers loans in Brazil and Mexico," www.reuters.com/article/us-mercadolibre-mexico/leveraging-big-data-mercado-libre-offers-loans-in-brazil-and-mexico-idUSKBN19E233.
81 Arias, I. 2014. "Supporting entrepreneurs: Breaking down barriers for access to finance," 14 November, https://blogs.worldbank.org/voices/supporting-entrepreneurs-breaking-down-barriers-access-finance.
82 Ibid.
83 IFC. 2016. "Collateral registries: A smart way to expand access to finance," October, www.ifc.org/wps/wcm/connect/news_ext_content/ifc_external_corporate_site/news+and+events/news/impact-stories/collateral-registries-smart-way-to-expand-a2f.
84 Woodman. 2017.
85 Rodrigues. 2017.
86 IFC. 2016.
87 Ibid.
88 Arias. 2014.
89 IFC. 2016.
90 Ibid.
91 Garrison, C. 2017. "Soros, Cohen among big name investors betting on Argentine startups," www.reuters.com/article/us-argentina-economy-startups/soros-cohen-among-big-name-investors-betting-on-argentine-startups-idUSKBN1DG32R.
92 finnovista.com. 2017.
93 Ruvolo, J. 2016. "Why have some of Silicon Valley's top investors started investing in Latin America?," Sep. 28, https://techcrunch.com/2016/09/28/why-have-some-of-silicon-valleys-top-investors-started-investing-in-latin-america/.
94 Guthrie. 2017.

95 KPMG. 2018. "Venture Pulse Q4 2017 Global analysis of venture funding," *KPMG International Cooperative.*

96 Ruvolo. 2016.

97 larepublica.co. 2018. "Conozca varias aplicaciones para hacer mercado sin salir de casa," www.larepublica.co/internet-economy/aplicaciones-para-hacer-mercado-sin-salir-de-casa-2595645.

98 Izquierdo, D. 2017. "Can Colombia's one-stop app become profitable?," 15 November, https://rctom.hbs.org/submission/can-colombias-one-stop-app-become-profitable/

99 Whymedellin. 2017. "Rappi: A Colombian startup who wants to deliver everything," 12 May, http://whymedellin.com/2017/05/12/rappi-a-colombian-startup-who-wants-to-deliver-everything/.

100 Egusa. 2018.

101 andina.com. 2016. "Wayra Perú impulsó US$ 1.8 millones de inversión para startups en 2016," www.andina.com.pe/agencia/noticia-wayra-peru-impulso-18-millones-inversion-para-startups-2016-652614.aspx.

102 Espejo, S. 2017. "Leveraging big data, Mercado Libre offers loans in Brazil and Mexico," 23 June, www.reuters.com/article/us-mercadolibre-mexico/leveraging-big-data-mercado-libre-offers-loans-in-brazil-and-mexico-idUSKBN19E233.

103 WorldBank. 2018. "Research and development expenditure (% of GDP)," https://data.worldbank.org/indicator/GB.XPD.RSDV.GD.ZS.

104 Daza, E. 2016. "Driving the Colombian economy with entrepreneurs," https://thecitypaperbogota.com/business/driving-the-colombian-economy-with-entrepreneurs/13794.

105 Intellectual Property Watch. 2017. "Brief: Government-Financed R&D Declining; Private Sector, Tax Incentives Rise, OECD Finds," www.ip-watch.org/2017/02/07/government-financed-r-private-sector-tax-incentives-rise-oecd-finds/

106 Stunt. 2017.

107 Matthews, H. 2015. "Colombia seeks to provide internet to 63% of population by 2018," http://colombiareports.com/2018-63-colombians-will-connected-internet/

108 Lee, T. 2014. "Colombia a surprising leader in high tech," www.sfgate.com/business/article/Colombia-a-surprising-leader-in-high-tech-5452591.php.

109 Speedtest. 2018. "Speedtest Global Index," www.speedtest.net/global-index.

110 Espinosa, J.E.A. 2015. "Why Chile and Colombia lead the world for entrepreneurship," www.weforum.org/agenda/2015/01/why-chile-and-colombia-lead-the-world-for-entrepreneurship/.

111 Griffin, O. 2017 "The secret new startup hub," www.raconteur.net/current-affairs/the-secret-new-startup-hub.

112 Seed, "Start-Up CHILE EN ES," www.startupchile.org/programs/seed/

113 Ventureburn. 2018. "Start-up Chile opens applications to accelerator programme, increases funding," http://ventureburn.com/2018/01/start-up-chile-opens-applications/

114 West, D. M., & Karsten, J. 2015. "Start-up Chile: A "start-up for start-ups" in Chilecon Valley," 19 August www.brookings.edu/blog/techtank/2015/08/19/start-up-chile-a-start-up-for-start-ups-in-chilecon-valley/

115 Larsson, N. 2016. "Welcome to Chilecon Valley: a startup hub with its own special charm," www.theguardian.com/small-business-network/2016/dec/22/chile-accelerator-startup-grants.

116 www.startupchile.org/the-s-factory-announces-a-new-application-process/

117 Ibid.
118 "Start-up Chile," www.fastcompany.com/company/startup-chile.
119 "Start-up Chile (Scale Factory)," www.globalinnovationexchange.org/funding/startup-chile-scale-factory.
120 Griffin, O. 2017. "The secret new startup hub," 6 February, www.raconteur.net/current-affairs/the-secret-new-startup-hub.
121 Egusa, C. 2016, "A Look into Chile's innovative startup government," 16 October, https://techcrunch.com/2016/10/16/a-look-into-chiles-innovative-startup-government/
122 Scott, I.E. 2013. "Want to create American jobs? Remove American Barriers to Immigration," www.forbes.com/sites/realspin/2013/09/06/want-to-create-american-jobs-remove-american-barriers-to-immigration/#2c58a6816c84.
123 West & Karsten. 2015.
124 Espinosa. 2015.
125 West & Karsten. 2015.
126 Noto, A. 2016. "8 facts to know about startup accelerators across the globe," www.bizjournals.com/newyork/news/2016/06/14/8-facts-to-know-about-startup-accelerators-globe.html.
127 Hinchliffe, T. 2017. "Visa Tech: Chile is streamlining 15 day visa process for foreign startups, tech workers," 7 April, https://sociable.co/business/chile-visa-tech/.
128 West & Karsten. 2015.
129 Cruz. 2017.
130 Mark, D. 2014, "New Chilean insolvency law promotes reorganizations," November, www.jonesday.com/new-chilean-insolvency-law-promotes-reorganizations-12-01-2014/.
131 West & Karsten. 2015.
132 Hinchliffe, T. 2017. "Visa Tech: Chile is streamlining 15 day visa process for foreign startups, tech workers," 7 April, https://sociable.co/business/chile-visa-tech/.
133 Margolis, M. 2017. "Latin America's Star Pupil Needs Some New Ideas Chile can't rely on copper to pull it out of its middle-income funk," www.bloomberg.com/view/articles/2017-11-24/latin-america-s-star-pupil-needs-some-new-ideas.
134 Ravanona, A. 2016. "How start-up Chile put their ecosystem on the global map and became a benchmark for other countries," 2 February, www.huffingtonpost.com/anne-ravanona/how-start-up-chile-put-th_b_9140198.html.
135 Cruz. 2017.
136 Ravanona, A. 2016. "How start-up Chile put their ecosystem on the global map and became a benchmark for other countries," 2 February, www.huffingtonpost.com/anne-ravanona/how-start-up-chile-put-th_b_9140198.html.
137 West & Karsten. 2015.
138 Griffin. 2017.
139 Larsson, N. 2016. "Welcome to Chilecon Valley: a startup hub with its own special charm," December 22, www.theguardian.com/small-business-network/2016/dec/22/chile-accelerator-startup-grants.
140 Egusa. 2016.
141 Larsson, N. 2016. "Welcome to Chilecon Valley: a startup hub with its own special charm," www.theguardian.com/small-business-network/2016/dec/22/chile-accelerator-startup-grants.

142 Egusa. 2016.
143 Espinosa. 2015.
144 Insight, E. 2014, "Start-up Chile: Heading toward failure or success?," 9 September, www.ecosysteminsights.org/start-up-chile-heading-toward-failure-or-success/.
145 The Economist. 2012 "The Chilecon Valley challenge in the war for talent, America can learn a lot from Chile," 13 October, www.economist.com/node/21564564.
146 LAVCA. 2016. "Latin America venture capital: Five-year trends," https://lavca.org/industry-data/latin-america-venture-capital-five-year-trends/
147 West & Karsten. 2015.
148 WIPO. 2016. "WIPO IP Facts and Figures 2016," *World Intellectual Property Organization, at* www.wipo.int/edocs/pubdocs/en/wipo_pub_943_2016.pdf.
149 Egusa, C. 2013. "The silicon valleys of Latin America: A tale of 3 nations," https://venturebeat.com/2013/09/29/the-silicon-valleys-of-latin-america-a-tale-of-3-nations/.
150 Cutler, J. 2013. "The Brazilian government is doing a startup program, too, and they're putting a call out for entries," https://techcrunch.com/2013/04/15/startup-brasil-brazil/.
151 Egusa. 2017.
152 Egusa. 2013.

ICI: mPedigree's Innovative Solution to Fight Counterfeit Drugs

The nonprofit organization, *mPedigree* has developed innovative solutions to fight fake drugs. Using mPedigree's Goldkeys product (http://gold keys.org/), manufacturers, and regulators can effectively monitor the supply chain. Drug manufacturers register their products with mPedigree's database.

While buying a drug at a pharmacy store, a customer can find a 12-digit code by scratching a sticker on the surface of the package and then send a text message to a given number. The code sent by the customer is matched with the ones registered by pharmaceutical companies in the cloud database maintained by *Hewlett-Packard* (HP). The customer then receives a response back that tells whether the drug is counterfeit or genuine. In addition, information such as the batch number, expiry date, and dosage can also be sent in the same message. In order to maintain the system's integrity, sophisticated enterprise technologies are required to incorporate the secure labelling process with industrial and logistic processes.[1]

In Nigeria, the technology is being used by regulators to pinpoint where frauds are taking place. As of September 2016, more than 2,000 products had been registered. The company estimated that 75 million people in Africa had benefited from the company's efforts to fight fake drugs.[2]

In 2014, mPedigree added another product to the Goldkeys Suite—EarlySensor, which is a data-analytics, mass notifications framework. EarlySensor uses pattern-recognition algorithms to monitor for anomalies and irregularities in the consumer authentication ecosystem *on a real-time basis*. When certain conditions are breached, it promptly sends location-based warnings to diverse stakeholders such as brand owners, regulatory bodies, and consumers.[3] In the near future, consumers are expected to receive warnings before purchasing products when suspicious activities are discovered in the supply chain near them.[4]

Most developing countries have underfunded regulatory offers its solutions to potential clients at a cost that is within 1% of a product's wholesale value.[5]

Some Challenges Faced

Sub-Saharan Africa (SSA)-based firms often face challenges in mobilizing resources. For instance, *mPedigree's* founder Bright Simons reported that pharmaceutical companies showed unwillingness to do business with *mPedigree*. VC firms often do not find local funds attractive to fund. Regulators show tendency to ignore local companies. After the detection of a counterfeit product, due to the lack of coordinated actions to *remove fake products* from the shelf.[6]

Lax Regulatory Oversight Leading to Pervasiveness of Fake Drugs

Most developing countries have underfunded regulatory agencies in the areas related to drug development, use, and sales. Some government officials in these countries are reported to accept bribes to approve medicines.[7] An upshot is the pervasiveness of fake drugs. The widespread distribution of fake drugs is a significant problem that has been linked to a large number of deaths in SSA economies. One study, published by the *American Journal of Tropical Medicine and Hygiene*, found that in just one year, fake and poorly made malaria drugs contributed to the deaths of more than 100,000 children in Africa. According to the World Health Organization, 700,000 deaths occur due to counterfeit antimalarial and tuberculosis drugs.[8]

Estimates suggest that in some countries in Asia, Africa, and Latin America, counterfeit medical goods account for up to 30% of the market.[9] The global counterfeit medicine market is valued at US$75 billion annually.[10]

According to the Interpol, the Internet has worsened the situation. Counterfeit and illicit goods can be bought more easily online without a prescription.[11]

Fake drugs often completely lack active ingredients or just enough to pass quality-control tests. However, there are often no noticeable differences with real drugs *in terms of their visual* characteristics.[12]

The problem can be attributed to the system's porosity. For instance, most drugs sold in Ghana come from China, India, and Malaysia, which are imported by Ghanaian distributors. These drugs are then sold to chemical sellers, pharmacies, and hospitals.[13] Some manufacturers *lack control over their supply* chains. For instance, one drug distributor's warehouse manager was reported to be selling batches of a new malaria treatment drug from a different company.[14]

Innovations like *mPedigree* become subject to a number of obstacles and constraints in SSA economies. A single authentication code was checked 1,500 times in a *period of few days*.[15] In another case, *mPedigree* used its data to track down a warehouse that was full of fake malaria medications.

In still another case, a counterfeiter reportedly took a genuine code and used to make thousands of copycat labels, which *were used on* counterfeit morning-after pills. *mPedigree* called everyone who had tested the code to find out where they bought. It then alerted regulators and law enforcement agencies.[16]

Finally, among the most notable of big data-related developments in SSA is that *in* some countries such as Nigeria, scratch-off codes have become mandatory on all malaria drugs and antibiotics.[17]

Technology and Infrastructures

In most African economies, costs associated with managing data centers and using ICTs such as broadband are prohibitively high. For instance, watching a three-hour video online could cost the user a US$50 prepaid package in Congo.[18] Among the biggest needs of *mPedigree* were cloud servers to manage data and partnerships with major cell phone networks. In December 2010, HP announced it would run the data centers to host *mPedigree's* codes. Simons estimated that it saved company US$10 million in infrastructure costs. Simons also persuaded Safaricom (a Vodafone subsidiary), MTN Group, and other mobile carriers to subsidize the cost of text messages.[19]

Many African countries also lack basic infrastructure such as electricity, which restrict the availability of ICTs to businesses and consumers. For instance, blackouts can last twenty-four hours in Ghana. Partly because of this problem, *mPedigree's* data centers are located on three continents.[20]

Competition

MPedigree is not the only company fighting fake drugs. The U.S.-based companies PharmaSecure and Sproxil and the Norwegian company Kezzler have also introduced scratch-off codes and other forms of technologies such as holograms and RFID chips to fight counterfeit drugs. As of 2015, PharmaSecure was reported to have its labels on 1.5 billion packs of medicines, mostly in India. Kezzler has worked with Pfizer in Hong Kong and Royal Dutch Shell in Kenya.[21]

Sproxil has developed a Mobile Product Authentication (MPA) system. As of 2012, Sproxil operated in Ghana, Kenya, Nigeria, and India. Sproxil has attracted venture capital to develop anti-counterfeit technologies.[22] Drug manufacturers have utilized Sproxil's MPA system for other purposes. For instance, using the MPA, it is possible to gain insights into locations that are *counterfeit hotspots and assess* the quantities of *counterfeit drugs*. Sproxil's cloud database analyzes the text messages to spot counterfeit drug activity.[23] Big data- and cloud-based tools such as Sproxil's MPA system can realize economies of scope. Manufacturers of other products have also started using Sproxil's MPA system to eliminate counterfeiters. As of 2012, Nigeria's hair- and skin-care product manufacturers and the Swiss company O'tentika had started collaboration with Sproxil.[24]

mPedigree's International Expansion

The pervasiveness of fake medicines in developing countries increases the attractiveness of mPedigree's solutions. One study conducted in 21 SSA countries found that a third of malaria drug samples failed chemical testing and one-fifth were confirmed as fake.[25] Likewise, one in three medicines sold in Ghana is estimated to be counterfeit, compared to 1% in the U.S. and Europe.[26]

By 2015, *mPedigree* had opened offices in Egypt, Ghana, India, Kenya, Nigeria, and Tanzania. However, only four—Egypt, Ghana, India, and Nigeria—had a sufficient number of companies that had signed up to make *mPedigree's* solution profitable.[27] It was exploring for business opportunities in Bangladesh, Rwanda, Sierra Leone, South Africa, Uganda, and Zambia. As of September 2016, mPedigree was operating in 12 countries across Asia and Africa.[28]

mPedigree also outsources its resources to other developing countries. For instance, mPedigree's labels are printed in China and India.[29]

Expanding to New Market Segments

mPedigree has expanded beyond medicine to fight counterfeiting. Its clients include manufacturers of veterinary medicine, electrical products, baby food, cosmetics, and high-yield seeds used in agriculture.[30] For instance, Dutch luxury fabric company Vlisco adopted mPedigree's system since March 2015 to fight the problem of counterfeit and fake products in Ghana. Pirated versions of Vlisco's products sold nearby for a fraction of the price had cut the company's market share from 50 to just 15% during 2005–2014. It uses *mPedigree's* system and uses the data to send text-message advertisements to customers.[31]

Skill Shortage

As noted in Chapter 7, the shortage of skills is a key challenge facing entrepreneurial firms in Africa. A further problem noted by Simons was that talented developers in the continent do not like to work for local companies.

Africa's low education level poses additional challenges. While the service helped consumers to detect specific fake product packs at retail level, counterfeiters penetrated the parts of the market with lower consumer education level.

Case Summary

Although mPedigree's application provides obvious commercial benefits to drug manufacturers and patients, one of the most important benefits is that it helps save lives by enabling the customers to check the authenticity of life-saving drugs. mPedigree's solutions are thus an effective tools to fight healthcare problems facing the developing world. The above discussion suggests that successful innovations such as those of *mPedigree* can bring favorable regulatory changes.

Notes

1 Disrupt-africa.com. 2015. "mPedigree EarlySensor: Ahead of its Tim," http://disrupt-africa.com/2015/08/mpedigree-earlysensor-ahead-of-its-time.
2 Wall, M., 2016, "Counterfeit drugs: People are dying every day," www.bbc.com/news/business-37470667.
3 Disrupt-africa.com. 2015.
4 Ibid.
5 Yeebo, Y., 2015, "Taking on fake drugs in Africa," www.businessweekme.com/Bloomberg/newsmid/190/newsid/1187/Taking-On-Fake-Drugs-in-Africa#cnttop (accessed 17 February 2016).
6 Disrupt-africa.com. 2015.
7 Ossola, A. 2015. The fake drug industry is exploding, and we can't do anything about it, 15 September, www.newsweek.com/2015/09/25/fake-drug-industry-exploding-and-we-cant-do-anything-about-it-373088.html.
8 Rudd, M. 2012. "Fake anti-malarial drugs could cost 'millions of lives," http://tinyurl.com/oo7uktm.
9 Clasper, J. 2017. "Cracking the code: using SMS verification to spot fake drugs," www.virgin.com/virgin-unite/cracking-code-using-sms-verification-spot-fake-drugs-0.
10 Blackstone, E.A., Fuhr, J.P., & Pociask, S. 2014. "The health and economic effects of counterfeit drugs," www.ncbi.nlm.nih.gov/pmc/articles/PMC4105729/.
11 Interpol, 2017, "Pharmaceutical crime," www.interpol.int/Crime-areas/Pharmaceutical-crime/Pharmaceutical-crime.
12 Yeebo, 2015.
13 Ibid.
14 Ibid.
15 Ibid.
16 Ibid.
17 Ibid.
18 Ekekwe, N. 2016. "What Africa's banking industry needs to do to survive," 28 July, https://hbr.org/2016/07/what-africas-banking-industry-needs-to-do-to-survive.
19 Ibid.
20 Ibid.
21 Ibid.
22 Ibid.
23 McBride, R. 2012. "Software provider to Merck taps IBM cloud to fight fake drugs," http://tinyurl.com/7uo9pta www.fiercebiotechit.com/story/software-provider-merck-taps-ibm-cloud-fight-fake-drugs/2012-05-03.

24 Bowman, A. 2012. "Scratching out Africa's counterfeit medicines." http://blogs.ft.com/beyond-brics/2012/08/28/scratching-out-africas-counterfeit-medicines/.
25 lancet.com. 2012. "Poor-quality antimalarial drugs in southeast Asia and sub-Saharan Africa," www.thelancet.com/journals/laninf/article/PIIS1473-3099%2812%2970064-6/fulltext.
26 Yeebo, 2015.
27 Ibid.
28 Wall. 2016.
29 Yeebo, 2015.
30 Douglas, K. 2014, "How Cameroon's Rolex award winner created Africa's first medical tablet," www.howwemadeitinafrica.com/how-cameroons-rolex-award-winner-created-africas-first-medical-tablet/41552/.
31 Yeebo, 2015.

IC2: The Impacts of Big Data, Cloud Computing, and the Internet of Things in Farm Entrepreneurship

TH Milk in Vietnam

In 2010, Vietnamese dairy company TH Group started dairy breeding and centralized milk-processing project at an industrial scale in North-Central Vietnam's Nghe An province. The milk facility has been constructed in 8,100 hectares. It was the biggest private project undertaken in the Vietnamese agricultural sector.[1]

A group of Israeli companies led by the milking technology developer Afimilk based in Kibbutz Afikim near the Sea of Galilee teamed up with TH Group. The initial agreement was signed in 2009 and construction began in October of that year.

It is the largest Israeli dairy farming project in the world. It was reported that the original cows for the dairy were from New Zealand. They were inseminated with Israeli and European cows' sperms to maximize the milk's quality and the yield.[2]

As of early 2011, 12,000 cows had arrived from New Zealand of which 2,000 were milked daily. About 300 workers had been hired. As of March 2015, TH Group had invested US$450 million on importing and raising cattle.[3]

This project was the largest turn-key dairy farm project worldwide. As of July 2016, the project included seven dairy farms that had 30,000 cows and heifers. The daily milk production was 400,000 liters per day.[4] Afimilk management system provides data on each individual cow at any moment.[5] For the first two years, Afimilk managed all the aspects of the TH project. After that, it only provided consulting services and training to the local teams. 1,200 Vietnamese workers received training on the use of milking technology and the management of an integrated complex of industrial-size dairy farms. The workers did not have prior experience in dairy herd management.[6] Afifarm experts in nutrition, agronomy, veterinary, and animal husbandry offered on-site consultation.[7]

The venture started selling milk in December 2010. The goal is to increase the number of cows to 137,000 by 2017 and about 203,000 by 2020 and increase the total investment to more than US$1.2 billion.[8] TH

Group's 2014 revenue from milk was over $200 million, which accounted for a third of the fresh-milk market in Vietnam.[9] After the completion of the project, TH Milk's goal is to capture 50% market share in the Vietnamese fresh milk market. TH Milk will then become the biggest milk producer in Vietnam overtaking Vinamilk.[10]

Regulations and Policy

Vietnam has embraced advanced technologies enthusiastically in key areas of agricultural and environment thanks to the political support at the highest level. Tsafrir Asaf, the commercial attaché of Israel's Economics Ministry in Vietnam, noted,

> Vietnam has a clear understanding at all governmental levels that their objectives will be achieved only through the implementation of advanced technologies in all areas of the agricultural sector. The central government and the provinces are trying to promote this process, and many private companies are also examining ways to improve the product quality of their yields.[11]

Industrialized world–based big data firms can internalize and exploit their big data–related knowledge, experience, technology, and other resources in the developing world markets. The case of AfiMilk and other Israeli firms in Vietnam indicates that MNCs in big data area can engage in high value-adding activities in developing countries. For instance, it was reported that the TH Milk project is reported to be 11 times larger than the biggest milking facility in Israel with a capacity to produce milk equivalent to 15% of Israel's dairy.[12] It is arguably one of the world's largest projects of its kind.

The experience of Vietnam indicates that big data projects are more likely to be launched in countries with political will at the highest level of the government. Vietnam is one of the world's biggest exporters of rice, coffee, and seafood. However, poor farming techniques often result in high costs to farmers. Moreover, due to degrading quality of water resources and land, several major outbreaks of disease have been reported in fish and animals. These factors have led to a decrease in agricultural production.[13] According to Vietnam's agriculture ministry, the country had 170,000 cows in 2013. The goal is to increase to 500,000 cows by 2020. In addition to low yield, the milk produced in Vietnam lacks quality due primarily to the fact that farmers use agricultural by-products to feed cows. Vietnam has exhibited a high degree of reliance on imported materials for its dairy industry. Vietnam was estimated to spend US$812 million on dairy imports in 2012 and about US$1 billion tin 2013. The country's annual milk imports are about one million tons.[14] Vietnam is thus facing a strong pressure to increase agricultural productivity using ICTs.

Technologies and Infrastructures

Each cow is tagged with a chip. A warning is provided in case of illness *such as* breast inflammation. The milking machine then automatically stops working; this process ensures that the milk is of high quality.[15]

One of AfiMilk's flagship products is the milk meter, which is customized for goat-milking. The meter has been approved for goat-milking by the International Committee for Animal Recording (ICAR). AfiMilk's system uses electrodes to measure milk's quality and quantity. AfiMilk also produces tags to attach on each animal's leg to collect movement data. For instance, the leg tag tells whether a goat is moving, standing, or lying down. The farmer will be alerted when an animal is lying down for longer than normal or at unusual times, which can indicate an illness.[16] The data can be used to choose the next generation of goats. If a farm has a capacity for 100 goats, the farmer can decide the baby goats to grow based on the mother goat's health records.

Big data and the cloud has also helped to improve the efficiency of the distribution channel. In 2013, TH Milk switched to Cloud ERP platform provided by the software firm, Acumatica. A single database is hosted on TH Milk's private cloud, which provides real-time information to staff, distributors, and salespersons. By June 2014, all of TH Milk's 180 distributors were connected to Cloud ERP platform. The company's 1,000 salespersons gather at the distributors' offices each morning to get sales plans. TH Milk salespersons synchronize their sales data with TH Milk's server via an app. It allows them to get new pricing or sales promotion.[17]

There was the lack of basic physical infrastructures such as mechanized infrastructures for unloading the cows at the port. Such infrastructures needed to be built.[18]

Skills

Vietnam severely lacked key ingredients needed to successfully deploy mega big data projects. For instance, the lack of professionals such as veterinarians as well as animal health products and other critical resources such as medicines and vaccines significantly increased the costs of the project. This fundamental reality needs to be kept in mind in the launch of big projects.

Big data projects do not exist in a vacuum. It was reported that all the infrastructure needed for TH Milk in Vietnam including veterinarians, medicines and vaccines were built around this project.[19] In order to reduce costs, Vietnamese dairy farmers were trained and given as much responsibility as possible.[20]

Another challenge that TH Milk faced was that the Vietnamese lack a professional knowledge of dairy farming. This means that the Israelis needed to develop systems, manage the farms, and train the Vietnamese in different procedures. In order to teach the most basic jobs to the Vietnamese team, Afimilk uses relevant examples. For more skilled jobs, manuals are used which describe the process step-by-step protocols. Specially created courses in Israel and Vietnam are used for upper-level management jobs.[21]

Impacts

The product and the benefits to diverse stakeholders such as the users, customers, or the organization's employees can be used as possible criteria to measure a project's success.[22] Some impressive accomplishments have been achieved in increasing milk production. The average cow in TH Milk facility was reported to generate 9,300 liters of milk annually despite tropical conditions.[23] This means that a cow at the TH Milk facility has about the same level of milk productivity as in the U.S. An average cow in Vietnam is estimated to produce about 3,500 litters of milk a year.[24]

The nature of impacts may vary across big data projects. Specifically, the use of ICT in SMEs and big firms such as TH Milk facility may lead to different impacts. The benefits of economic growth in most developing economies are highly concentrated and disproportionately distributed to the well-connected and wealthiest individuals. In this regards, mega big data projects such as those implemented by TH Milk, notwithstanding overall positive impacts on economic growth, may have limited effects on poverty reduction.

The impacts of projects such as TH Milk go beyond purely economic considerations. For a mega-project such as TH Milk, environmental concerns also deserve attention. According to the U.S. Environmental Protection Agency (EPA), a dairy operation with 2,500 cows creates as much waste as a city of 400,000 people.[25] This means that TH Milk could be producing as much waste as 22 million people.

Case Summary

TH Milk facility is a massive capital-intensive mega-project, which uses advanced technologies to modernize the milk production process. Main sources of data are from Internet of Things sensors. This case indicates that businesses in developing countries driven by advanced technologies may disrupt existing business models, practices, and operations.

TH Milk is likely to contribute to the economic growth via higher productivity. However, a project such as this tends to perform poorly in terms of other impact indicators such as reducing poverty and formalizing informal businesses. Deployment of ICTs in micro- and small enterprise could be more effective in reducing poverty compared to mega-projects discussed in this case. Mega agricultural projects such as those undertaken by TH Milk are also likely to leave a significant ecological footprint.

Notes

1 Vietnam Development Bank. 2014. "TH Milk factory construction project: a proof of state credit's efficiency in the agricultural sector," http://en.vdb. gov.vn/news2021/th-milk-factory-construction-project-a-proof-of-state-credits-efficiency-in-the-agricultural-sector.
2 Udasin, S. 2015. "Israeli-Vietnamese commercial milking venture nears completion," www.jpost.com/Business/Israeli-Vietnamese-commercial-milking-venture-nears-completion-390874=.
3 Tung, T. 2015. "Vietnam's dairy queen courts fame," http://english.vietnam-net.vn/fms/business/125135/vietnam-s-dairy-queen-courts-fame.html.
4 AfiBlog. 2016. "TH Milk supplies a daily glass of fresh milk to Vietnam," www.afimilk.com/afiblog/th-milk-supplies-daily-glass-fresh-milk-vietnam.
5 Ibid.
6 Ibid.
7 Ibid.
8 Tung, 2015.
9 Ibid.
10 Rabinovitch, A. 2015. "RPT-Milking it: Israel leads the way in dairy tech," www.reuters.com/article/2015/05/19/israel-dairy-idUSL5N0Y44V820150519.
11 Shamah, D. 2012, "Dairy diplomacy yields stronger ties with Vietnam," www. timesofisrael.com/dairy-diplomacy-yields-stronger-ties-with-vietnam/.
12 Udasin, 2015.
13 Shamah, 2012.
14 Hoang, T. 2013. "Dairy farming in dire need of high tech," http://english. thesaigontimes.vn/32197/Dairy-farming-in-dire-need-of-high-tech.html.
15 Vietnam.vnanet.vn. 2015. "The true milk-a leading brand in Vietnam's fresh milk market," http://vietnam.vnanet.vn/english/th-true-milk-a-leading-brand-in-vietnams-fresh-milk-market/190058.html.
16 Chan, L.Y. 2013. "How Israel became the world leader in milking technologies," http://nocamels.com/2013/03/how-israel-became-the-world-leader-in-milking-technologies/.
17 Acumatica, 2015, "Vietnam's leading fresh milk producer transforms distribution management system with Acumatica."
18 Udasin, 2015.
19 Ibid.
20 Bland, B. 2011, "Israelis teach Vietnam how to milk it." www.ft.com/cms/s/0/7ee50218-50c7-11e0-9227-00144feab49a.html.
21 Leichman, K.A. 2011. "Milking Israel's dairy expertise in Vietnam," www. israel21c.org/milking-israels-dairy-expertise-in-vietnam/.

22 Atkinson, R. 1999. "Project management: Cost, time and quality, two best guesses and a phenomenon, its time to accept other success criteria," *International journal of project management*, 17(6), pp. 337–342.
23 Udasin, 2015.
24 Leichman. 2011.
25 MacDonald, M. 2014. "Will 'milk life' go global? Big dairy sets its sights on Asia," www.huffingtonpost.com/mia-macdonald/will-milk-life-go-global-_b_5249166.html.

Online Sources of Global Entrepreneurship-Related Data and Statistics

The sources below provide data and statistics on a variety of indicators, mainly at the macro-level, related to determinants, performance indicators, and impacts of entrepreneurship.

The Global Entrepreneurship Monitor

The Global Entrepreneurship Monitor (GEM) (www.gemconsortium. org/) is a not-for-profit academic research consortium. It has stated its goal as "making high quality information on global entrepreneurial activity readily available to as wide an audience as possible." The GEM is the arguably the "largest single study of entrepreneurial activity in the world." The GEM started studying worldwide entrepreneurship in 1999 with 10 countries. By 2009, it covered 54 countries.

Data on entrepreneurial activities covered in GEM studies can be accessed by clicking the link to "Data" *tab at the top of* the GEM homepage (www.gemconsortium.org/).

The GEM's policy is to make the full datasets publicly available only three years after the yearly data collection cycle. As of August 2010, GEM data for 1999–2009 were publicly available. One needs the SPSS statistics software to open the GEM datasets. A GEM requires a researcher to provide some information to *download the datasets.*

The World Bank Group

The World Bank Group has created *rich datasets and databases for various macro-level indicators,* mainly related to worldwide development. The Data Catalog (http://data.worldbank.org/data-catalog) has a list of World Bank datasets and *databases, and* provides access to over 2,000 indicators from various sources.

The World Development Indicators

The World Development Indicators (WDI) (http://data.worldbank.org/data-catalog/world-development-indicators) is the World Bank's premier compilation of development-related, macro-level data. The WDI provides a comprehensive selection of economic, social, and environmental indicators *as back as 1960*. These indicators are based on data from the World Bank as well as over 30 partner agencies. Most of the WDI-related statistics *are* from national statistical agencies of respective countries. As of August 2010, the WDI covered over 900 indicators for 210 economies.

Doing Business Survey

Of special importance is the Doing Business Survey (www.doingbusiness.org/), which provides the most comprehensive comparative survey on the regulatory aspects of entrepreneurship affecting the ease of up and running a business. This survey provides objective measures and comparisons of regulations and their enforcement affecting businesses and is especially relevant for SMEs. The 2013 ease of doing business index ranked the world's 185 economies (from 1 to 185). the index of economy was the simple average of its percentile rankings on the following ten indicators: (1) starting a business, (2) dealing with construction permits, (3) employing workers, (4) registering property, (5) getting credit, (6) protecting investors, (7) paying taxes, (8) trading across borders, (9) enforcing contracts, and (10) closing a business.[1]

The Central Intelligence Agency (CIA) World Factbook

The World Factbook (www.cia.gov/library/publications/the-world-factbook/) is probably the most highly used online reference for *country-level economic, political, legal, geographic, military, demographic,* and social indicators. The CIA World Factbook is constantly updated and contains the latest *data on indicators such as* population size, terrain, and per capita GNP.

The first unclassified version of the Factbook was published in 1971 and the 1975 edition was the earliest that was made available to the public by the U.S. Government. The CIA has been providing online editions of the Factbook since. According to the CIA, "Hard copy editions for earlier years are available from libraries."[2] One limitation of the Factbook is that since it is updated on a regular basis, new changes overwrite the previous versions of the report. Researchers thus need to refer to the hard copy editions if past data about some indicators are needed.

The Organization for Economic Cooperation and Development

The Organization for Economic Cooperation and Development's *(OECD)* Statistics Portal *(*www.oecd.org/statsportal/0,3352,en_2825_293564_1_1_1_1_1,00.html*)* is a useful data source *for various macro-level* *indicators, mainly for the members of OECD.* Some datasets are available for free download, while others require subscription. The OECD collects data related to a wide range of public policy areas. They include agriculture, education, environment, taxation, trade, science, technology, industry, and innovation.[3]

The Statistics Portal provides links to two key tables: Country statistical profiles and OECD Factbook: Country statistical profiles (http://stats.oecd.org/Index.aspx?DataSetCode=CSP2010) contains data selected from over 40 statistical databases from the OECD's online library, SourceOECD. This statistical profile is updated annually. Links to data sources are provided with red's, where one can also find up-to-date and time series data.

The OECD has been publishing the OECD Factbook (www.oecd-ilibrary.org/content/book/factbook-2010-en) annually since 2005. In 2010, the OECD Factbook was in its sixth edition, which cost US$70. The OECD Factbook 2010 provides statistics on over 100 indicators. Areas covered include population, economic production, foreign trade and investment, energy, labor force, information and communications technologies, public finances, innovation, environment, foreign aid, agriculture, taxation, education, health, and quality of life.

The OECD Factbook 2010 also contains a special focus section on The Crisis and Beyond.

The International Telecommunication Union

The *International Telecommunication Union (ITU)* (www.itu.int/en/pages/default.aspx) *is a* United Nations agency for information and communication technology (ICT) issues. The ITU makes available a wide range of indicators for the ICT sector. By clicking the "Statistics" *tab at the top of* the *ITU* homepage (www.itu.int/en/pages/default.aspx), one can access various ICT-related statistics (www.itu.int/ITU-D/ict/index.html). The ITU also publishes World Telecommunication/ICT Indicators Database. The 14th Edition, World Telecommunication/ICT Indicators Database 2010, was published in June 2010. CD-Rom as well as Online versions of this publication are available for purchase at www.itu.int/ITU-D/ict/publications/world/world.html#Order%20now.

Human Development Report

The *United Nations Development Program (UNDP)* has been publishing the *Human Development Report* (HDR) (http://hdr.undp.org/en/reports/) annually since 1990. The HDR presents a wealth of statistical information on various aspects of human development. HDRs contain national-level data on indicators that are the causes of and associated with three components of human development—life expectancy, education and GDP. The data are freely available for download on UNDP's website (http://hdr.undp.org/en/statistics/data/). The UNDP also publishes regional, national, and subnational HDRs.

The Heritage Foundation

The Heritage Foundation (www.heritage.org/) publishes data on economic freedom of economies every year. The Foundation measures ten components of economic freedom. Each component is assigned a score in each component (in a 0–100 scale, 100 representing the maximum freedom). The overall economic freedom for an economy is the average of the scores for the ten components. The ten components are: Business Freedom, Trade Freedom, Fiscal Freedom, Government Spending, Monetary Freedom, Investment Freedom, Financial Freedom, Property rights, Freedom from Corruption, and Labor Freedom.[4]

The Political Risk Services

The political risk services (PRS) (www.prsgroup.com/) publishes International Country Risk Guide (ICRG) and other publications, which rate 161 countries on political, economic, financial and other risks related to international businesses. Since 1980, *ICRG* is being published on a monthly basis. The PRS makes ICRG available to subscribers online, in print, and on CD-ROM. However, free samples of some data and reports are also available.

Euromonitor

Euromonitor (www.euromonitor.com/) is a private sector research firm, which publishes various market research reports and global business and market intelligence. Some content such as summaries of reports and articles on the *Euromonitor* websites are free, while most need to be purchased.

Euromonitor covers many industry sectors such as those related to consumer goods, health care, and travel services. In-depth reports, analyst comments, statistics, and external sources are included in each category. There are multiple search options available and results can be integrated across categories.[5] Data and information on Industries, Countries and Consumers, and Companies can be searched by country or region. Under Industries, indicators such as market share and trends as well as country-specific industry reports are available. In Countries and Consumers, country-specific statistics and reports on consumer behavior and lifestyles are available. Under Companies, there are data and information on company profiles, market analysis, and key trends. To ensure comparability, *Euromonitor* also provides standardized international definitions for variables.

There are five major constraints related to the use of international secondary data: accuracy, age, reliability, lumping, and comparability.[6] Euromonitor largely addresses these constraints and its data are considered to be of high quality.[7]

Notes

1 doingbusiness.org. 2018. "Doing Business", www.doingbusiness.org/economyrankings/.
2 Buneman, P., Müller, H., & Rusbridge, C. 2009. "Curating the CIA World Factbook," *The International Journal of Digital Curation*, 4(3), www.ijdc.net/index.php/ijdc/article/viewFile/132/171.
3 oecd.org. 2010. "OECD work on statistics," www.oecd.org/dataoecd/18/49/44652140.pdf.
4 heritage.org. 2010a. "How do you measure economic freedom?", www.heritage.org/index/.
5 Bentley University Library. 2010. Database of the Month: Euromonitor, 10 July, http://blogs.bentley.edu/intheknow/.
6 Kotabe, M., & Helsen, K. 2001. *Global Marketing Management*. New York: John Wiley.
7 Kotabe, M. 2002. "Using Euromonitor database in international marketing research," *Academy of Marketing Science Journal*, 30(2), pp. 172–175.

Preparing an International Business Plan (IBP)

A business plan is a written document prepared by an entrepreneurial firm, which is based on a current and future state analysis of the firm (e.g., management team, product, or services) and the environment facing it. It defines the short-term and long-term goals and how they will be accomplished.[1] The most common readers of a business plan include potential funders, who make their funding decision based on the company's business plan.

An international business plan (IBP) describes internal and external elements associated with internationalizing a business. An IBP thus demonstrates the feasibility of internationalizing and helps organize associated activities. As is the case of any business plan, a good IBP is based on sound international market research (see Appendix 2 for various information sources) and accurate financial projections.

Elements of an IBP

Executive Summary

The most important component of an IBP is probably the executive summary. The executive summary must be clear, concise, convincing, appealing, and effective so that it is able to capture the reader's interest. At a time of intense funding competition, potential investors often dismiss an IBP after reading the executive summary. An effective executive summary tells the reader, inter alia, what the business is about and helps understand the main points the entrepreneur is making. Whereas there may be some disagreement as to the length of an executive summary, a single page is probably the best length.

The first part of the executive summary normally includes name and location of the business, the product, or service being sold and purpose of the IBP. Other important elements to be included in the IBP are as follows:

a   Business description: Nature and unique features of products or services, how they will fit in the foreign market and whether they are going to change in the future.

b   Strategic direction and strategy formulation: Appraisal of the current status of the company, direction and goals of the company for the next 5–10 years, and how they will be achieved.

c   Description of the foreign market: Profile of the market segment in the foreign country that the company is targeting, the channels through which they are reached and value proposition to the target groups of the company's products or services.

d   Management team: Professional background, responsibilities, and potential contributions to the company of the founders and top management.

e   Financial aspect: Expected revenue and net earnings for the next five years and contributions of the foreign operations, capital needed, and how it will be used, expected returns to investors and how and when they will get their money (e.g., IPO or sale of the company through an acquisition).

The rest of the business plan consists of information about the following:

I   History and overview of the company

   a   History of the company: History of the company's product and services and evolution to the current stage.

   b   Background information: Backgrounds and experiences (including international experience) of the owners, number of years in business, number of employees, why and by whom the organization was formed, whether the organization's mission changed since the organization was formed, strategic fit of the company's international business activities with the existing resources.

   c   Current status of the company: Definition, scope, nature, and importance of the business (the company's product or services, where and how they will they be used, number of countries in which the company is doing business, profile of the customer), technical specification, features and design (for technologically complex products).

   d   The business concept: Key factors that determine the success in the industry (e.g., low price, high quality, and technological/ marketing capability), how the company's products meet these requirements, unique selling propositions of the products or services, evidence and reasons as to why buyers in the foreign market are likely to prefer the company's products over its domestic and international competition.[2]

   e   Objectives: Overall objective, specific objectives for sales, profitability, market share, product, innovation, branding, management development, employee morale, social responsibility.

II Foreign market entry and expansion
The elements to be included in this section include the following:

a   Whether the company has received inquiries from foreign markets for its products or services.
b   Availability of the financial resources to perform market research and promote the product in the foreign market.
c   Whether the company has personnel export skills, customer service, and networking skills required for the operation in the foreign market.
d   Whether a new position will be created in the company to develop international markets
e   The level of control the company wants to maintain in the foreign country over sales, customer service, and customer credits.
f   Choosing a market entry method (e.g., licensing, joint venture, or investment as possible options).

III Industry and market analysis
The following are described in this section:

a   Overall market: Description of present and projects markets in terms of locations, sales, growth rate, profitability, and trends.
b   Projected industry sales: Over the next three to five years and the company's market share and whether they will be different in the foreign market.
c   Specific market segment: Description of present and future market segments and major competitor in each segment, Expected strategic changes about market segments, detailed information about major customers and prospects.
d   Competitor analysis: Expected effects on sales due to existing competitors, potential competitors, buyers substitute products, detailed information about the leading competitors (e.g., sales volume, market share, and profitability), whether the company's domestic competitors are exporting similar or closely related products or services, whether foreign competitors in the industry are active in the home country.

IV Macroeconomic factors
Some important indicators related to macroeconomic features include the following:

a   GDP growth.
b   Inflation rate.
c   Effects of disruptive economic events such as the GFC and whether such events have differential effects in the foreign country.
d   Infrastructural situation.

   e   Credit rating of the country.

   f   Currency fluctuation issues and how they will affect customers' ability and willingness to buy the company's product.

V Development, production, and logistics

It is important to explain in detail about the following with necessary diagrams:

   a   Stages involved in the development and production process and budget and time for each stage.

   b   A comparison of production versus subcontracting.

   c   Whether the factory will be located in the target country, the home country, or a third country.

   d   A description of engineering and operations department.

   e   Production requirements (raw materials, supplies, and labor).

   f   Details of plant facilities, machinery, and equipment required.

   g   The most appropriate form of transportation.

   h   Shipping and associated costs.

   i   The degree and location of R&D activities.

   j   How quality assurance will be undertaken.

   k   Whether the product requires special storage and if the foreign country has such facilities

   l   The current status of the company's production capacity (operating at full capacity, running under capacity) and difficulty involved in increasing the capacity to meet international demand.

   m   Whether there is a minimum order requirement and if this requirement is different for international sales.

   n   Whether the company uses a freight forwarder for export shipments.

   o   Packaging and labeling needed for the product to reach the foreign country.

   p   Documentation needed to meet the government regulations in the home country and the foreign country.

   q   The bank to be used for international transactions.

   r   Acceptable payment methods in the foreign market.

VI Political and legal forces that are likely to shape the industry and the business

It would be important to explain in detail about the following:

   a   Whether there are special policies favoring the industry.

   b   Whether subsidies are available for the industry.

   c   Special Economic Zones benefits (e.g., Kaspersky Lab in Tianjin, China benefited from a Chinese government's special economic zone for start-ups, Chapter 5).

   d   Tax breaks and import tariff reductions.

e   Political stability condition.
f   The legal system and rule of law status.
g   Whether the foreign country has a special trade relation with the home country and if so how it would affect the company's business.
h   Laws and enforcement mechanisms to protect from the infringement of copyright and related rights (for products with copyright issues).
i   Whether there are certain business ownership restrictions for foreigners.
j   Whether accreditation from agencies such as professional associations are needed.
k   Whether the product can be manufactured in a cost-effective way to meet the overseas regulatory requirements or standards.

VII   Social forces that are likely to shape the industry
The potential readers of an IBP would be interested to know about the following aspects:
a   Demographic profile of the customer: age, gender, income, occupation, etc.
b   Predicted shift in the demographic makeup of the foreign country's population and how it will affect the company's business.
c   The public's perception of the industry.
d   Whether there are some cultural aspects that influence the product's acceptance in the foreign market (e.g., religious beliefs, taste preferences, habits, and lifestyles).
e   Crime rates including organized crimes and cybercrimes and how they will affect the company's business in the foreign country.

VIII   Technical forces that are likely to shape the industry
It would be necessary to discuss in detail about the following:

a   Penetration rates of various technologies in the foreign market and their effect on the company's business.
b   The foreign country's position in the adoption of emerging technologies and its effect on the success of the business.
c   The level of the product's technology (simple, advanced, and state of the art).
d   Degree of fit of the technology in the foreign market.
e   Potential profitability of the industry in the foreign market.
f   Important trends in the industry in the foreign market.

IX   SWOT analysis
An analysis of a firm's strengths, weaknesses, opportunities, and threats (SWOT) entails the process of analyzing the firm and its

environments and is commonly used to assist the firm in identifying strategic direction.

X Organizational overview
   The typical contents of this section are as follows:

   a   Organizational structure
   b   Human resource strategies
   c   Key personnel and other personnel
   d   International staffing requirements and degree of fit with the available resource skills in the organization

XI Financial overview
   The primary components of this section are the following:

   a   Business financing issues.
   b   Selected financial ratios (e.g., return on assets, net sales to net worth ratio and net income to net sales ratio, and earnings per share).
   c   Projected profit and loss statement.
   d   Projected balance sheet.
   e   Capital needed and how it will be spent: working capital, marketing, R&D, export budget, international overhead expenses, and starts up costs.
   f   Break even analysis.
   g   Seasonal effect on financial performance.
   h   Receivables and payable management.

XII Marketing strategy
   The major components of this section are as follows:

   a   Results of international marketing research.
   b   Segmentation: Selection of market segments and rationales, environmental analysis of various market segments.
   c   Products: Description of products and services and comparison with major competitors, selection of possible products and services to be exported, importance of the protection of proprietary methods, trademarks, and intellectual property rights for the product, product adaptations (e.g., technical, design, content, functionality, and cosmetic changes) needed to meet regulative, cultural, economic, and technical conditions in the foreign country, modifications needed in product packaging, instructions, manuals and translations involved, whether there are technical terms that might be difficult to translate in the language of the foreign country, differences in geography- or climate-related factors (e.g., humidity, heat, cold, rain, wind, sand, dust, and terrain) that may affect product functions in the foreign country,

buyer preferences in the foreign country with respect to various product features (e.g., size, packaging, and color), warranty and servicing standards in the foreign market and whether the company needs to include this in pricing, stage of the product life cycle (introduction, growth, maturity, and decline) and whether the stage is different in the foreign market, *w*hether and how after-sale services will be provided in the foreign country.

d   Pricing: Pricing strategy, whether the company prefers to have the ability to change price, terms and conditions, profit margin in the company's domestic price, relative price sensitivity of the foreign market and its effect on profit margin, whether the company's price is competitive after adding export-related costs and tariffs to the product's price, direct materials and labor costs involved in the production for export.

e   Distribution: Standard distribution practice in the foreign market, how the company's domestic competitors sell in the foreign market, distribution channels to be employed by the company in the foreign country, selection of distribution partners, types of discounts (trade, cash, and quantity) or allowances (advertising, trade-off) commonly given to a member of the distribution channel for similar products in the foreign market, agent and distributor markups in the foreign country.

f   Promotions: Advertising tactics and other promotional measures, whether different benefits of the product will be emphasized in the foreign country, activities related to branding, packaging, and labeling.

g   Sales forecast for the next five years.

XIII Strategic gap analysis
The elements of this section constitute the following:

a   Company's current position.
b   An alternative strategy better suited to the current context (due to change in objectives, decision makers, or performance levels).
c   Ideal outcome corresponding to the alternative strategy.
d   Changes needed to achieve the ideal outcome.

XIV   Ownership
Key elements of this section should include the following:

a   Legal form of ownership (e.g., sole proprietorship, partnership, and corporation).
b   Whether there has been a change in ownership in recent years.
c   Investment made by the business founders.
d   Debt and equity funding needed.

e   Condition for doing business if it is established as a partnership.

f   List of owners (e.g., individuals, corporations, and trusts) if the business is established as a corporation.

g   Proportion of stocks owned by the employees.

h   The company's share price.

i   The number of shares owned and investment by each director.

XV   References

XVI Appendices and supporting information

Notes

1 Schilit, W.K. 1987. "How to write a winning business plan," *Business Horizons*, 30(5), pp. 13–22.

2 Murphy, P. 2004. "International business plan workbook," Massachusetts Export Center, www.msbdc.org/publications/intlbizplan/intl_busplan.pdf.

Index